$195-198

MUIRHEAD LIBRARY OF PHILOSOPHY

An admirable statement of the aims of the Library of Philosophy was provided by the first editor, the late Professor J. H. Muirhead, in his description of the original programme printed in Erdmann's *History of Philosophy* under the date 1890. This was slightly modified in subsequent volumes to take the form of the following statement:

'The Muirhead Library of Philosophy was designed as a contribution to the History of Modern Philosophy under the heads: first of Different Schools of Thought – Sensationalist, Realist, Idealist, Intuitivist; secondly of different Subjects – Psychology, Ethics, Aesthetics, Political Philosophy, Theology. While much had been done in England in tracing the course of evolution in nature, history, economics, morals and religion, little had been done in tracing the development of thought on these subjects. Yet "the evolution of opinion is part of the whole evolution".

'By the co-operation of different writers in carrying out this plan it was hoped that a thoroughness and completeness of treatment, otherwise unattainable, might be secured. It was believed also that from writers mainly British and American fuller consideration of English Philosophy than it had hitherto received might be looked for. In the earlier series of books containing, among others, Bosanquet's *History of Aesthetic*, Pfleiderer's *Rational Theology since Kant*, Albee's *History of English Utilitarianism*, Bonar's *Philosophy and Political Economy*, Brett's *History of Psychology*, Ritchie's *Natural Rights*, these objects were to a large extent effected.

'In the meantime original work of a high order was being produced both in England and America by such writers as Bradley, Stout, Bertrand Russell, Baldwin, Urban, Montague, and others, and a new interest in foreign works, German, French and Italian, which had either become classical or were attracting public attention, had developed. The scope of the Library thus became extended into something more international, and it is entering on the fifth decade of its existence in the hope that it may contribute to that mutual understanding between countries which is so pressing a need of the present time.'

The need which Professor Muirhead stressed is no less pressing today, and few will deny that philosophy has much to do with enabling us to meet it, although no one, least of all Muirhead himself, would regard that as the sole, or even the main, object of philosophy. As Professor Muirhead continues to lend the distinction of his name to the

A

Library of Philosophy it seemed not inappropriate to allow him to recall us to these aims in his own words. The emphasis on the history of thought also seemed to me very timely: and the number of important works promised for the Library in the very near future augur well for the continued fulfilment, in this and other ways, of the expectations of the original editor.

H. D. LEWIS

The Elusive Mind by H. D. LEWIS
Indian Philosophy by RADHAKRISHNAN 2 vols revised 2nd edition
Introduction to Mathematical Philosophy by BERTRAND RUSSELL 2nd
    edition
Kant's First Critique by H. W. CASSIRER
Kant's Metaphysic of Experience by H. J. PATON
Know Thyself by BERNADINO VARISCO translated by GUGLIELMO
    SALVADORI
Language and Reality by WILBUR MARSHALL URBAN
Lectures on Philosophy by G. E. MOORE
Lecturers on Philosophy by G. E. MOORE edited by C. LEWY
Matter and Memory by HENRI BERGSON translated by N. M. PAUL
    and W. S. PALMER
Memory by BRIAN SMITH
The Modern Predicament by H. J. PATON
Natural Rights by D. G. RITCHIE 3rd edition
Nature, Mind and Modern Science by E. HARRIS
The Nature of Thought by BRAND BLANSHARD
On Selfhood and Godhood by C. A. CAMPBELL
Our Experience of God by H. D. LEWIS
Perception by DON LOCKE
The Phenomenology of Mind by G. W. F. HEGEL translated by SIR
    JAMES BAILLIE revised 2nd edition
Philosophy in America by MAX BLACK
Philosophical Papers by G. E. MOORE
Philosophy and Illusion by MORRIS LAZEROWITZ
Philosophy and Political Economy by JAMES BONAR
Philosophy and Religion by AXEL HAGERSTROM
Philosophy of Space and Time by MICHAEL WHITEMAN
Philosophy af Whitehead by W. MAYS
The Platonic Tradition in Anglo-Saxon Philosophy by J. H. MUIRHEAD
The Principal Upanisads by RADHAKRISHNAN
The Problems of Perception by R. J. HIRST
Reason and Goodness by BLAND BLANSHARD
The Relevance of Whitehead by IVOR LECLERC
The Science of Logic by G. W. F. HEGEL
Some Main Problems of Philosophy by G. E. MOORE
Studies in the Metaphysics of Bradley by SUSHIL KUMAR SAXENA
The Subject of Consciousness by C. O. EVANS
The Theological Frontier of Ethics by W. G. MACLAGAN
Time and Free Will by HENRI BERGSON translated by F. G. POGSON
The Transcendence of the Cave by J. N. FINDLAY
Values and Intentions by J. N. FINDLAY
The Ways of Knowing: or the Methods of Philosophy by W. P.
    MONTAGUE

Muirhead Library of Philosophy

EDITED BY H. D. LEWIS

OUR KNOWLEDGE OF RIGHT AND WRONG

OUR KNOWLEDGE
OF RIGHT AND WRONG

BY
JONATHAN HARRISON

LONDON · GEORGE ALLEN & UNWIN LTD
NEW YORK · HUMANITIES PRESS, INC

PREFACE

This book falls into two parts. It would be an over-simplification to say that the first part was true, but not new, and that the second part was new, but not true. Some of the first part is new, and it may even be that some of the second part is true. The second part of the book, however, is not nearly as clear as I could wish. My excuse must be that I felt that if I spent any more time trying to get the second part any clearer, I would never finish the book at all. Whether this is a good excuse will depend upon its merits, which I must leave my reader to determine.

My thanks are due to the Philosophy Department at Northwestern University for giving me a light teaching programme when I was working on the final chapters; to Professor H. H. Price for his generous encouragement – he told me, among other things, that it was better to finish a bad book than not to finish a book at all; to my late wife for her moral support; and to Mrs. Vera Peetz who, besides encouraging me, has taken a very great deal of trouble in reading the proofs and correcting a large number of careless mistakes of my own.

J.H.
Nottingham 1970

CONTENTS

CHAPTER I

FIRST-ORDER/SECOND-ORDER

It is very natural for those unacquainted with moral philosophy to suppose that moral philosophers spend their time propounding and discussing various theories about the difference between right and wrong, between actions which are duties and those which are not, between the things which are good and ought to be sought after and the things which are bad and ought to be avoided, the difference between virtue and vice, and between good men and bad. Such discussions, it is assumed, are aimed at answering such questions as 'What actions are right, and what actions are wrong?', 'What sorts of action ought we to perform, and what other sorts of action ought we to refrain from performing?', 'What things ought men to aim at, for themselves and for others?' and 'What traits of character are virtues, and what traits of character are vices?' It is further supposed that, if moral philosophers were successful in their quest, ordinary men, should they come to know of the answers which had been given to these questions, would be helped thereby to solve any moral problems with which they might be faced: that these theories would give them some practical guidance in the conduct of their life, would tell them how to live, and at what they ought to aim.

In fact, only a proportion of moral philosophy is directed at answering questions such as these. Modern moral philosophers sometimes distinguish between first-order questions and second-order questions. Questions of the type of which I have just given examples would be called first-order questions, and they ask what actions are right and wrong, what actions are duties, and at what ought we to aim? Second-order questions are questions *about* first-order questions, and they ask such things as 'What exactly are we asking, when we ask whether an action is right?' or 'What is meant by "right"?' or 'How do we answer questions which ask whether a given action is right or wrong, and how does the method – if it can be called that – of answering such questions differ from the method by which we answer other sorts of question, for example, historical questions or scientific questions?'

Philosophers who distinguish between first-order and second-order moral questions would not limit this distinction to ethics. They would hold that ethics is one of a number of first-order enquiries, such as history, physics, biology, economics, and that each one of these enquiries gives rise to a second-order enquiry, the object of which is to investigate the methods and concepts of the respective first-order enquiry, the nature of the assertions those pursuing it make and of the evidence by which they are properly established, their relation to other enquiries, and the extent to which such first-order enquiries can give us knowledge. Such enquiries are sometimes called 'meta-enquiries', and philosophers talk about 'meta-history' or 'meta-biology', though more often the more old-fashioned phrases 'the philosophy of history' or 'the philosophy of biology' are preferred.

A great many modern philosophers would hold that the *only* function of philosophy was to engage in meta-enquiries of the sort I have mentioned; that philosophers can give us no first-order knowledge of the actual world, but only second-order knowledge about the nature of this knowledge, and how it is obtained by others.[1] This answer is particularly attractive to empiricist philosophers, for if you hold that information about the world can only be obtained by observation and experiment, philosophers, who neither observe nor experiment, will inevitably seem peculiarly ill fitted to get it. Some modern philosophers, however, have held that philosophy does have another function, which is to synthesize the specialized information given by particular first-order enquiries into the aspects of the world with which they are especially concerned, to get the general gist of it, and to piece it together in order to present a synoptic view of the world as a whole.[2] Such a task must inevitably get more difficult as the various first-order enquiries amass more and more information, become more and more specialized, and more and more technical.

Philosophers in the past, and some contemporary modern philosophers, have held that the function of philosophy is not confined to pursuing meta-enquiries, nor in condensing and combining information about the world acquired by others, but

---

[1] A defence of a wider view of the function of philosophy may be found in 'Clarity is not Enough,' by H. H. Price, in a volume of the same name edited by H. D. Lewis (Allen & Unwin, 1963).

[2] See C. D. Broad, *Scientific Thought*, (Routledge & Kegan Paul, 1923). Introduction.

that there are certain questions about the world which cannot be answered by the ordinary first-order enquiries, but which can be answered by philosophers, without recourse to observation and experiment, by the exercise of reason alone. The most important of the questions have been 'Is there a God?', and 'If so, what is he like, and what is his relation to the world he has created?' But nowadays those philosophers who think that philosophy can provide the answer to such questions are in a minority.

To return to the distinction between first-order and second-order *ethical* questions, there is at least one reason why the distinction is important. A great many modern moral philosophers would hold that moral philosophers are in no better position to answer first-order ethical questions than anyone else;[1] that such questions are best answered by the ordinary good man, who has by practice developed and made more sensitive his moral perception; that moral philosophers are neither better nor more morally discerning than other people, and that the type of ratiocination at which a philosophical training may be supposed to make one more adept does not enter into the solution of moral problems. If, of course, first-order questions were the only sort of question, moral philosophy, for such philosophers, would be pointless, but, since they are not the only sort of question, moral philosophy is not prohibited by those philosophers entirely, but merely confined to the solution of second-order questions. The statement that reasoning is not involved in solving moral problems would be, for example, a partial answer to the question 'How do we know what is right?' In attempting to provide an answer to such second-order questions, it is held, moral philosophers are performing an enlightening, if purely academic, task, for these are not questions which ordinary people usually find it necessary to ask, or would be particularly well-fitted to answer; nor does the fact that reasoning of the sort a philosopher may be expected to be better at than other people is not involved in answering first-order questions mean that it is not the most important thing involved in answering second-order questions about the first.

The division of the questions of moral philosophy into first-order questions and second-order ones, however, does not seem to me to be exhaustive. Moral philosophers quite properly discuss

[1] The view that it is not part of the business of a moral philosopher to answer moral questions has been held, for example, by A. J. Ayer in *Language, Truth and Logic* (Gollancz, 1946), Chapter VI.

a very large number of questions which are neither moral questions nor questions about moral questions, though, of course, what answer we give to these would have a bearing upon what answers we give to certain moral questions. Examples of the sort of thing I have in mind would be problems about motives and choice and the freedom of the will. Moral philosophers discuss problems concerning the interpretation of the writings of other moral philosophers, problems concerning the bearing of other studies, such as theology, biology, medicine, psychology, physiology, anthropology, economics, politics and law, upon moral philosophy. Other philosophical problems, the existence of God, the immortality of the soul, the mind/body problem, also have a bearing upon moral philosophy. It would also be unwise to consider second-order questions about ethics entirely in isolation from similar second-order questions about other branches of knowledge. Indeed, a neat classification of the problems of moral philosophy is impossible; any questions may be of interest to the moral philosopher, and it is impossible to say off-hand which problems will be relevant and which will not.

The important question now arises, whether it is possible to separate first-order questions about moral philosophy from second-order questions; whether it is possible to commit oneself to some second-order assertion about the meaning of ethical words or the manner in which ethical knowledge, if there is any, is obtained, without committing oneself to some answer to a first-order question, i.e., without committing oneself to the view that such-and-such a thing is good, or such-and-such an action right. On the face of it, it seems impossible to divorce the two kinds of question. In support of this view it can be argued that someone committing himself to any first-order moral view is implicitly claiming that the method by which he has arrived at it is sound, and therefore committing himself to the second-order view that methods of this kind are sound methods of reaching moral views. It can also be argued that anyone claiming that a certain method of arriving at a moral view is a sound one – which is a second-order moral view – is committing himself to claiming that views arrived at in this way are sound, that is, committing himself to a first-order moral view.

On the other hand, it certainly looks as if it should be possible to hold a theory about the definition of ethical terms, i.e., to hold a second-order moral view, without having any first-order theory at all about what things these terms apply to. Where second-order theories about the nature of scientific reasoning are concerned, it is possible to hold, say, that any theory established inductively is correct, without committing oneself to any view about what theories actually are established inductively. Similarly, the contention, whether true or not, that moral judgments are known to be true by a moral sense, or the contention that moral judgments are known to be true by reason, does not commit the person making these contentions to any view about what moral judgments the moral sense or reason does establish. Furthermore, it is possible to reason correctly on any given subject, without being able explicitly to state what the principles according to which one reasons are. As Locke said, it was not the case that man could not reason until Aristotle discovered the principle of the syllogism, and, just as one can play a game well without being able to say how one does it, one can reason well, without being able to say what in general constitutes the difference between good reasoning and bad.

Nevertheless many moral philosophers in the past who have been purporting to say according to what principles correct moral reasoning proceeds, have in fact done nothing more than give some very general moral judgment, which is in just as much need of justification as the moral judgments of which it is supposed to be the rationale. If one says that moral arguments with factual premises and a moral conclusion are valid, then all one is doing is to make the moral judgment that these actions of which the premises are true have a certain moral quality. For example, if I say that all ethical arguments which reason from the fact that an action has good consequences to the fact that it ought to be done are valid arguments, then all I am doing is to assert that one ought to act in such a way as to produce good consequences, which assertion is itself a moral judgment, and not a principle which can be used to test the validity of moral judgments. This, however, does not mean that ethics and meta-ethics cannot be kept separate, but simply that some moral philosophers have failed to separate them.

It must also not be forgotten that though a meta-ethical view *by itself* does not entail any ethical view, it may do so in conjunction with some other additional premises. For example, the meta-ethical view that 'right' means 'conducive to the survival of the race' does not entail any view at all about what actions are in fact right, but if you add the premise that warfare is not conducive to the survival of the race, then the moral view that warfare is wrong does follow.

Not only are there first-order and second-order problems in moral philosophy; there are also third-order problems. Third-order problems, of course, are problems about second-order problems. To the extent that philosophy consists in a consideration of the nature and methods of disciplines which study the world or make value-judgments about the world, it is a meta-enquiry, and the philosophy of history and the philosophy of science consist at least partly in a discussion of meta-problems about history and about science. What might be called the philosophy of philosophy, therefore, consists of meta-meta-problems, and the philosophy of moral philosophy consists in a third-order consideration of the nature of second-order problems about moral problems and the manner in which they may be solved.

It seems fairly obvious that the problems of meta-philosophy are not solved in the way in which problems about the nature of the world are solved, and problems about meta-ethics are not solved in the way problems about ethics are solved. I shall later, for example, argue that we do not have a moral sense. But it does not just so happen that we do not have a moral sense, though, had nature been organised differently, we might have had. Hence meta-ethical problems are solved by *a priori* reflection rather than by observation. But reflection upon what? The facts with which second-order moral philosophy starts is that we have in the English language, together with equivalents in other languages, words such as 'right' and 'wrong', 'good' and 'bad', 'duty', 'ought' and so on, which words have, roughly, the function of appraising people and things and states of affairs and of directing behaviour. It is, of course, just a matter of fact that languages possess words which have this function, and just a matter of fact that these particular words, and not others, perform this function. But those engaged in second-order moral philosophy are not so much interested in the fact that a particular word has the function it does, so much as that there is a function, which some particular word has, the nature of this function, and a comparison of this function with the function of other non-ethical words. Such statements are not known to be true by observation and experience, but by means of reflection on the functions of words. That the function, which in chess a pawn has, is a different function from the function a king has, is not an empirical statement, though the statement that the function of a king is different from the function of a pawn is an empirical statement. Similarly, that the function which it so happens the word 'good' has is a different function – and that it is different in such-and-such ways – from the function which the word 'green' has, is not an empirical statement, though that the word 'good' has a different function from the word 'green' is an empirical statement. Hence meta-ethics consists in solving problems which can be solved by reflection, rather than by observation. Meta-ethical truths are known in the same manner in which we know that, though it is an empirical fact that the English phrase 'larger than' means what it does mean, it is necessarily the case that if two terms A and B are related by the relation which is 'named' by the English phrase 'larger than', and B is related in the same way to another term C, then A must be larger than C.

CHAPTER II

IS KNOWLEDGE OF MORALITY A DELUSION?

Perhaps the first question we ought to consider is whether or not the whole of our apparent knowledge of morality is not some all-prevalent, insidious, but nevertheless inescapable delusion. Views roughly to this effect have been hinted at by Greek Sophists, Marxist economists, Freudian psychologists and Existentialist moralists. However, in the following pages I shall examine the question in my own way.

Hume, who rejects the views of those who deny the reality of moral distinctions,[1] himself produces little argument against the view he so cavalierly dismisses, and most moral philosophers have followed him in not taking it very seriously, or ignoring it altogether.

By the question 'Is knowledge of morality a delusion?' I do not mean 'Is it a delusion that men ever act morally?' Philosophers who answer this latter question in the affirmative presumably maintain something like this. Men never behave as they ought or, if they do, this is only from base or selfish motives. They never perform kind or generous or noble or unselfish actions, but only persuade others or delude themselves that they do. Consequently all men are bad, or, at least morally indifferent, and it is a delusion to think that virtue is ever exemplified in the motives or actions of human beings at all.

It should be noticed that those who hold this view are implicitly assuming that there is nothing radically wrong with man's moral faculties as such. They are not disputing, but, rather, implicitly presupposing, that some motives or traits of character are better than others, and also that we know that they are; they are just maintaining that, as a matter of fact, men do not have the better ones. They do not doubt that some ways of behaving are better than others, that there are some things which men ought to do, and others which they ought not to do; they are just asserting that men never behave in the better ways, or do

[1] David Hume, *An Enquiry Concerning the Principles of Morals*, ed. by L. A. Selby-Bigge (Oxford University Press, 2nd edition, 1902), pp. 169–70.

as they ought, unless it suits them. They do not wish to maintain that there is anything radically wrong with man's capacity for making moral judgments; they themselves are quite prepared to make moral judgments, uncomplimentary ones, about mankind as a whole. It is man's moral achievements, not his moral insight, that they think badly of, though they must also think badly of man's moral insight, to the extent that they are presumably bound to maintain that the vast majority of mankind have too high an opinion of their own virtue. Even those who think we have no duties because our will is not free, are not suggesting that there is anything wrong with man's moral *insight*. His moral insight tells him the hypothetical proposition that he would have certain duties, if he were free, but unfortunately, he is not free.

The view I want to discuss is the more interesting and more radical one that there is something fundamentally wrong with the belief, which most men seem to have, that there *is* a better or a worse in matters of conduct; with the belief that some things are fitting, admirable or obligatory, while others are base, ignoble or wrong. Whereas those who hold the view, which I do not intend to discuss here, that morality is a delusion, in the sense that it is a delusion that men ever behave well, those who hold this latter view maintain that it is a delusion that there *are* proper or improper ways of behaving at all. Presumably, since that all men behave badly, or that sin is ineradicable from human nature, are themselves moral assessments, it would be just as much a delusion that men are all evil as that some of them are good. We must distinguish, therefore, between the claim to see through *men*, and the more interesting claim to see through *morality*.

We must beware, of course, of saying that morality is a delusion that it is *better* to be without, for this would presuppose that some things were *better* than others, and this would presuppose the falsity of the very view which is being contended for. But perhaps it could be said that all that is being contended is that a morality which demands sacrifice, a morality of duty, a morality of categorical imperatives which must be obeyed, irrespectively of the interests of the agent, is a delusion; but that it is no delusion that some things are better *for* people than others; no delusion, for example, that food is better for people than starvation, and hence no delusion that it is better for people to be free from the delusion of morality than to remain its slave.

The view that morality is a delusion, in this more radical sense, however, is not at all clear. Those who maintain it may mean one or other of the following three things.

1. They may mean that the moral judgments which we normally and often unreflectingly believe, are all *false*, and the things we describe as having moral attributes do not ever have them. According to this view, it is always *false* that we have a duty to do something, whether we want to do it or not, and always false that some men are admirable, others vile, and that some ways of behaving are better and more desirable than others.

2. They may mean that certain words, like 'right' and 'wrong', 'good' and 'bad', 'ought' and 'ought not', and others which it would be tedious to enumerate, are words *without meaning*. Consequently, though men think they are saying things which are true and important when they use these words, they are in fact saying nothing at all. They suppose that they are talking sense when they use such words, but this supposition is delusive. It is a delusion, of course, which may have a profound effect on the behaviour of the men who suffer from it, but a rational man will not have it, for a rational man would not suppose he was talking sense when he was in fact talking nonsense.

3. It may be held that, though moral words are not meaningless and do express moral judgments, some of which are in fact true, men are never in a position to *know which* of these moral judgments are true and which false, and that the only proper attitude to such judgments is one of complete and total scepticism. Men's moral beliefs, or at any rate some of them, may be true, but men never have any good reason, or even any reason at all, for supposing that any given belief is true, and so all such beliefs are alike irrational. A rational man will realize that the truth on moral matters is something he can never attain, and will take up the only proper attitude to such issues, which is one of thoroughgoing scepticism.

It is worth noticing that no-one ought to hold all three of these views, or even any two of them, simultaneously. The second is straightforwardly incompatible with the first and the third; if moral words are meaningless, then they can express no moral judgments which can be described as being all false, which is what the first view holds, and no moral judgments which can be described as unfounded, which is what they are according to the third view. And though there is, so far as I can see, no *logical* incompatibility of the normal sort between the first view and the third, for there is no reason why it should not be the case that, though all moral judgments are in fact false, we never *know* which of them are true and which of them are false, no philosopher ought to maintain both views for, if he asserts that they are all false, he is implicitly claiming that at least one person, namely himself, knows or has reason for thinking that they are all false, and so implicitly claiming that not all moral judgments can be unfounded. *His own* moral judgments must be in a specially privileged position, exempt from the rule that no-one can ever know, or even have any real reason for thinking, that any moral judgment is true rather than false, or false rather than true.

The second of the three views is, I suppose, the most difficult for anyone to find credible. It is true that, when God gave man the gift of speech, he gave him also, as the other side of the coin, the capacity to talk nonsense, which capacity man has, ever since, made the fullest use of. Nevertheless, it is difficult to believe that a whole class of sentences, or a whole area of discourse, can as such be meaningless, particularly when it has survived, and so presumably performed a useful function, since time immemorial. But the arguments which have been used to show that moral discourse, though it may be abused, must in general be meaningful, are not very convincing. It is true that ethical terms are used and so, presumably, there are rules for their use and so, if for a word to have meaning is for its use to be governed by rules, moral terms must have a meaning. But meaning admits of degrees. Theological discourse cannot be wholly meaningless, but it might be, as some have maintained, *in the last resort* meaningless, and the same might be said for moral discourse. People do not *fully* understand everything they read or hear. Their understanding is frequently partial, and when it is only partial, it is impossible for them to tell whether what they only partially understand is fully meaningful, or only partially so. It is because of men's partial understanding, it might be argued, that they have continued to use theological discourse, although theological discourse is meaningless, and the same is true of the language of morals. I do not myself think this view is very plausible, however, though I do not see how it can be refuted.

The view that all *judgments* (not just moral ones) are false would appear to be self-contradictory. If all judgments are false, then, since that all judgments are false is itself a judgment, *it* is false, and so some judgments are true. It might be possible to escape from this difficulty by arguing, plausibly or otherwise, that no judgment can be about a class of judgments of which it is a member; any judgment about judgments must be of an order one higher than the judgments it is about. Hence the judgment that all judgments are false, must be about judgments of the order n, but since it itself will be of the order $n+1$, it will not be about itself, and so will not imply its own falsity.

However, even the view that only all *moral* judgments are false is initially faced with what might appear to be an insuperable objection. Not *all* moral judgments can be false, because some moral judgments are the contradictories of others, and if a given moral judgment is false, its contradictory must be true. The statement that incest is *not* wrong is just as much a moral judgment as the statement that incest *is* wrong. The statement that it is not our duty to help others is just as much a moral judgment as the statement that it is our duty to help others. It is possible for someone to *refrain from making* either judgment, or to say that he does not know which of them is true, but it scarcely seems possible to deny that one or other of them must be true.

There are various possible ways of escaping the above difficulty. Firstly, it is possible to say that statements such as 'It is our duty to help others' and 'It is not our duty to help others' are not strict contradictories, but only contradictories on a given assumption, and that this assumption is false. To take an example from a sphere other than the sphere of morals, it might be argued that 'The King of France is bald' and 'The King of France is not bald' are not contradictories, but only contradictories on the assumption that there is a King of France. If there is a King of France, it must be the case that he is either bald or not bald, and that he cannot be both; but if there is not a King of France, then it may be (or even must be) the case that neither are true. (It might be held, incidentally, that this is because they are both false, or because they are both neither true nor false.) Similarly, it might be argued that 'It is our duty to help others' and 'It is not our duty to help others' are not strict contradictories, but only contradictories on the assumption that we can help what we do. If we *can* help what we do, then it must either be the case that it is, or that it is not, our duty to help others, but if we can *not* help what we do, then these statements are either both false, or (what is less plausible) both neither true nor false. Such a view, however, does not maintain that there is anything wrong with our moral faculties as such, but merely that there is something

wrong with a factual assumption, namely, that we can help what
we do, which most of our moral beliefs presuppose. Consequently
I shall not discuss it any further.

Secondly, we may escape the argument which maintains that
since some moral judgments contradict others, some moral judgments must be true, by denying that truth and falsity are applicable to moral judgments at all. Those philosophers who have held
this view, however, have not generally wished to say that there
was anything radically wrong with our moral faculties, so much as
that moral philosophers had totally misunderstood the nature of
moral discourse, which is not to report the discoveries which our
moral faculties enable us to make, but to do something more like
commanding, exhorting or persuading. Consequently discussion
of this view will be reserved for a later chapter.

The only way I can think of of escaping the above refutation –
that since some moral judgments are the contradictories of others
they cannot all be false – of the view that all moral beliefs are
false is this. Moral beliefs may be divided into two classes, which
I shall call 'positive' and 'innocuous' respectively. Among positive moral beliefs I shall count both the opinion that a certain
thing ought to be done and the opinion that it ought not to be
done; among innocuous moral beliefs I shall count the opinion
that a certain thing is permissible but that, since it does not matter if we do not do it, it is not actually obligatory, that is, it is
also permissible to omit it. Among positive moral beliefs would be
the belief that a certain action or man was worthy of praise or of
blame; among innocuous moral beliefs would be the opinion that a
certain action or man was neither worthy of praise nor of blame.
Though there is something logically wrong with the view that all
moral beliefs are false, there is nothing, so far as I can see, *logically*
wrong with the view that only non-innocuous moral beliefs are false.

What we have called innocuous moral beliefs, however, are
just as moral as positive ones are, and the view that only such
moral beliefs are true is just as much a moral theory, though a
queer one, as any that have been held. Hence it is not as radical a
view as the one that the whole area of our moral beliefs is a delusion. According to it, men are the victims of a delusion only when
they hold *positive* moral views, and a holder of the theory who holds
no *positive* moral view, though he does hold a *moral* view, is not
a victim of this delusion at all. However, since it is itself a moral
theory of sorts, it cannot be supported by any *general* argument,

if such an argument is possible, which argument would purport to show that *all* moral beliefs were false or that there was something radically and inveterately wrong with our faculty for arriving at and considering moral judgments, for the user of such an argument would be cutting the ground from under his own feet, or sawing off the branch on which he himself was sitting. For if his argument did show that moral beliefs were false, it would show, *a fortiori*, that the belief that all innocuous moral beliefs were true, was false.

Before going on to consider what sort of argument might be used in support of the 'anti-moralist' position that *all* ethical beliefs are false, let us consider arguments in favour of this rather queer moral position, which anyone who held that only innocuous moral judgments are true must be committed to, which view might be called 'moral nihilism', according to which, roughly, everything is permissible.

Sometimes it has been held that though in fact everything is alike permissible, those who are of the contrary opinion are so because they are the dupes of certain interested people.[1] Sometimes it is suggested that it is the strong who are responsible for this deception; the strong, who govern us, persuade us that it is, among other things, our duty to obey the law, which law the strong make in their own interest, whereas in fact we have neither this nor any other duty. Sometimes a view directly opposite to this is held, namely, that it is the *weak* who dupe the *strong*; the weak, who realize that the strong have the power to take at will both their lives and their property, have cleverly persuaded the strong, as their best means of defence against them, that it is their duty not to do these things.

Both the view that the strong dupe the weak, and that the weak dupe the strong, seem to me to have difficulties which are insuperable. First of all, it is not just the strong, or the weak, who benefit from the performance of duty, but everybody. We do not benefit from *every* performance of what is generally supposed to be a duty; sometimes other people have what is generally supposed to be a duty, the performance of which would harm us; and sometimes we ourselves have what is generally supposed to be a duty to sacrifice our own interests to that of others. Nevertheless, it is obvious that in a society where people did not think they had duties, and were not in any way guided by the moral beliefs

[1] See Plato, *The Republic*, Book I.

which to some extent guide us, *everybody* would be very badly off indeed. Secondly, it is just an empirical fact that the weak as well as the strong (or the strong as well as the weak) suppose they have duties. Therefore the strong (or the weak) must not have duped others only; they must also have somehow succeeded in duping themselves. Lastly the person holding the theory that we have been duped into thinking we have duties is implicitly claiming that he himself has seen through the machinations of those responsible for this delusion, i.e. he is claiming that he himself is exempt from some of the weaknesses which beset his neighbours. On the whole, it is unlikely that he is right.

Some psychiatrists seem to be opposed to what they are pleased to call 'morality', and appear to suppose themselves to hold something approximating to the view that all things are permissible. Some seem to think that, by and large, morality is bad for people, and that people in general, and their patients in particular, would be better off without it. They sometimes class man's belief that there are certain things he ought to do as a delusion, along, perhaps, with his belief that there is a God, and that we have immortal souls. In forming such an opinion it seems very likely that these people have been to a large extent influenced by the effect of certain moral prohibitions upon the health and happiness of some of their patients. Some people – and these are the people who seem more likely than most to find their way into psychiatrists' consulting rooms – appear to think that certain forms of sexual relationship – or perhaps even any form of sexual relationship – are immoral, and it would also appear that they would live much more satisfactory lives if they were not prevented or impeded from forming such relationships by their belief that they are immoral. Well, perhaps these beliefs are harmful, and perhaps, too, they are not only harmful, but mistaken, and the things these psychiatrists' patients think are wrong not wrong at all. Nevertheless, we must not be misled by the charming English euphemism by which it is customary to speak of departures from the commonly accepted standard of sexual behaviour as 'immorality' into supposing that sexual morality is the whole of morality, or that sexual prohibitions are the only prohibitions. It is very unlikely that any psychiatrist would wish to say that murder or rape was not wrong, on the ground that preventing themselves from committing it was bad for their patients. Perhaps, too, psychiatrists think they are opposed to morality, when they are merely opposed to a stringent or exacting morality, or merely to a stringent or exacting sexual morality. Or perhaps they are inclined to think they think that all positive moral judgments are false, when all they really think is that a certain sub-class of positive moral judgments are false, namely, those stating that certain people deserve to be praised, or, more particularly, blamed, for performing certain actions, or that some men are better than others. It may be that, because all men are alike actuated by self-interest, no men are better than any others, or that, because all human actions are the inevitable outcome of a heredity and environment over which the agent has no control, no one can very properly be praised or blamed for what he does. Nevertheless, these are not the only sorts of moral judgment there are, and, unless our psychiatrist is prepared to hold the view that murder and cruelty and violence are not wrong, he does not adhere to the moral nihilist position we are at the moment discussing. Indeed, once it is seen that what I have called 'moral nihilism', since it maintains the moral proposition that all things are permissible, is itself a moral position, it is difficult to see how anyone could hold it. One might maintain, in one's study, as a flight of speculative fancy, that absolutely all moral beliefs, not simply what we have called positive ones, have something radically and inherently wrong with them and, in a way, escape confrontation with hard reality by the mere fact that such a view, if it militates against any moral view, militates against all alike, and so is somehow felt to be not quite serious. A man who holds it may say to his daughter, or his servant, or his pupil, 'It is false that it is wrong to sleep with whom you please,' and his pronouncement is deprived of all seriousness or effect by the fact that he is, or ought to be, if he sticks to the logical consequences of his own view, also prepared to say to them, 'It is also false that it is perfectly all right to sleep with whom you please'. Pointing in both directions at once, he escapes responsibility for pointing in either. The view we have called moral nihilism, however, is not intellectually frivolous in this way; where two moral propositions are contradictory, it asserts one, and denies the other. The very fact that one assumes some responsibility in putting it forward – or would do so, if there were any chance of one's being taken seriously – means that it is the less likely to be held, and so, though logically less vulnerable than the view that all moral beliefs are false, it is at the same time psychologically less attractive.

When we go on to consider what sort of argument could be used in an attempt to support the anti-moralist view that *all* moral beliefs (not just the ones which are not innocuous) are false, I think it is clear that such arguments do not support the view that they are all false, but the different view that no one has any reason, or any good reason, for supposing them to be true, and that consequently such beliefs are all alike irrational, which brings us to a discussion of the third of the three views distinguished above.

The view that no one has any reason, or any good reason, for his moral beliefs escapes the objection which appeared conclusive against the view that all moral beliefs were false. According to this view, it is not both false that cruelty is wrong, and also false that cruelty is not wrong; one of these is true, and the other false, but no one has ever any good reason for believing the one rather than the other. It is held that all our moral beliefs are unfounded, because it is held that it is always possible to explain how it comes about that any man, or any community of men, accepts certain beliefs and not others. The sorts of explanation which might be given are these.

When one considers certain classes of belief – moral, religious and political beliefs are the most outstanding examples of the sort of thing I have in mind – one cannot fail to be impressed by the fact that different beliefs are distributed unevenly about the globe and that, furthermore, they tend to *stay* distributed that way over fairly long periods of time. This distribution – partly, though not entirely, because of the fact that people move about – is somewhat higgledy-piggledy, but in certain areas you find Christians, while in others you find Buddhists; in some areas you find democrats, in others you find communists; in some areas you find people who regard polygamy with abhorrence, whereas in others you find that people regard it as the right and proper form of matrimony. This is doubtless largely due to the fact that we tend very largely to accept our moral, religious and political beliefs from those round about us, our parents, or those responsible for our upbringing, in particular. Though we sometimes react against these beliefs, we generally react against them only within a context, i.e. react against some of them while accepting others, and it is quite likely that our rejection of them is no more rational than our acceptance of them would have been. Hence it is at least plausible to suggest that we have the moral, political and religious beliefs we do have, not because we perceive that there are good grounds for accepting them, but because they have been stamped upon us in our youth. If the President of the United States of America had been born in Leningrad and the Prime Minister of Soviet Russia had been born in New York, it is difficult to believe that, had their force of character and political acumen brought each to equally high positions in the other's country, each would not have been condemning the beliefs which each now so enthusiastically supports. It is difficult not to believe that if by an accident of birth the Archbishop of Canterbury had been born a Jew, he would not now be employing his outstanding talents in furthering a very different cause.

I think it must be allowed that it is obvious that irrational forces do play a very large part in moulding our political, religious and – which is what we are here concerned with – moral beliefs. Our moral beliefs are bound to be irrationally affected by the moral beliefs of the people amongst whom we are brought up, by our emotions, our interests, our social and economic position, and even by our physiological state, which may predispose some to a melancholy asceticism, and others to a cheerful worldliness (though, by and large, only the former go to the lengths of writing books on moral philosophy). It must be remembered, however, that the view we are considering holds, not simply that, in forming the moral beliefs we do, we are at every moment liable to be irrationally motivated by such logically irrelevant but causally effective factors as a middle-class upbringing, a domineering mother, or a poor digestion, but that absolutely every belief which has ever been held is influenced solely by such factors. Now the reason why I said previously that such arguments as these would be very unsatisfactory if used in favour of the view that all moral beliefs are false is that the fact that I arrive at a certain opinion irrationally does not mean that it is *false*. I may irrationally believe, solely because I want to, that there are a class of beings whose function it is to watch over me, help and care for me, and my life and property – but so there are (I speak, of course, of the police force). I may wake up unreasonably convinced that evil will befall me, and so it may. Things I believe for the worst of reasons, or without any reason at all, may, nevertheless be true. Hence an argument to the effect that all moral beliefs are unfounded does not at all show that they are all false. To show that a moral belief is false, one must oneself use the type of argument, whatever it may be, appropriate to a moral issue, and this is a very odd thing for people who wish to discredit moral argument in general to do.

Hence you do not show that a belief is *false* merely by being able to produce a causal explanation of how it comes to be held. Do you, by giving such a causal explanation, show it to be *irrational*? Now the facts which seem to show that moral beliefs, amongst others, are irrational, can be put, if we wish, in a much less damaging way. There can be a history of truth and discovery, as well as one of error and blind alleys, and the ideal historian would have to explain not only why people came to make certain mistakes at certain times and not others, but also why they came to hit upon truths at certain times and not at others. The fact that there is a perfectly good causal explanation of how it comes about that the Greeks believed the sun went round the earth, but we do not, does not mean that our belief that the earth goes round the sun is irrational. Why, then, should the fact that it is possible to explain why the Greeks did not believe that infanticide was wrong, while we do, mean our belief that it is wrong is irrational? Perhaps both man's insights and his errors alike admit of a causal explanation. Perhaps Jones would not have believed some mistaken theory were it not for his great respect for the teacher who propounded it. On the other hand, perhaps Smith would not have hit upon an important truth were it not for his detestation of the eminent men whose opinions it overthrew. One may be made to think aright by being influenced by the people among whom one is brought up, as well as prevented from doing this by them. One's position in life may free one from certain blindnesses, as well as prevent one from having certain insights. A physiological state of one kind may produce delusions, but so a different physiological state may sharpen one's capacity for following difficult arguments which men in a different physiological state cannot follow. Some drugs may refine our faculties, though others blunt them.

The fact, then, that a man would not have believed a given doctrine had he not lived in a certain environment, at a certain period of history, been brought up in a certain way, had certain wishes, or possessed a certain type of physiological make-up does not by itself tend to show that his belief in this doctrine is irrational, or that he has no good reasons for accepting it. Beliefs, in other words, may have *necessary* conditions in the past history of the believer – in events in his life which are such that, if they had not occurred, he would not have believed what he did – without being made irrational thereby. But what if they have *sufficient* conditions in the past history of the believer, in events which are such that, if they occur, he *must* believe what he does? What if certain things happen to a man which enable us to say, not just that, if they had not happened, he would not have believed such-and-such a thing, but that, since they have happened, he must believe such and such a thing? Even this, it seems to me, would not force us to say that his beliefs must be irrational. A knowledge of a man's past life may, for all I can see to the contrary, enable us to say that, at a later date, he will form, in a certain way, a certain belief which goes against the evidence, or that, at a later date, he will quite correctly perform certain mental operations which result in his apprehending a truth.

There is, however, another sense in which our beliefs may have sufficient conditions in our past lives. The statement that our beliefs have sufficient conditions in the past histories of the believers may mean that we believe certain things *only* because we were jealous of our fathers, frightened of losing our money, or addicted to opium. Since the word 'only' means, in this context, 'and not for any other reason', it does indeed follow that the beliefs of people who arrive at their conclusions *only* for these reasons are irrational. But though an empirical investigation of the *genesis* of our beliefs might well show that they all had necessary conditions, or even that they all had sufficient conditions, in the first of the two senses distinguished above, could such an investigation show that they had sufficient conditions in the second of these two senses?

It seems to me that, should a sociologist or a psychologis' or a physiologist pronounce that our moral beliefs are irrational, on the grounds of something he has discovered by means of a study of sociology or psychology or physiology, then he is unwittingly stepping out of the sphere in which his training makes him an expert into one in which it does not. We have already seen that, should someone claim that a study of one of these subjects has shown him that a given moral view is false, we can reply to him that the statement that a moral view is false is as much a moral judgment as the statement that it is true, and so that, to show that it *is* false, a study of psychology or sociology or physiology is not enough. It must be shown to be false by means of the use of the proper methods appropriate to moral argument, whatever these may be. It may *seem* that the sociologist or psychologist or physiologist escapes this difficulty if he stops short of saying that a given moral view is false, and simply says that, though it may be true, a study of its causal factors has shown that there are no reasons for thinking that it is. Though it may not be obvious, however, the statement that a moral judgment is *unfounded* is as much a moral judgment as the statement that it is *false*, and one is passing over from sociology or psychology or physiology to moralizing when one says that a moral judgment is irrational just as much as when one says that it is mistaken or erroneous. When one says that a given moral judgment is irrational, what one means is that the reasons the people who hold it have for thinking it is true are not good reasons for thinking it is true, or not reasons for thinking it to be true at all. Now it may be a matter of empirical fact that someone's reasons for thinking so-and-so are such-and-such, and it may also be an empirical fact that these reasons would not have weighed with him but for certain causal factors such as that he wished very much to believe the conclusion, or that he had been brought up in an environment where such reasons weighed with everybody else, or that he was at the time in a certain physiological or psychological state. But if the psychologist goes on to say that these reasons do not at all support the belief in question, then he is doing something over and above what this empirical investigation of the causes of this belief entitle him to do. If the belief in question is a belief about the past, what he is doing, over and above sociology, psychology or physiology is history; if the belief in question is a mathematical one, then what he is doing, over and above these things, is mathematics; if it is a political belief then, in pronouncing upon the adequacy of the reasons given in support of it, he is trespassing into politics; finally, if the belief is a moral one, then he is stepping over the borders of sociology, psychology or physiology, and moralizing. To add the *coup de grâce* to this position, it is only necessary to point out that if all moral beliefs are without foundation, then, since the belief that certain moral beliefs are inadequately supported is *itself* a moral belief, it, too, must be without foundation. So this anti-ethical theory, like the last, ends by digging its own grave.

The matter, however, does not rest here. In discussing the third of three possible anti-moralist positions (the fourth position, if you count the view that only 'innocuous' moral judgments are true as an anti-moralist position) we took it that it was not being disputed that there were good reasons for or against moral beliefs to be found, if only man was not blinded by his desires and his upbringing and his physiological endowment from ever seeing them. A more sophisticated version of the same position would hold, not that there were such reasons, though man can never see them (much as, presumably, there is a proof of the four-colour theorem, but no mathematician has yet discovered it) but that there are not even any good or bad reasons for or against moral beliefs to be discovered. According to this more sophisticated view, the notions of good and bad reason, of satisfactory argument, or conclusive proof do not go together with the notion of moral judgment. Moral judgments are not the sort of thing for which one can have reasons, good or bad. It simply does not make sense to talk of moral judgments being formed rationally or irrationally. Whereas on the more unsophisticated view, moral judgments escape being formed rationally in the sense in which a boy may escape being clean, viz. by being dirty, on the more sophisticated view moral judgments escape being formed rationally only in the sense in which a neutron or a rainbow or an equation or God escapes being clean; just as these things are neither clean nor dirty, so neither the notions of rationality nor irrationality apply to moral judgments.

Of course, anyone who holds that moral judgments are neither rational nor irrational, in that it does not make sense to speak of there being good or bad reasons for holding them, is also very likely, though not necessarily, to hold that they are neither true nor false, that is, to hold that it does not make sense to say that they are true, and does not make sense to say that they are false. Obviously, there is no point in trying to arrive at true answers to moral questions if the notion of truth is inapplicable to moral judgments, and no chance of success in our efforts to think rationally about moral questions if it does not make sense to say that our methods of answering them are either rational or irrational. However, the view that the notion of truth is inapplicable to moral judgments themselves, and the notion of rationality inapplicable to the manner in which we form them, need not lead to this distressing conclusion. After all, clothes or figures or faces are neither true nor false, rational nor irrational, and yet some are preferable to others. Perhaps moral judgments are like this in that, though there are appropriate criteria for preferring some to others, these have nothing to do with truth or falsehood, and the means of arriving at truth. These questions will have to be discussed in a later chapter.[1] For the time being, it is perhaps worth pointing out that the view that falsehood and irrationality are not applicable to moral judgments can no more be established by an empirical scientist pursuing his vocation than can the view that they are all false or all irrational. You cannot show that a moral judgment is false or irrational without departing from the sphere of empirical science and entering the sphere of moral epistemology. Similarly, you cannot show that the notions of truth and rationality are inapplicable to moral judgments and the methods by which these are arrived at without departing from the sphere of empirical science and crossing the bounds of that area where philosophy and the study of lanaguage intermingle, the area containing discussions about what things can properly be said of what, or the question of what it makes sense to say.

[1] Chapter XII.

CHAPTER III

SOME PRELIMINARY DISTINCTIONS

The refutation of moral scepticism given in the preceding chapter – we shall see later that it must be regarded as merely provisional – can scarcely satisfy unless it is backed up by some positive account of the rationale of the process by which we arrive at our moral beliefs, or by some explanation of the manner in which we arrive at them which makes manifest their justification. It is the investigation of this problem with which this work is concerned. But in order to carry out this investigation, it is first necessary to elucidate some distinctions common among epistemologists. This I shall attempt to do in this chapter. We shall be concerned with the distinction of propositions into those which are analytic and those which are synthetic, into those which are *a priori* and those which are empirical, into those which are necessary and those which are contingent, into those which are inferred from other propositions and those which can be known without inference, and with some reflections upon the manner in which we acquire *concepts*.

ANALYTIC/SYNTHETIC

The first philosopher to divide judgments into those which were analytic and those which were synthetic was Immanuel Kant.[1] According to him, a judgment was analytic if its predicate could be obtained by analysis from its subject. Otherwise it was synthetic. For example, the judgment that every effect has a cause is analytic, for the predicate, having a cause, can be obtained by analysis from the subject, and to deny such a proposition is self-contradictory. On the other hand, since the predicate, having a cause, cannot be obtained by analysis from the subject of the proposition 'Every *event* has a cause', this latter proposition is synthetic.

Kant's distinction has had to be widened by later philosophers. Kant supposed, wrongly, that every proposition ascribed a predicate to a subject, and hence supposed that an account of the distinction between analytic and synthetic propositions which

[1] See the Introduction to the *Critique of Pure Reason*, trans. by Norman Kemp Smith (Macmillan & Co. Ltd., 1933.)

would apply to subject/predicate propositions like 'Every effect has a cause' would apply to all propositions. Since it is impossible to describe with plausibility judgments such as 'If you drop it, it will break', or 'Either he is telling the truth or is a very good liar', as ascribing a predicate to a subject, Kant's account must be modified to fit these and other judgments which are not of subject/predicate form.

An account of analytic judgments which is wider than Kant's and would, if it were correct, apply to analytic propositions of all sorts, is this. A judgment is said to by analytic if it is true simply by virtue of the meanings of the words in the sentence which expresses it; otherwise it is synthetic. To know that an analytic proposition is true, all one needs to know is what the words used to formulate it mean; no knowledge of anything over and above this is necessary. Hence it is sometimes said that a proposition is analytic if its truth can be deduced from the definitions of the words which express it, and that it is synthetic if it cannot be deduced from these definitions. Hence 'Bachelors are unmarried' is analytic, for that they are unmarried follows simply from the definition of 'bachelor' as a man who is not yet married. For this reason it is sometimes said that analytic propositions, such as 'All bachelors are unmarried', unlike synthetic propositions, such as 'All bachelors are unhappy', are true by convention – true by convention because it is simply a matter of convention that words like 'bachelor' and 'unmarried' are used in the way English people in fact do use them.[1]

This account of the distinction between analytic and synthetic propositions must certainly be wrong.[2] It is just a matter of brute fact that the words 'bachelor' and 'unmarried man' mean what they do; indeed, this is even part of what is meant by saying that their meaning is a matter of convention. The word 'man' might have meant what the word 'mother' means now, in which case the sentence 'Bachelors are unmarried men' would simply not express a proposition which is analytic; it would express a proposition which is actually false, the one now expressed by the words 'Bachelors are unmarried mothers'.

However, an analytic proposition is supposed to be incapable of being false. A bachelor cannot possibly be married. But

---

[1] See A. J. Ayer, *Language, Truth and Logic*, (Gollancz, 1946), Chapter IV.
[2] See W. Kneale, 'Are Necessary Truths True by Convention?' in *Clarity is not Enough*, ed. by H. D. Lewis (Allen & Unwin, 1963).

circumstances might arise, and would arise if the words 'bachelor' and 'unmarried man' meant something different from what they do, when the definition 'The word "bachelor" means "unmarried man" ', was incorrect; hence, if analytic propositions were true simply because they followed from definitions, circumstances could arise in which analytic propositions would be false. No circumstances, however, can conceivably arise in which a bachelor can be unmarried.

The view that analytic propositions are true by convention, then, is a product of confusion, and the confusion which has produced it is this. Propositions are not the same thing as sentences, though they can be formulated by means of sentences. The proposition that the sea is wet is not true by convention, but the sentence which English people use to formulate this proposition has the meaning it does, and so expresses the proposition it does because of the meaning, which certainly is conventional, that English people attach to the words in it. If they were to change these conventions, so that the word 'sea' came to mean 'earth' then the sentence 'The sea is wet' would express a false proposition, the proposition which we now express by the sentence 'The earth is wet'. This does not make any difference to the proposition which we may describe as the proposition expressed by the sentence 'The sea is wet', given the conventions which at the moment govern the use of the words in that sentence. The truth of that proposition cannot be altered by a change in mere verbal conventions. What happens when we do alter verbal conventions which apply to the words in the sentence 'The sea is wet' is that these words, since their meaning is now altered, do not express the proposition which is now expressed by this sentence, but express some other proposition instead, a proposition which may be a false one.

'The sea is wet' is a synthetic proposition, but the same is true of an analytic proposition such as 'Every effect has a cause'. To alter the conventions which determine the meaning of the word 'effect' or the word 'cause' would not alter the truth of the proposition which we now express by means of these words. What it would do would be to make the sentence which now expresses this proposition express some other proposition, a proposition which might not be an analytic one, and which might even be a false one. The truth of the proposition 'Every effect has a cause', however, is independent of verbal conventions: this must be so, because the truth of analytic propositions which are necessarily true, cannot be altered, but verbal conventions quite easily can be.

From this it follows that, contrary to what is often said, the truth of an analytic proposition cannot be deduced from definitions, if these are propositions about the meanings of words. This is because propositions about the meanings which words have are always capable of being false, whereas an analytic proposition is not capable of being false, and a proposition which is not capable of being false cannot be deduced from a proposition which is capable of being false.

The best definition of analyticity is in terms of entailment.[1] Thus the rather complicated hypothetical proposition 'If all men are mortal, and Socrates is a man, then Socrates is mortal' is analytic if and only if the antecedent 'All men are mortal and Socrates is a man' *entails* the consequent 'Socrates is mortal'. 'All bachelors are unmarried' is analytic if and only if that someone is a bachelor *entails* that he is unmarried. 'A thing cannot both be and not be', or the more modern version of this ancient principle, 'Not both p and not-p' (where the symbol p means 'any proposition', much as the symbols x and y in mathematics mean 'any number') is analytic if and only if that a thing is *entails* that it is not the case that it is not, or if p entails not not-p). Again, 'A thing must either be or not be' or its more modern version, 'Either p or not-p', is analytic if and only if that it is not the case that it is, *entails* that it is not.

One must learn to recognise cases of entailment by being presented with examples of them, and some people are not very good at doing this, but this does not mean that entailment cannot be defined. One proposition entails another if the state of affairs which would make the first proposition true would also make the second proposition true, or, what amounts to the same thing, if any state of affairs which would make the second proposition false would also make the first proposition false. Hence that someone is a bachelor entails that he is unmarried because the state of affairs which would make it true to say that he was a bachelor would automatically also make it true to say that he was unmarried. The proposition 'All men are mortal, and Socrates is a man', entails the proposition 'Socrates is mortal' because any state of affairs which would make the first proposition true would *ipso facto* make the second proposition true.

Whether the relation of entailment holds between two proposi-

[1] The view which follows is not as unlike as might appear the view which Hume puts forward in *A Treatise of Human Nature*, Book I, Part III, Section I.

tions or not does not depend on human convention. The meanings of the words in the sentences 'All men are mortal and Socrates is a man' and 'Socrates is mortal', are of course, a matter of human – or rather English – convention, which could be changed if there were any point in doing so, and if we could persuade enough people to go along with us. But given the conventions which determine the meanings of the words in the first and second of these two sentences, then there is no need for a further set of rules to determine whether the proposition expressed by the first sentence entails the proposition expressed by the second sentence, nor is it possible to have such rules. Given that the words in these two sentences mean what they do mean, the first sentence could not express a proposition which did not entail the proposition expressed by the second sentence. Hence there is not any need to have rules determining what propositions entail one another, over and above having rules which determine what the words in the sentences expressing those propositions mean; indeed, it would be impossible to have such rules, for one could not have a rule which, in spite of the meanings allocated to words like 'bachelor' and 'unmarried man', determined that a man's being a bachelor does not entail that he is unmarried.

PROPOSITIONS WHICH ARE NEITHER ANALYTIC NOR SYNTHETIC

It is sometimes maintained that there is a class of propositions which are neither analytic nor synthetic.[1] This view seems to me to be correct, though not necessarily for the reasons that have been given for it. Words come to have the meaning they do by a series of decisions. We use a word to describe a certain kind of thing, and then we come across something which is like, but not quite like, the things which we have in the past described by that word. When this happens, we have to *decide* whether to describe these things by this word, or not. If we do decide to describe them by this word, it is not that we have altered the meaning of the word in question, in the sense that the word was previously used in such a way that these things were not to be described by this word, but now they may be. Rather we have specified whether these

[1] See Willard Van Orman Quine, 'Two dogmas of Empiricism', in *From a Logical Point of View*, (Harvard University Press, 1953) and F. Waismann, Verifiability', in *Essays on Logic and Language*, First Series, ed. by Antony Flew (Blackwell, 1951).

things are to be described by this word or not; formerly there was no rule saying whether or not these things were to be so described, but now there is. If we decide to call these things by this word, it will be a synthetic proposition that some X things (where X is the word in question) are Y (where Y is a description of the new case in terms which do not include the word in question). If we decide not to call these things by this word, it will be an analytic proposition that X things are *not* Y. For example, before English-speaking people have come across any black swans, it will be simply undecided whether birds which otherwise resemble swans, but are black, are to be called swans or not. If English people decide to call them swans then it will become a (true) synthetic proposition that some swans are black. If they decide not to call them swans, then it will be an analytic proposition that all swans are white. But this is the situation after the meaning of the word 'swan' has been specified to meet the demands of a case which had not been previously met with. *Before* the rules for the use of the word 'swan' had been so specified, it was neither an analytic and true proposition that no swans were black, nor a synthetic and false proposition that no swans were black, though after the rules for the use of this word had been made determinate, this sentence expressed a false synthetic proposition. (If English-speaking people had decided not to call these black birds swans then the sentence 'No swans are black' would have expressed a true analytic proposition.)

Cases arise which have more relevance to ethics than the example we have just been considering. Consider the question 'Does a woman who has artificial insemination by donor commit adultery?' It is no use trying to resolve this question by appealing to the actual use of the word 'adultery'. Since no such cases had until quite recently been met with or envisaged, there is no rule for the use of the word 'adultery' which either permits or proscribes applying this word to artificial insemination by donor. Hence, until such a rule has been created, the proposition 'A woman who has artificial insemination by donor commits adultery' is in the same position as the proposition 'A bird with characteristics A, B, C, etc. (where A, B and C stand for the characteristics swans are usually expected to have) and is black is a swan'. There simply is no rule which determines whether artificial insemination by donor is or is not adultery until the rules for the use of 'adultery' have been made more determinate.

It is sometimes supposed that, if there are some propositions which are neither analytic nor synthetic, it follows that there is something, the truth of these propositions, which we can know neither by observation – as we would if they were synthetic – nor because to deny them would be self-contradictory – as we would if they were analytic. And it is sometimes supposed that *moral judgments* are neither analytic nor synthetic, and hence that we may know them to be true neither by observation nor because to deny them would be self-contradictory. This conclusion, however, does not follow. For example, we have nothing other than the ordinary means of obtaining information about birds; if the statement that all swans are white was neither analytic nor synthetic, this simply means that in view of this information, acquired by means of observation, the question whether these black birds in Australia, which otherwise resemble swans, are to be called swans or not, has not been decided. Resolving this problem is not a matter of acquiring any further information; it is simply a matter for deciding how to use a word.

EMPIRICAL/*A PRIORI*

A proposition is empirical if in order to find our whether or not it is true, it is necessary to make observations. Hence that the earth is round is an empirical truth; for all we could know about it prior to observation, it might be flat or cylindrical like a penny. On the other hand, it is not necessary to make observations in order to know that seven and five are equal to twelve; that, if the axioms of Euclidian geometry are true, the sum of the angles of a triangle equals 180 degrees; that if all men are mortal and Socrates is a man, then Socrates must be mortal; or that all uncles are male.

According to Kant[1] the reason why we do not need to make any observations in order to know that an analytic proposition is true, is that the subject and predicate of an analytic proposition, unlike a synthetic one, are not two *different* things, which might conceivably be separated, so that we have to find by observation whether or not they are connected in fact. Since the predicate is already contained in the subject, if the subject applies to something, the predicate must do so also. When we describe something as an effect, we have already described it as having a cause, and

---

[1] Immanuel Kant, *op. cit.*, pp. 49.

so there is no need to have recourse to observation to find out whether or not effects have causes.

Again, if you accept the more modern view, that an analytic proposition is one which is true solely in virtue of the meaning of the words in the sentence which expresses it, or the truth of which follows solely from the definitions of the words in this sentence, it is quite easy to see why analytic propositions should be known to be true *a priori*. They can be known *a priori* because all you need in order to determine whether or not they are true is simply to know what the words in the sentences which express them mean. Once we know what 'unmarried' and 'man' and 'bachelor' mean, we do not need any further information in order to be able to determine whether or not the proposition 'All bachelors are unmarried' is true.

If, as I have tried to do, you define 'analytic' in terms of 'entails', it may seem that perhaps you need to appeal to intuition, to say that we need to have a capacity for knowing intuitively when a proposition entails some other proposition and when it does not. This, however, is not the case. We have defined 'entails' in terms of 'make true', and said that one proposition entails another if any state of affairs which would make the first true would also make the second true. No intuition is necessary in order to see that a state of affairs which makes the proposition 'Smith is a bachelor' true, also makes the proposition 'Smith is unmarried' true. If we know how to establish whether or not Smith is a bachelor, and know how to establish whether or not he is un-married, nothing further is necessary in order to establish the proposition that he is a bachelor entails that he is unmarried.

NECESSARY/CONTINGENT

Propositions are also classified into those which are necessary and those which are contingent. Necessary propositions must be true, and cannot be false. Contingent propositions, if they are true, might have been false, or, if they are false, might have been true. That seven and five are twelve, that bachelors are unmarried, that if all men are mortal and Socrates is a man then Socrates is mortal, and that, given the axioms of Euclidean geometry, the square on the hypotenuse of a right-angled triangle equals the sum of the squares on the other two sides, are all generally held to be necessary propositions. That the earth is flat, that most men have hair, and that there are no unicorns, are generally held to be contingent. There might have been unicorns, though, unfortunately, there are not, but if all men are mortal and Socrates is a man, Socrates cannot be anything other than mortal.

Before we go on to discuss the relation between the classification of propositions into those which are necessary and those which are contingent, and the classification of propositions into those which are empirical and those which are *a priori*, and the classification of propositions into those which are analytic and those which are synthetic, there is a confusion which must be cleared up. Some philosophers describe as a necessary proposition a proposition which asserts that something is necessary, that is one which, if expressed in English, would need the word 'necessary' or an equivalent in the sentence which formulates it.[1] On this view, 'It is necessarily the case that all crows are black' would count as a necessary proposition, although crows are not necessarily black – indeed, not all crows are black, for there are some albino crows – and the proposition that they are necessarily black is not true. Conversely, according to this definition that seven and five are twelve would not be described as a necessary proposition, even though it cannot be false, because it does not contain the word 'necessary' or an equivalent in the sentence which expresses it.

I think the best definition of 'necessary proposition' is that a proposition is necessary if some other proposition *about* it, that is the proposition that it is a necessary proposition, is *true*. This definition would not only have the advantage that 'Crows are necessarily black' no longer counts as a necessary proposition, because it is not true; it would also mean that propositions such as that if you want to be rich it is necessary to be economical, do not count as necessary propositions, although they are both true and contain the word 'necessary' in their verbal formulation, because the proposition *about* them, saying that they are necessarily true, is false. Hence 'It is necessary to eat to live' is not a necessary proposition, for the proposition ' "It is necessary to eat in order to live" is a necessary proposition' is itself a false proposition. Even though it is necessary to eat to live, it is not necessarily the case that it is necessary to eat to live; men could have been constructed, though in fact they are not, so that they could live on air, or on nothing at all. I believe a great deal of confusion has been caused by philosophers' failure to notice this distinction

[1] See R. Robinson, 'Necessary Propositions', *Mind*, Vol. LXVII, 1958.

between propositions which assert that something is necessary and propositions which can truly be asserted to be necessary. There is no reason, for example, why there should not be a necessary connection between a cause and its effect,[1] no reason why, for example, arsenic should not necessarily result in death, though of course the proposition that arsenic necessarily results in death is not a necessary proposition, because the proposition asserting that it is a necessary proposition is false. This means of course, that there are two senses of 'necessary' or two sorts of necessity, the sort of necessity which is possessed by propositions which are necessarily true, and the sort of necessity which is possessed by such things as connections between events, or by tin-openers (because tin-openers are necessary to open tins, though the proposition that this is so is not a necessarily true proposition).

THE SYNTHETIC *A PRIORI*

When we come to consider how these three classification of propositions, into those which are analytic and those which are synthetic, into those which are empirical and those which are *a priori*, and into those which are contingent and those which are necessary, are connected with one another there are eight possible kinds of proposition. There are:

(1) those which are synthetic, empirical and contingent;
(2) those which are synthetic, empirical and necessary;
(3) those which are synthetic, *a priori* and contingent;
(4) those which are synthetic, *a priori* and necessary;
(5) those which are analytic, empirical and contingent;
(6) those which are analytic, empirical and necessary;
(7) those which are analytic, *a priori* and contingent;
(8) those which are analytic, *a priori* and necessary.

However, all but at most three of the above eight classes are certainly empty or null. The reason why at least five of these classes must be empty is this. All analytic propositions must be *a priori*. There is no need to have recourse to observation to know that a predicate may be affirmed of a given subject if the predicate is already contained in the subject; no need to have recourse to observation if all that is necessary in order to know that a proposi-

---

[1] The first philosopher to deny that there was a necessary connection between a cause and its effect was David Hume. See *A Treatise of Human Nature*, Book I, Part III, Section III.

tion is true is to know the meanings of the words in the sentence that expresses it; no need to have recourse to observation to know that if one proposition is true, another proposition is true, if what makes the first proposition true also makes the second proposition true. If all analytic propositions are *a priori*, then classes (5) and (6) above are empty. (Incidentally, whether a proposition is *a priori* or not, does not depend upon whether or not it is in fact known without observation, but upon whether or not it could be. A child may in fact know that seven and five are twelve by counting on his toes, and so know it by observation, but it is nevertheless proper to classify it as an *a priori* proposition because it could be known *a priori*, by someone with the necessary maturity or intelligence, even though it is known to Timothy only by observation.)

Again, analytic propositions must be necessary truths. If the predicate of a proposition is actually contained in the subject, it will obviously not be possible for the subject to apply to something without the predicate also applying to it. If a proposition is true by definition, its truth is guaranteed by the fact that its contradictory cannot be true if the words in the sentence expressing it are used in their accepted sense; the only way for the sentence 'Bachelors are not always unmarried' to express a truth would be for the words 'bachelors' or 'unmarried' or some other word in the sentence to mean what they ought not to mean if the English language is being used correctly. Again, if two propositions are so connected that the state of affairs which makes the first true also makes the second true, the first cannot be true if the second is false, or the second false if the first is true. This means that classes (5) and (7) are empty. (We have already decided that class (5) must be empty, on the grounds that there are no analytic propositions which are empirical.)

All *a priori* propositions must be necessary, and all necessary propositions must be *a priori*. This is because, as Kant pointed out,[1] observation can tell you only what is the case, but not what must be the case, and because, if something is necessarily so, there is no need to have recourse to observation in order to discover that it is so. This means that classes (2), (3), (6) and (7) must be null. (We have already decided on other grounds that classes (6) and (7) were null.)

[1] See Immanuel Kant's *Critique of Pure Reason*, trans. by Norman Kemp Smith (Macmillan & Co. Ltd., 1933), p. 44.

This leaves us with classes (1), (4) and (8), viz. the class of propositions which are synthetic, empirical and contingent; the class of propositions which are synthetic, *a priori* and necessary; and the class of propositions which are analytic, *a priori* and necessary. Some philosophers have held that all true propositions are analytic and necessary, and capable of being known *a priori* by a being with sufficient intelligence.[1] Others, for example, John Stuart Mill,[2] have held that all propositions, even those of arithmetic and logic, are synthetic, empirical and contingent. Almost all philosophers, however, are now agreed that there are some propositions which are synthetic, empirical and contingent, and others which are analytic, *a priori* and necessary. Not all philosophers have been agreed, however, upon whether there are any propositions (4) which are synthetic, *a priori* and necessary and this question is still a controversial one.

Immanuel Kant held that there are some propositions which are synthetic as well as being both known *a priori* and also necessarily true.[3] The propositions of arithmetic and geometry were, he thought, examples of these, as well as propositions such as that every event has a cause and that substance is permanent. This presented Kant with a problem. Though he did not have any difficulty in seeing how the truth of synthetic propositions could be established empirically, by observation, nor any difficulty in seeing how we could know analytic propositions *a priori*, he did have great difficulty in seeing how we could know *a priori* the truth of a synthetic proposition. In these cases we could know them to be true neither because we found the subject and the predicate terms together in fact, nor because the predicate was not something distinct from the subject, but contained in it. The explanation of this puzzling fact, he thought, was that *a priori* synthetic knowledge was knowledge of the form of all possible experience, and it was possible to know prior to our having experience what form

[1] Leibniz, for example, appears to have held that everything that happens to a substance, and everything about it, follows from its nature, and can be known *a priori* by God, though he also, inconsistently, maintains that there is a distinction between *a priori* and contingent propositions. See Bertrand Russell, *A Critical Exposition of the Philosophy of Leibniz* (5th impression, 1958), pp. 213, A. J. Ayer, in *Language, Truth and Logic*, Chapter VIII, maintains that the view that all propositions are analytic is implied by monism. (He is presumably thinking of F. H. Bradley.)

[2] See *System of Logic*, Book II.

[3] In the introduction to the *Critque of Pure Reason*.

it must take because an investigation of the mind's capacity for having experience showed that should the phenomena we experience not have this form it would not be experienced. The form of experience was the mind's own contibution to it, and it was possible to have *a priori* knowledge of it for this reason. That we have *a priori* knowledge of space and time, and of such things as that substance is permanent and that every event has a cause, is due to the fact that this is knowledge of the form of experience, and the form of experience is something imposed upon experience by the mind in the process of having it. But the very reason for the fact that we can have *a priori* knowledge of the form of experience, that this is something the mind imposes upon experience, shows that experience is 'subjective', that experience is experience of a mere world of appearances, or of phenomena, and that we cannot know any synthetic propositions – Kant thinks only synthetic knowledge would be informative and useful – about things as they are (that is, about things in themselves or noumena). We cannot have *empirical* synthetic knowledge of things in themselves, because empirical knowledge is based on observation, and only phenomena, and not things in themselves, are observed. We cannot have *a priori* synthetic knowledge of things in themselves, because we could only have this if we imposed a form on things in themselves in the process of experiencing them, and we do not experience things in themselves, and if we did, they would be modified by the fact that they were experienced, and so would not be things in themselves, that is, things as they really are, but phenomena. The analogy that is sometimes given is our knowledge of the fact that if we are wearing blue spectacles, everything looks blue. We can only know *a priori*, when we are wearing blue spectacles, that everything will look blue, because we contribute the blueness ourselves, and hence things are only apparently blue, and not blue independently of being perceived by us.

It is impossible to give here a detailed criticism of Kant's view. Suffice it to say in refutation that either the proposition that a mind with cognitive capacities like ours cannot experience a world in which those synthetic *a priori* propositions which Kant mentions about the form of experience are not true is itself either a synthetic proposition or it is not. If it is a synthetic proposition, then, since it must be known *a priori* – we can hardly go about *observing* what experience is like for minds *without* cognitive capacities like ours – it presents as many difficulties as the synthetic propositions it is used to justify, and Kant is no better off than he was when he started. If, on the other hand, it is analytic, then the cognitive capacities of the mind must be defined in terms of the sort of world it experiences; the proposition, that a mind with cognitive capacities like ours must experience a world having the form that our world has, simply means that a mind, which is such that it experiences a world with the form that our world has, will experience a world with the form that our world has. This proposition is hypothetical, and means that if we define the cognitive capacities of our mind as being such that it can experience only a world of which Kant's synthetic *a priori* propositions are true, then any world which it experiences will be one of which these propositions are true. This, unfortunately for Kant, does not mean that we can know anything synthetic about experience prior to our having it. All it does mean is that, if it turns out that we experience a world of which these synthetic propositions do not hold good, we shall have to say that the cognitive capacities of our mind have changed.

There is, however, an element of truth in what Kant says. There are certain beliefs which are such that, if we had had to wait for their empirical confirmation before we acquired them, we would not have survived. Baby deer run for cover when they see any shape in the sky which resembles a hawk. They therefore behave as if they believed the proposition that the presence of hawks means danger for baby deer. Since they run away the very first time they see such a shape, they can have acquired no empirical evidence for the truth of this proposition and, indeed, if they had been rational and waited for the evidence, they would not have survived to have profited by it. It could be argued with some plausibility that if men had not believed without evidence, that every event has a cause, that substance is permanent, and that material objects are organized three-dimensionally, they would not have been able to find their way about the world well enough to have survived. These beliefs, therefore, are *a priori* beliefs. This, however, is quite different from *a priori* knowledge. Neither we nor the baby deer had to begin with any rational foundation for our beliefs, and hence they cannot be counted as knowledge. They are true beliefs which are such that, had they had to be acquired rationally, the person acquiring them would not have survived; a benevolent nature has seen that they grow up in us prior to our having those experiences upon which they are subsequently grounded.

THE VERIFICATION PRINCIPLE

Though Kant believed that there were propositions of which we could have synthetic *a priori* knowledge, many philosophers have thought we could only know synthetic propositions to be true by recourse to observation, and some philosophers – Logical Positivists – have held that there can be no synthetic propositions the truth of which could not be determined at all, that all propositions other than analytic ones can in principle be discovered to be true or false by means of observation and experience, and that, though there can be sentences which purport to express synthetic *a priori* propositions, there cannot in fact be any such propositions, because all such sentences must be meaningless.[1] According to them, it is not so much that there are some propositions the truth of which, because it cannot be established by observation, cannot be established at all, as that there are no propositions (excluding analytic ones) the truth of which cannot in principle be decided by observation. The truth of all synthetic propositions is empirically discoverable.

What has been known as the verification principle, that all propositions are either analytic and *a priori* (and necessary) or synthetic and empirical (and contingent) has too often been put forward as a dogma, but there are things to be said in its favour, and I shall proceed to state them in my own way. To understand a word is to know how to use it, that is, to be able to operate with it correctly according to certain rules. There are two sorts of rule which govern the use of words: rules which dictate how they are to be combined with other words, and rules which dictate what words we are to use when confronted with actual situations. The rule that permits 'The cat is on the mat' and prohibits 'Is cat the the mat on?' is a rule of the former kind; the rule that says that 'cats' is the word to use for cats is a rule of the second kind. Rules of the second kind are essential. If we know only rules of the first kind, we do not understand what words mean. The person who combines the word 'cats' quite correctly with other words, but applies the word 'cat' indifferently to all mammals, does not know what the word 'cat' means – for it means to him what 'mammals' means to the rest of us – but it is not meaningless for him. And if he has no rules at all for applying it to the situation he comes across, but applies and withholds it haphazardly and unpredictably, then the word is meaningless even for him.

[1] See A. J. Ayer, *Language, Truth and Logic* (Gollancz, 1946).

The second kind of rule is more fundamental than the first kind. If the words you use in a sentence, or the order in which you use them, make no difference to the sort of situation which it would be proper to describe by using the sentence, then we use them simply because it is elegant or customary. If, however, they do make a difference to the sort of situation which it would be proper to describe by the sentence, then they do this because of a rule of the second kind, which relates the sentence to actual situations which we might come across.

The rules which dictate what sentences are to be used in the various kind of situation we come across are also the rules which determine whether what we state by means of the sentence is true or false. If there is a rule which dictates that 'cats' is the word for cats, when we come across a cat, and say 'That's a cat' then what we say is true. Hence if there is a rule connecting the word with a kind of situation, it should be possible by finding the situation, to discover whether, when we describe situations by using this word, we are making a true statement or a false one. From this it follows that if it is not possible to discover in such a way whether what we are trying to say by a sentence is true or false, there is no rule connecting the sentence with any situations, and the sentence is meaningless, and so fails to enable us to state any proposition.

To put what I think is the same arguemnt in a different way, it is possible to contend that to understand a sentence is to know what it would be like to come across a situation which can correctly be described by using this sentence, and to know that this is the situation the sentence describes. We understand the sentence 'There is an elephant in the garden' if we know what it would be like to find an elephant in the garden, and know that the sentence 'There is an elephant in the garden' is used to describe what we find. If we do not know this, then we do not know what the sentence as a whole means. Perhaps, though we do know what the word 'garden' means, we do not know what the word 'elephant' means. What this comes to is that we understand a sentence if we can use it to assert a proposition which we know how to *verify*, in some sense of 'verify'; to know what it would be like to go into the garden and find an elephant is to know how to verify in one sense of 'verify' the proposition that there is an elephant in the garden. If we do not know what it would be like to go into the garden and find an elephant, we do not know how to verify, in any sense of 'verify', the proposition that there is an elephant in the garden. Hence, if there is a sentence which does not express any proposition which we know how to verify at all, it cannot be the case that we understand what this sentence means; the sentence is meaningless to us and if this sentence conveys nothing which anybody knows how to verify, then the sentence is meaningless to everybody.

I am not saying that the argument for the verification principle which I have stated is valid, merely that it is plausible. It is plausible, however, only in those cases where one can perceive the thing in question. Here it does seem, at first sight at any rate, reasonable to suggest that if we describe something we see as red or as a cat when it is not, this must be because we do not know what the word 'red' or the word 'cat' means, that to get right the rules for using the word 'red' or the word 'cat' correctly is to assert a proposition, 'That is red' or 'That is a cat', which is true. But when we are not in the presence of something red, or in the presence of something which is a cat, and so require evidence for thinking that it is red or is a cat, it is much less plausible to suggest that someone who thinks that there is a cat in the next room, say, when there is not, is simply getting the meaning of the word 'red' or the word 'cat' wrong.

The question then arises: 'How do we know that there are no synthetic *a priori* propositions; how do we know that all propositions are either analytic and *a priori* or synthetic and empirical?' It is sometimes argued that such a proposition can itself neither be analytic and *a priori*, nor synthetic and empirical. If it were synthetic and empirical, we should know it to be true by reviewing a very large number of propositions and discovering that, as a matter of fact, we come to know them either by observation or because they are logically true. But this would be a very difficult feat to accomplish, for the number of propositions which one might wish to assert is at least very large, and quite possibly infinite. Even the very idea of trying to discover such a thing empirically is rather odd. Could it be just an empirical fact that whereas we discover that the earth is flat by observation, the fact that things which are each equal to a third thing are equal to one another is something which may be known *a priori*? On the other hand, it is argued, it cannot be an analytic proposition that all propositions are either analytic and *a priori* or synthetic and empirical, for this would make this assertion simply an arbitrary consequence of the way in which we decide to use the word 'meaningful', and there is no particular reason why we should use it in the way in which logical positivists wish to use it. Hence the proposition that all propositions are either synthetic and empirical or analytic and *a priori* is itself neither synthetic and empirical nor analytic and *a priori*. It itself is a proposition which does not fall into the alleged dichotomy, and so the dichotomy cannot be exhaustive.[1]

For myself I am inclined to think that the proposition that all meaningful sentences express propositions which can be either verified empirically or which are analytic is both true and analytic, but only, as we have seen, in a very narrow sense of 'verify'. It is true that we cannot find a clearly formulated verbal rule which makes it apparent that it is analytic, as we can with propositions such as that bachelors are unmarried, or that if water is boiling at sea level on the earth, its temperature is 212 degress Fahrenheit. As has been pointed out by Professor J. L. Austin,[2] there are many propositions, however, which may justly be called analytic, where there are no such rules. Take, for example, the proposition that if some object of stable size, such as a motor-car, starts looking smaller and smaller, this is good (though not conclusive) reason, for saying that its distance from the observer is increasing. One would not be able to arrive at the fact that such a proposition was analytic by consulting any verbal rule for the use of 'smaller' or 'farther away'. In order to come by it, we have to envisage carefully what sorts of situations would make us say that something was getting farther away from us, and, when we do this, we find that we cannot envisage a situation in which something was looking smaller and where we would not be at least strongly inclined to say that it is getting farther away. It seems to me that the proposition that all synthetic propositions are empirically verifiable is arrived at in the same sort of way. If we reflect carefully on the sort of connection with reality which makes us say that a sentence has meaning, we see that the process of showing that a sentence has meaning by means of showing in what sort of situation it would be proper to use it would be the same as the process of showing a situation which would make true the proposition asserted by that sentence.

Hence the verification principle is both true and analytic.

[1] See A. C. Ewing, 'Meaninglessness', *Mind*, Vol. XLVI, 1937.
[2] *Sense and Sensibilia* (O.U.P., 1962), pp. 120 f.

However, it must be reaffirmed that it is only true and analytic if we construe the word 'verification' in an unusually narrow way. It is true that if we count seeing a cat as verifying the proposition 'That is a cat', then someone who does not know how to verify that that is a cat does not know what the sentence 'That is a cat' means. But sometimes philosophers who have attempted to identify the meaning of a proposition with its verification have wanted to identify the meaning of a proposition with what we normally say is evidence for the truth of that proposition, and to go on to say that propositions for which there is no evidence are either analytic or meaningless. There is no justification whatsoever for this latter view.[1] Part of our evidence for saying that the cat is locked in the airing cupboard may be that someone remembered seeing her go there, that there are miaows coming from the cupboard, and that she is attracted by places which are warm, but it would be most implausible to maintain that these things are part of what we mean when we say that the cat is in the cupboard. Hence there is no justification whatsoever for saying that sentences which purport to express propositions for which there is no *evidence* are meaningless sentences. There is, however, no reason why we should *believe* such propositions if there is no evidence for them, so we can accept the view that we have no *a priori* knowledge of synthetic propositions.

BASIC PROPOSITIONS AND INFERENCE

Some things we know to be true because we remember them, or believe them to be true because we think we remember them. Memory, however, is never an independent means of acquiring knowledge – even if it is proper to speak of it as a way of acquiring, as opposed to retaining, knowledge at all. We can remember only what we have been told, or seen, or heard, or inferred. Hence it is not possible for men to have acquired their knowledge of what things are right or wrong by memory, for they could only remember that certain things were right if they had first acquired the knowledge that these things were right in some way other than by memory, just as I can only remember that the square on the hypotenuse of a right-angled triangle is equal to the sum of the

---

[1] See G. J. Warnock, 'Verification and the Use of Language,' in *A Modern Introduction to Philosophy*, ed., by Paul Edwards and Arthur Pap (Collier-Macmillan, 1965); and H. H. Price, *Belief*, (Allen & Unwin, 1969), p. 194.

squares on the other two sides if I have first acquired this piece of information by being told, or by having worked it out for myself. Indeed, the very notion of remembering what is wrong is odd, and I doubt whether it makes sense to speak of remembering that, say, promise-breaking is wrong at all.[1]

Many other things we know to be true because we have been told them by reliable informants; indeed, since our experience is too limited to have observed everything ourselves, and our intellectual capacities too limited to have worked everything out for ourselves, most of our knowledge is of propositions accepted upon the testimony of others, or upon their authority. Testimony, however, like memory, cannot be an independent means of acquiring knowledge, for we can reliably be informed of something only by somebody who himself has acquired this piece of information by some way other than by testimony, or who has himself been informed of it by someone who has acquired this information by some way other than by testimony. Hence, if some people know what actions are right and wrong because they accept this on the authority of others, the people whose authority they accept must have found out what actions are right and wrong in some other way. I must confess, however, that the idea of believing that something is wrong because one has been told it is wrong by someone else seems to me to be as odd as the idea of believing that something is wrong because one remembers that it is wrong. (Perhaps the idea of believing that something is wrong because we remember that it is wrong or because we have been told that it is wrong is odd because believing that something is wrong implies taking up some hostile emotional attitude to it, and we cannot possibly take up a hostile attitude to something as a result of memory or testimony.[2])

If we exclude memory and testimony, we are left with the things we know without making an inference at all, and the things we know because we have inferred them from other things we know. This brings one to an important distinction, the distinction between basic propositions and propositions which are not basic.

Sometimes philosophers say that in order for us properly to be said to *know* that something is the case, three conditions must be

[1] See Gilbert Ryle, 'On Forgetting the Difference between Right and Wrong', in *Essays in Moral Philosophy*, ed. by A. I. Melden (Univ. Washington Press, 1958).

[2] For a discussion of this problem see W. H. Walsh, 'Moral Authority and Moral Choice', *Aristotelian Society Proceedings*, Vol. LXV, 1964–5.

fulfilled. Firstly, the proposition someone is said to know must be true. Obviously, Smith cannot know that today is Tuesday if today is not Tuesday. Secondly, he must be sure that today is Tuesday. If, for example, though today is Tuesday, Smith is not sure that it is, perhaps because he is guessing, then, again, he cannot know that today is Tuesday. Thirdly, it is often said that one cannot know that today is Tuesday if one's reasons for thinking so are not conclusive ones, or, at any rate, good ones. Smith, for example, cannot know that today is Tuesday, if his reasons for thinking this are that he lectures today, and that he lectures on Tuesdays, if Tuesday is not the only day on which he lectures.

This last condition, however, is certainly not one which must necessarily be fulfilled before anyone can properly be described as knowing something.[1] It implies that a man cannot be said to know something unless he infers it from other propositions. But what about these other propositions themselves? If he knows these propositions, must this man not have also *known* the propositions from which he inferred this proposition? It is no good saying, for example, that Smith knows it is Tuesday because he is lecturing and he is fortunate enough to lecture only on Tuesdays, if he does not also *know* that he is lecturing today, and know that he lectures only on Tuesdays, but is merely guessing. But if we are to say that a man must know the propositions from which he infers what he is said to know, then an infinite regress is generated. For must he not also, if he is to know the propositions from which he infers what he claims to know, infer these propositions from yet other propositions? And since he must also know these, must he not infer these from yet other propositions again, and so *ad infinitum*?

Fortunately there are many propositions which we can quite correctly be said to know to be true, though they are not inferred from any other propositions at all. I do not, for example, normally infer what day of the week it is (though I may do). Mostly I just remember what day it is, and what I remember I do not infer. Normally, too, I do not infer that I have a toothache – though I may infer that Jones has a toothache from his bandages and swollen cheeks and the groans and moans that emanate from him. Nor do I normally infer that I am angry or tired or wondering when I will next get a meal or pondering upon a philosophical

[1] See, for example, D. M. Armstrong, *A Materialist Theory of the Mind* (Routledge, 1968), p. 188.

problem or that what I see at least *looks* brown and elliptical –
though many philosophers have given accounts of things like
thoughts and feelings which would allow us to know what we
were thinking of and what we were feeling only by inference.

The propositions I have just stated have all been examples of
empirical propositions, but we can also know *a priori* propositions
without inference, for example that two and two are four, that
things which are each equal to a third thing are equal to one
another, and that if all whales are mammals, and all mammals
suckle their young, whales suckle their young. Propositions like
these, whether they be empirical or *a priori*, I shall call 'basic'
propositions or 'non-inferential' propositions.

There is, however, strictly speaking no class of empirical
propositions which are basic, that is to say, no class of empirical
propositions which are basic as such.[1] This is because the notion
of being basic is a relative notion so far as it applies to empirical
propositions. I do not need to infer that I am wishing that Jones
would stop talking, but Jones, if he knows this at all, will have to
infer it, from the expression on my face or something of the sort.
Jones may not have to infer that he is seeing double, but I have to
infer it from his slurred speech and unsteady gait. Jones, perhaps,
does not have to infer that it is raining, for he can see through the
window, but I am confined to my bed, and can only infer that it is
raining from noises which sound like rain falling on the roof.
Today I have to infer that tomorrow I will be suffering from a
hangover, for I know that I always have a hangover after a party
like this one, but tomorrow I do not need to infer that I have a
hangover; I know without inference that I am feeling ill. Hence
basic empirical propositions are always relative, relative to a
person, relative to a place, or relative to a time.

That some propositions about one's thoughts and feelings and
sensations and intentions are basic to the person who has these
thoughts or feelings or sensations or intentions, is the important
fact insisted upon, quite correctly, by those philosophers who have
believed in introspection.[2] Unfortunately, however, the view that

---

[1] See J. L. Austin, *Sense and Sensibilia* (O.U.P., 1962), p. 111. Austin seems
to be under the misapprehension, however, that philosophers who hold the
sense-datum theory would deny this.

[2] See William James, *The Principles of Psychology*, (Dover Publications Inc.,)
Vol. I, Chapter VII. pp. 185 f. For a criticism of the doctrine that we know
things about ourselves by introspection see Gilbert Ryle, *The Concept of Mind*
(Hutchinson's University Library, 1949), Chapter VI, pp. 163 f.

we know some things by introspection has been associated with the view that introspection is infallible, and with the view that we can know things about our thoughts and feelings and so on, only by introspection. There is no reason to believe that either of these two latter views is correct. For example, we can, after introspecting, think we believe something which we do not, and often we are driven to inferring what our motives are from seeing how we ourselves behave.

Where *a priori* propositions are concerned, again, some are inferred and others are known without inference. I may infer that cubes have six sides and twelve edges because my mathematics teacher says that this is so, and I do not believe that he would say anything about mathematics which is wrong. But Smith may see, without inference, that this must be so. Smith, too, may be able to infer it from some general principles about solid geometry, though I am not capable of doing anything so difficult. There is a difference, however, between these two cases. My knowledge that cubes have six sides and twelve edges may only be arrived at empirically, for I infer it from an empirical fact about what my mathematics teacher has said. (We have seen that we can have empirical knowledge of a proposition which is *a priori*.) Smith, however, has *a priori* knowledge of this proposition, even when he infers it, if he infers it because he sees that it necessarily follows from certain propositions which are necessarily true.

Though it may be necessary for one person to infer an empirical proposition which another person, situated at another place, living at another time, does not need to infer, there are some empirical propositions which might be described as essentially non-basic or essentially inferential. Anyone at all who knows these propositions will *have* to know them as a result of making an inference. Personally, I should wish to contend that propositions about material objects were propositions of this class, but this is a highly controversial assertion which it would take me too far from my subject to justify here. But I think it would be generally agreed that propositions about protons and electrons, since these are not capable of being observed by anybody, would belong to this category of propositions which are essentially non-basic.

Although, as we have seen, some *a priori* propositions are inferred, and others are not, I am personally inclined to think that no *a priori* proposition *has* to be inferred. A being with the intellectual capacity could, I believe, just see without inference the necessary truth of all the propositions which in many mathematical systems are theorems, that is, which are inferred from the axioms, provided the axioms themselves are necessarily true. People of only moderate intellectual powers can do this sometimes. Most people – or most undergraduates, at any rate – can see that p implies not not-p, that is, that any proposition implies that its own contradictory is false. But in *Principia Mathematica* there is a quite complicated proof of this proposition, self-evident though it is. So perhaps all the propositions which follow from a set of self-evident and necessarily true axioms are themselves capable of being seen to be self-evident by a being with the necessary intelligence.

Of course, it is not the case that the axioms of every mathematical system are self-evident or even necessarily *a priori* true. The axioms of Euclidean geometry were once supposed to be like this, but are so no longer. In this case the fact that a theorem can be shown to follow from an axiom does not show that the theorem is necessary and self-evident, only that it must be true if the axioms are true, which they do not have to be. In this case however, what is necessary is the proposition that the axioms imply the theorems, or that if the axioms are true, then the theorems also must be true.[1] Presumably, too, we must be able to grasp this necessity, of the axioms implying the theorems, if we are to be capable of inferring the theorems from the axioms. We need not do this all in one step. We may see that the axioms imply Theorems 1 and 2, that Theorems 1 and 2 imply Theorem 3, and so on down to the theorem we are trying to prove, but at each step in the proof we shall have to grasp the necessity of a hypothetical proposition, the hypothetical proposition that if the axioms are true, Theorems 1 and 2 must be true, that if Theorems 1 and 2 are true, Theorem 3 must be true, and so on. We must be capable of grasping the truth of these hypothetical propositions without proof, that is to say, our knowledge of them must be non-inferential, and they must be self-evident to us. If we attempted to prove that the axioms did imply Theorems 1 and 2, that Theorems 1 and 2 did imply Theorem 3, and so on, we would still need to be able to grasp, without proof, that the propositions we used as our premises in this proof implied that the axioms implied Theorems 1 and 2, and that Theorems 1 and 2 implied Theorem 3, and so on. And this process, once started upon, would need to be prolonged

[1] See John Stuart Mill, *System of Logic*, Book II, Chapter IV.

indefinitely. Hence all proof, even when what is proved is shown to follow from premises which are not necessarily true, involves the apprehension of something which can be seen to be true without proof.

A proposition is sometimes said to be demonstrated if it is shown to follow from certain other propositions. However, a proposition is more commonly said to be demonstrated if it is shown to follow from certain propositions which are themselves not only true, but self-evidently true. To be self-evidently true, a proposition has to be both *a priori* and necessary (and, if all *a priori* necessary propositions are analytic, it also has to be analytic). As we have seen, a proposition which is self-evident can also be demonstrated, if it can be shown to follow from certain *other* self-evident propositions. Some moral judgements can certainly be demonstrated, in the looser sense of 'demonstrate', in that some moral judgments can be shown to follow from others. If there are any moral judgments which are self-evidently true, then some moral judgments could probably be demonstrated in that they could be shown to follow from these. Not *all* moral judgments could be demonstrated by being shown to follow from moral judgments which were self-evidently true, however; though this might be done for some, it could not be done for all without an infinite vicious regress. Whether there are any moral judgments which are self-evidently true is a question which we shall consider later. One might be tempted to say that moral judgments could be demonstrated if they could be shown to follow from certain true factual judgments, but they would not be demonstrated in the sense of having been shown to follow from propositions which are necessarily true, unless they were shown to follow from factual propositions which were necessarily true, and it is very unlikely that this can be done. The question whether any moral judgments do follow logically from factual judgments will also have to be considered later.

It must not be assumed that the question 'How do you know?' always means 'From what propositions do you infer . . . ?' A perfectly proper answer to the question 'How do you know that there are twenty-seven people at the party?' would be 'Because I have counted them'. A perfectly proper answer to the question 'How do you know that it rained yesterday?' would be 'Because I remember that it did'. A perfectly proper answer to the question

'How do you know that is a monkey?' would be 'Because I can see that it is'. It does not follow from this, however, as some philosophers have supposed, that there are some propositions which we know, although we have neither inferred them nor not inferred them; indeed, it is difficult to see how there could be a species of knowledge which was neither inferential nor non-inferential. What it does mean is that there are different ways of arriving at knowledge which we do not infer, and different ways of arriving at knowledge which we do infer. What we remember, we know in a different kind of non-inferential way from what we introspect, and the inference from the fact that all Smith's predecessors have died before they were 150 years old to the fact that Smith will die before he is 150 years old is not quite like the inference from the deflection of an observed planet's course to the existence of some unobserved planet. And sometimes, of course, it is difficult to say whether a given piece of knowledge is inferential or not. For example, when we know that there are twenty-seven people at the party because we have counted them, is this something we have inferred from something else – for example, that we have mentally correlated each one of the first twenty-seven numerals with a person at the party, and not correlated any numeral with more than one person at the party – or do we know what we know by counting non-inferentially?

A PRIORI AND EMPIRICAL CONCEPTS: OSTENSIVE DEFINITION

A concept is said to be empirical if we acquire it by abstracting it from its instances. It is said to be *a priori* if we do not acquire it by abstracting it from its instances.[1] For example, we acquire the concept of redness by seeing things which are red. It is alleged by some philosophers, however, that though we have a concept of causation, we never actually come across any instances of it, for all we are actually aware of, when we see a cause being followed by its effect, is the regular succession of events, like the effect, upon events, like the cause, together perhaps with the fact that the cause is contiguous in space and time with its effect. The actual causal transaction always lies behind the observed phenomena, which are symptoms of it, but not identical with it. Hence, it is

[1] See C. D. Broad, *Examination of McTaggart's Philosophy* (C.U.P., 1933), pp. 42 f.

argued, since we have a concept of what it is for one event to cause another event, we must have this concept in spite of not having had the opportunity to abstract it from actual observed instances of causation. Hence it is what has been called an *a priori* concept. (The distinction between *a priori* and empirical concepts is now considered old fashioned.)

An *a priori* concept must not be confused with an *a priori* proposition. To say that a proposition is *a priori* is to say something about the way we come to know that it is true; to say that a concept is *a priori* is to say something about how we come to have it. Obviously it would not make sense to say that concepts were *a priori* in the sense in which propositions are *a priori*, for it does not make sense to say of concepts that they are true, and so it cannot make sense to talk about the way in which we come to know that they are true. Again, there is no reason why the concepts involved in our *a priori knowledge* should be *a priori concepts*. The proposition that if all men are mortal and Socrates is a man, then Socrates is also mortal is an *a priori* proposition, but we obviously acquire the concepts of being a man and being mortal in a perfectly normal way. The same is true of the proposition that everything that is coloured is extended.

Though not all *a priori* propositions involve *a priori* concepts, however, it seems not implausible to suggest that all propositions involving *a priori* concepts must be *a priori* propositions. If, for example, we do not acquire our concept of causation by abstraction from actual instances of it, then, presumably, we cannot know by observation when it is present, because we never do observe cases of it. Presumably, then, we know that it is present only because we know *a priori* the truth of some such proposition as that whenever regular succession and contiguity in space and time are present, then causation must also be present.

The process described earlier as acquiring a concept by abstracting it from its instances is more commonly known nowadays as the process of learning the meaning of a word by ostensive definition.[1] The view that we know the meaning of some words by ostensive definition, that is, by being shown examples of the sort of things they mean, appears to have difficulties. One of these, I think, can quite easily be overcome. It might seem that we cannot

---

[1] For a detailed account of ostensive definition, see H. H. Price, *Thinking and Experience*, (Hutchinson's University Library, second edition, 1969), Chapter VII.

teach someone the meaning of a word by ostensive definition, for this consists in explaining to him what is meant by 'dog' by showing him a dog, for example, or by explaining to him the meaning of the word 'cat' by showing him a cat. How, however, can he possibly, by being shown a cat, understand from this that the word 'cat' means what it does, and not 'mammal' or 'vertebrate' or 'four-legged animal' or 'Persian cat', if the animal we select to teach him the meaning of 'cat' is, as well as being a cat, a mammal, a vertebrate, a four-legged animal, and a Persian cat?

The answer is that we cannot teach the meaning of a word by ostensive definition by means of showing our pupil only one thing to which the word may properly be applied. If we show him a red equilateral triangle and say 'That's red', he will not be justified in taking it that we mean red by 'red' rather than triangle, or equilateral triangle, or equal-sided figure, or red triangle, or red equilateral triangle. In order to provide him with sufficient reason for thinking that it is the colour red which we mean by the word 'red' we must show him more figures, one of which must be red but not triangular, or even equilateral, and say 'That is red, too,' and other things which are triangular, but not red, and say 'Those are not red,' and things which are coloured, but not red, and say 'Those are not red'. Ideally, we define a word ostensively not by producing a single object, but a set of objects which are such that they have in common the characteristic or attribute or relation, the word for which we are defining, and which is also such that this is the only thing they have in common.

Not all words which can be defined ostensively are so defined in fact. It is possible to define the word 'whale' by showing people whales, or by saying that a whale is a fish-like mammal that lives in the sea, though 'showing people whales', in order to provide a satisfactory ostensive definition, would have to include more than familiarizing them with the outward appearance of whales, but cutting them open and allowing them to acquire an adequate amount of information about their insides and their internal functioning. In fact, in order to understand what a whale was, the person for whom we were providing the definition would have to understand what the sea was, what a fish was, the difference between whales and fish, what mammals are, which means understanding (at least) the difference between the way in which fish reproduce themselves and the way in which mammals reproduce themselves, and that in its turn involves understanding at least something about the very complicated process of reproduction, and so on, and so on, and so on. I think it is probably this that gives strength to the case of those who say we cannot learn the meaning of words by ostensive definition. It appears that we do not learn what is meant by 'whale' simply by being shown a whale; we have to have explained to us in words a lot of things about whales, such as how they differ from fish in their manner of reproduction and from other mammals in their habitat. But this does not mean that the manner in which we learn the meaning of 'whale' differs fundamentally from the manner in which we learn the meaning of 'red', for in the last resort, we do have to be shown things in order to understand the verbal explanations of what mammals are, what the sea is, what reproduction is, and so on. And if it is possible to explain these words by using yet other words, at some point or other the words we use must 'latch on' to reality, and if there were no rules at all connecting words with actual states of affairs, such as the rule which lays down that the word for the colour red is 'red', they would be meaningless.

Some philosophers have held that this is not true of all words.[1] It is true, they have argued, with words like 'red' and 'round' and 'whale' and 'mammal' and even of terms like 'parliamentary government' and 'internal combustion engine' and 'quadratic equation', but it is not true of what were once called 'syncategorematic' words, or 'logical' words, like 'all', 'some', 'most', 'not', 'if . . . then', 'either . . . or' and 'and'. You can show people things which are red or round, or which are internal combustion engines; you can even, in an indirect and complicated way, show them examples of parliamentary government and quadratic equations, but you cannot show them ifs or ands or nots.[2]

It is not true, however, that words like 'and' and 'if' and 'not' cannot be ostensively defined. One cannot define them ostensively by showing people things which are cases of them; they are not the sort of word which can have or fail to have cases. Nothing can be an if, nor fail to be an if. Nevertheless, it is possible ostensively to explain their meaning by showing in what circumstances whole sentences containing them are properly used. For example, though you cannot show anyone a not, you can show him what is

[1] See P. T. Geach, *Mental Acts* (Routledge, 1957), Sections 6–11.
[2] *Op. cit.*, pp. 22 f.

the difference between the sentence 'There is cheese in the larder' expressing something true, and the sentence 'There is not any cheese in the larder' expressing something true. In the first case you say to someone 'There is cheese in the larder', and take him to the larder, and show him the cheese. In the second case you say to someone, 'There is not any cheese in the larder,' and you take him to a larder which does not contain any cheese. He learns to connect the first sentence expressing a truth with a larder with cheese in it, and the second sentence's expressing a truth with a larder with no cheese in it. You can say to someone, 'All the men in the room are bald', and show him a room containing bald men and no men who are not bald. You can say to someone, 'Some of the men in the room are bald', and show him a room containing some bald men and some men who are not bald. There is not of course a one–one relation between a sentence's expressing a truth and some state of affairs with which it may be correlated, and which the person to whom you are teaching the words in the sentence may be shown. In the case of teaching someone the meaning of 'Some of the men in the room are bald' one would have to teach him not only that this sentence expressed a truth in the event of some (at least one) of the men in the room being bald and some (at least one) of the men in the room having hair; one would also have to teach him that this sentence expressed a truth in the event of all the men in the room being bald. And he would have to learn that it did not matter how many men there were in the room or what proportion of them were bald. Hence you learn, when you learn the meaning of a sentence and the words contained in it, not what is the state of affairs about which it expresses a truth, but what range of states of affairs make it true to say that it expresses a truth and what range of states of affairs make it true to say it expresses a falsehood.

This is how you teach the meaning of the words 'not' and 'all' and 'some' by means of a process of ostensive definition, without doing what is impossible, that is, showing people nots and alls and somes. The case of 'if . . . then' 'either . . . or' and 'and' is similar. You teach someone the meaning of 'and' by teaching him how sentences containing it correlate with states of affairs. You teach someone the meaning of 'There is cheese in the larder *and* there is butter in the larder' by showing him a larder containing cheese and butter, then a larder containing cheese but no butter, a larder containing butter but no cheese, and a larder containing

C

neither cheese nor butter, and explaining that the sentence 'There is cheese in the larder and there is butter in the larder' expresses a truth in the first of these four cases, but a falsehood in the other three. One would teach him the meaning of 'Either there is cheese in the larder *or* there is butter in the larder' by showing him that this sentence expressed a truth in the first three of the above four cases, but a falsehood in the fourth. The case of 'If there is cheese in the larder, there is butter in the larder' is a little more difficult, for this sentence, though it is false in the event of there being cheese in the larder but no butter, is not necessarily true in the event of the other three cases, the case when there is cheese and butter, no cheese but some butter, no cheese and no butter, obtaining. One must show him – for one such 'if' at any rate – that repeatedly, when there is cheese in the larder, there is butter, but to go into the question of the meaning of 'if . . . then' would take us too far away from the object of our present enquiry.

There is another, more formidable, difficulty about the alleged process of ostensive definition, which difficulty is not often mentioned. It is this. We appear successfully to learn the meanings of many words, even though the things which we would use ostensively to define them cannot fully be shown in one perceptual act. The whale we talked about earlier is a good example of this. We saw that, in order to understand, by a process of ostensive definition, the meaning of the word 'whale', it was not sufficient to be familiar with the outward appearance of whales; one would also have to understand something about their internal functioning, the manner in which they were related to their environment, and some of the structural and functional differences and similarities between them and other things. This cannot be done all at once, but must be done piecemeal, a bit at a time. While we are examining the whale's organs of reproduction, our attention is necessarily drawn away from its looks, and when we concentrate upon its looks, we are for the most part oblivious of its environment. Even so far as the outward appearance of whales goes, we do not learn what whales look like in one single perceptual experience, by looking at them once and once only. That an animal that looks as a whale does from on top will look as a whale does from behind is not something self-evident of which our knowledge is innate. It has to be learnt by experience. Hence not only knowing what whales are like, but what they look like, is something that is done a bit at a time, and coming to learn the meaning of the word 'whale' is something which cannot be done all at once, but only bit by bit, rather like building up a picture in a jig-saw puzzle by being shown the pieces one by one. But that such a process occurs is not so much a difficulty with the contention that we know the meaning of (some) words by ostensive definition, so much as an elucidation of the nature of the process of ostensive definition itself. That we should have a capacity for acquiring concepts although their instances can be revealed to us only a bit at a time is a necessary condition of our having any knowledge which goes beyond the immediate content of what we experience at any one moment.[1]

There are also a number of other words and phrases which cannot be defined ostensively in the way in which words like 'cat' and 'dog' can be ostensively defined. Take, for example, the word 'please'. You cannot explain to anybody what this word means by showing him things which are please, and saying, 'These are the things I am talking about', and then showing him things which are not please, and saying, 'These are not the things I am talking about'. Nor can you explain to anybody the meaning of the word 'please' by showing what difference its insertion in a certain place in a sentence makes to the truth or falsity of what the sentence is being used to assert, for adding the word 'please' to the sentence 'Pass the salt' does not make *any* difference to its truth or falsity; 'Pass the salt' was neither true nor false in the first place, and 'Please pass the salt' is not true or false either. Words and phrases like 'please', 'I hereby undertake . . .', or the differences between sentences such as 'The door is shut', 'Shut the door' and 'Is the door shut?' cannot be explained by the difference between the situations which they each describe, for only the first of them does describe any situation. Nevertheless, these expressions can be ostensively defined, in a rather wider sense of 'ostensively define' than that used hitherto. A person who does not understand them can be shown how to use them, by being shown what is accomplished by them. For example, the difference between 'Shut the door' and 'Please shut the door' can be explained by showing in what situations it is proper to use them – you should say 'Shut the door' only when you are in a

[1] See Immanuel Kant, *Critique of Pure Reason*, trans. by Norman Kemp Smith, (Macmillan, 1968), pp. 131 f; and H. H. Price, *Perception*, (Methuen, second edition 1950), p. 310.

position of authority, for example – and what they are designed to accomplish, even if it cannot be shown what states of affairs can properly be described by them. The possibility must be born in mind that words like 'right' and 'wrong' may be capable of ostensive definition only in the wider way just explained.

HOW DO MORAL JUDGMENTS FIT INTO THE PRECEDING CATEGORIES?

Having, without going into them in any great detail, made clear to the best of my ability the preceding distinctions, between propositions which are analytic and those which are synthetic, between propositions which are *a priori* and those which are empirical, between those which are necessary and those which are contingent, and those which are inferred and those which are not inferred, and between concepts which are *a priori* and those which are empirical, the question must be borne in mind during the following chapters: 'Into which of these categories do moral judgments and moral concepts fit?' To anticipate a little, may I say that, if we ignore our epistemological prejudices, the most natural view to take of moral judgments is that they are synthetic, *a priori* and necessary. They seem to be synthetic, for it does not seem at all plausible to suggest that statements such as that homicide is wrong are true simply in virtue of the meaning we attach to the word 'homicide'. They seem to be *a priori*, because it does not seem to be the case that a knowledge of the facts of any situation settles the question whether it is right to do one thing in that situation rather than another; once we have all the empirical evidence at our command, it seems that we have to make a decision, with which decision no empirical evidence can be any help. And it would seem to me to be odd to suggest that it just so happens that homicide is wrong; of course, it might have been that human nature was very different from what it is, and, in *that* case homicide might not have been wrong, but, given that the facts about human nature are as they are, then it seems as if homicide has to be wrong. And again, the natural view to take of 'wrong' would be that it was not capable of ostensive definition in quite the same way as the word 'red', that our 'concept' of wrong is acquired in a different way from our concept of round. These are questions which we shall have to go into in greater detail in the following chapters.

CHAPTER IV

MORAL JUDGMENTS AS *A PRIORI* AND ANALYTIC: THE PLACE OF DEMONSTRATIVE REASONING IN ETHICS

The first question to be considered is whether moral judgments can be regarded as *a priori* and analytic, of the same type as that two and one is three, or that if two things are each equal to a third thing, they are equal to one another. If they were, of course, our answer to the question 'How do we know what things are right and wrong?' would be a simple one. We would know that certain things were right because, if we were to say that they were not right, we would be contradicting ourselves. Hence no more than ordinary logical insight, or a capacity to recognize logical contradictions when we came across them, would be necessary in order to know what things were right and what things were wrong. And if we say that something can be proved to be true when we can show that to deny it is contradictory, we would, if this view were correct, be able to prove moral judgments for, if they were analytic, to deny them would result in contradictions. A view rather like this appears to have been held by Aquinas and by John Locke.[1]

However, no such simple way out is possible. It is true that it is possible to deduce some moral judgments from others. It is

---

[1] John Locke, *An Essay Concerning Human Understanding*, Book IV, Chapter III, and St. Thomas Aquinas, Summa Theologica, Question XCIV, Second article. Similar views have been held by Cudworth and Clarke. See Ralph Cudworth, *A Treatise Concerning Eternal and Immutable Morality;* and Samuel Clarke, *A Discourse of Natural Religion*. Excerpts from their writings may most easily be found in *British Moralists*, ed. by D. Daiches Raphael (O.U.P. 1969). It was not common in those days to draw a distinction between analytic and synthetic propositions, and hence it is not easy to tell whether rationalists of the period held the view that moral judgments were self-evident or capable of proof because they were analytic, or followed from propositions which were analytic, or whether they thought we had rational insight into certain synthetic *a priori* truths of morality. A criticism may be found in David Hume, *A Treatise of Human Nature*, Book III, Part I, Section I.

possible to deduce the moral judgment 'You were wrong to do that' from the judgments 'You promised you wouldn't' and 'It is wrong to break your promises'. This, however, is not the same thing as proving that you ought not to do that, for something is not proved by being deduced from other propositions. It has to be deduced from other true propositions, and, moreover, propositions which are known to be true, and the question arises 'How do we know that we ought to keep our promises?' This judgment would seem to stand in as much need of justification as the original judgment 'You were wrong to do that'. It is true that the judgment 'It is wrong to break one's promises' can itself be deduced from other judgments, for example, from the judgments that breaking promises harms other people, and that to do what harms other people is wrong, but then the question arises, 'How do we know that it is wrong to do what harms other people?' We can deduce this judgment from yet other judgments, for example, from the judgments that God has commanded us not to harm other people, and it is wrong to disobey God's commands, but still the question remains 'How do we know that it is wrong to disobey God's commands?' Obviously the process of deducing some moral judgments from others, and those from yet others, cannot be pushed back *ad infinitum*; it must stop somewhere, and stop with moral judgments which are known to be true although they cannot be proved in this way.

If moral judgments could be proved in the way suggested, then we would know them to be true because we would see that a contradiction would be involved in accepting the premises but denying the conclusion. Perhaps if it could be further shown that a contradiction would be involved in rejecting the premises, we would have done what we set out to do, for we would have shown that we could not consistently reject certain moral judgments without rejecting other moral judgments the rejection of which would involve a contradiction. This would mean, of course, that the premises from which we deduced the moral judgment we wished to prove were analytic judgments.

There certainly do seem to be some moral judgments which look as if they might very well be analytic. It is possible to argue that 'It is wrong to steal' is analytic, for 'stealing' just means 'the wrongful taking of what is not one's own'. 'Murder is wrong' will be analytic if 'murder' just means 'killing some other human being wrongfully', and 'It is wrong to eat and drink too much' will be analytic if 'eat and drink too much' just means 'eat and drink more than it is right to eat and drink.'

On the other hand, there are certainly moral judgments which are not analytic. Even if 'Stealing is wrong' is analytic, 'Taking what is not one's own is wrong' is not analytic; even if 'Murder is wrong' is analytic, 'Killing other people is wrong' is synthetic; even if 'It is wrong to eat and drink too much' is analytic, 'It is wrong to eat a whole large haggis and drink a bottle of whisky in an evening' is synthetic. And though a contradiction would be involved in denying the analytic judgments, no contradiction would be involved in denying the synthetic ones. Nor could the synthetic judgments be deduced from the analytic ones, for no synthetic judgment *can* be deduced from an analytic one. An analytic judgment is in a certain sense uninformative; whether it is right to kill Smith, Jones or Robinson, it still remains true that murder, if 'murder' means 'wrongful killing', is wrong, and hence, from that wrongful killing is wrong, it cannot be deduced that it is wrong to kill Smith, Jones, Robinson, or anyone else one cares to think of.

Furthermore, an argument to a conclusion about what it is right to do which attempts to use an analytic premise must always beg the question. You cannot argue that it would be wrong to kill Smith because to kill Smith would be murder, and murder is, by definition, wrong, for until you have first established the very thing that you were attempting to prove, namely that it *is* wrong to kill Smith, you have not established that to kill Smith would be a case of murder. Hence all analytic moral judgments are practically useless, that is, useless as a guide to action. Moral judgments such as that murder is wrong or that stealing is wrong never tell you what it is right or wrong to do in any particular circumstances with which you may be faced. They only tell you that unless what you are contemplating doing is wrong, it is not stealing, or that unless what you are contemplating doing is wrong, it is not murder. They do not tell you that what you are contemplating doing is wrong; and that, after all, is what you wanted to know.

It must not be concluded from the foregoing discussion that there is anything peculiar about moral reasoning in this respect. Demonstrative reasoning plays just as much, or just as little, a part in moral reasoning as it does in any other branch of reasoning. This is because the part of demonstrative reasoning in any subject is always hypothetical. By logical reasoning you are able to know that *if* you accept certain propositions, you must also accept certain others, or, what comes to the same thing, that propositions cannot be held in certain combinations, that certain propositions are incompatible with others. But though logical reasoning can tell you that if you accept proposition *p*, you must also accept proposition *q*, or that if you hold proposition *r*, you cannot also hold proposition *s*, logical reasoning cannot choose between the alternatives. It cannot tell you whether or not to accept *p* and so also accept *q*, or, on the other hand, to reject *q*, and so also reject *p*. If *r* is incompatible with *s*, logic can tell you that you cannot accept both *r* and *s*, but it cannot tell you whether to accept *r* and reject *s*, or accept *s*, and reject *r*. Logical reasoning alone will enable us to keep our beliefs consistent with one another, but it is possible for all our beliefs to be consistent with one another, and yet be false. Hence logical reasoning alone, in morals or any other subject, will not tell us what to believe; it will merely tell us which combinations of beliefs are impossible, without enabling us to choose among the many logically possible combinations.

CHAPTER V

MORAL JUDGMENTS AS *A PRIORI* AND SYNTHETIC: INTUITIONISM AND THE NATURALISTIC FALLACY

Moral judgments, then, are not all analytic, and not all capable of being denied without logical inconsistency. Moreover, the ones which are analytic are practically useless, in that they give no guidance to anyone faced with a moral problem. Though, too, some moral judgments can logically be deduced from other moral judgments which we use as premises, this is not enough to establish any moral judgment, unless we can find some way of establishing these premises themselves, and, though we might deduce the premises from yet other premises, obviously this process cannot be pushed back *ad infinitum*. At some point or other we must find some way of establishing the moral judgment, which we intend to use as a premise, other than by deducing it from yet other moral judgments. For example, we may argue that this action is wrong because it is a case of lying, and lying is wrong; and we may argue that lying is wrong because it causes unhappiness and causing unhappiness is wrong; and we may deduce that causing unhappiness is wrong because God has forbidden us to make others unhappy and what God has forbidden is wrong, but at some time or other we must try to show the truth of one of our premises – in this example, the statement that what God has forbidden is wrong – in some way other than deducing it from yet other propositions which are themselves in as much need of justification as the conclusion deduced.

We have seen that logic alone cannot guarantee the truth of any of our premises unless it is analytic, and that, if it is analytic, no practically useful conclusion can be deduced from it. Some philosophers have held, however, that there are certain moral judgments which, though they are synthetic, not analytic, can just be seen to be true without the need of embarking upon the infinite regress of trying to find other propositions from which they may be deduced. These philosophers have held that, though moral judgments such as 'Lying is wrong', 'Promise-breaking is wrong',

'Stealing is wrong', and so on, are synthetic, we can nevertheless, if we reflect upon them, apprehend that they are necessarily true, without having to produce any reasons for them. Since our knowledge of such propositions, according to this theory, is a question of insight, rather than one of collecting empirical evidence which supports them, our moral knowledge, if the theory is true, will be *a priori*. Since what we have insight into, according to the theory, is that promise-breaking, lying and stealing *cannot* be right, moral judgments, if this theory is correct, will also be necessarily true. Indeed, as we have seen, it is difficult to see how we can have *a priori* knowledge of the truth of a proposition if it is not necessarily true, for, if it is not necessarily true, then it is just a matter of fact that it is true, and how one can know *a priori* that something is so as a matter of fact, though it does not have to be so, it is impossible to see.

The theory that we just see certain moral judgments to be true, without argument, and without the need to collect any empirical evidence in their favour, is known as intuitionism.[1] Intuitionism, as I have defined it, is often confused with two other theories which are in fact totally different. Intuitionism, in the sense in which we are talking about it, is a meta-ethical theory, a theory about the manner in which we acquire our knowledge of right and wrong and of good and evil. But there is also a theory, known as intuitionism, which is not a meta-ethical theory at all; this sort of intuitionism is a theory about what we ought to do, rather than a theory about how we come to know what we ought to do. It consists, in the main, of a denial of utilitarianism. Utilitarians have held that there is one single supreme principle of morality, from which all other moral principles, which are only subsidiary and derivative, can be deduced. According to utilitarianism, the one ultimate (ultimate in the sense that it cannot be derived from any principle more fundamental than it) moral principle is that all men ought to act in such a way as to bring into existence the greatest possible balance of good over evil. If utilitarianism, as just defined, is combined with the view that there is only one thing which is good, namely, happiness or pleasure, then the utilitarian philosopher is known as a hedonistic utilitarian. If he

[1] See Sir David Ross, *The Right and the Good* (Clarendon Press, 1930), and *The Foundations of Ethics* (O.U.P., 1938). See also Richard Price, *A Review of the Principal Questions in Morals* (O.U.P., 1948) edited by D. Daiches Raphael.

thinks that things other than pleasure – knowledge, for example – can also be good, not just because they are pleasant themselves or give rise to pleasant consequences, then the utilitarian philosopher is known as an ideal or agathistic utilitarian.

If either of these kinds of utilitarianism is true, then moral rules, such as that we ought to keep our promises, pay our debts, and tell the truth, are obligatory to the extent that doing any of these things brings into existence a greater balance of good over evil than anything else the agent could have done. If they do not do this, then there is no reason why we should tell the truth, keep our promises or pay our debts, and if doing these things actually brings into existence a smaller balance of good over evil than something else the agent could have done, then he will be under a positive obligation not to keep his promises, not to pay his debts or not to tell the truth. Hence, if utilitarianism is true, promise-keeping, debt-paying, truth-telling and so on, are obligatory only if and when in keeping our promises, paying our debts or telling the truth we are acting upon the one supreme principle of morality which utilitarians recognise, namely the principle that we always ought to act in such a way as to bring into existence the greatest possible preponderance of good over evil.

In reply to utilitarianism, some philosophers have held that it is just self-evident that we ought to keep our promises and pay our debts and tell the truth, and that, consequently, these principles are obligatory in their own right, and not just because and to the extent that they can be deduced from the principle of utilitarianism. They have also held that we are under at least some obligation to keep our promises, pay our debts and tell the truth even when no preponderance of good is brought into existence thereby, and sometimes even when some preponderance of bad over good results from what we do.

Though I think it is clear, once it is pointed out, that this theory, which is also known as intuitionism,[1] is not a meta-ethical or epistemological theory at all, and is a theory about how we ought to behave, not one about how we know how we ought to behave, there is some excuse for those philosophers who have called both this and the view which is the subject of the present chapter by the one name 'intuitionism'. The excuse is this. If utilitarianism is true, then a reason can be given why we

---

[1] Both Richard Price and Sir David Ross were intuitionists in both senses of this word.

ought to keep our promises, pay our debts and tell the truth; we ought to do these things because by doing so we bring into existence the maximum balance of good over evil. If, however, these principles are obligatory in their own right, then it seems to follow that no reason can be given why we ought to act in accordance with them, and from this it seems to follow that we must just see that they are obligatory, that is, know intuitively that they are obligatory.

There is no reason, however, why the two theories known as intuitionism, the epistemological theory and the moral theory, need be held in conjunction. Even if we accept, as an explanation for the fact that we ought to keep our promises and pay our debts, that we ought to do so because good is maximized as a result, we still need to answer the question 'How do we know that we ought to act in such a way as to bring about a maximum balance of good over evil?' and there is no logical reason why the answer to this question should not simply be that we know this, although no reasons can be given for it, by intuition. If so, of course, one can be an intuitionist, in the epistemological sense of 'intuitionist', without being an intuitionist in the moral sense. On the other hand, there is no reason why we should not hold that though it is indeed the case that we ought to keep our promises, pay our debts and so on even when a preponderance of good over evil is not produced by our doing so, we do not intuit the truth of this, but know it in some other way. It might perhaps be held, for example, that statements about how we ought to behave are just statements about what are in fact the accepted standards of behaviour in our society, and that the accepted standards of behaviour in our society cannot be given a utilitarian justification or, at any rate, not a complete one. In this case, though it would be true that we ought to keep our promises even when evil resulted from our doing so, this would not be something which we just intuited, but something which we discovered empirically, by finding out what the accepted standards of behaviour in our society in fact are. (More will be said later[1] about the view that our knowledge of morality is just knowledge about the accepted norms in our society.)

Intuitionism in the sense in which it is a theory about how we know what we ought to do and intuitionism, in the sense in which it is a theory about what we ought to do are thus logically independent.

[1] Chapter X.

The second theory sometimes confused with intuitionism, is the theory which is more correctly known as a moral sense theory. It has presumably been confused with intuitionism because, both if it is true and if intuitionism is true, we do not arrive at a knowledge of moral principles by a process of reasoning or ratiocination. According to moral sense theories, we know that promise-breaking is wrong in the same sort of way that we know that grass is green and pillar-boxes in Great Britain are red, that is by means of perception, and, of course, if we know something because we perceive that it is so, we do not know it because it is the end-product of a process of reasoning. It is not the case, however, that everything we do not know by reasoning we do know by intuition, and it would certainly not be plausible to hold that we know by intuition that pillar-boxes are red and grass is green. Hence a moral sense theory, though it agrees with intuitionism in holding that we cannot argue for moral principles or give reasons for them, is quite different from intuitionism in other ways. The confusion between the two may have been helped by the fact that we speak of seeing that pillar-boxes are red and grass is green, and the fact that intuitionists also speak of 'seeing' that promises ought to be kept and debts paid, but the sense of 'seeing' in which intuitionists use the word is something like a metaphorical sense. We do not see anything with our eyes or with any other sense, even a moral sense, according to intuitionism; we just intellectually grasp, without argument, that certain moral principles are necessarily true.

Intuitionism, the epistemological theory which is the subject of this chapter, has been objected to by philosophers for a variety of different reasons, but I doubt whether any of these objections are conclusive. If intuitionism is true, moral judgments or propositions are like mathematical propositions – and intuitionists often liken our knowledge of moral principles to our knowledge of the axioms of mathematics. The proposition that two and two are four is not true in some places and false in others, nor true at some times and false at others; nor true when asserted by some people, false when asserted by others. If a mathematical proposition is true at all, it is true everywhere and at all times. It is not the case that that two and two are four is true in England, but false in Malaya, or true today, but false several centuries ago, or true when asserted by Smith, but false when asserted by Robinson. It is argued, however, that the same is not true where moral propositions are concerned; it is perfectly possible for polygamy to be wrong in England but right in India, for patricide to be wrong in Europe, but right north of the Arctic circle, for infanticide or slavery to be wrong at the present time, but right before the birth of Christ. Circumstances, it is held, alter cases, and so there is no reason why patricide, for example, which would be wrong in a wealthy country where the aged are well provided for, should not be right in a very poor country, where the aged can not only not be looked after, but are a serious impediment to the survival of their communities; and the same is supposed to hold good for many other cases.

Up to a point, the intuitionist can reply to this objection fairly easily. Firstly, he may point out, as Hume did,[1] that the fact that the law of gravity holds everywhere and at all times does not make it puzzling that some rivers flow east while other rivers flow west, nor that some objects fall to the ground while others do not. This is because the law of gravity states how things will behave under certain circumstances and, if the circumstances are different, so will be the behaviour of the things to which these laws apply. Similarly the same moral principles, when applied to different circumstances, tell us to do different things. If there is a moral principle enjoining fidelity to wives, Tom will be obeying it by being faithful to his wife Mary, while Dick will be obeying it by being faithful to his wife, Jane. If there is a moral principle enjoining promise-keeping, Jones will be obeying it by doing what he has promised, and Smith will be obeying it by doing what he has promised, even though *what* they have promised is different. A doctor may give antibiotics to one man and a placebo to another, but on both occasions be doing his professional duty. Hence the fact that in one place or at one time it may be right to care for the aged, but in another place or at another time, where, owing to the difficulty of surviving, circumstances are very different, not right to care for the aged, does not mean that there is not some one moral principle, which enjoins care for the aged upon one set of people, but enjoins patricide upon another set of people, nor that the principle is not the same for both times and places, and for the people living at those times and places. Both people, for example, may be acting on the principle that the welfare of their community

---

[1] In 'A Dialogue', in *Hume's Enquiries*, ed. by L. A. Selby-Bigge, (Clarendon Press), 2nd edition, 1902, p. 333.

must be maximized, but it so happens that the kind of behaviour which maximises one community's welfare is different from the sort of behaviour which maximises the welfare of the other.

Secondly, he may point out that not only do the circumstances to which moral principles have to be applied vary from one place to another and from one time to another, thus leading to our having different duties at those times and places; people's opinions about the circumstances also vary. There may be no *moral* disagreement between one doctor who recommends that a patient be given drugs, and another doctor who recommends that the same patient have an operation. The difference in what they think they ought to do may be due not to a disagreement over moral principles, but to a different assessment of the factual situation to which these moral principles may be applied. Similarly, there may be no moral disagreement between a community which regards cannibalism with moral abhorrence and one where cannibalism is enjoined as a duty. They may both accept the same moral principles, and the different conclusions they come to about what they do in particular circumstances may be due to a difference of opinion on a matter of fact; the community which regards eating one's enemies as a duty may believe that by doing so one assimilates their virtues oneself, whereas the community which prefers to bury them may not believe this. Hence the same moral principles may produce a difference of opinion about what one ought to do, because people's beliefs about the situations to which these are applied are different, even though the situations to which they are applied are not in fact different in any relevant respect at all.

The first and the second intuitionist answer to the difficulty stated above are not on a par. The first answer says that, owing to the different circumstances which obtain at different places and at different times, an action can actually *be* right at one place and time, and another similar action actually *be* wrong if performed at a different place or at a different time, and then proceeds to explain that the *same* moral principles applied to *different* circumstances enjoin different actions. The principle that one ought to drive safely, for example will enjoin driving on the left-hand side of the road in England, but on the right-hand side of the road in the United States. The second answer says that, owing to different people or groups having varying opinions on matters of fact, they may *think* that moral principles, which they both accept, enjoin different actions in circumstances which, though they suppose them to be different, are in fact the same. (There is no reason incidentally, why the intuitionist should not give both these answers at once, since they are in no way incompatible with one another.) The difference in these two answers shows that there are in fact two different objections. The first is that some things really are right at one time and wrong at another, and right at one place and wrong at another. This objection is, I think, correctly answered. The second objection is that people at one place suppose things to be right which people at another place suppose to be wrong, and that people at one time suppose to be right things which people at a different time suppose to be wrong. This objection would be answered only if it were clear that had these different people the same beliefs on matters of fact, they would agree with one another on questions of moral principle. It is answered only if differences of opinion on moral matters were always entirely due to differences on matter of fact; but that this is so is not clear. It is quite possible, for example, that a missionary would not agree that killing elderly relatives is right, even if he does come to see that keeping them alive reduces the mobility, and so the chances of survival, of their tribe. And though it could be argued that many differences of opinion on moral matters arise because people suppose that moral rules, which may perfectly well be justified in the community to which they are accustomed, apply the world over, without their realizing that circumstances in different parts of it may be very different from those which obtain in the place in which they themselves live, it seems certain that many people would adhere to the moral views to which they had been accustomed, even after they had realized how different life in other parts of the world was. It seems possible, for example, that a well-brought-up Englishwoman would not come to approve of polygamy for the people who practise it, even after she realised that the reason for it was that wives, in their community, were a great financial asset, which she knows is not the case in her own.

Hence people genuinely do disagree over moral principles; it is not the case that all apparent disagreements over questions of moral principle can be explained away as being due to people accepting the same moral principles, but deriving different conclusions from them owing to different opinions on matters of fact. Is there any reason, however, why an intuitionist *should* hold that all people do have the same beliefs about moral principles? In the case of mathematics, which intuitionists sometimes hold up as an example, it is clear that we sometimes think we can grasp truths which we do not in fact grasp, either because, though it so happens that what we think we grasp is true, we do not really clearly apprehend the necessity of its truth, or because what we think we grasp is not even true. Why should the intuitionist not hold that the same is true where our intuition of moral truths is concerned? It is true that he may wish to hold that intuition is infallible, that what we intuit must be true, but this may be no more than a terminological matter. Though what we intuit must be true, this does not mean that we may not sometimes seem to intuit that which is false; it means only that, if what we seem to intuit is not true, the intuitionist would rather – and, I think, quite rightly – not describe it as being intuited.

So far, though we have discussed certain objections to intuitionism, we have said nothing about the reasons for being an intuitionist, nothing about what makes intuitionism a tempting theory to hold. The reasons for being an intuitionist are almost entirely the reasons for not being a naturalist. According to naturalism, moral judgments are just ordinary statements describing the natural world. Some naturalists have identified them with statements about what is conducive to survival, others with what produces happiness, others with statements about what is approved of, or desired, or with statements about the conventions which a given community accepts. It is clear that if any of these theories are correct, moral judgments will be *synthetic*, *contingent*, and that, since we can know only by observation and experience what people desire, or approve of, what is conducive to survival or happiness, or what accords with a community's conventions, moral judgments will also be *empirical*. Naturalism is a theory which is bound to be attractive to a moral epistemologist, for, if it is true, moral judgements are just a sub-class of ordinary empirical judgments describing the world as it is, and though, of course, there are problems enough about the manner in which we come to know that they are true, there will, if naturalism is right, be no *special* problems about moral judgments, no problems over and above the problems to which ordinary empirical judgments describing the natural world give rise. Moral judgments are, if naturalism is true, in no way mysterious, esoteric or elusive; they are just like judgments to the effect that the giraffe's neck is useful to the giraffe, that bigamy is illegal in England or that good-tempered people are more likely to be happy than bad-tempered people.

Some philosophers wish to identify naturalism with the view that moral problems can be settled by the methods of empirical science, but this is not strictly speaking correct. It is true that, if moral judgments are judgments about what is conducive to survival moral problems will be settled by biologists, for it is the biologist who settles questions about what is conducive to survival; if moral judgments are judgments about what is desired, then moral questions will be settled by psychologists, for it is psychologists who investigate the nature and objects of human motivation; if moral judgments are judgments about what accords with the customs of the agent's society, then moral questions will be settled by anthropologists, because it is anthropologists who must investigate the customs of different societies. It is not the case, however, that the only empirical judgments there are, are judgments the truth of which scientists can settle, and about which they are entitled to have an expert opinion, an opinion more to be relied upon than that of ordinary men and women. That grass is green is an ordinary empirical judgment about the natural world, but ordinary men and women are in just as good a position to discover its truth as any scientist is. That my shoe pinches or that I am seeing double are, again, ordinary empirical judgments about the natural world, and some people – the person whose shoe pinches or the person who is seeing double – are in a much better position to discover that they are true than anyone is by application of scientific method.

THE NATURALISTIC FALLACY

It is objected to naturalism that it commits what is known as the naturalistic fallacy.[1] Any attempt to identify the characteristic, property or quality which we are attributing to anything when we are describing it as good or bad, right or wrong, etc., with any of the 'natural' properties of things must be mistaken, and there is quite a simple way of showing that it is. If we attempt to identify being wrong with the natural property of being prohibited by

[1] See G. E. Moore, *Principia Ethica* (C.U.P., 1903), Chapter i.

law, for example, it will follow that the words 'wrong' and 'prohibited by law' are different words for what is one and the same thing. However, it seems perfectly sensible to ask questions such as 'Is what is prohibited by law always wrong?' If 'wrong' simply meant 'prohibited by law', if there were not two things, being prohibited by law and being wrong, but only one thing, which was referred to either by 'wrong' or by 'prohibited by law', then it would not be sensible to raise the question 'Are things which are prohibited by law always wrong?', for asking the question presupposes that there are two different things, and suggests that these two things might not always be found together, and hence, if there were only one thing, the question could not be raised.

The above argument can be put in a different way. If 'wrong' and 'prohibited by law' mean the same thing, it ought to be possible to substitute either for the other in any sentence in which one of them occurs, just as, since 'uncle' and 'parent's brother' mean the same thing, it is possible to substitute either for the other in any sentence in which one of *them* occurs. But, it is argued, it is possible to find a sentence in which 'wrong' cannot be substituted for 'prohibited by law', the sentence considered above: 'Is what is wrong always prohibited by law?' If you substituted 'wrong' for 'prohibited by law' in this sentence, what results is the sentence 'Is what is wrong always wrong?', or if you make the converse substitution, and replace 'wrong' by 'prohibited by law', what results is the sentence 'Is what is prohibited by law always prohibited by law?' It seems, it is then argued, quite obvious that when we ask the question 'Is what is prohibited by law always wrong?' we are not simply asking 'Is what is prohibited by law always prohibited by law?' or 'Is what is wrong always wrong?' Since these questions are not equivalent, 'wrong' cannot just mean the same as 'prohibited by law', for if it did, these three questions would be equivalent.

Again, it is argued that someone making the statement 'It is always wrong to do what is prohibited by law' is clearly ascribing to a class of thing, viz. those things prohibited by law, a further characteristic, the characteristic of being wrong. He is making a statement of some substance, a moral judgment from which something of practical importance would follow if it were true, one which it is sensible to doubt or to deny. If, however, 'wrong' simply meant 'prohibited by law', all he would be saying would be that 'It is always wrong to do what is wrong' or 'It is always prohibited by law to do what is prohibited by law'. Anyone making such a statement would not be attributing to the class of things which are prohibited by law an attribute over and above, different and distinct from, their being prohibited by law; nothing of any practical importance would follow from it if it were true, nor would it be sensible to doubt it or to deny it. Since the statement 'It is always wrong to do what is prohibited by law' would not be a moral judgment of substance if being wrong and being prohibited by law were identical, and it *is* a moral judgment of substance, it follows logically that being wrong and being prohibited by law cannot be identical. Indeed, some philosophers, who have accepted some such definition of 'wrong' as the one we have been considering, have themselves in practice treated their own definition as if it were incorrect,[1] by themselves asserting some such thing as, 'It is always wrong to do what is prohibited by law,' as though it were a moral judgment of substance, one from which consequences of importance for the practical guidance of everyday life would follow if it were true.

This argument against defining words like 'wrong' naturalistically – it is thought that the case is not altered if we consider 'right' or 'good' or 'bad' instead of 'wrong' – is not, however, flawless. It is simply not the case that, if two words mean the same thing, it is possible to substitute either for the other in *any* sentence in which one of them occurs.[2] For example, though 'uncle' and 'parent's brother' mean the same thing, it does not follow that 'He said, "I had tea with my uncle" ' is equivalent to 'He said, "I had tea with my parent's brother" '. The latter, after all is a very unlikely thing for anyone to say, whereas the former is something which comes quite naturally. Hence, there is at least one kind of case when words which have the same meaning cannot be substituted for one another, that is, when the words in question are being actually quoted, as in direct speech. This is because, in such statements, information is being given about the actual words used, and, of course, to say that someone used the word 'uncle' is not at all to say that he used the words 'parent's brother', even though these words do mean the same thing.

Hence, the rule, that if two words (or phrases) have the same

---

[1] Jeremy Bentham, for example. See *An Introduction to the Principles of Morals and Legislation*, ed. by Wilfred Harrison (Blackwell, 1948), pp. 125 f.

[2] See R. M. Hare, *The Language of Morals* (O.U.P., 1952), Chapter V.

meaning, either can be substituted for the other in any sentence in which one of them occurs, does not apply when the words in question occur in quotation marks, thus indicating that the statement which this sentence is being used to make is about the words themselves. It must not be assumed, however, that the substitution can always be made when the words do *not* occur in quotation marks. In the sentence ' "Puppy" means "baby dog" ', the substitution obviously cannot be made, even though the words 'puppy' and the phrase 'baby dog' do mean the same thing, but in the sentence 'A puppy is a baby dog' the substitution still cannot be made – it would result in the sentence 'A puppy is a puppy' or the sentence 'A baby dog is a baby dog' – even though the words 'puppy' and 'baby dog' are not in fact in quotation marks. Someone saying 'A puppy is a baby dog' is actually defining the word 'puppy', even though he does not put 'puppy' in quotation marks. Similarly with 'A bachelor is an unmarried man' and 'A triangle is a plane figure bounded by three straight lines'. There is no grammatical difference between 'A puppy is a baby dog' and 'A puppy is a delightful companion', although the first does, but the second does not, serve to define the word 'puppy'. Somehow, one is supposed to be able to judge from the context whether the statement being made is telling you, as in the case of 'A puppy is a baby dog', what the essential characteristics of the thing are, the essential minimum which anything must possess in order properly to be described by the word in question, or whether, as in the case of 'A puppy is a delightful companion', 'extra' characteristics are being attributed to it. If one judges that it is the former that is being done, then one can infer that it is the possession or lack of these characteristics on account of which one applies or withholds the word, and hence infer what this word means, in the sense in which to know what the word 'so-and-so' means is to know what characteristics a thing must possess in order to qualify to be described as so-and-so.

It is an interesting question whether statements such as 'A puppy is a baby dog' or 'A triangle is a plane figure bounded by three straight lines' are analytic propositions or synthetic propositions. These propositions ought to be analytic, for the predicate terms, being a baby dog, and being a plane figure bounded by three straight lines, can be obtained from the subject terms, puppy and triangle, 'by analysis': all the attributes being ascribed to a thing when it is called a baby dog or a plane figure bounded by three straight lines have already been ascribed to it by calling it a puppy or a triangle. However, it is obvious that the statement 'A puppy is a baby dog' and 'A triangle is a plane figure bounded by three straight lines', although allegedly analytic, do give empirical information to a person who does not know what the words 'puppy' and 'triangle' mean, which information he could not get by any amount of a *a priori* reflection. For they inform him of the meanings of the words 'puppy' and 'triangle', and it is just an empirical and contingent fact that English people use these words in the way they do, that is, as equivalents for one another.

Perhaps the explanation of how we can get empirical information from these analytic propositions is this. The proposition 'A puppy is a baby dog' is an analytic one, but empirical information can be deduced from the fact that it is analytic, together with a knowledge of what the words in the sentence used to express it actually are. Anyone knowing that the statement 'A puppy is a baby dog' is analytic, and supplying for himself the additional premise, which he can quite easily do because he hears the sentence being spoken or sees it written on paper, that the statement 'A puppy is a baby dog' is expressed in the words 'A puppy is a baby dog' and using this additional premise, together with his knowledge, which is acquired by experience, of English syntax, can infer that the word 'puppy' and the words 'baby dog' mean the same.[1] He cannot make this inference from the statement that a puppy is a puppy, or that a baby dog is a baby dog, for to get this information he needs a sentence in which the word 'puppy' and the word 'baby dog' both occur, and in each of these sentences only one of these word occur.

Does this mean that we can say that the sentences 'A puppy is a baby dog' and 'A puppy is a puppy' express the same statement (which is an analytic one), although because this statement is expressed in different words in the two cases, inferences about the meaning of words can be drawn from the first sentence, which inferences cannot be drawn from the second? It is presumably a

---

[1] Strictly speaking, he cannot infer this from knowledge of the fact that 'A puppy is a baby dog' is analytic, for this would be analytic, so long as being a puppy entailed being a baby dog, but being a baby dog did not entail being a puppy. From the fact that 'A bachelor is unmarried' is analytic you cannot deduce that to be a bachelor means to be unmarried, for this is not true. The premise you need in order to deduce that 'puppy' means 'baby dog' is not that 'A puppy is a baby dog' is analytic, but that 'A puppy is a baby dog' states that being a puppy and being a baby dog are (unlike 'The evening star is the morning star') analytically equivalent.

belief that these two sentences do express the same statement which makes some philosophers wish to describe analytic statements as taulologies, for it would, I suppose, be correct to describe 'A puppy is a baby dog' as a tautology. However, it seems implausible to describe the statements which each of these two sentences express as the same, even though, since the first can be deduced from the second and the second can be deduced from the first, they are logically equivalent to one another. It is true that the second occurrence of the word 'puppy', in the sentence 'A puppy is a puppy', connotes exactly the same attributes that 'baby dog' in the sentence 'A puppy is a baby dog' connotes, so somehow one feels that the two sentences ought to be saying exactly the same thing. There is, however, over and above the fact that an inference about the synonymity of the words 'puppy' and 'baby dog' can be drawn from the statement 'A puppy is a baby dog' which cannot be drawn from the statement 'A puppy is a puppy', a psychological difference between the two statements. 'A puppy is a baby dog' mentions separately two features a thing must possess to be counted as a puppy, being a dog and being a baby, whereas 'A puppy is a puppy' does not do this. The difference, perhaps, is like seeing a certain figure as a duck and seeing the same figure as a rabbit. The former statement causes us to see two features separately which the latter lumps together, thus causing us to treat them as a whole.

This digression, upon the nature of statements such as 'The word "puppy" and the words "baby dog" mean the same' and 'A puppy is a baby dog' shows that the objection to naturalism, which has had enormous influence upon moral epistemologists during the twentieth century, must be rejected as unsound. The objection was that, to revert to our original example, 'wrong' cannot mean 'prohibited by law', because if it did, one could substitute, in the sentence such as 'Is what is wrong always prohibited by law?' or 'It is always wrong to do what is prohibited by law', the words 'prohibited by law' for 'wrong', without altering the meaning of the sentences, whereas in fact making this substitution does alter the meaning of these sentences. The reply is that one might just as well argue that 'puppy' cannot possibly mean 'baby dog' because, if it did, one could substitute 'baby dog' for 'puppy' in the sentence 'A puppy is a baby dog' without altering the meaning of this sentence, whereas, again, one obviously does in some sense or other alter its meaning. 'A puppy is a baby dog' does supply one with information which 'A puppy is a puppy' does not supply one with, viz. that 'puppy' means 'baby dog'. Similarly, 'It is always wrong to do what is prohibited by law', even if 'wrong' did just mean 'prohibited by law', would not be at all the same as 'It is always prohibited by law to do what is prohibited by law', for from the first – or, more accurately, from knowledge that the first expresses an analytic equivalence – one can infer that 'wrong' and 'prohibited by law' mean the same, while from the second one cannot infer this. For the same reason, even if 'wrong' did mean 'prohibited by law', it would not follow that the question 'Is what is wrong always prohibited by law?' was the same as the question 'Is what is prohibited by law always what is prohibited by law?' Hence it does not follow that, because it is just silly to answer the second question in the negative, it is just silly to answer the first question in the negative. It is possible to see, simply from the form of the second question, that the answer to it must be affirmative (indeed it would be possible to see this, even if one did not know what the words 'prohibited by law' meant), but it is not possible to see that an answer to the first question, 'Is what is wrong always prohibited by law?' must be in the affirmative without in some sense knowing what the words 'wrong' and 'prohibited by law' mean. Indeed, there is a way in which, though the answer to the question 'Is what is prohibited by law prohibited by law' has to be in the affirmative, the answer to the question 'Is what is wrong always prohibited by law' does not have to be in the affirmative, even if 'prohibited by law' *is* just what the word 'wrong' means. For though both the proposition 'What is prohibited by law is prohibited by law' and the proposition 'What is wrong is prohibited by law' are, if 'wrong' just means 'prohibited by law', necessarily true, and also equivalent to one another, it is possible to say that the second statement might be false, meaning that its verbal form does not preclude its being false, whereas it is not possible to say this of the first statement.

The matter does not rest here, however. It is true that from the fact that 'wrong' is given some definition, which we may call X, it does not follow that the definition is incorrect because statements such as 'Wrong actions are X' are not equivalent to 'Wrong actions are wrong' or 'X actions are X'. Nevertheless, certain propositions will be analytic and practically useless if the definition 'Wrong means X' is correct, which will be synthetic and have consequences of importance if the definition is incorrect. Hence it may be argued against any given form of naturalism that certain propositions, which will be analytic if the definition in question is satisfactory, are in fact synthetic. Indeed, it does seem to me that, to go back to our original example, the statement 'If an action is wrong, it is prohibited by law', so far from being analytic, practically uninformative, and true, is in fact synthetic, practically important, and false.

The fact that it is possible to reject certain proffered definitions of ethical words like 'right' and 'wrong', 'good' and 'bad' for this reason, gives no *automatic* way of refuting any definition of ethical words. The substitution argument we have been considering, however, is a spurious attempt to provide such an automatic method. Whatever definition of ethical words we offer, it would always be possible to find a sentence, for example, the sentence 'Wrong actions are inconducive to the survival of the species', and argue that the definition must be incorrect, because the definition cannot be substituted for the word defined in this allegedly analytic statement. But even if it were a fact that 'wrong' meant 'inconducive to the survival of the species', this would still not mean that we could substitute 'inconducive to the survival of the species' for 'wrong' in the sentence 'Actions which are wrong are inconducive to the survival of the species'. 'Actions which are wrong are inconducive to the survival of the species' would, if true, allow us to make a deduction which 'Actions which are wrong are wrong' or 'Actions which are inconducive to the survival of the species are inconducive to the survival of the species' would not allow us to make, namely, the deduction that the words 'inconducive to the survival of the species' and 'wrong' are synonymous. Hence the substitution argument would rule out even a correct definition of ethical words if there is one. The process of considering whether propositions which will be analytic if a certain definition is correct are really analytic in fact, must be undertaken afresh with each new definition; each case must be considered on its merits, and there is no method of rejecting all definitions of ethical words on principle.

The substitution argument which we have rejected would, if valid, do more than dispose of definitions of ethical words in terms of words for natural characteristics, the presence of which can be detected by an empirical investigation of the natural world.

It would also dispose of definitions of some ethical words in terms of others, although such definitions would not normally be considered to have committed the naturalistic fallacy.[1] Take, for example, the definition of 'good man' as 'man better than most men', which definition is probably correct so far as it goes. This is not a naturalistic definition of 'good', for 'good' is defined in terms of 'better than', which is itself an ethical phrase. Nevertheless, if the substitution argument were valid, it would be possible to reject this definition on the grounds that, if it were correct, it would be possible to substitute 'better than most men' for 'good man' in the sentence 'A good man is better than most men', which would give you 'A good man is a good man' or 'A man who is better than most men is better than most men', both of which are obviously not equivalent to the original statement. It would also be possible to reject out of hand certain definitions of ethical words in terms of words which are not names for empirically detectable characteristics of the natural world, which definitions have usually been considered as committing the naturalistic fallacy. The definition ' "Wrong" means "prohibited by God" ', though it does not attempt to define 'wrong' in terms of any empirically detectable characteristic of the natural world, could be rejected out of hand on the grounds that the statement 'It is wrong to do what God prohibits' does not simply mean 'It is wrong to do what is wrong' or 'To do what God prohibits is to do what God prohibits'. Though this definition is, I dare say, incorrect, it cannot be rejected for the reason supposed.

Even if the above attempt to dispose wholesale of all attempts to define ethical words in terms of words for empirically detectable characteristics of the natural world were successful, it would still not have refuted naturalism. What the argument would show is that ethical words were indefinable, and quite apart from the fact that it does not even show this (it would, as we have already seen, dispose of the quite correct definition of 'good man' as 'man better than most men') it would not follow from the fact that ethical words were not *definable* that they were not words for *empirically detectable characteristics of the natural world*. It is true that the argument, if valid, would show that ethical words

---

[1] It would follow that not all theories which commit the naturalistic fallacy are naturalistic ethical theories, and Moore himself clearly regarded *metaphysical* ethical theories as committing the naturalistic fallacy.

could not *be defined in terms of* natural characteristics – this would follow from the fact that they were indefinable – but they might *be* words for such characteristics none the less. There is no reason why a word should not both be indefinable and a word for a natural characteristic – the word 'red' is such a word – and though, like the word 'red', the word 'good' could not be defined in terms of any words for natural characteristics, this would not show at all that it was not a word for a natural characteristic, so long as this was an *indefinable* natural characteristic. A moral sense theorist then might hold that 'good', like 'red', was a name for an indefinable natural characteristic the presence of which we detect by means of a moral sense. Indeed, the argument which deduces that moral terms are not natural from the premise, whether true or false, that they are not definable, is little more than a howler.

In spite of this, I think many people will feel that it is just self-evident that ethical words and non-ethical words *cannot* be defined in terms of one another, and that a naturalist must be maintaining that they *can* be defined in terms of one another. I think that the reason for this feeling is as follows. Let us suppose we are asked to draw up a list of ethical words on the one hand, and of non-ethical words on the other, and we then raise the question whether any members of the first group can be defined in terms of members of the second group. Now, I think many people will feel that if any member of the first group can be defined in terms of a member of the second group, it must *ipso facto* become a member of the second group, and they feel that for this to be so is logically impossible, for we started with a division of words into ethical words and non-ethical words, which division was intended to be exclusive as well as exhaustive, which was intended to put every word into either one group or the other, and none in both.

However, from the fact that the division of words into two sets is exclusive, it does not logically follow that no member of either set can be defined in terms of the other. To take an example, the division of words into definable words and into indefinable words is exclusive; no words fall into both categories. Nevertheless, it obviously does not follow that no members of the first group can be defined in terms of members of the second group. On the contrary, many – and perhaps, in the last resort, all – definable words can be defined in terms of indefinable words. So, too, can many mathematical words be defined in terms of non-mathematical (logical) words, and many biological words may be defined in terms of non-biological (e.g. biochemical) words.

It will only be logically impossible to define ethical words in terms of non-ethical words if we make this impossible by definition; if we widen our definition of 'non-ethical words' to mean not simply 'word which is not an ethical word', but 'word which is neither an ethical word nor a word in terms of which an ethical word can be defined'; or, conversely, if we widen our definition of 'ethical word' in such a way as to refuse to call a word an ethical word if it turns out that it can be defined in terms of non-ethical words. If we do this, we must produce some good reason for doing so, and the only reason I can think of is that this is what 'ethical word' in fact means. But is this what 'ethical word' means? Now I am not myself at all clear what 'ethical word' does mean, but it seems to me perfectly possible that an ethical word, or, at any rate, the ethical word 'good', may be so called partly because it evinces a certain kind of favourable attitude to the thing described by the word. We call something good, perhaps, only if we are in favour of it, or prepared to advise others to seek it, or to recommend their adopting it. It may perfectly well be that, though the word 'good' can be defined in terms of words for natural characteristics, when we use these words for natural characteristics by themselves, they evince no such favourable attitude. The favourable attitude is evinced by the word 'good', but not by its definition. Hence, though it is an ethical word, the words in terms of which it is defined are not.

In general there seems to me to be no reason why the characteristic of being an ethical word might not belong to certain words, although it does not belong to the words in terms of which they are defined, though perhaps not for the reason suggested above for the word 'good'. The relation between a concept and its definition is not unlike the relation of a whole to its part. If I say that a brother is a male sibling, I am 'splitting up', so to speak, the notion of being a brother into two constituent notions. This is because there are two features which anything has to possess to count as being a brother; it must have the relation of being a sibling (i.e. having the same father and mother) to something else, and it must be male, and these two features severally are related to being a brother in the same sort of way that a part is related to the whole to which it belongs. Again, when I say that an uncle is a parent's brother (or a parent's male sibling) I am doing something like mentioning severally two parts which in this case are themselves relations which the relation of being an uncle consists in (logicians recognize this fact by describing 'being the uncle of' as a compound relation, a relation compounded of 'being the parent of' and 'being the brother of').

Where ordinary wholes and parts are concerned, there are *often* characteristics which belong to the wholes, but which do not belong to any of the parts separately. To take a well-known example, being difficult to break is a characteristic which can belong to a bundle of rods collectively, although it does not belong to any of the rods taken by themselves. It is not obvious to me that the characteristic of being ethical is not a characteristic which might belong to certain sets of characteristics taken as a whole, but which does not belong to the parts, in terms of which they are defined, taken by themselves. Certainly it is possible for an emotional reaction, such as one of approval, to be prompted by the presence of a number of characteristics collectively, though it is not evoked by the presence of any of these characteristics severally. If this is so, however, there is no logical reason why ethical words should not be capable of being defined in terms of words which are not ethical words.

But what bearing has the question whether *ethical* words can be defined in terms of *non-ethical* words upon the question whether it is possible to define ethical words in terms of words for *empirically detectable characteristics of the natural world*? From the fact, if it were a fact, that you could not define ethical characteristics in terms of *non-ethical characteristics* it would only follow that you could not define ethical characteristics in terms of *empirically detectable characteristics* of the natural world if that non-ethical characteristics are the only empirically detectable characteristics of the natural world could be assumed. This cannot be assumed without begging the question, however; for that non-ethical characteristics are the only empirically detectable characteristics there are, will only be true if ethical characteristics are *not* empirically detectable characteristics of the natural world, and this is precisely what anyone using this argument is attempting to prove. Indeed, that ethical characteristics cannot be defined in terms of non-ethical characteristics, even if it were true, would not show that ethical characteristics were not any kind of characteristics you care to think of. As G. E. Moore suggested, ethical characteristics are indeed what they are, and not another thing, but from this truism nothing at all can be deduced about what *sort* of thing ethical characteristics are.[1]

If ethical characteristics cannot be defined in terms of any empirical characteristics of the natural world, it seems to follow that all moral judgments in which some ethical assessment is made of some actual feature of the world, or of something which might happen or which someone might do, are synthetic, not analytic. (It would not follow as has been supposed that all moral judgments without exception were synthetic and not analytic. That murder is wrong is analytic, whether ethical characteristics can or cannot be defined in terms of empirically detectable characteristics of the natural world.) Any judgment which, like 'Promises ought to be kept' or 'Happiness is a good', connects something ethical – being a good or being something which ought to be done – with something in the natural world, such as being a promise, or being a state of happiness, would be an example. It is being said that anything which answers to the description of a promise has the ethical features of being obligatory, or that anything which is a case of happiness, is to that extent good. Now, presumably, if ethical characteristics are not empirically detectable features of the natural world, it cannot be ascertained just by observation and experience that the things which answer to the natural descriptions possess the ethical characteristics in question. Hence, if one rejects naturalism, it is difficult to see how one can answer the question 'How do we know that certain things possess certain ethical characteristics?' except by saying that we know this by intuition; that we just intellectually grasp that certain non-ethical characteristics and certain ethical characteristics must go together; that we just see that anything which possesses the non-ethical natural characteristics must also possess the ethical non-natural characteristics also. Hence, if we reject naturalism, it seems difficult to avoid accepting intuitionism. (We shall see later[2] that there are other alternatives to rejecting naturalism than accepting intuitionism; I have here assumed, for the sake of argument, that ethical words are words for characteristics, which is something that many philosophers have denied, and I shall say more later[3] about the possibility

---

[1] See W. K. Frankina, '*The Naturalistic Fallacy*,' *Mind*, Vol. XLVIII, 1939.
[2] Chapter XII.   [3] Chapter XIV.

that they are not names for characteristics at all.) It would also seem to follow that if ethical words are not names for empirically detectable features of the natural world, ethical concepts must be *a priori* concepts.

We have now discussed certain commonly made *objections* to intuitionism, and seen that they are invalid. We have also seen that the strongest reason for being an intuitionist, is that naturalism is untenable, and this too, we have seen some reason to question. It is now necessary to return again to the question whether it can really be plausible to maintain that we simply intuit the truth of true ethical propositions. (It is worth pointing out that though non-naturalism entails intuitionism, intuitionism does not entail non-naturalism. It is logically possible to hold that, though both the concept of happiness and the concept of goodness are natural characteristics, we intuit a necessary connection between the two.) The ethical propositions which we intuit, if, indeed, we intuit any at all, must be all of a certain kind. We might possibly intuit the proposition that all promises ought to be kept, but we could not possibly intuit that Smith ought to have tea with his aunt (because that is what he has promised) for this would involve our intuiting that Smith has promised to have tea with his aunt, which is obviously something we establish empirically, by asking him or hearing him do it. Hence, the ethical propositions which we might conceivably know by intuition will all be hypothetical; they will state that if something in the natural world answers to a certain description, then some ethical characteristics must be predicated of it. Obviously, however, we can know only by observation that something in the world does answer to this description, and so, any judgment such as 'Smith did wrong to break his promise, or 'Jones is kind, honest, industrious and reliable, and so better than most men are' cannot be known solely by intuition. We establish by observation – if we include accepting things on others' testimony under the head of observation – that he did break his promise, and by intuition that, given that he did, what he did was wrong. The moral judgments which are known wholly by intuition will be the ultimate principles of morals, and certain other general judgments which can be deduced from them. We can know by intuition that all promises ought to be kept, which may be a proposition which cannot be deduced from any true ethical proposition more general than it, and so, presumably, we can know by intuition that all lying promises ought to be kept, for, since lying promises are promises this second judgment would follow logically from the first. But, for example, assuming that we know by intuition that we ought to act in such a way as to maximize happiness, we cannot maintain that we know by intuition that we ought to keep our promises, for this cannot be deduced solely from the judgment that we ought to maximise happiness; we must assume a premise which could be established only by observation, that promise-keeping does maximise happiness. In general, we can intuit only the ultimate principles of morals, and then derive other principles, or particular moral judgments, from these by means of premises stating that certain actions or classes of action fall under them, which premises can be established only empirically.

Whatever we think of the view that we intuit the truth of certain general ethical propositions, I think it certainly has to be maintained that there are *some* things which we know by intuition, though maybe moral judgments are not among them. A capacity for intuiting is necessary if we are to be able to grasp the validity of any logical argument or mathematical proof. If we are to deduce a proposition q from some other proposition p, we must be capable of simply seeing, without proof, that q follows from p. If we attempt to prove that q follows from p, by deducing this from some third proposition r, intuition will still be necessary if we are to see that the proposition, that q follows from p, follows from r. For example, if we attempt to prove, what may seem self-evident, that if the antecedent of a true hypothetical proposition is true, its consequent must be true too, we must still intuit that this proposition follows from the propositions we use to prove it. Hence understanding any argument or proof involves intuition in a sense, for understanding an argument or proof involves seeing without argument that the premises of the argument or the proof entail the conclusion.[1] This is just as much true of *deductive* moral arguments as it is of any deductive arguments at all. This is not, however, enough to establish the truth of intuitionism, for all it shows is that, given some propositions, other propositions may be intuitively seen to follow from them. This by itself, however, does not validate one single judgment. We need some way of knowing not only that *if* certain moral judgments are true, certain other

[1] See Lewis Carroll, 'What the Tortoise Said to Achilles,' *Mind*, Vol. IV, 1895.

moral judgments are true, but also of knowing that these moral judgments, our premises, *are* true.

Furthermore, not only does a capacity for this kind of intuiting, though we must agree we actually have it, not establish the premises of any moral proof, it is a capacity for grasping only analytic connections, whereas we have earlier argued that, if any moral judgment is to give any practical guidance, it must be synthetic, not analytic. (I say the connection between the propositions p and p implies q, and the proposition q, is analytic, because the proposition that p and p implies q entails q can be shown to be an analytic proposition, in that it will be true whatever combination of the possible truth-values of p and q holds; it can be shown that it will hold whether p and q are both true, whether p is true and q false whether p is false and q true, or whether p and q are both false. Hence it is analytic and uninformative, in the sense that it rules out no possible combination of the truth or falsity of p and the truth or falsity of q. Indeed, it is just because it is uninformative that it is necessarily true. If it were informative, then some possible combination of the truth and falsity of p and q would make it false. Since we could not know *a priori* that this combination did not obtain, the proposition that p and p implies q entails q could not be necessarily true.)

Hence the fact that we intuit that certain premises imply certain conclusions, in moral reasoning just as much as in any other, is not enough to establish the truth of intuitionism. We need to show that we also intuit the truth of the premises. Can this be shown? Let us consider parallels in mathematics and logic. There are, in mathematics and logic, a number of cases where this certainly cannot be shown, where no case can be made out for saying that we intuit the premises or axioms of the mathematical or logical system, as well as the fact that the theorems can be deduced from them. In certain kinds of geometry, for example, there may be alternative sets of axioms; the axioms of Euclidean geometry are not the only ones which might be true, and mathematicians have, in the course of time, produced more and more bizarre geometries, starting first by combining the contradictory of Euclid's axiom that parallel lines do not meet, however far they are produced, with the rest of Euclid's axioms. We cannot intuit these axioms because, though that the axioms of these systems imply the theorems is a necessary truth which may be grasped intuitively,

D

that the axioms are true is an empirical statement – and usually not even a true empirical statement at that. Hence *a priori* geometers simply confine themselves to finding sets of axioms which might be true, and deducing theorems from them, and it is up to natural scientists to find which out of large numbers of possible sets of axioms holds good of the actual world.

There are other cases too where we cannot hold that we intuit the truth of the axioms as well as intuiting that the theorems follow from the axioms. This holds true of uninterpreted axioms. Uninterpreted axioms consist of what are called propositional functions rather than propositions. A propositional function is a verbal and/or symbolic formula which will give a proposition if words of known meaning are substituted for certain of the symbols used in it. For example, 'X loves Y' is a propositional function, and a proposition can be obtained from it if we substitute the word 'Tom' for the symbol X and the word 'Mary' for the symbol Y. Clearly, this propositional function cannot itself be true or false, but it is such that, if certain words are substituted for 'X' and 'Y', the resulting proposition will be true, but if certain other words are substituted for 'X' and 'Y', the resulting proposition will be false. It may be true, for example, that Tom loves Mary, but false that Mary loves Jane. Some words may even be substituted for 'X' and 'Y' which yield a result which is meaningless, for example, 'Jam loves triangularity'.

A still more 'abstract' or generic propositional function can be obtained if, instead of 'loves', which has a constant meaning, we substitute another variable, say '*' giving 'X*Y'. This is more abstract or generic than 'X loves Y' because, in order to obtain an actual proposition, we need to substitute words for '*' as well as for X and Y; hence it is one more step removed from being an actual proposition than is 'X' loves Y'. An example of a set of substitutions which would yield a proposition which was true might be 'Harold hates Ted'; an example of a set of substitutions which would make it false might be 'Evelyn worships George'. It would not make sense to say of 'X * Y' itself that it is true or that it is false.

Now it is possible to have axioms called uninterpreted axioms, which are not propositions but propositional functions, and, oddly enough, possible too, to deduce theorems from them.[1] (The theor-

---

[1] Morris R. Cohen and Ernest Nagel, *An Introduction to Logic and Scientific Method* (Routledge, 1934), Chapter VII.

ems, of course, will be propositional functions, as are the axioms.) It is perhaps a little puzzling what the nature of the deduction of the theorems from the axioms can be. Normally deducing something from something else consists in seeing that if the first thing is true, the second thing must be true also. Hence it looks as if the notion of deduction is tied to the notion of proposition or statement; only propositions can be deduced, and these can be deduced only from propositions, for only propositions are capable of being true or false. But here we have something that seems to be deduction, but where both what is deduced and what it is deduced from are not propositions, but propositional functions, and are not capable of being true or of being false. Hence there seems something paradoxical about the deduction of theorems from sets of uninterpreted axioms. This appearance of paradox can, I think, be removed when we see that the process of deduction of a theorem from an uninterpreted axiom consists not in seeing that if the axioms are true, the theorem must be true too – for it does not make sense to say that uninterpreted axioms are true or false – but in seeing that any actual proposition – which of course can be true or false – which one can obtain by substituting words for the variables in the axioms entails the proposition which one obtains by substituting the *same* words for the same variables when they occur in the theorems.

However, though there are certain cases when we certainly cannot say that we intuit the axioms in a mathematical or logical system, either because it is simply an empirical fact, if it is a fact at all, that the axioms are true, or because it does not make sense to say that they are true, there are other cases when I think it is very plausible to hold that we do intuit the truth of the axioms. For example, given that we understand the meanings of the words in the axiom (from the first edition of *Principia Mathematica*) that, if a proposition q implies another proposition r, then the statement that either a third proposition p is true or q is true implies the statement that either this third proposition p is true or r is true, we can see that there is no possible alternative to this axiom's being true. To take another example, one of Euclid's axioms, that if two things are each equal to a third thing, they are equal to one another, it is possible, if we understand the meaning of the words in this sentence, to see that there is no alternative to their expressing something true.

This has often been denied, but I think the denial rests upon a confusion. It has been denied because it has been held that it is possible, for example, to have a mathematical system in which 'equals' is not a word for a transitive relation, or in which propositions can take more than the two truth-values true and false, in which case the logical properties of 'implies' or 'either . . . or' have to be appropriately modified. However, this does not mean that we can have a system which contains as an axiom the contradictory of the axiom that things which each equal a third thing must equal one another, or of the axiom that that if X equals Y and Y equals Z, X must equal Z. What it does mean is that someone can use the symbol 'equals' not as a word for a transitive relation, which is the way in which it is used at present, but for a relation which is not transitive. Hence the new axiom is not the contradictory of the old axiom; it is just that it *seems* to be the contradictory of the old axiom because the verbal formulation is what would have been the verbal formulation of the contradictory of the old axiom, if the meaning of 'equals' had not been changed. The process of producing axioms which appear to be contradictories of old axioms, which old axioms were such that we would see there was no possibility of their being false, if we understood the meaning of the words in the sentential or other formulae expressing them, is normally twofold. In the axiom that if X equals Y and Y equals Z, X must equal Z, the word 'equals' has a constant meaning, the same meaning that it has in ordinary parlance. In any system in which this axiom is denied, however, it becomes not a word with a constant meaning, but a variable symbol; the new axiom which results from the (apparent) denial of the old axiom is not a proposition, but a propositional function, and the axiom is an uninterpreted axiom, not an interpreted one. (This is because, since 'equals' obviously cannot mean what it used to mean, and no attempt is made to explain what it does mean, we simply manipulate it in accordance with the rules the axiom lays down without 'cashing' the sentential formulae involving this word in terms of any words we know the meaning of or in terms of mental images, and without knowing how to relate such formulae to any situation we might actually come across.) In apparently denying the old axiom we produce a new one, which is uninterpreted where the old one was interpreted. Where the old one had to be true because of the way in which the word 'equals' is actually used, one cannot properly say that the new one is either true or false, but only that it will yield propositions which are true or propositions which are false, according as to what word we substitute for the symbol 'equals' in the uninterpreted axiom. Hence our 'new' axiom is neither true nor false, and so cannot constitute a denial of anything, and the word 'equals' which it contains is not being used in the same way as it was in the 'old' axiom, where it had a constant meaning, the meaning which it has in ordinary speech, but as a variable for which it is possible to substitute various words for relations; some of these substitutions will produce results which are true, while others will produce results which are false.

My conclusion from the foregoing discussion is that there are some axioms which are necessarily true, and the truth of which we do intuit. These are axioms which are such that we can see that, if the words in the sentences formulating them are properly used, there is no alternative to their being true. This is because, if we put the axiom in a hypothetical way – for example, that *if* a first thing equals a second thing, and the second thing equals a third thing, the first thing must equal the third thing – any situation or state of affairs which would make the antecedent of the hypothetical proposition true would be identical with some state of affairs which would make the consequent of the hypothetical proposition true.

Such propositions, the axioms of mathematical or logical systems, can be seen or grasped or intuited as necessarily true because the very same situation or state of affairs which would make true the antecedent of the proposition into which they are translated when they are put hypothetically would also make true the consequent. This shows that the same account cannot be given of our knowledge of the basic principles of morals. The whole point of the basic principles of morals is that they should make an estimate of some possible or actual situation, or that they should tell one how one ought to behave in such a situation. If we frame them hypothetically, they become 'If anything is a case of such-and-such, then this thing is good' or 'If any action which one could perform answered to a certain description, then one ought to perform it'. If the very same situation or state of affairs which made the antecedent of these hypothetical propositions true were to be identical with the situation or state of affairs which made the consequent of this hypothetical true also, then there would be no possibility of an actual or possible situation being assessed, or of an action being directed or enjoined. The evaluation or assessment would be no different from the statement that the situation being evaluated or assessed obtained, and the 'moral directive' no different from the statement describing the action open to the agent. But if this were so, there would be no possibility of different evaluations of the same situation, or different injunctions concerning whether an action was or was not to be performed. The moral assessments or moral directions would simply be entailed by the statements describing the situations assessed or the actions prescribed. Even if it were possible for a moral assessment or a moral directive to consist in no more than this, the resulting proposition, formulating the assessment or expressing the directive, would, as we have seen, be uninformative and practically useless, and would in no way enable us to choose between different possible assessments of the same man or action or state of affairs, or give us any guidance about how we ought to behave in any given situation. Hence an account of the manner in which we see the necessity of the truth of the axioms of a mathematical or a logical system will not at all help us to see how we know, if we do know, that the world ought to be assessed in certain ways, or that certain things ought to be done in certain situations. What does not matter in mathematics and in logic, which are simply techniques for drawing out the implications of information which has already been given, imposes an important limitation in morals. In morals there has to be a difference between describing the situation and assessing the situation described, and between describing an action which is open to the agent, and saying whether the action ought or ought not to be performed. If there were no such difference it would be impossible, so to speak, to point in one direction rather than another, and the whole object of moral language, which essentially involves the possibility of assessing different situations differently, or directing people in different alternative directions, is lost.

Of course, all that this amounts to is that moral judgments, or moral judgments of a kind which are important, informative and properly action-guiding – and only such judgments can serve as the ultimate principles of morals – must be synthetic, not analytic. It is still open to an intuitionist to hold that such moral judgments are just seen to be true, in spite of the fact that it is simply not true that the way we use words excludes any possibility of these judgments being false.

This contention of the intuitionist does indeed fulfil two important conditions, which any satisfactory theory of moral epistemology must give some account of. It does at least seem as if our knowledge of morality is *a priori*. When we have collected all the facts about a person or a state of affairs, it seems that we do not need to collect any more facts in order to make our moral assessment. Indeed, the idea that we can collect any more than *all* the facts seems to be contradictory. If there are no more facts which we can, or need to, have in order to make our moral pronouncement, it looks as if our moral pronouncement must be made *a priori*, for what is an *a priori* pronouncement or judgment but one which is made without having recourse to any further knowledge of matters of fact? Furthermore, it does at least seem as if moral judgments, if true, must be necessarily true. If someone thinks that the only proper way of behaving is to try to bring into existence the maximum amount of human happiness, he cannot think that this just happens to be so, and might very well turn out not to be so, if things were different. He must think that this *must* be the right and proper way of behaving. It is true that there are many cases where something may seem to be the right and proper way of behaving, but where it turns out that this is not the proper way to behave when a more detailed or more accurate account has been established of the situation in which the action has to be performed. And it may very well be that there are many things which it is right and proper to do in some circumstances, but which are not *necessarily* right and proper things to do, for they would not be the right way of behaving if circumstances were different, or in places or at times in which circumstances are in fact different. And, of course, it is just a contingent fact that circumstances are as they are, and so it cannot be necessarily the case that such-and-such is the right and proper way of behaving, if it is the right and proper way of behaving only in circumstances which arise as a contingent matter of fact.

This difficulty, however, will apply only to *derivative* moral judgments, not to the ultimate principles of morality, whatever these may be. The reason for this is as follows. A derivative moral principle is always derived from some ultimate or non-derivative moral principle by the mediation of some factual proposition, which serves as a necessary premise, without which the deduction of the derivative from the ultimate principle could not be made. If we assume, for the sake of argument, that we ought to act in such a way as to maximize happiness, we can derive from this that we ought to keep our promises, provided it is the case that keeping one's promises does in fact maximize happiness. Since keeping one's promises, if it is a fact at all, is a contingent fact, it can only be contingently the case, given this utilitarian view, that we ought to keep our promises, for it would not be true that we ought to keep our promises, if doing so did not bring into existence the maximum amount of happiness. However, this very way of showing that certain moral judgments, like the judgment that we ought to keep our promises, are only contingent, will, if valid, suggest that the ultimate principles of morality cannot be contingent for this reason. An ultimate principle of morality is, by definition, just a principle which cannot be derived from any other principle of morality *via* the mediation of, or taken in conjunction with, some factual premise. Hence, where ultimate moral principles are concerned, there is no contingency, such as keeping one's promises either bringing or not bringing into existence the maximum amount of happiness, which is such that, if it obtained, we would have an obligation to act on the ultimate principle, but which, if it did not obtain, we would not have this obligation. I am not suggesting that this argument proves that the ultimate principles of morality must be necessary, though ordinary people habitually treat them as if they were necessary. But one thing it does is to rebut an argument which is designed to show that the principles of morals must all of them be contingent. This argument will only show that derivative principles are contingent, and a reason which can be given for showing that a derivative principle is contingent cannot possibly apply in the case of an ultimate moral principle.

The main difficulty with intuitionism, it seems to me, is that it provides too easy a solution to the problem of how we know what things are right and what things are wrong. Granted that there is an overwhelming case for thinking that our moral knowledge is not all analytic, that there is a strong case for thinking that it is *a priori*, and a strong case for thinking that moral judgments are necessarily true, to say that we know them to be true by intuition does not really do more than provide a name to cover up our ignorance. To say that we know moral judgments to be true by intuition is simply to assert that we know them, but to refuse to explain how it is that we do know them to be true. Just to say this, without attempting to provide any rationale of such knowledge, is altogether too crude a way of dealing with the problem. To this it might be replied that to say that moral judgments are synthetic, *a priori* and necessary is all that the intuitionist asserts, and that I have conceded that there is a strong case for thinking that they are synthetic, *a priori*, and necessary. We must see, however, whether some other solution can be found to the problem of explain-their *a priority*[1] and their necessity later in this book.[2]

OUGHT AND IS

A question often discussed by moral philosophers is whether it is possible to derive statements about what ought to be done from statements or sets of statements about what in fact is the case; whether it is possible to accept certain factual premises and at the same time without logical inconsistency to reject any moral conclusions which may be alleged to follow from them.

A number of spurious arguments are sometimes adduced as reasons for thinking that no *ought* can be derived from any *is*. For one thing, from the fact that a man is doing something, it does not follow that he ought to be doing that thing; but all this shows is that statements about what a man ought to be doing do not follow from factual statements describing what he is doing, not that they do not follow from any factual statements at all. It is sometimes supposed that because questions of fact can be contrast-ed with questions of right, questions of right cannot be questions of fact, and so cannot be settled simply by settling questions of fact. But from the fact that questions of right can be contrasted with questions of fact, it does not follow that there is not a sense of 'fact' in which questions of right are questions of fact. Similarly, from the fact that you can contrast questions of law with questions of fact, it does not follow that it is not, in a different sense of 'fact', as much a question of fact whether what the accused is alleged to have done is prohibited by law as it is whether he really did what he is accused of having done. Fact may not simply be contrasted with moral judgments or with legal judgments, but also with theories or with fiction or with mathematical truths or with scientific laws. Lastly, it is sometimes supposed that, because we must settle all the facts about what someone did before we pass

[1] Chapter XIV.
[2] For a discussion of naturalism and the naturalistic fallacy, see A. N. Prior, *Logic and the Basis of Ethics* (O.U.P., 1949).

moral judgments upon what he did, it follows that the moral judgment we pass cannot itself be a matter of fact, but this may simply mean that we have to settle all the non-moral matters of fact before we can pronounce upon a matter of moral fact. For again, from the fact that we must settle the facts about what the accused actually did before we decide whether what he did was contrary to law or not, it does not follow that the question whether what he did was contrary to law is not itself a question of fact.

A short way with the question whether an *ought* can be derived from an *is*, is this. It can be maintained that a judgment is only purely factual if it morally neutral, if it simply describes what the facts are without making or implying any evaluation of them or committing the person making this judgment to any view about what ought or ought not to be done. If it can be deduced from my apparently factual judgment that I would evaluate the situation I am judging in one way rather than another, or that I would be in favour of one thing rather than another being done in that situation, then my judgment is not purely factual. It would seem to follow from this that it is simply a tautology that judgments about what ought to be done cannot follow from purely factual judgments, for, if they do follow, then, by definition, these judgments are not purely factual. But even this does not, strictly speaking, follow, for it is possible that from a set of judgments which is such that no conclusions about value or about what ought to be done follow from any one of them individually, conclusions about what is of value or about what ought to be be done do follow when they are taken collectively. One might argue that from judgments not imputing guilt to any individual person no judgments which do impute guilt to an individual person may follow, but though 'My last client was a murderer' does not impute guilt to any individual person, and nor does 'Smith was my last client', it does follow from these two together that Smith is a murderer, which does impute guilt to an individual person.

But *is* it part of the definition of 'factual' that no moral judgment may follow from a factual judgment? Even if being factual entails not being moral, it does not necessarily follow from the fact that a judgment is X that it is not not-X, for from the fact that a judgment is formulated in a sentence written in green ink it does not follow that it is not formulated in a sentence written in ink which is not green, or from the fact that it is asserted on a Tuesday it does not follow that it is not asserted on some day other than a Tuesday.

This is because it is a feature of judgments that they can be expressed by different people, situated at different places, at different times, in different words, in different ways, and with different ends in view, and so from the fact that a judgment is expressed on one occasion with one end in view, it does not follow that the same judgment may not be expressed on a different occasion with a different end in view. Hence, if the dichotomy 'moral/non-moral' refers, not to the content of a judgment, but, say, to the ends the person making it has in view, there is no reason why the same judgment should not both be moral and non-moral, i.e. moral on one occasion and non-moral on another, and, since every judgment entails itself, no reason why a non-moral judgment should not entail a moral judgment.

There do, indeed, seem to be certain cases where it is very difficult to deny that factual judgments do entail moral judgments. This is especially the case of moral judgments saying what someone ought to do in order to attain certain ends, and of moral judgments expressing that certain actions are required by certain rules. For example, if it is the case that the way and the only way to become a concert pianist is to practise for eight hours a day, then it seems difficult to deny that if Smith wants to become a concert pianist, he *ought* to practise eight hours a day. Anyone accepting the premise but denying the conclusion would seem to be failing to understand what the word 'ought' meant. Again, if it is a rule of chess that a pawn may not be moved forward by more than a square at a time after it has once been moved, then it seems difficult to deny that Smith, who is playing chess, ought not to have moved his pawn from KB4 to KB6. Or, to take another similar example, if it is a rule of society that promises are to be kept, it seems to follow that Smith, who has made a promise, ought to keep it. And, if an 'ought' judgment is defined as one which is expressed in a sentence which contains the word 'ought', there is no reason at all why an 'ought' should not follow from an 'is', for there is no reason at all why a judgment expressed by means of the word 'ought' should not follow from a judgment – perhaps one and the same judgment – not expressed by means of the word 'ought'.

My conclusion is that there is no obvious reason why an 'ought' should not follow from an 'is', but this is a subject to which I shall return in a later chapter.[1]

[1] Chapter XIV.

CHAPTER VI

MORAL JUDGMENTS AS SYNTHETIC, CONTINGENT AND EMPIRICAL: SUBJECTIVISM

I. THE VIEW THAT MORAL JUDGMENTS ARE ABOUT THE SPEAKER'S FEELINGS.

If intuitionism is true, and judgments about ultimate moral principles are like the propositions of mathematics and logic, a number of important consequences follow. One of these we have already seen. If intuitionism is true, then a true moral judgment will be like a true logical judgment or a true mathematical judgment in that its truth is independent of the person who makes it, the time at which he makes it, and the place at which he makes it. It does not matter who the person is who says that two and two are four, for it will be true whoever says it. Nor does it matter where he is when he says it, nor the time of day, the week or the year when he says it. The same is supposed by intuitionists to hold good of the ultimate principles of morality. It will not hold good of derivative principles, of course, for these, as we have seen, are derived from ultimate moral principles *via* the mediation of certain factual propositions, and these factual propositions may be true of one place and false of another, or true of one time but false of another, and true about some people, but false about others. Though, for example, if one is both an intuitionist and a utilitarian, one will have to think that the ultimate principle that one ought to act in such a way as to maximize happiness is true regardless of who says it, where he is when he says it, and the time of his saying it; nevertheless, from an ultimate principle such as this it is possible to derive many moral judgments which do not hold good of all people, places and times – for example, the judgment that one ought not to eat pork, which may be true in hot countries where pork does not keep, but false in cold ones.

It is possible to call any theory such as this, which holds that there are some ultimate moral judgments, which are true irrespective of person, place and time, an objective moral theory, though the word 'objective', as we shall see later, is a misleading one. But there are many theories, known as 'subjective' ethical theories, which deny this. The word 'subjective', however, is as misleading as the word 'objective', and I do not think the nature of these 'subjective' theories will become clear until we have examined some examples of them. It will also appear, perhaps, that, though subjective ethical theories all have something in common, there are many differences between them, and that many of them are subjective in different degrees or in different ways.

It is sometimes held that what one means when one says that some action is right is that one personally approves of it, or that the thought of the action arouses in one a feeling of approval. Similarly, one can hold that to say that an action is wrong is to say that the thought of the action arouses in one a feeling of disapproval.[1] To avoid the difficulty[2] that, though every action is either right or wrong, and cannot be neither, there are many actions of which one neither approves nor disapproves, it would be best to define the theory as holding that to say that an action is wrong is to say that thinking of it arouses in one a feeling of disapproval, and that to say it is right is to say that thinking of it does *not* arouse in one a feeling of disapproval.[3] It is sometimes objected to this theory that we can disapprove of an action only while we are actually thinking of it, which we do only periodically, but the action is wrong even during the intervals when we are not thinking of it. This objection can quite easily be overcome by pointing out that when we say we disapprove of something we we are making a *dispositional* statement about ourselves, and that to say that we disapprove of something is not to say that we are feeling anything here and now, but that if certain circumstances arose, we would feel something – for example, that if we were to

---

[1] David Hume sometimes speaks as if he held this view; for example, when he says that you can find the viciousness of an action only 'when you turn your reflexion into your own breast, and find a sentiment of disapprobation, which arises in you towards the action'. *A Treatise of Human Nature*, ed. by L. A. Selby-Bigge, (O.U.P., 1897), Book III, Part I, Section I, pp. 468–9.

[2] Many of the objections discussed in the following pages, together with some I have not mentioned, may be found in *Ethics*, by G. E. Moore (O.U.P., 1960), Chapters III and IV; in *The Foundations of Ethics* (O.U.P., 1938), by Sir David Ross, Chapter IV; and in *The Definition of Good* (Macmillan, 1947), by A. C. Ewing, Chapter I.

[3] Though this is a refinement which I shall frequently ignore.

think of the action, even though we are not thinking of it now, the thought of it would arouse a feeling of disapproval in us. This may be true of us even at times when we are not thinking of the action we disapprove of.

It is also sometimes objected to the theory we are considering, the theory that when we say that some action is wrong, what we mean is that thinking of that action arouses in us a feeling of disapproval, that to say we approve of some action is not to make a statement about it, so much as to give our consent to its being performed or, if it has already been performed, to actions like it being performed in the future. When a civil servant writes 'I approve' on a document, he is not making a statement about it, but giving his consent or permission to the proposal the document contains going forward.

This objection rests upon a failure to notice that 'approve' has different senses or functions. When I say that I *approve* some action or proposal, then I am giving my consent to it, rather than making a statement about it. When I say I approve *of* some action or proposal, I am not giving my consent to it, but making a statement about my attitude to it. It is approving *of*, not *approving*, that philosophers who hold the theory are talking about when they argue that, when we say that some action is right, what we mean is that we approve of that action. The more precise circumlocution, 'thinking of the action arouses in us a feeling of approval', should make this quite clear.

What, however, is this feeling, in terms of which this theory attempts to define 'right 'and 'wrong'? It has been held that it is possible to identify the feeling of approval only as that feeling which is aroused in us by the thought that an action is right, and that it is only possible to identify the feeling of disapproval as that feeling which is aroused in us by the thought that an action is wrong. If this is so, of course, the view we are considering will have to be rejected out of hand for, if it is true, we will have to identify a wrong action by the feeling of disapproval which it arouses in us, whereas in fact we can identify the feeling only as that feeling which is aroused in us by the prior thought that the action is wrong. However, I think it is possible to give some account of the feeling of disapproval, though possibly not a very satisfactory one, without saying that it is that feeling which is aroused in us by the thought that an action is wrong. For one thing, the feeling of disapproval belongs to the genus 'hostile feelings'. To the extent that people arouse a feeling of disapproval in us, we are hostile to them, and to the extent that actions arouse this feeling in us, we are against their being performed. This is not enough, of course, for there are hostile feelings other than the feeling of disapproval. We may be against actions being performed because they are contrary to our own interest or to the interest of those we love or the interest of some institution of which we are a member, but this sort of hostility is not the same as moral disapproval. It may be, however, that the difference between this latter kind of hostility and moral disapproval is that, where the former is concerned, we are hostile to actions of the kind in question only so long as they are contrary to our interest, or the interests of other people or institutions we are concerned about; we are not hostile to any members of the class in question, irrespectively of how they affect us or people or institutions with whom we identify ourselves. Hence perhaps we are not very far from the truth if we say that a feeling of disapproval is a feeling of hostility which is aroused by any of a class of actions, irrespectively of how they affect us personally, or of how they affect people or institutions with whom we are connected. If so, there is no reason why we should not identify the feeling of disapproval without having to fall back on saying it is simply that feeling which is aroused in us by the thought that an action is wrong.

I now come to some more serious objections to the theory that what we mean when we say that an action is wrong is that the thought of it arouses in us a feeling of disapproval. It has been argued that the theory must be rejected because, if it is true, it will be possible *firstly* for one and the same action to be both right and wrong,[1] and *secondly* for an action to change from being right to being wrong, both of which are alleged to be impossible.[2] The argument which purports to show that, if the theory is true, an action may be both right and wrong is as follows. Let us suppose that there are two people, Jones and Smith, and that thinking of Brutus's assassination of Caesar arouses a feeling of approval in Jones, but arouses a feeling of disapproval in Smith. Then, if Jones says that Brutus was *right* to assassinate Caesar, what, on the theory, he will mean will be that the thought of Brutus's assassination of Caesar arouses in him a feeling of approval, which *ex hypothesi* it does; hence, when he says that

[1] See G. E. Moore, *Ethics* (O.U.P., 1966), pp. 44 f.   [2] *Ibid.*, p. 97.

Brutus was right to assassinate Caesar, he will be making a true statement, and so Brutus's action will be right. Smith, on the other hand, when he says that Brutus was *wrong* to assassinate Caesar, will also be making a true statement, for all *he* means is that he feels disapproval of Brutus's action, which *ex hypothesi* he does; hence, he too will be making a true statement, the true statement that what Brutus did was wrong, and if Smith truly says that Brutus's action was wrong, it seems that it must be wrong. Therefore one and the same action must be both right and wrong – right because it is truly judged to be right by Jones, and wrong because it is truly judged to be wrong by Smith.

A rather similar argument is used to show that one and the same action could, if the theory were true, change from being right to being wrong. Robinson, in the days of his rebellious youth, felt approval of Brutus's assassination of Caesar, but he has become conservative with greater age, and now feels disapproval of it. However when, many years ago, he said it was right, all he meant, according to the theory we are considering, was that he felt approval of it, and since, *ex hypothesi*, he did, he must have been judging truly that it was right, and so it must have been right. A similar argument shows that when he is older, and says that Brutus's action was wrong, he is also making a true judgment. All he means, according to the theory, is that he disapproves of it, and since *ex hypothesi* he does, his judgment that Brutus was *wrong* to assassinate Caesar must be true, and so Brutus's action must have been wrong. But if a long time ago he could truly judge that Brutus's action was wrong, but now can truly judge that it was right, it follows that a long time ago it must have *been* wrong and that now it must *be* right; hence it must have changed from being right to being wrong and, since, it is said that this is impossible, the theory must be rejected.

But *is* it impossible for an action to change from being right at one time to being wrong at another, and conversely? We have already seen that an action can be right at one time but, because circumstances have changed in the meanwhile, be wrong at another. Here, however, we are talking of classes of action and, put more precisely, the statement that an action can be right at one time, but wrong at another, means that *instances* of a class of action, performed at one time, can be right, while *other instances* of the *same* class of action, performed at another time can, because circumstances are different, be wrong. For example, once upon a time it might have been wrong to marry your deceased wife's sister, but now, because the law prohibiting this has been repealed, it is quite all right to do so. In the case we are considering, however, we are not concerned with a class of actions, some instances of which can be right and others wrong, but one individual action, Brutus's assassination of Caesar, and, of course, it would not make sense to say of Brutus's assassination of Caesar, or of any other single individual action, that it could sometimes be right and at other times be wrong.[1]

But things, it is obvious, do change, and possess attributes at one time which they do not possess at another; why should not actions be among them? I think the answer which would usually be given to this question is that a thing is something relatively permanent which endures through time, and so there is no reason why things should not be true of it at early stages of its history which are not true of it at later stages of its history. Actions, on the other hand, are a species of event, and events are not even relatively permanent, and do not endure through time. It cannot be that things are true of them in early stages of their histories which are not true of them at later stages of their histories, for events, unlike substances, do not have histories. Events happen, but it does not make sense to say that they change, while substances change, but it does not make sense to say that they happen. Since events cannot change, they cannot change from being right to being wrong, and any theory which entails that they do change must be rejected.

However, though events do not strictly speaking change, it nevertheless remains the case that statements can be true of them at one time which are not true of them at another. In the days of Robinson's youth, it was a true statement about that event which is described as Brutus's assassination of Caesar that it aroused feelings of approval in Robinson. Later, when he was much older, it was not a true statement about Brutus's assassination of Caesar that it was approved of by Robinson. It is true that we do not say that Brutus's assassination of Caesar has changed because of this, but this does not alter the fact that something can be true of it at one time which is not true of it at a later time. Perhaps, although we ought not to say that Brutus's assassination of Caesar has *changed* from being right to being wrong, there is nothing wrong

[1] See G. E. Moore, *op. cit.*, pp. 81 f.

in saying that at one time it was true of Brutus's assassination
of Caesar that it was right, and at another time true of Brutus's
assassination of Caesar that it was wrong, although it is improper
to describe this as a kind of change which takes place in the event
itself.

In any case, neither argument against the variety of subjectivism we are considering is quite watertight as it stands.[1] Let us
consider the first argument, that if all we mean when we say
that something is wrong is that we personally disapprove of it,
some actions will be both right and wrong at the same time.
If we reflect, we ought to see that the theory cannot entail this
consequence, for if we say that an action is both right and wrong
at the same time we will, if the theory is correct, simply mean
that we both disapprove and do not disapprove of one and the
same action at the same time. Though we may approve of an
action in some repects and disapprove of it in other respects, it
is obviously impossible both to disapprove of some action and not
to disapprove of it *on the whole* at the same time. Hence the
theory, so far from entailing that an action can be both right and
wrong at the same time, actually entails that an action cannot be
both right and wrong at the same time, so the argument against
it must somewhere be mistaken.

The mistake the argument against the theory makes, is to
pass from the statement that Jones truly judges an action to be
right to the statement that it is right, and from the statement that
Smith truly judges an action to be wrong to the statement that
it is wrong. The fact that I say that Jones truly judges that Brutus's
assassination of Caesar is right does not, if this theory is correct,
mean that I can say that it is right, for I can say that Jones judges
that Brutus's assassination of Caesar is right – because all he
means is that he approves of it, and he does – without having
to say that it is right, for this would simply mean that *I* approved
of it, and, of course, from the fact that Jones approves of it it
does not at all follow that I do. Similarly, I can judge that Smith
truly judges that Brutus's assassination of Caesar is wrong – for
he says that it is wrong, meaning that he disapproves of it, which

[1] A criticism of Moore's arguments may be found in 'Moore's Arguments
against certain forms of Ethical Naturalism,' by Charles L. Stevenson in *The
Philosophy of G. E. Moore* (Tudor Publishing Company second edition 1952),
ed. by P. A. Schilpp.

he does – without having to say that it is wrong, for this would mean that I disapprove of it, and again, from the fact that Smith disapproves of it it does not at all follow that I do. Hence, if the theory is right, I can concede that Jones is making a true statement when he say that Brutus was right to assassinate Caesar, and that Smith is making a true statement when he says that Brutus was wrong to assassinate Caesar, without having to say that Brutus's assassination of Caesar is both right and wrong. This could only mean that Brutus's assassination of Caesar is both approved of and disapproved of by me, which is as impossible on this theory as it is on any other.

The second argument against this variety of subjectivism also fails as it stands. From the fact that Robinson is making a true judgment when, in his youth, he says that Brutus was right to assassinate Caesar, and the fact that he is also making a true judgment when, in his old age, he says that Brutus was wrong to assassinate Caesar, it does not follow that Brutus's assassination of Caesar was right and is wrong. For one thing, it does not follow from the fact that Robinson can truly say today that Brutus was wrong to assassinate Caesar that I can truly say that Brutus was wrong to assassinate Caesar, for, if the theory is true, I will be saying that I disapprove of it, and that I disapprove of it does not at all follow from the fact that Robinson (now) disapproves of it. For another thing, it will not, if the theory is correct, follow from the fact that Robinson could once truly say that Brutus was right to assassinate Caesar that anyone at all, even Robinson as he is today, can say that Brutus was right to assassinate Caesar. In fact, Robinson can *not* say that Brutus was right to assassinate Caesar, for, *ex hypothesi*, he disapproves of this. The assumption the argument against this variety of subjectivism makes is that 'Brutus was right to assassinate Caesar' means 'I *formerly approved* of Brutus's assassination of Caesar' (which Robinson did) whereas in fact what it means is 'I now approve of Brutus's *former action* of assassinating Caesar,' (which Robinson does not). The past tense in 'Brutus *was* wrong to assassinate Caesar' indicates that the action is a past action, not that my disapproval is in the past. Similarly, from the fact that I now feel disapproval of Brutus's action, it does not at all follow that Brutus *is* wrong to assassinate Caesar; this would mean that Brutus's assassination of Caesar was in the present, which it is not. (I suspect what it would actually mean is that Brutus is acting wrongly in from time to time assassinating Caesar – an impossible feat – just as 'Richard is wrong to beat his children' means 'Richard is wrong in that he beats his children from time to time'.) Hence the fact that Robinson now disapproves of Brutus's assassination of Caesar does not mean that Brutus's action is (now) wrong – for this would mean that Brutus's assassination of Caesar was contemporary with Robinson's judging it to be wrong – and the fact that Robinson once approved of Brutus's assassination of Caesar does not mean that it was formerly right – for this would mean that he approved of it now. However, if this argument against this variety of subjectivism is to be regarded as satisfactory, this is what these things would have to mean; but they do not.

Nevertheless, these two unsatisfactory arguments against the variety of subjectivism we are considering, that is, the theory that what I mean when I say that an action is wrong is that I personally disapprove of it, do point to difficulties which seem to me to be conclusive reasons for rejecting it. The flaw in the first argument against subjectivism is that it assumed that, if Jones truly judged that some action was right, it would follow that this action was right, and that if Smith truly judged that some action was wrong, it would follow that the action was wrong. Now, of course, if all we mean when we say that an action is right is that we approve of it, and all we mean when we say that an action is wrong is that we disapprove of it, this does not follow. Though Jones may truly say that an action is right, meaning that he approves of it, and I can concede that what he says is true, I can say that what he says, when he says that an action is right, is true, without having to agree that the action which he says is right, *is* right; if I said it was wrong, this would mean that *I* disapproved of it. Similarly, I can agree that what Jones says when he says that an action is wrong is true, without having to say that the action *is* wrong, for when I say that what Jones says is true all I am saying is that he is right in thinking he disapproves of it, and from this it does not follow that I disapprove of it, which is what would be meant by my saying it was wrong.

However, it is surely evident that though this subjectivist theory implies that I can agree that someone who says that something is wrong is making a true judgment without conceding that what *he* says is wrong *is* wrong, I cannot possibly in fact do this. Obviously, if I say that someone is making a true judgment when he say that something is wrong, this implies that *I* must think that this action *is* wrong; the two statements 'Jones thinks rightly that Brutus was wrong to assassinate Caesar' and 'Brutus was not wrong to assassinate Caesar' are incompatible with one another. However, if the view, that what I mean when I say that an action is wrong is simply that the thought of it arouses disapproval in me, is right, these two statements will *not* be incompatible with one another. Since they are inconsistent in fact, the theory which implies that they are not inconsistent must be rejected.

Again, one flaw in the argument against this theory, which purported to show that, if the theory were true, an action could be right at one time and wrong at another, was in the passage from 'In the days of his youth, Robinson truly judged that Brutus was right to assassinate Caesar' to 'Brutus *was* right to assassinate Caesar'. If the theory is true, this latter statement does not follow from the former, for all the former means is that Robinson, in his youth, judged that he felt approval of Brutus's assassination of Caesar, and both I and Robinson can concede this without ourselves now feeling approval of Brutus's assassination of Caesar, and so without being able truly to judge that Brutus's assassination of Caesar was right.

Again, however, it is surely obvious that, if I do say, 'When Robinson, fifty years ago, said that Brutus was right to assassinate Caesar, he was making a true judgment', I am logically committed to 'Brutus was right to assassinate Caesar'. I cannot say, 'Robinson, fifty years ago, truly said that Brutus was right to assassinate Caesar', and, 'Brutus was not right to assassinate Caesar', without inconsistency. Since the theory, that all 'Brutus was wrong to assassinate Caesar' means is that the person making the judgment felt approval of Brutus's assassination of Caesar at the time at which he made the judgment, implies that the two aforementioned propositions, 'Robinson truly judged that Brutus was right to assassinate Caesar' and 'Brutus was not right to assasinate Caesar' are consistent, even when it is Robinson himself who makes them, and since they are not consistent, the theory must be rejected.

2. THE INTER-TEMPORAL AND INTER-PERSONAL NEUTRALITY OF MORAL JUDGMENTS

Some of the peculiarities of the theory that what I mean when I say that an action is wrong is that it evokes in me personally a feeling of disapproval, arise from the fact that, in the sentence offered as a definition, there occurs the word 'I'. The word 'I' is one of a class of words, which class contains words like 'me', 'you', 'here', 'there', 'today', 'tomorrow', 'yesterday', 'next week', 'soon', and so on, which are such that the person or thing or time or place which they refer to depends upon the context in which they are used, that is, upon the identity of the person who uses them, the place at which he is situated when he uses them, and the time at which he uses them.[1] Hence, the sentences 'It is now raining' or 'Today is Tuesday' express different propositions or judgments when these sentences are used at different times or on different days. This is because the word 'now' refers to the time at which it is being used which is, of course, a different time when 'now' is being used on different occasions, and 'today' refers to the day on which it is being used and this, naturally enough, is a different day when 'today' is being used on different days. Similarly 'here' refers to the place where the speaker is, and so will refer to different places when the speaker is situated at different places, and 'there' will refer to a place where the speaker is not, and so may refer to a different place when the speaker is at different places. The word 'I' is just like these others in that it refers to the person using the word 'I', and so will refer to a different person when the word 'I' is being used by different people. When Tom says 'I', 'I' will refer to Tom, and when 'Dick' says 'I', 'I' will refer to Dick. (Hence pronouns are more sophisticated than proper names, for though 'Tom' always refers to Tom and 'Dick' always refers to Dick, 'I' will refer to Tom if it is Tom who uses it, but to Dick if it is Dick who uses it; hence children find it more difficult to learn to use pronouns than they do to learn how to use proper names, and so, for example, tend to refer even to themselves by their own name.)

Another feature of the sentence, given by the variety of subject-ivism we have been discussing as a definition of what we mean

[1] See Bertrand Russell, *An Inquiry into Meaning and Truth* (Allen & Unwin, 1967), Chapter VII.

when we say that something is wrong, is that it is in the present tense. Though it does not actually contain the word 'now', it would be possible to insert this word without altering the meaning of the sentence into which it was inserted. 'I feel approval of Brutus's assassination of Caesar', since it is in the present tense, means 'I *now* feel approval of Brutus's assassination of Caesar'.

It is these two features of the sentence, put forward by this variety of subjectivism as a definition of what we mean when we say that something is wrong, that give rise to the two difficulties that we have been discussing. The statement which is expressed by the sentence 'I feel disapproval of Brutus's assassination of Caesar' will depend upon who it is who uses this sentence. When this sentence is used by Jones it will express the statement 'I (Jones) feel disapproval of Brutus's assassination of Caesar'; when this sentence is used by Smith, it will express the statement 'I (Smith) feel disapproval of Brutus's assassination of Caesar'. Clearly, since these two statements are about the feelings of two totally different people, there can be no logical relationship between the truth of the one and the truth of the other; they may both be true, the first may be true and the second false, the first may be false and the second true, or they may both be false. Again, they are expressed in the present tense, and it would be possible to introduce the word 'now' without altering the meaning of these sentences. Hence the sentence 'I (now) feel disapproval of Brutus's assassination of Caesar' will express different statements when it is used at different times, just as it expresses different statements when used by different people. Hence at one time it is about the disapproval which the person using this sentence feels at *this* time, and at a later time it is about the disapproval he feels at *this later* time; there is no logical connection between the truth of a statement saying that a given person feels approval or disapproval at one time and the truth of a statement saying that the same person feels approval or disapproval at a different time. The first and the second statement may both be true; the first may be true and the second false, the first may be false and the second true, or they may both be false. If this account of what is meant when I say that an action is wrong is correct, there will be no logical connection between the judgments which are made when ethical sentences are used by different speakers, and no logical connection between the judgments which are made when ethical sentences are used by the same or by different speakers at different times. When Jones says 'Brutus was wrong to assassinate Caesar,' he is not contradicting Smith, or anybody else for that matter, who says 'Brutus was not wrong to assassinate Caesar'; and when Robinson says 'Brutus was wrong to assassinate Caesar' he is not saying anything which is incompatible with any proposition which he may have, at some other time, expressed when he said 'Brutus was not wrong to assassinate Caesar'.

However, when we come to look at how the words 'right' and 'wrong' (and other ethical words) are used, it is quite obvious that what would be a feature of ethical discourse, if the view that moral judgments were about the feelings of the speaker were correct, is not in fact a feature of ethical discourse at all. It is as obvious as anything can be that, if Jones says 'Brutus was wrong to assassinate Caesar' he *is* saying something which is the contradictory of what Smith is saying when he says 'Brutus was not wrong to assassinate Caesar.' And it is as obvious as anything can be that, when Robinson says 'Brutus was wrong to assassinate Caesar' he *is* saying something which is the contradictory of what he said in his youth when he said 'Brutus was right to assassinate Caesar.'

Hence it is a feature of moral judgments that they are *inter-personal* and *inter-temporal*. They are inter-personal in that, if one person says something like 'Brutus was wrong to assassinate Caesar', any other person saying 'Brutus was not wrong to assassinate Caesar' is saying something which is the contradictory of what he has said. In other words, it is not permissible for the second person to say to the first person 'What you say when you say that Brutus was wrong to assassinate Caesar is perfectly true; nevertheless Brutus was not wrong to assassinate Caesar.' (On the theory that moral judgments were about the speaker's feelings, this *would* be a perfectly permissible thing for him to say). Moral judgments are inter-temporal in that if someone at one time says 'Brutus was wrong to assassinate Caesar' then if he himself at a later time, or anyone else at a later time says 'Brutus was not wrong to assassinate Caesar', he is making a judgment which is incompatible with the earlier judgment. It is not permissible to say, 'When, a while ago, I said Brutus was wrong to assassinate Caesar, what I said was true, but, nevertheless, Brutus was not wrong to assassinate Caesar.' (If the theory that moral judgments were about the speaker's feelings were correct, this *would* be a perfectly permissible thing to say.) In other words, sentences like 'Brutus was wrong to assassinate Caesar' and 'All promises ought to be kept' each express the same judgment, whoever it is who uses them, and whenever he uses them (and also wherever he is when he uses them); the sentences 'Brutus was wrong to assassinate Caesar' and 'All promises ought to be kept' express propositions which are incompatible with the propositions expressed by the sentences 'Brutus was not wrong to assassinate Caesar' and 'Not all promises ought to be kept', regardless of who uses these sentences and the time at which he uses them (and where he is when he uses them).

However, it is not the case that *all* moral judgments are inter-personal and inter-temporal (or that they are all inter-spatial either). If I say, 'It would be wrong for me to tell him (as I do not know him well enough)', this is obviously not incompatible with someone else's statement, 'It would *not* be wrong for *me* to tell him (because I *do* know him well enough).' If I say in June, 'It would be wrong to sell them now (because prices are going up)', what I say is not incompatible with what I say in October when I say, 'It would not be wrong to sell them *now* (because prices are going down).' If I say, 'It would be wrong to leave one's house unlocked in this part of the world (because it is a very squalid district)', what I say is not incompatible with what someone who lives somewhere else says when he remarks, 'It would not be wrong to leave one's house unlocked in *this* part of the world (as it is a very secluded neighbourhood).' However, what a philosopher who maintains that, when I say that some action is wrong, all I am saying is that the thought of the action arouses disapproval in me personally, *is* committed to is the view that *all* moral judgments have some reference to some person or some time such that they are about only the person speaking and the time at which he is speaking.

Those who hold the theory are further committed to holding that, though it is possible for someone else to deny the moral judgment that I make when I say that some action is wrong, the judgment which he makes when he contradicts my moral judgment is not itself a moral judgment. He contradicts my moral judgment, 'Brutus was wrong to assassinate Caesar', by saying, 'You say you approve of Brutus's assassination of Caesar, but you do not,' but his judgment, 'You do not approve of Brutus's assassination of Caesar', is not a moral judgment; although it is about someone's feelings, namely, mine, it is not about the speaker's own feelings, and only judgments about the speaker's own feelings of approval or disapproval count, on the theory we are considering, as moral judgments. This, incidentally, points to another difficulty with this view, quite apart from the fact that it leads to the paradoxical conclusion that the contradictory of a moral judgment need not itself be a moral judgment. If Smith were to say, 'I approve of Brutus's assassination of Caesar', it would be perfectly appropriate, though possibly a little impolite, for me to say, 'You don't'; but if he were to say 'Brutus was right to assassinate Caesar' it would not be at all appropriate for me to say to him, 'You don't'; if I were to say this, he would think that I could not properly have heard what he said.

The view that what I mean when I say that something is wrong is that it arouses in me a feeling of disapproval is also open to another, quite fatal, objection. If the theory is correct, the only thing necessary to make a moral judgment of mine true is that the action in question really should arouse in me this feeling of disapproval. So long as it does this, the action really is wrong, and if it does not do this the action is not wrong. Nothing else whatsoever is relevant to the truth of my moral judgment. However, the fact that I disapprove of the action rather than approve of it will have an explanation, which explanation will take into account partly the sort of person I am and partly the sort of upbringing I have been subjected to, but the explanation of how it comes about that I feel disapproval rather than approval will not alter the fact that I do disapprove, and so will have nothing to do with the truth of my moral judgment. So long as it really is the case that I disapprove of an action, then my judgment that it is a wrong action is true, regardless of how it comes about that I feel this disapproval of it. It may be that I disapprove of the action because I have indigestion or toothache, and would not disapprove of it if I did not have indigestion or toothache. It may be that I disapprove of it because I was brought up as a communist or a Catholic, and would not disapprove of it if I had not been brought up as a communist or a Catholic, but this, though others would normally regard it as a reason for suspecting – though it does not conclusively prove – that my moral judgment was biassed, irrational and unfounded, and that I myself was prejudiced, has nothing whatsoever to do with the truth of my moral judgment, if the theory we are considering is correct.

So long as I correctly believe that I disapprove of an action, this action is wrong, and the explanation of how it comes about that I disapprove of it is entirely irrelevant. The distinction between a rational and an irrational judgment is simply the distinction between a rational belief about one's own feelings of approval and an irrational belief about these feelings. If I believe that I disapprove of something because I very much want to be the sort of person who disapproves of things like that, then my belief that I disapprove, and so my equivalent belief that the things of which I disapprove are wrong, *is* irrational.

Among the most important reasons why I believe that something is right or that it is wrong is that I believe certain things about it, and approve or disapprove of it in consequence. The beliefs I have about the thing I approve of or disapprove of cannot be a sufficient condition of my feeling approval or disapproval of that thing. I might have had the same beliefs about it, and not disapproved of it, if I had been brought up differently, or if my nervous system had been in a different state, or if my digestion had been better, or if my glands had been functioning differently. Nevertheless, given that my upbringing and character and the state of my nervous system and brain is what it is, there are certain factual beliefs which will cause me to approve of a thing, and certain other factual beliefs which will cause me to disapprove of it. Given that my nervous system, my upbringing and my character are standing conditions of my approving of what I do, my beliefs about the actions approved of will be differential conditions. Now on the theory that the moral judgments I make are about my own feelings of approval or disapproval, the question whether the factual beliefs I have about the action I approve or disapprove of are true or false will be entirely irrelevant to the question whether or not I am right in saying that the action I approve of is right, or am right in saying that the action I disapprove of is wrong. Let us suppose that I approve of capital punishment because I believe that, when there is no death penalty for murder, the number of murders is vastly greater than when there is a death penalty for murder. We would normally suppose that, if this is why I believe that it is right to have the death penalty for murder, my belief that it is right is totally unfounded, for the statements I give as my reasons for thinking that it is right are false statements; it may, we think, turn out that my belief that it is right to have the death penalty for murder is correct for some reason other than the one I have actually given, but nevertheless the reasons I give do not justify my belief, though it may so happen that it is true. However, if the view that moral judgments are about the feelings of the person making the judgment is correct, my judgment that it is right to have the death penalty for murder is true so long as, as a matter of fact, the thought of having the death penalty for murder really does arouse in me the feelings I say it does. If the thought of having a death penalty for murder really does arouse in me a feeling of approval, then, when I say that it would be right to have the death penalty for murder, I am making a true statement, regardless of whether the factual beliefs about the death penalty which *cause* me to have this feeling of approval are correct or incorrect. Obviously, however, we would in fact say that my belief that it was right to have the death penalty was unfounded if the beliefs which caused me to feel approval of it were false. Hence the theory that, when we make moral judgments, we are making judgments only about our own feelings and about nothing else whatsoever, must be rejected.

It is, indeed, if the theory that moral judgments are about the speaker's feelings is correct, rather odd to talk at all about having reasons for the moral judgments we make. We may well have reasons for thinking that someone else disapproves of cruelty – he may tell us that he does, refrain from being cruel himself, and behave in an antagonistic way to other people when they behave cruelly – but what reasons can we have for thinking that we ourselves feel disapproval of cruelty? Though our belief that other people disapprove of cruelty is a belief which we need to infer, our belief that we ourselves disapprove of cruelty would seem to me to be a basic proposition; we do not infer it, and do not need to infer it, from other propositions, but know it to be true, without making an inference, because we are immediately aware of or are acquainted with this feeling of disapproval for cruelty itself. We are not aware of other people's feelings of disapproval, and so we do need to infer what they are, but, since we are aware of our own feelings, we do not need to infer what they are; it would indeed, be very odd to suggest that I know I disapprove of something because I infer that I do so from what I hear myself say about it and because I observe myself behaving in a disapproving way towards the thing in question and because, when I look into a glass, I see a disapproving look on my face. Perhaps in *some* cases this is how I know that I disapprove of something. I may be very reluctant to admit that I disapprove of my parents, which provides me with a strong motive for failing to notice that they arouse feelings of disapproval in me, and, perhaps I only come to believe that I disapprove of my parents when it is pointed out to me that I do behave in a disapproving way towards them, but such cases are in a minority; usually I have no difficulty in discovering by introspection that I feel approval of certain things and disapproval of other things.

Indeed, it is a difficulty for the view that moral judgments are about the speaker's feelings that it is easier to find out what things I approve of and disapprove of than it is to find out what is right and what is wrong. If the theory is correct, all I need to do to find out what actions are right and what actions are wrong is to introspect carefully, whereas one would normally think that, in order to come to a decision on a difficult question of right and wrong it would, at the very least, be necessary to collect a great deal of factual information about the nature of the action and the consequences of performing it. Of course, it is a psychological fact about people that, very often, when they know they have very little factual information, they neither approve of the thing about which they are so ignorant, nor disapprove of it either. In a case such as this, their acquiring more factual information may *cause* them to feel approval of it or disapproval of it, as the case may be. On the theory we are considering, however, this recently acquired factual information is not related to their recently acquired belief that the action is wrong, as reasons for thinking an action wrong are related to the belief that the action really is wrong. If beliefs about the rightness or wrongness of the action are just beliefs about my own feelings, the factual information I acquire about the action cannot be reasons for thinking that the action is right at all, for one thing because beliefs about the action itself are not by themselves reasons for thinking that I react to it favourably rather than unfavourably; for another thing, because acquiring these beliefs cannot provide me with a reason for thinking that I feel either approval or disapproval, for, until I acquired these beliefs, I neither felt approval nor disapproval. Though, on the theory that moral judgments are about the feelings of the person making the judgment, my factual beliefs about the action are related to my feelings of approval or disapproval as (part) cause to effect, they are not related to my beliefs about these feelings, that is, to my belief that the action is right or that it is wrong, as grounds for a belief are to the belief for which I have grounds. This is another oddity about the theory we are considering, for there is no doubt that we normally do regard our factual beliefs about the action as our *grounds* for thinking that it is right or as our *grounds* for thinking that it is wrong.

The next question to be considered is about the sense in which the view that when we say that an action is wrong we are making a statement to the effect that thinking of this action arouses in us a feeling of disapproval can properly be described as 'subjective'. First of all, let me point out that there are some ways in which this theory is certainly not subjective. Sometimes to say that a belief is subjective is to say that it is very difficult to form an opinion, on its truth, which is not highly influenced by the emotions and prejudices of the believer. There is no particular reason why the theory itself, which is, of course, a belief *about* moral judgments, should be subjective in this sense. Nor is there any particular reason why the theory, although not subjective in this sense itself, should have to hold that our *moral judgments* are subjective in this sense; there is no reason why it should hold that moral judgments, besides being *about* our feelings, are particularly prone to be *biased by* our feelings. There is no reason why it should not hold that, in the majority of cases, at any rate, we can form a perfectly objective, unbiassed and impartial opinion on whether we approve of a certain kind of action or not.

There is also another sense in which the theory itself is not subjective. (By saying it is not subjective, of course, I mean not that the belief itself which constitutes the theory, which is a belief about moral judgments, is not subjective – though it is *not* subjective – but that this theory does not hold that *moral judgments* themselves are subjective in this sense.) The theory does not hold that what is right and wrong depends in any way upon our *beliefs* about what is right and wrong; it does not hold that thinking that something is right or that it is wrong makes it so. What the rightness or wrongness of an action does depend on, if the theory is true, is our *feelings*, but moral judgments, which are beliefs about our feelings, are not made true by our holding the moral judgments themselves; they are made true or false by our having or not having the feeling which the moral judgment in question says we have. There is no reason why we should not have a feeling of approval without believing that we have it, and no reason why we should not believe that we have a feeling of approval although we do not in fact have it. Hence the theory does not hold that anything's being right or wrong depends upon our believing it is right or wrong. On the contrary, it implies that a thing which is right is right whether we believe it to be so or not.

Nevertheless, the theory is a subjectivist theory, in that it holds that there are certain ways in which moral judgments are subjective. If you say that an attribute of something is an 'objective' attribute when it is an attribute which it would have whether there were any human minds to be aware of it or not or to have beliefs about it or not, it would appear that the theory must hold that being right and being wrong are not objective attributes of actions; for if to say that an action is right or wrong is to say how an observer would react to that action, then it would appear that were there no observers, there would be no reactions, and so, in the absence of observers, actions themselves would be neither right nor wrong.

The most characteristic feature of the view that what we mean when we say that an action is wrong is that it evokes in us a feeling of disapproval, however, is one of which the word 'subjectivism' is not a wholly accurate description. As we have seen, if this theory is true, the moral judgments of each person will be about his own feelings; Smith's moral judgments will be about Smith's feelings, and Jones's moral judgments will be about Jones's feelings. This in fact gave rise to the difficulty that, since Smith's moral judgment that something is wrong simply states that Smith disapproves of it, and Jones's apparently incompatible moral judgment that the same thing is right simply means that Jones approves of it, no two moral judgments of two different people can ever contradict one another – nor, for that matter, can they stand in any other logical relationship to one another. The theory also implies that since Smith's moral judgments are about the feelings Smith has at the time he makes the judgment, no moral judgment made by Smith at one time can be incompatible, or indeed stand in any other logical relationship, to any other moral judgment made by Smith at a later time. At one time Smith can say that something is right, and at a later time say that the same thing is wrong, and what he says at these two different times are in no way incompatible with one another. These two features of the theory might be described by saying that it implies that moral judgments are (a) self-referential and (b) present-referential, that is, each moral judgment is about the feelings of the speaker, and about the feelings he has, and has at the time the judgment is made. It is, of course, these two features of the theory which, together with the fact that, if it is true, it does not matter what causes us to feel approval or disapproval of an action, nor whether the beliefs about the action, on account of which we either approve of it or disapprove of it, are true beliefs or false ones, which make this theory one which it is totally impossible to accept.

3. THE VIEW THAT MORAL JUDGMENTS ARE ABOUT THE FEELINGS OF A GROUP OF PEOPLE

The view, that when we make a moral judgment, we are talking about the feelings which the action or person or state of affairs about which we are making the judgment arouses in ourselves personally, is, of course, not the only type of theory according to which moral judgments are judgments about the way people react to the things being judged of, or according to which moral judgments describe the feelings which contemplating the things, about which these judgments are made, arouse in people. It is possible to hold that moral judgments are about the feelings of some person other than the speaker, in which event it may be held either that moral judgments are about some one identified person, or that they are about the feelings of some unspecified person or other. Neither of these theories is remotely plausible, and I shall not waste much time on them. It is impossible to hold that all moral judgments are about the feelings of one identified person, for who could such a person be? If we decide that he must be an Englishman, then who is the Englishman whose feelings are regarded as of such paramount importance that whether he approves of something or not determines whether the thing he approves of is right or wrong, and why should Indians and Chinese be supposed to be talking about *his* feelings, when they ascribe moral characteristics to actions? On the other hand, if when we say that some action or class of actions is wrong, we are simply supposed to be saying that someone or other, whose identity is not specified, disapproves of the action or class of actions in question, an insuperable difficulty immediately arises. There must be many things which arouse approval in some people, but disapproval in others. Hence, if when I say that this thing is right, I mean that it arouses approval in someone, and when I say that it is wrong, I mean that it arouses disapproval in someone, both these judgments will be true. Hence this theory does lead to the conclusion that one and the same person can both truly say that an action is right and at the same time truly say that the same action is wrong. This conclusion is so obviously a travesty of how we actually use the words 'right' and 'wrong' that the theory must be rejected out of hand. (One special version of the view that, when we make moral judgments, we are talking about some specified person's reactions to the things judged of, is the view that moral judgments are about what God approves of, wills, commands or prohibits. This theory has had considerable importance in the history of moral philosophy, and will be considered in more detail in a later chapter.)[1]

A more plausible view, according to which moral judgments about actions or people or states of affairs are judgments about the way people react to these actions or people or states of affairs is the view that moral judgments are judgments not about the reactions of the speaker, but about the reactions of some group of people. Again, the theory must hold either that all people's moral judgments are about the reactions of the same group of people, or that they are about the reactions of different groups. The former seems most implausible. Other nationalities use moral language besides Englishmen, and, though it may be impossible to translate what Englishmen mean by 'wrong' quite accurately into, say, Tibetan, and though other people may have words, which are properly described as ethical words, which it is impossible to translate quite accurately into English, to the extent that translations can be found for what English people mean by 'right' and 'wrong', to that extent they must mean the same thing by these words as we do. This gives rise to a dilemma. If we suppose that Englishmen, when they say that something is wrong, mean that Englishmen disapprove of it, we must also suppose that Tibetans, if they have an equivalent for our word 'wrong', must also mean that Englishmen disapprove of it, which is absurd.

[1] Chapter IX.

On the other hand, if we suppose that Tibetans, when they say that something is wrong, mean that Tibetans disapprove of it, we must suppose that this is what Englishmen mean by 'wrong', which is equally absurd. Nor does it seem at all plausible to suggest that there is some neutral group of actual people, whom Tibetans and Englishmen use as referees, about whom both Englishmen and Tibetans may be supposed to be talking when they make moral judgments.

Hence the only plausible thing to suggest is that Englishmen, when they say that something is wrong, are talking about the reactions of Englishmen, and that Tibetans are talking about the reactions of Tibetans. To obviate the difficulty, that in this case Tibetans and Englishmen will not mean the same thing when they use the word 'wrong', it will have to be held that both Tibetans and Englishmen are talking of the reactions about the group of people of which they are a member. Englishmen and Tibetans will in this case mean the same thing by 'wrong', for when they say 'That is wrong' both Englishmen and Tibetans will mean 'My community disapproves of that'. But, of course, though they mean the same thing when they use moral words, for each will be talking about the reactions of the community of which he is a member, they will be talking *about* the reactions of a different community, for the community of which an Englishman is a member is not the same community as that of which a Tibetan is a member.

The view, that what I mean when I say that something is wrong is that the community of which I am a member disapproves of it, shares some, though not all, of the logical characteristics of the theory that what I mean is that I, personally, disapprove of that thing. (Hence it will not be necessary to discuss it in great detail.) It will not be the case, as it is the case on the view that moral judgments are about the judger's own reactions, that no two moral judgments made by different people can ever be incompatible with one another – or ever be equivalent to one another. If Tom and Dick are both Englishmen, then Tom's judgment that the community to which he belongs approves of hanging will be incompatible with Dick's judgment that the community to which he belongs disapproves of hanging, for in this case Tom and Dick both belong to the same group, and so are talking about the feelings of the same group. But if Tom is an Englishman and Kai Lung a Chinaman, then Tom's judgment that hanging people is wrong will not be incompatible with Kai Lung judgment that hanging people is not wrong, for Tom will mean that the community in which he lives disapproves of hanging people, and Kai Lung will mean that the community in which *he* lives does not disapprove of hanging people, and, since Tom and Kai Lung are talking about the reactions of different communities, there is no reason why what each of them says should not be true.

Again, though on the view that what I mean when I say that something is wrong is that it arouses disapproval in me, I discover which actions are right and which actions are wrong by, in Hume's words, 'looking within my own breast', and finding there a feeling either of approval of disapproval, moral judgments, on the view that they are about the reactions, to the action judged, of the community to which the person making the judgment belongs, will be discovered to be true in a totally different way. It is no use Tom's *introspecting* to find out what his community approves of; it may be the case that what arouses approval in him also arouses approval in other members of the same community, but, on the other hand, it may not be. In order to find out what arouses the feeling of approval in other members of his community, Tom has to do something like what he would have to do if he wanted to know which way members of his community were going to vote, or whether or not they preferred tea to coffee. Presumably he will have to go about asking them what they approve of, whether or not, for example, they approve of hanging or abortion or homosexuality, or go about noting whether most of them behave in the way characteristic of approving of these things or in the way characteristic of disapproving of these things. Since it is unlikely that he will be able to ask or observe every individual member of the community to which he belongs, he will presumably have to take a sample, which he believes will fairly represent the attitudes of his community, and assume that the same preponderance of approval over disapproval, or *vice versa*, which he finds in the sample, is also to be found in the community, which he belongs to, as a whole. Obviously this method is empirical and, to the extent that the methods of survey employed in the social sciences can be described by the word, scientific.

The difficulty, presented by this account of our manner of finding out what actions are right and what actions are wrong implied by the theory, I shall discuss later in the chapter. In the meantime it is necessary to point out that, though the theory, that moral judgments are judgments about the reactions of the community to which the speaker belongs to the actions judged of, implies that the moral judgments of Frenchmen cannot be incompatible with the apparently inconsistent moral judgments of Englishmen – that it implies that a Frenchman saying fornication is not wrong is not saying anything incompatible with what an Englishman who says that fornification is wrong is saying – it seems clear that the moral judgments of Frenchmen do sometimes contradict the moral judgments of Englishmen; that when the moral judgments of a Frenchman and the moral judgments of an Englishman *seem* incompatible, this is almost always because they in fact *are* incompatible. It is important to remember that the moral judgments, the incompatiblity or otherwise of which I am considering, are the moral judgments 'Fornication is wrong' (made by an Englishman) and 'Fornication is not wrong' (made by a Frenchman). Of course, if all the Frenchman says is 'Fornication is not wrong in France', and all the Englishman says is 'Fornication is wrong in England', then their judgments are not incompatible, either in appearance or in fact, for there is no reason why something that is wrong in England should also be not wrong in France, if circumstances are appropriately different in the two countries.

We saw, when discussing the view that moral judgments are judgments about the reactions of the person making the judgment to the thing judged, that, if this view were correct, the moral judgment a man made at one time would not be really incompatible with the apparently contradictory moral judgment he made at a later time. Since his moral judgments are, on the theory, judgments about the reaction he has now, and since there is no reason why someone should not have different reactions to the same thing at different times, there is no reason why his judgment, made at one time, that something is wrong, should not be true, and also his judgment, made at a later time, that this very thing is right, should not also be true. The theory that moral judgments are about the reactions, to the thing judged, of the community to which the person making the judgment belongs, leads to the same implausible conclusion. Since the feelings about an action which my community has at one time may be quite different from the feelings it has about the same action at a different time, there is no reason why my moral judgment that something is wrong – which means that my community feels disapproval of it – made at one time, should not be true, and why my judgment, made at a different time, that the same action is right, should not also be true. However, it seems clear that, in actual fact, when we say that something is right, we are logically committed to saying that when, on a former occasion, we said that it was wrong, we were mistaken. It is not logically possible to say that something is right, and also to say that we were right when, formerly, we said it was wrong. This fact, that the view that moral judgments are about the reactions, to the thing judged, of the speaker's community leads to this unacceptable conclusion, is a sufficient reason for rejecting it.

The theory that moral judgments are about the reactions of the speaker's community also leads to another of the unacceptable conclusions, to which the view that they are about the speaker's own reactions also leads. We saw that the view that moral judgments are judgments about the way the speaker reacts to the thing judged leads to the conclusion that it does not matter what causes the speaker to react in the way he does, nor whether the beliefs on account of which he approves or disapproves the action judged of are true or false; so long as he actually has the reaction he asserts himself to have when he makes the judgment, his judgment is true, no matter how bizarre are the causes of his having the reaction, nor how wide of the mark are his factual beliefs about the action he is reacting to. The view that moral judgments are judgments about the reaction, to the action judged, of the speaker's community has precisely the same difficulty. If this theory is true, it will not matter in the least *why* the speaker's community approves of a thing rather than disapproves of it and it will not matter in the least that they might have a totally different attitude to the action if their false beliefs about it are replaced by true ones. So long as my community really does react to the action by disapproving of it, then my judgment that it is wrong is true, and nothing else whatsoever is relevant to the truth of my moral judgment except the mere fact that my community actually does have the reactions this moral judgment alleges that they have. This consequence alone would be sufficient to justify us in rejecting the theory, for it is quite obvious that we do in fact regard our moral judgments as being quite unfounded when we discover that the factual beliefs which gave rise to them are totally erroneous.

Though one difficulty to which the view that moral judgments are about the speaker's reactions gave rise, that no moral judgment one person makes can ever be incompatible with any other moral judgment another person makes, was slightly mitigated by the view that moral judgments are about the reactions of the community to which the speaker belongs – for sometimes, different speakers' moral judgments are capable of being incompatible, on this latter theory, for they are capable of being incompatible when the persons making the judgments belong to the same group, and so are talking about the reactions of the same group – there are other difficulties for the latter theory to which the view that moral judgments are about the speaker's own reactions does not give rise. One difficulty is that, if moral judgments are about the reactions of the community to which the person making the judgment belongs, it is difficult to see how a person can ever think that some action, of a kind which the community to which the speaker belongs approves of, can ever be wrong; yet it seems just a matter of fact that it is sometimes the case that people do think that an action of which a majority of their community approve can be wrong.[1] Wilberforce, for example, in thinking that child labour was wrong, did not appear to be thinking that the majority of his community disapproved of child labour, for he must have known perfectly well that they did not disapprove of it. Suffragettes, when they thought it was wrong that women should not have the vote, could not have been thinking that the majority of the community to which they belonged disapproved of women not having the vote for, again, they must have known perfectly well that the majority of their community did not disapprove of women not having the vote.

The statement of this difficulty, however, needs careful handling, and people who have levelled it against the view that moral judgments are about the feelings of the speaker's community have not always handled it carefully. It would, even if this theory were true, be perfectly possible for someone to think something right, and at the same time to think that the majority of his community thinks that this thing is wrong. What this amounts to, on the theory, is that it is perfectly possible for someone to think that the majority of his community thinks that most of the community feel disapproval of the thing in question, while he himself thinks that the majority of his community feels approval of the

[1] See G. E. Moore, *Ethics* (O.U.P., 1966), pp. 111 f.

thing in question. This is possible, because it is possible for one person to be the only person who gauges correctly what are the feelings, towards the action, of the majority of his community. What is not possible, on the theory, is not for a man both to think that something is right and at the same time to think that the majority of members of his community think that it is *wrong*, but for a man to think that an action is right and also to think that the majority of members of his community feel *disapproval of* this action. That the former is possible while the latter is not arises from the fact that the theory defines what is wrong not as that which most people in the speaker's community think is wrong, but as that which most members of the speaker's community feel disapproval of. It is perfectly possible, on this theory, for most people in a community to feel disapproval of a thing themselves, and at the same time to think that most members of the community feel approval of it, or *vice versa*.

The difficulty we are considering, however, still remains; it is obviously possible for a person of strong and independent moral convictions to think that something is wrong and at the same time to think that the majority of members of his community feel approval of that thing. Of course, if all he meant when he said that it was wrong was that the majority of members of his community felt disapproval of it, it would be quite impossible for his belief that something was wrong and his belief that this thing aroused approval in the majority of members of his community to coexist.

The account, implied by the theory, of the way in which we *find out* what actions are right and what actions are wrong, is also not a very plausible one.[1] The theory implies that, when I am in doubt about whether an action is right or wrong, what I do to resolve my doubt is to make an enquiry concerning the way in which other people in my community feel about the action; when this enquiry is completed, and I know how other members of my community feel, then this settles the matter. It is surely obvious, however, that quite often I am capable of resolving my doubt without bothering to find out how other members of my community react to the action, and that, when I do bother to find this out, I regard the information I have gained

[1] See C. D. Broad, *Five Types of Ethical Theory* (Routledge, 1930), pp. 114–5.

not simply as settling the matter beyond all further argument, but simply as a pointer to what the correct solution is. If the majority of members of my community disapprove of taking drugs, for example, this is some reason for thinking that taking drugs really is wrong, but it is not a conclusive reason for thinking that, and I may set aside the attitudes of others if it seems to me that I have strong enough reason for doing so.

The view that, when I say that some action is wrong, I am saying that this action arouses in me *personally* a feeling of disapproval does not give rise to the difficulty that, if it is correct, I cannot believe that an action is wrong and at the same time believe that the majority of members of my community feel approval of it. I can, on *this* theory, perfectly well believe that the thought of the action arouses disapproval in me, but at the same time believe that the thought of it arouses approval in the majority of my community. It is, however, a difficulty with the theory, that it *is* possible to know that the thought of an action arouses disapproval even in oneself, and at the same time to think that the action which arouses this feeling of disapproval is not wrong, which is something which would be impossible, if the theory were true. If I have been brought up by puritanical parents to regard drinking as wrong, it is quite possible that I may continue, in spite of myself, to feel disapproval of drinking long after experience of the world has caused me to revise the opinion which was once inculcated in me. If the theory that thinking that an action is wrong consists simply in thinking that the thought of this action arouses disapproval in me were correct, it would not be possible both to think that something, drinking, for example, was not wrong and to think or know that the thought of this action aroused disapproval in me. The fact that this is possible, therefore, constitutes another reason for rejecting the theory.

Does the view that what I mean when I say that an action is wrong is that contemplating this action arouses disapproval in *me* imply a more plausible account of the way in which we find out what actions are right and what actions are wrong than does the theory that what I mean when I say that an action is wrong is that contemplating this action arouses feelings of disapproval in the majority of the members of the *community to which I belong*? If the former theory is true, then I discover what is right and wrong by a process of self-examination, for it is by introspection that

I come to know that I approve of one thing and disapprove of another. It is surely wrong, however, to think that I can find out what actions are right and what actions are wrong simply by a process of self-examination. If this were the way in which I found out these things, then it would not be necessary to gain further information about the nature and consequences of the actions about whose rectitude I am in doubt of, for one can find out what one in fact at the moment approves of or disapproves of without doing this. Since it is necessary to acquire information concerning the action, the rectitude of which one is pondering about, the account of the manner in which we resolve our moral perplexities which is implied by the theory that moral judgments are simply judgments about our own feelings, must be rejected.

It seems quite reasonable to describe the theory that moral judgments are about the reactions to the actions judged of by the majority of members of the community to which the speaker belongs as a 'subjective' ethical theory, but, if so, it must be noticed that it is subjective in a rather different way and to a lesser degree than the theory that moral judgments are judgments about the speaker's feelings. First of all, there are two ways in which the theory is *not* subjective, that is to say, two ways in which *moral judgments*, if the theory is true, will not be subjective. There is no particular reason why people should not arrive at 'objective', impartial assessments of the nature of the reaction of the community, to which they belong, to an action or class of actions. Nor, on this theory, will it be the case that what makes an action right is its being *thought* to be right, for this would mean that what makes the community to which I belong feel approval is the fact that I believe that they feel approval of that thing, and, of course, there is no reason why my community should not feel approval of something, although I do not believe they do, nor why I should not believe that my community approve of something, although in fact they do not.

The view that moral judgments are about the speaker's feelings is subjective in the sense that the rightness or wrongness of actions depends upon something about the speaker, that is, upon whether or not these actions arouses approval in him personally. The view that moral judgments are about the feelings of the speaker's community is not subjective in this sense; whether an action is right or wrong will not depend upon anything at all about the person making the judgment that this action is right or the judgment that this action is wrong. What it will depend upon, of course, is the feeling which other members of his community have about the action, but this is something which will remain entirely unaffected by anything which he himself thinks or feels, and entirely unaffected even by whether he exists or not. However, though the truth of the judgment a person makes when he says that something is right or that it is wrong is wholly unaffected by anything about *him*, it still remains the case that, if moral judgments describe the reactions of the community to which the person making the judgment belongs, action will not be either right or wrong in the absence of any observers at all; in this case, however, the observers, whose existence is a necessary condition of actions possessing moral predicates, is not the observer making the moral judgment himself, but other members of his community.

The most characteristic feature of the view that moral judgments are about the *speaker's* reactions to the actions judged of is that moral judgments are alleged to contain a covert reference to the speaker and the time at which the speaker is making his moral judgment. This covert reference is made explicit in the sentence which the theory offers as a translation of sentences expressing moral judgments, for example. 'This action arouses in *me* a feeling of approval *now*'. The same covert reference to the speaker occurs in the sentence given as a translation of moral sentences by the theory that moral judgments are about the feelings of the community to which the person making the judgment belongs. The logical characteristics of the word 'my' as it occurs in '*my* community' are the same as the logical characteristics of the word 'me' as it occurs in the phrase 'arouses approval in *me*', that is to say, it refers to a different person when it is used by different people, because it always refers to the person who is using it. The difference between the two theories arises because one person's community may be numerically identical with another person's community; though two people may belong to the same community, one person's feeling of approval can never be numerically identical with another person's feeling of approval. It is because of this that sometimes the moral judgments of different people may, on the view that moral judgments are about the feelings of the speaker's community, be incompatible with one another, while at other times they may not be. They may be incompatible with one another when it so happens that the two people belong to the same community, but it is impossible for them to be incompatible with one another when these people belong to different communities. However since one person's feelings can never be numerically identical with another person's feelings, it would *never* be possible for two people's moral judgments to be incompatible with one another if moral judgments were about the feelings of the person making the judgment. On the version of subjectivism according to which moral judgments are about the feelings of the community to which the person making the judgment belongs, moral judgments will also contain a covert reference to the *time* at which the judgment is made; they will be about the feelings of the community to which the person who makes the judgment belongs at the moment the judgment is made. Hence, though it is not the case that, if it is true, the moral judgments made by different people can *never* be incompatible with one another, it is the case that if I say at one time that something is right, and at a later time that the same thing is wrong, my first judgment is *never* incompatible with my second. I can, if the theory is true, always judge that something is wrong without ever being logically committed to saying that I was mistaken when, on a previous occasion, I said it was right. This, together with the fact that the apparently contradictory judgments of people belonging to different communities are not, on this theory, in fact incompatible with one another – surely I cannot agree with anyone at all, when he says it is right to torture political prisoners, and at the same time think that it is *wrong* to torture political prisoners – and the fact that it does not matter on the theory how erroneous are the beliefs on account of which my community feels approval or disapproval of the things about which I am making my moral judgment, are more than sufficient to cause us to reject it.

4. THE VIEW THAT MORAL JUDGMENTS ARE JUDGMENTS ABOUT THE FEELINGS OF MEN AS SUCH

The third variety of subjectivist theory I shall consider is the view that, when I make moral judgments, I am talking not about my own attitude to the action judged of, nor about the attitude to it of the community to which I belong, but the attitude to it of the whole of mankind.[1] On this view, to say that an action is wrong is to say not that I disapprove of it, nor that my community disapproves of it, but that all or most men disapprove of it.

There is no need to spend much time on this theory after the detailed treatment that the former two varieties of subjectivism have already received. Clearly there is one difficulty for the two former theories which is not a difficulty for the view we are now considering; if one man says that something is wrong and another man say the same thing is right, their moral judgments will always be incompatible with one another, no matter who these two men may be, for according to this theory what one man is saying is that the action arouses disapproval in the majority of men, and what the other man is saying is that it does not arouse disapproval in the majority of men, and these two judgments cannot both be true. This theory, however, will have the same difficulty as the other two about moral judgments made at different *times*. There is no reason why it should not be true at one time that something arouses approval in the majority of men, and at a later time true that it does not arouse approval in the majority of men; hence it will be perfectly possible, if we accept this theory, for one now to judge an action is wrong without having to withdraw one's former judgment that it was right. Again, so long as the majority of mankind actually do disapprove of something it will not matter whether they have true or false beliefs about the action they disapprove of; our judgment that the action they disapprove of is wrong will be true in either event, for *all* it means is that they disapprove of it, which they do. This theory will be subjectivist in that the rightness or wrongness of actions will depend upon the emotions these actions arouse in people, but *not* subjectivist in the sense that whether or not actions are right or wrong depends on anything about the person actually making the judgment that it is right or the judgment that it is wrong. There is, again, no reason why the theory should hold that the fact that an action is right or wrong depends in any way upon my *belief* that it is right or wrong; obviously my belief that most people approve of something will have no tendency to *make* them approve of that thing. The theory will not hold that moral judgments are self-referential, for there is no reference

---

[1] This view has been attributed by Professor Broad to Hume, and Hume certainly does sometimes speak as if he held it. See C. D. Broad, *op. cit.*, Chapter IV.

made to the speaker in the sentence 'The majority of men disapprove of incest'. The theory does, however, imply that there is a covert reference to the *time* at which the judgment is made, for it holds that moral judgments are about the attitude which most men have to the action judged of at the time of the judgment, that is, it holds that 'Incest is wrong' means 'All or most men *now* disapprove of incest'. It is because of this that the theory must hold that my present belief that something is wrong is quite consistent with an earlier judgment that the same thing is right, for it may be both true that something arouses disapproval in all or most men now, and also true that it aroused approval in all or most men a while ago. It is obviously impossible, however, for what I say now when I say that something is wrong to be true and for what I said earlier when I said that that thing was right to be also true. The theory must be rejected because it leads to this impossible conclusion, and also because it regards the question whether the beliefs which cause all or most men to feel approval or disapproval of the action in question as irrelevant to the truth of our judgment that the action is right or wrong. It must furthermore be rejected because, if it is true, it becomes logically impossible to believe both that most men feel approval of an action, and that that action is wrong, and logically impossible to believe both that most men disapprove of an action and that this action is right. Both these things are obviously perfectly possible in fact.

5. THE VIEW THAT MORAL JUDGMENTS ARE ABOUT WHAT PEOPLE THINK

All the three subjectivist theories which we have recently been considering have one thing in common; they all hold that what we mean when we say that an action is wrong is that it arouses disapproval in some person or group of persons, either in the person making the judgment himself, or in the community to which he belongs, or in all or most men. It would be possible, however, to hold that what we mean when we say that an action is wrong is not that we or that members of our community, or that most men have a certain *feeling* about this action, namely, a feeling of disapproval of it, but that they have a certain *thought* about the action, namely, the thought that the action is wrong. Hence, corresponding to the three theories we have already considered, there will be, firstly, the theory that what I mean when I say that an action is wrong is that I personally think that it is wrong; secondly, the theory that what I mean when I say that an action is wrong is that most members of the community to which I belong think that is it wrong; and, thirdly, the theory that what I mean when I say that an action is wrong is that all or most men think that it is wrong.[1]

All these three theories are open to the very same objections as the corresponding theories, which hold that moral judgments are judgments about how people feel about the actions judged of. The theory, that what I mean when I say that something is wrong is that I personally think that it is wrong, for example, will be open to all the objections to which the theory that what I mean when I say that an action is wrong is that I personally feel disapproval of it is open. For example, if all Smith means when he says that something is wrong is that he thinks it is wrong, and all Jones means when he says that it is right is that he thinks that it is right, there is no reason why Smith's moral judgment and Jones moral judgment should not both be true, for there is no reason why it should not both be true that Smith thinks that something is right and that Jones thinks that the same thing is wrong. Again, since Robinson may think at one time that Brutus's assassination of Caesar is right and at another time think that Brutus's assassination of Caesar is wrong, there is no reason why the judgment he makes when he says that it is right should not be true – for all it means, according to this theory, is that he thinks that it is right, which he does – and why his later judgment that it is wrong should not also be true – for all he means, according to this theory, is that he thinks that it is wrong, which he also does. Hence, if this theory is right, there is no reason why I should not both say that Brutus was wrong to assassinate Caesar, and also say that when, earlier, I said that Brutus was right to assassinate Caesar, I was making a true judgment. Obviously, however, it is not possible for me to say that Brutus was wrong to assassinate Caesar without committing myself to saying that when formerly I said Brutus was right to assassinate Caesar I was mistaken. Lastly, according to the theory that what I mean when I say that an action is wrong is simply that I personally think that it is wrong, it will not matter what are my reasons for thinking it is wrong, nor whether the beliefs I hold about the actions, which beliefs are my reasons for thinking

[1] See G. E. Moore, op. cit., pp. 119 f.

that the action is wrong, are true or false; so long as I really do think that the action is wrong, the action is wrong, regardless of why I think that it is wrong, for all I mean when I say that it is wrong is that I think that it is wrong, which I do. And all the other objections we have been considering to the three views, that to say that an action is wrong means that it arouses feelings of disapproval in the speaker, that to say that an action is wrong means that it arouses feelings of disapproval in members of the speaker's community, and to say that it arouses feelings of disapproval in all or most men, apply, with the appropriate modifications, to the three corresponding views, that what I mean when I say that an action is wrong is that I personally think that it is wrong, that what I mean when I say that an action is wrong is that most members of my community think that it is wrong, and that what I mean when I say that an action is wrong is that all or most men think that it is wrong.

These three latter theories, however, are less plausible than the three former theories, for not only are they open to all the objections to which the first three are open; they are also open to some objections to which the first three theories are not open. One objection is that the theory is circular, and defines being wrong in terms of itself. It defines being wrong in terms of being thought to be wrong, but if you did not understand what was meant by being wrong in the first place you would hardly be likely to understand what was meant by being thought to be wrong. To take another example, if you did not properly understand what was meant by the word 'tetrahedron' you would not be much enlightened by being told that something was a tetrahedron if it had the characteristic shape of a tetrahedron; nor, if you did not know what was meant by the expression 'thoroughbred horse' would you be much enlightened by being told that a horse was a thoroughbred horse means that both of its parents were thoroughbred horses. Hence the statement that to say that an action is wrong means that it is thought, by the speaker or anyone else, to be wrong is scarcely helpful, for, if you did not know what 'wrong' meant in the first place, you would not know what it meant to say that something was thought to be wrong.

It is an objection to theories, which define being wrong in terms of being thought by some persons or other to be wrong, that they prohibit certain ways of speaking which would seem to be perfectly natural and proper. It seems perfectly natural and proper, for example, to say some such thing as that most members of my community mistakenly think that abortion is wrong, or that most men mistakenly think that incest is wrong. On the view that to say that an action is wrong means most members of my group think it is wrong, however, it would not be a permissible way of speaking to say that most members of my community mistakenly think that abortion is wrong. Such a statement would lead to a contradiction. By saying that they *mistakenly* think that abortion is wrong I imply that abortion is right, but by saying that they *think* that abortion is wrong I imply, according to the view that to say that an action is wrong means that most members of my community think that it is wrong, that abortion really *is* wrong. Hence the statement that most members of my community mistakenly think that abortion is wrong implies, if 'wrong' means 'thought to be wrong by a majority of members of my community', a contradiction; this statement does not, however, appear to be in the least contradictory, and so this definition of 'wrong' must be rejected. A precisely parallel argument shows that, if we accept the view that wrong means 'thought to be wrong by all or most men' the statement 'All or most men mistakenly think that incest is wrong' leads to a contradiction. The statement is not contradictory, however, and so this definition of 'wrong', too, must be rejected.

The same argument cannot be used against the view that what I mean when I say that something is wrong is that I personally think that it is wrong. I cannot possibly say that I mistakenly think that something is wrong, for to say this would be to say both that I believe that something is wrong and that – because I think I am mistaken – that I do not believe that it is wrong. It is, however, possible to believe that something one believes *may* be mistaken; I may say ,'I do not think it is wrong to take cannibis, but I may be mistaken.' If all one meant when one said that something was wrong was that one *thought* that it was wrong, this would not be a possible thing to say, for if one knew one thought it was wrong, one would have to know that it was wrong, and, if one knew it was wrong, one could not suggest that, perhaps, in thinking it was wrong, one was mistaken.

Quite apart from anything else, it is very difficult to see how an action, or anything else, can come to have a predicate as a result of being thought to have that predicate. Saying that an action may come to have a predicate or attribute because it is thought to have *that* very predicate or attribute must be distinguished from saying that an action can come to have a predicate or attribute as a result of being thought to have some *other* predicate or attribute. There is no difficulty at all about the latter, for there is no difficulty in seeing how, as a result of being supposed to have one predicate or attribute, an action comes to have another, different, predicate or attribute. For example, though it is difficult to see how an action can come to be wrong as a result of being thought to be wrong, it is not at all difficult to see how, as a result of being thought to be wrong, the action comes to have the different predicate, being *thought* to be wrong. Though it is difficult to see how, as a result of thinking he is inferior, a man can come to have the very same predicate which he thinks he has, actually being inferior, it is not at all difficult to see how he can come to have, because he thinks he is inferior, the different predicate, having an inferiority complex. Again, though it is difficult to see how, as a result of thinking he is ill, a man can come to have the predicate he thinks he has, which is being ill, it is not at all difficult to see how he can come, as a result of thinking he is ill, to have the different predicate, being a hypochondriac.

At this point it may be replied that very often our thinking that we have some characteristic does actually cause us to have the characteristic we think we have. Very often, because we think we can do something, we are actually able to do it, when we would not have been able to do it if we had thought we could not do it. We are much more likely to be able to lecture successfully, for example, if we think we can lecture successfully than if we think we cannot lecture successfully. Very often a man's belief that he is inferior actually makes him inferior, and quite often we think that, once we can eradicate his belief in his own inferiority, he will cease to behave in an inferior way. Very often, too, a man's belief that he is ill actually causes him to be ill. Hence, it might be argued, there are quite a number of cases where a man's belief that something has a predicate actually causes the thing he thinks has that predicate actually to have the very same predicate he thinks it has. So why should not being right or being wrong be one of these cases?

It might be replied that all these are very special cases; they are all cases where the beliefs I have are beliefs about myself, and so where, if I am sufficiently suggestible, something about myself, for example, that I believe that I am ill, may cause another thing about myself, in this case, cause me actually to be ill. It is very difficult to see, however, how my belief that anything *other* than myself has a certain attribute or characteristic could cause that thing actually to have the attribute or characteristic I suppose it to have; and, of course, the great majority of our moral beliefs will be about the virtue of people other than ourselves and the rectitude of actions other than our own.

In any case, it is not at all clear that the examples given above are really examples of my believing that something has a certain attribute actually bringing about that thing's having the very same attribute I believe it to have. There are two reasons for doubting this. In the first place, my belief that I am ill does not *immediately* make it true that I am ill. I believe that I am ill and then, after what may be quite a long interval, I actually become ill. Again, I believe that I am inferior and, after an interval, my belief that I am inferior actually causes me to become inferior. But, of course, where right and wrong are concerned, the theory we are considering held not that I believe that something is wrong and then, after an interval, the thing I think wrong actually becomes wrong as a result of this; the theory holds that all there is to being wrong is being thought to be wrong, not that one thing, an action's being thought to be wrong, can, after an interval, bring about another thing, an action's actually being wrong. In any case, at the time when my belief that I am ill first springs up in my mind, it is false, and it is only after an interval that I become ill; whereas the theory we are considering wishes to maintain that my thinking an action is wrong is identical with this action's being wrong, and is so from the very first moment that I acquire the belief that it is wrong.

The second reason for thinking that the examples I have given, of my belief that I am inferior causing me to be inferior, and of my belief that I am ill causing me to become ill, are not examples of an action's having a predicate because it is thought to have it, is that it is not at all clear that I do, *even after an interval*, come to have the identical attribute which I started by supposing myself to have. Perhaps I believe I cannot lecture because I do not know enough about the subject, but it may cause me to be unable to lecture, or to lecture well, because I am nervous. In other words,

I do not simply believe that I cannot lecture, but that I cannot lecture for a certain reason, or that I cannot lecture well in a certain way, and this belief does not bring about its own truth, but the truth of a rather different belief, the belief that I cannot lecture for a different reason, or that I do not lecture well in a different way. Again, when my belief that I am ill actually causes me to become ill, it is not the case that, even after an interval, I come to have the very same attribute that I started by simply believing I had. I start, let us say, by believing I have cancer and this belief does not cause me to be ill in that I have cancer; it causes me to be ill in that I am neurotic, or to be ill in that, because I believe I have cancer, I do not take enough exercise, and so come to suffer from a degenerate heart. Even if you grant that sometimes my belief that I am ill in a certain way actually causes me to become ill in the way I originally suppose myself to be ill, it is still the case that the belief does not become true simply because I have it, at the very moment at which I first acquire it. For a while the belief is false, and then, after an interval, certain things happen to me; I change in such a way that I actually have the characteristic which at one time I only supposed I had. This is clearly not a case of my belief that I have a characteristic being identical with my having that characteristic, nor a case of all there is to my having a characteristic being my believing that I have the characteristic. If this were so, there would be no need of the interval, during which I actually change in such a way as to make a belief, which was false when I first had it, become true. I think it might even be argued that the belief which, when I become ill, is true, is not the same belief which caused me to become ill. For the belief which caused me to become ill was the belief that now, at the moment of my having the belief, I am ill, which belief is false. If, as a result of my having this false belief I actually become ill, the belief which is true is the belief that now, at this different moment, I am ill. The two beliefs, that I am ill at the time at which the thought that I was ill first entered my mind, and the belief that I am ill after this false belief has had time to work its unfortunate influence upon me, are different beliefs. It is the former belief which brings about the state of affairs which makes the latter true, but this is not the same thing as saying that my having this first belief causes this first belief itself to be true.[1]

[1] See H. H. Price, *Belief* (Allen & Unwin, 1969), Series II, Chapter 6.

Though, so far as I can see, there is only one interpretation that can be put upon the view that to say that an action is wrong means that most members of my community think that it is wrong, and only one interpretation which can be put on the view that to say that an action is wrong means that all or most men think that it is wrong, the view that to say that an action is wrong means that *I myself* think that it is wrong can be taken in two ways, one of which is more plausible than the other. On one interpretation, the one that we have already discussed, the view, that when I say that an action is wrong I simply mean that I think that it is wrong, is trying to substitute for some statement which purports to be about the action, namely, the statement that the action is wrong, a statement about my cognitive attitude to the first statement, namely, the statement that I *believe* the statement that the action in question is wrong. And it is a serious, indeed insuperable, difficulty with the theory that it is very hard to see how two such statements, a statement which appears to be about the action, and a statement which appears to state that my cognitive attitude to the first statement is one of believing it, as opposed to disbelieving it or doubting it, can possibly be equivalent.

It has been held, however, that, when I say I believe that something is so or that I think that something is so, I am not making a statement different from the statement that it is so; what I am doing is to assert the statement that it is so, but at the same time to indicate that I am not very confident of its truth.[1] The difference between 'The cat is on the mat' and 'I think the cat is on the mat', according to this view is not that the former is a statement about the cat's whereabouts, whereas the latter is a statement about my cognitive attitude to the statement about the cat's whereabouts, asserting that this cognitive attitude is one of belief. Both are simply statements about the cat's whereabouts, but whereas in the first I say confidently where I take the cat to be, in the second I say the same thing with a certain amount of hesitation. If this were a correct account of believing or thinking that something is the case, then someone, who held that to say that something is wrong simply means that the speaker thinks that thing is wrong, would not be identifying a statement about the action, to the effect that it is wrong, with a different statement about my cognitive attitude to the first statement, for

[1] See J. O. Urmson, 'Paranthetical Verbs,' *Mind*, Vol. LXI, 1952.

there are not, if this view is to be believed, two different statements, 'Homicide is wrong' and 'I think homicide is wrong'. What he would be saying is that all moral judgments are asserted with a certain amount of diffidence, for he is maintaining that, where moral judgments are concerned, a judgment like 'Homicide is wrong' is always equivalent to 'I think homicide is wrong'; since, on this account of belief, saying 'I believe homicide is wrong' is simply saying 'Homicide is wrong', but saying it with hesitation, anyone who both holds this theory of belief and thinks that 'Homicide is wrong' is equivalent to 'I think homicide is wrong' is simply holding that all moral judgments are asserted with diffidence, for there is always a covert 'I think' to be read into a moral judgment. To this view it can only be replied that men do not always assert all their moral judgments with diffidence, though perhaps it would be a very good thing if they did.

On all the theories we have discussed in this chapter, moral judgments will be established empirically. If the theory that moral judgments are about the feelings or beliefs of the speaker is true, they will be basic propositions, that is, they will not be inferred from any other proposition, for we do not infer what we think or how we feel. On the other theories, they will be inferred from premises about how individual people, taken as a sample of the people in one's community or of the whole of mankind, think and feel. The argument will be roughly that individuals X_1 to X_n feel approval of A, and are a fair sample of my community or of the whole of mankind, so my community or the whole of mankind approves of A. We will establish that individuals X_1 to X_n approve of A by asking them, or inferring their feelings from the way they talk, their behaviour, or the expressions on their faces. On all these theories moral judgments will be synthetic, not analytic, for it is not part of the definition of a person or community of people or of mankind as such that he or they approve of one thing rather than another. (Some philosophers have argued that it is part of what it means to be a 'Person', with a capital 'P', to recognize one's obligations to other Persons, but in this sense of 'Person' it is highly questionable whether *people* are Persons – they do not all recognize their obligations to other people, unfortunately – and it is people, not Persons, we are talking about.) It will also, of course, be just a contingent matter of fact that people feel or think the way they do, and it is a difficulty with these views that we do in fact think that cruelty is wrong, even if it did so happen that people approved of it. Furthermore, on all these theories, moral concepts will be ordinary empirical concepts, acquired by a process of ostensive definition, for we know what is meant by words like 'approval' and 'belief' by being acquainted with feelings of approval and beliefs when we have these ourselves, and observing ourselves and others behaving in approving or believing ways. More is necessary, of course, to have a moral concept than to have a concept of approval or a concept of belief, on the theories that moral judgments are judgments about the feelings or beliefs of all or most people in a community or all or most people. We need also to understand the words 'all' or 'most', but we have already seen that an explanation of the work these words do in sentences can be given ostensively.

CHAPTER VII

IDEAL OBSERVER THEORIES

Theories according to which moral judgments are about the attitudes which people have to the actions or people or states of affairs to which these judgments ascribe moral qualities are not, as has been seen, very plausible, and the view that they are about the *beliefs* people have about the actions described in the judgment is even worse off than the view that these moral judgments are about the *feelings* the actions judged of arouse in people. That these theories are not satisfactory ought not to be a matter for surprise. They all try to identify the statement that something is wrong with some statement about the attitude to that thing of some actual person or actual group of people, and actual people are fallible in all sorts of different ways. One extremely important way in which actual people are fallible has already been mentioned; the information on account of which they have the moral beliefs or the moral feelings they do is always liable to be incomplete and erroneous. Why then, should we identify being wrong with the opinions or feelings of an actual person, when it is a known fact that actual people's opinions and feelings would very often be different from what they are, had they more information about the things which are the subjects of their opinions or the objects of their feelings?

Hence no theory which holds that moral judgments are statements about actual people's attitudes to the actions judged of can possibly be satisfactory. It might, then, be better to hold that moral judgments are not about the attitudes and beliefs of any actual person or observer or set of persons or observers, but about the attitudes and beliefs of some ideal person or ideal observer.[1]

Two crucial questions arise immediately: firstly, 'How is the expression "ideal observer" to be defined?', and secondly, 'How are we supposed to know what an ideal observer would or would not approve of?' It must be remembered, of course, that since there are not in fact any ideal observers, we cannot find out what ideal

[1] The first philosopher to my knowledge to put forward such a view was Adam Smith in *The Theory of Moral Sentiments*.

observers approve of by observing or asking an ideal observer, and noting whether or not he approves of actions the morality of which we are in doubt of.

Let us first consider the question how the expression 'ideal observer' is to be defined. (When one talks about an ideal observer, it is not necessary that an ideal observer should be in any sense an ideal person; it is his moral opinions or attitudes which are supposed to constitute a yardstick by which to determine the adequacy of our own, and whether the ideal observer is also virtuous in behaviour is entirely irrelevant.) There is one way in which the expression 'ideal observer' certainly must not be defined; he must not be defined as an obesrver who always approves of actions which are right, and disapproves of actions which are wrong, for such a definition would be circular. In order to understand it, we would have to know already what the words 'right' and 'wrong' meant, which is precisely what those who put forward this definition are trying to elucidate for us.

It would seem, however, that it must be stipulated that an ideal observer, unlike actual observers, must be omniscient. If he is omniscient, then it is not possible for his attitudes to be, as ours are, based upon inadequate knowledge of the actions or situations he is approving of or disapproving of, or for his attitude to be based upon mistaken beliefs about them. (I am assuming that, if some being is said to be omniscient this does not simply mean that he knows the truth of every true proposition, but that he is also incapable of believing any propositions that are false.) Perhaps, however, it is not necessary to go so far as to lay down that a being, to count as an ideal observer, must actually be omniscient. It is tempting to say, instead, that he must not be ignorant of or mistaken concerning any *relevant* matter of fact about the action or person he approves or disapproves of. What, however, is meant by a relevant matter of fact? One is inclined to say that a matter of fact is a relevant matter of fact if it is one which ought to be taken into account in our assessment of whether an action is right or wrong, but it is impossible to use this definition of 'relevant' in defining the expression 'ideal observer'. This is because the object of introducing the notion of an ideal observer was in order to give an elucidation of the meaning of the words 'right' and 'wrong', so if, in the sentence propounding this elucidation, one uses the expression 'fact which ought to be taken account of in assessing whether an action is right or wrong' one is, again, producing a definition of 'ideal observer' which is circular.

It is, however, possible to define 'relevant' in such a way as to be able to say that an ideal observer is not ignorant or mistaken concerning any relevant matter of fact without making circular our definition of 'right' and 'wrong' in terms of the reactions of an ideal observer to actions. One can say that a matter of fact about an action or person or situation is a relevant matter of fact if whether or not the ideal observer knows of it or is ignorant of it or is mistaken about it will make a difference to his attitude to the action or person or situation which it is a fact about. Hence, just as the theory defines 'right' and 'wrong' in terms of the attitudes an ideal observer would have to the actions whose morality is in question, so one can define 'relevant' in terms of what would make a *difference* to the attitudes of the ideal observer. This definition of relevance must, however, be made a little more precise than it is at the moment. It is possible that the reason why whether the ideal observer knows of or is ignorant of or mistaken about some matter of fact makes no difference to his attitude is that he is ignorant of or mistaken about some *other* matter of fact. It may be, for example, that the reason why the attitude of the ideal observer to an unfortunate episode involving Smith is not altered one way or the other by whether or not he knows Smith pulled the trigger (or is ignorant of this, or whether he mistakenly thinks that Smith did not pull the trigger) is that he is ignorant of the fact that the gun was loaded, or because he mistakenly believes that the gun was not loaded. Hence it is not sufficient to define a 'relevant' matter of fact as a matter of fact which is such that whether the ideal observer knows of it or is ignorant of it or is mistaken about it makes a difference to his attitude to the thing this fact is a fact about, for this would make the fact that Smith, in the example above, pulled the trigger, an irrelevant matter of fact. One must also stipulate that whether or not knowledge of, or ignorance concerning, or mistake about this matter of fact does or does not make a difference to the attitude of the ideal observer is not due to his being ignorant of, or mistaken about, any other matter of fact.

It has also been suggested that an ideal observer, besides knowing all the 'relevant' matters of fact concerning the actions he approves of, should be impartial, consistent, unbiased, dispassionate, and disinterested.[1] This gives rise to a difficulty, however. *Why* should we suppose that an ideal observer should be all these things? Is it not because we approve of these characteristics, and think that it is wrong not to possess them? But if this is why we think that an ideal observer ought to be consistent, and so on, then we are supposing that we already know what is right and what is wrong, which is just what we are not supposed to know until we have discovered, by whatever method turns out to be appropriate, what an ideal observer would approve of. In other words, though the feelings of an ideal observer are supposed to be the ultimate court of appeal on moral matters, we are now rigging the election, so to speak, in such a way that if the ideal observer turns out not to approve of what we already approve of, we will redefine the expression 'ideal observer' until we find a definition which is such that something which is an ideal observer, in this sense, does approve of what we approve of already.

One may attempt to answer this objection by distinguishing between the *formal* characteristics and the *material* characteristics of any moral code or set of moral beliefs. When I talk about the matter of a set of moral beliefs, I mean the actual principles which it contains. It appertains to the matter of a set of moral beliefs or principles that it contains an item saying that promise-breaking is wrong, or one saying that divorce is wrong. Where the matter of our moral beliefs are concerned, it is quite proper to say that we do not know, on an ideal observer theory, what set of moral beliefs we ought to have until we first find out what the attitudes of an ideal observer to things like promise-breaking and divorce are. This is because it is not possible, without 'moral insight', which the ideal observer theory is supposed to be giving an account of, to decide whether divorce or promise-breaking are right or wrong. Having moral insight into whether some kind of action is right or wrong, on an ideal observer theory, consists in knowing what the reactions of an ideal observer would be to members of this class of actions.

However, there are certain conditions which it is possible to say that any satisfactory set of moral beliefs must fulfil, without our possessing any moral insight at all. For example, it is possible to see, without having recourse to moral insight, that any set of moral beliefs must, whatever else they are, be *consistent* with one

---

[1] See Roderick Firth, 'Ethical Absolutism and the Ideal Observer', *Philosophy and Phenomenological Research*, Vol. XII, March 1952.

another. Whatever set of moral beliefs we accept, they must be consistent with one another, in two ways. It must not be possible to deduce from any one of someone's moral beliefs that some other member of the set of his moral beliefs is false. Not only this, no member of the set which constitutes a person's beliefs must enjoin some action such that, if it is performed, circumstances will make it inevitable that some action enjoined by another member of the same person's moral beliefs must be omitted. A set of moral beliefs which contained both a belief that all promises ought to be kept, and a belief that promises extracted by means of force ought to be broken would be an example of a set which contained moral beliefs which were inconsistent in the first kind of way. A set of moral beliefs which contained both a belief that all promises ought to be kept, and a belief that all debts ought to be paid, would, if it is sometimes impossible for a man both to keep his promise and pay his debt, be an example of a set of moral beliefs some of whose members were inconsistent with one another in the second kind of way.

Not only must any person's set of moral beliefs not contain any beliefs which are incompatible with one another – and this must be taken to include the condition that it must not be possible to deduce from any *combination* of them that some one of them is false – a person's moral beliefs ought to be *clearly sorted out into those which are ultimate and those which are derivative*. If a person's set of moral beliefs contains both a belief that it is wrong to cause other people inconvenience and a belief that it is wrong to talk in libraries, it should be clear that the latter belief is not ultimate, for it can be derived from the former. Strictly speaking, a person's moral beliefs need include only beliefs which are ultimate, for, since beliefs which are not ultimate can be derived from those which are, the latter are logically superfluous, and need be included only for the purpose of elucidating the implications which those beliefs which are ultimate, together with suitable statements about matters of fact, have for example, the statement that talking in libraries is one thing which causes inconvenience to other people.

A person's set of moral beliefs ought also to be *complete*. By saying that a set of moral beliefs is complete, I mean that it must be capable of giving guidance in every situation. That is to say, for every conceivable situation, it must be possible to tell by reference to a person's moral beliefs whether some action is enjoined in that situation, or whether some action is prohibited in that situation, or whether, in that situation, it is a matter of indifference what action we perform. This would seem to mean that, if a person's moral beliefs include a number of beliefs to the effect that certain kinds of action are prohibited, and a number of beliefs to the effect that certain kinds of action are enjoined, this person's set of moral beliefs must also include a belief to the effect that all other kinds of action are neither enjoined nor prohibited, that is, that all the actions which are enjoined are listed, and all the actions which are prohibited are also listed. That a person's set of moral beliefs is complete, of course, does not mean that they are all correct, or that it includes all the correct moral beliefs there are. For example, a person's set of moral beliefs might simply contain one belief to the effect that causing pain was prohibited, that nothing, except not causing pain, was enjoined, and that, apart from causing other people pain, it did not matter how anyone behaved. Such a set of moral beliefs would be complete in the sense of 'complete' which has just been explained, but it is quite likely that it does not include all the 'correct' moral beliefs there are, and possible that some kinds of action which are prohibited by this set of beliefs are not always morally reprehensible in actual fact. (There may well be some situations, for example, in which one has to cause some people pain in order to secure some large or essential benefit for others.)

A person's set of moral beliefs ought also to be *precise* and *unequivocal*. The latter condition is fairly easy to fulfil. I cannot, indeed, think of any actual example of a moral belief which can be taken in two entirely different ways. The former condition, however, is much more demanding. This condition lays down that a person's moral beliefs should be precise, in the sense that they should be the opposite of vague. A moral belief is imprecise if there are cases to which it is not clear whether or not it applies, and it is precise to the extent to which it eliminates the possibility of such borderline cases – and, I should add, not only cases which actually arise, but cases which can be thought of or imagined. Though I cannot think of a single example of a moral belief which is equivocal, I cannot think of any actual moral beliefs which are not in some degree or other imprecise, and leave open the possibility of cases which are such that one cannot tell whether the belief applies to them or not, even if such cases do not arise in actual fact. For example, it is not clear whether or not someone has made a promise if he says 'I promise . . .' jokingly, and is taken seriously by the person to whom he says these words, or if he says 'I promise . . .' putting one possible interpretation on the words describing what he has promised, while the person to whom he says 'I promise . . .' puts another interpretation on these words. It is not clear whether a woman who has been given artificial insemination by a donor who is not her husband has or has not committed adultery. It is unclear whether someone who deliberately refrains from resuscitating someone whose life he could quite easily save is guilty of homicide or murder or neither. It is unclear whether someone who asserts, with intent to deceive, a proposition which he is convinced is false, but which is in fact true, is lying. Innumerable cases such as this can actually be found, or be thought up, if they have not actually occured, by anyone with sufficient ingenuity. Every time such a case arises, it is necessary that the moral belief whose application to this case is in question should be made more precise, so that it may be determined without doubt whether the borderline case is or is not an example of the kind of action which the belief describes as right or wrong or obligatory.

That a set of moral beliefs is unsatisfactory in that its members are imprecise is something which someone without any 'moral insight' at all can quite easily determine. The question whether moral beliefs are precise is quite a different question from the question whether or not they are correct. The belief that all men ought to be hanged is at least as precise as any other moral belief, and a good deal more precise than most, but scarcely anyone would wish to maintain that it was correct.

It is also a necessary condition of a set of moral beliefs being satisfactory that those members of the set which are ultimate, and from which all other members of the set are derived in the manner previously explained, should be about 'open' classes only, and not about 'closed' ones. An example of an open class is the class of men, or promises, or cases of homicide. Examples of closed classes are all the men in England, all the promises broken by Smith, or all the cases of homicide whose perpetrators were hanged in England during the nineteenth century. A class is a closed class if its membership is limited by reference to some particular person or thing or event, which will be referred to either by a proper name, for example, 'England' or 'Smith', or by a description, such as 'the nineteenth century after the birth of Christ'. A class is open if its membership is not limited in this way, if it contains all men or all promises or all cases of homicide without restriction.

Ultimate moral beliefs must not mention closed classes, because this would offend against what has sometimes been called the *universalization principle*. The universalization principle states that if an action is wrong, then any precisely similar action performed by a similar person under similar circumstances must also be wrong; the same thing is supposed to apply also to those actions which are right, to those actions which ought to be done or omitted, and to those things which are good. I shall discuss whether the universalization principle is true or not in a later chapter.[1] The reason why mentioning a closed class in a belief about an ultimate moral principle infringes the universalization principle is this: if not all promise-breaking is said to be wrong, but only that promise-breaking which is done by Smith, then it is suggested that precisely similar cases of promise-breaking performed by a similar man, Jones, under similar circumstances might not be wrong. If they are not wrong, then an action is said to be wrong when it is done by Smith, but is not held to be wrong when done by Jones, even though the promise which is broken, the man who breaks it, and the circumstances under which it is broken, are all similar, and this offends against the universalization principle. If, on the other hand, they *are* held to be wrong, then there are actions which are held to be wrong by the person who thinks that promise breaking by *Smith* is wrong, which this person has not mentioned.

There is, of course, no reason why one should not hold that promise-breaking by Smith is wrong, so long as one does not hold it as an ultimate moral principle; indeed, the statement 'Promise-breaking is wrong' would entail the statement 'Promise-breaking by Smith is wrong', since the latter can be derived from the former. As an ultimate moral principle, however, 'Promise-breaking by Smith is wrong' is not satisfactory. For either promise-breaking by anybody is wrong, in which case the principle should say so, or promise-breaking is wrong only when it is Smith's promises that are broken, which is contrary to the principle that similar cases should be treated similarly.

Ultimate moral beliefs, or beliefs about ultimate moral principles should also be *universal*, in the sense that they should be to the effect that *all* actions which are cases of so-and-so are wrong, or

[1] Chapter XIV.

all actions which are such-and-such are right. If they are particular, that is, to the effect that *some* actions which are cases of so-and-so are wrong, or *some* actions which are such-and-such are right, then this suggests that other instances of actions which are so-and-so might be right, and that other actions which are such-and-such might be wrong. Now if some actions which are cases of so-and-so *are* right and others wrong, there must be some difference between the actions which are right and the actions which are wrong, which difference accounts for our assessing them differently in this respect. This simply follows from the aforementioned universalization principle, for the statement that if an action is right, then any other similar action (performed by similar people in similar circumstances) must be right, logically entails, by the operation known as contraposition, that if one action is right and another action is wrong, then they cannot be similar actions (or that they are performed by dissimilar people or in dissimilar circumstances). In this case, if some of a class of actions are right and others wrong, it must be possible to find the reason for this, and once this reason is found – let us suppose it is the possession of a characteristic which makes right the members of this class which are right, and makes wrong the members of this class which are wrong – it should be possible to say *all* actions which are both such-and-such and X are right, that is, to produce a principle which is universal and refers to the members of all of the class of actions which is being held to be right or to be wrong.

It is possible, of course, that in a case like this the fact that, when I say all actions which are both such-and-such and cases of X are right, the fact that they are cases of such-and-such subsequently turns out to be irrelevant; it may be that all Xs are right, whether they are also such-and-such or not. In this case, of course, the statement that all actions which are both such-and-such and X is not mistaken, but it is not an ultimate moral principle, since it can be logically deduced from the principle that all actions which are X are right. An example would be as follows. We may hold that sometimes it is right to keep our promises, which suggests, though it does not entail that it is also sometimes right to break them (i.e. wrong to keep them). There must be some reason, if the universalization principle is correct, why some actions which are cases of promise-keeping are right and others wrong; otherwise precisely similar actions would receive a different moral assessment. This reason may turn out to be that those cases of promise-keeping which are right promote the happiness of society while those cases of promise-keeping which are not right do not promote the happiness of society. It may then turn out that, so long as actions promote the happiness of society, they are right, regardless of whether they are cases of promise-keeping or not, so we may say simply that all actions which promote the happiness of society are right. It would, of course, follow logically from this that we must accept the principle, which can be derived from the principle that all actions which promote the happiness of society are right, that all promise-keeping which promotes the happiness of society is right.

Philosophers, for example, Kant, sometimes confuse the question whether a principle is universal or not with the question whether it is specific or not. The statement that all murderers ought to be hanged is just as universal as the statement that all men ought to be hanged, but the former is more specific than the latter, and the statement that all who have murdered policemen ought to be hanged is more specific than either of these. Though I have produced a reason for thinking that all ultimate moral principles must be universal, this is not the same thing as saying that ultimate moral principles must be highly inspecific. *Sometimes* it is possible to produce a reason why ultimate moral principles must be more specific than derivative moral principles. One can produce such a reason when one deduces a derivative moral principle from an ultimate moral principle *directly* because, if all Xs are right, then all XYs are right – and, of course, the class of XYs is more specific than the class of Xs. But when one derives a principle *indirectly*, by arguing that because all Xs are right, and Ys are in fact cases of X, all Ys must be right, it does not follow from the fact that the rightness of Ys is derived from that of Xs that the defining characteristic of the class of Ys is narrower than the defining characteristic of the class of Xs. For example, if all sinful men ought to repent, and all men are sinful men, it follows that the statement that all men ought to repent can be derived from the statement that all sinful men ought to repent. The class of men, however, is less, not more specific than the class of sinful men.

Many comparatively recent philosophers (Sir David Ross, for example[1]) have argued that there are no universal principles about what sort of action is right and what sort of action is wrong. The best one can do is to say that certain sorts of things always *tend*

[1] *The Right and the Good* (Oxford University Press, 1938), Chapter II.

to be right, or that certain other kinds of things always tend to be wrong. This tendency to be wrong, however, may be overridden if the agent cannot perform this action without omitting some other action which has, in the circumstances, an even stronger tendency to be right. Hence the best a moralist can do is give lists of actions which tend to be right and which tend to be wrong, and say that, when it is impossible to perform an action of a kind which tends to be right without at the same time performing an action of some other kind which tends to be wrong, the stronger tendency must override the weaker; it is claimed, however, that it is not possible to give rules about this. For example, one can say that keeping one's promises, though not always right, always tends to be right, and that the same is true of paying one's debts. Sometimes, as when I have only a limited amount of money, I cannot keep my promise to one man to give him five pounds without failing to pay the debt of five pounds I owe to another. In such a case, there is no rule which one can fall back upon; one must simply weigh the two conflicting tendencies or *prima facie* duties against one another, and decide which is stronger, that is, whether it is worse to pay the debt and break the promise or, on the other hand, to keep the promise and fail to pay the debt. Which of these two alternatives is right will depend upon the circumstances.

However, if paying a debt, even though this involves breaking a promise, is sometimes right and at other times wrong, it ought to be possible to hit upon the reason why this is right at some times but wrong at others. (That there must be a reason follows from the universalization principle, that if one action is right and another action is wrong, there must be some respect in which they are different.) Once this reason is hit upon, one can say that paying a debt, even though it involves breaking a promise, is always right when there is some further characteristic present. And if this can be done, it *may* be possible to go on to say that all actions which have this characteristic, X, are right, whether they are also cases of breaking a promise in order to pay a debt or not.

I have been arguing that any satisfactory set of moral principles or moral beliefs must fulfil the requirements I have been specifying, and also that it is possible to see that they must fulfil these requirements without making use of any special moral insight, for that a set of moral principles or moral beliefs fulfils these re-

F

quirements leaves it an open question what these moral beliefs, which belong to the set which fulfils the requirements, are. They may be principles to the effect that all promises ought to be kept, or principles to the effect that all enemies ought to be eaten, for all anything fulfilling the formal requirements I have been talking about can say to the contrary. Granted that we can know that no set of moral beliefs which does not fulfil the requirements listed above can be satisfactory, and know this without moral insight, this does not tell us how we know that a given set of moral beliefs, which fulfils these formal requirements, *is* satisfactory. Nor does it tell us how we know that a satisfactory set of moral beliefs must fulfil these requirements.

It has sometimes been suggested that we know that moral principles must fulfil the formal requirements – that they must be consistent, complete, precise, about open classes, and universal – because it follows from the definition of moral principles that what does not fulfil these formal requirements is not a moral principle. It may well be that *some* of these requirements do follow from the definition of 'principle'; it may well be, for example, that it is proper to refuse to call anything a *principle* unless it is universal. On the other hand, it would scarcely be reasonable to refuse to call something a principle on the ground that it was not consistent with other principles accepted by the same person; inconsistent principles are just as much principles as any other kind of principle.

A possible reason why moral principles must fulfil the formal requirements I have mentioned is that otherwise they would not do the work which we expect moral principles to do. Moral principles are intended to guide us in the way we should go, but if they were inconsistent, they would point in two different directions at once, and so be worse than useless. Moreover, it would be impossible to act upon them, for it is impossible to act upon principles which are inconsistent with one another, since acting on the one will entail failing to act on the other, and principles which demand the impossible will be useless. If they are not complete, they will leave areas in our lives in which they fail to give us guidance. If they are imprecise, it will sometimes be unclear whether they enjoin a given action or do not enjoin it. If they are not about open classes, they will enjoin an action, but irrationally and arbitrarily fail to enjoin a precisely similar action in similar circumstances, for no better reason than it is a numerically different action performed by a numerically different person. If they are not universal, but simply enjoin some of a class of actions, then it will be impossible to tell by consulting them which actions in this class one should perform and which actions in this class one should not perform; furthermore, it will follow that some actions in a class will be right and others wrong for no reason, and that there is no difference between the right ones and the wrong ones, which is impossible.

Unfortunately, however, the formal conditions which any satisfactory set of moral beliefs must fulfil are not at all the same as the characteristics which we must attribute to an ideal observer, tempting though it was to suppose that these must be identical. For example, one condition which any satisfactory set of moral beliefs must fulfil is that every member of the set must be consistent with every other member of the set. The ideal observer, however, so far from having to fulfil this condition, cannot possibly fulfil it, for he is an individual, not a belief or a set of beliefs. Nor need his beliefs fulfil this, or any other of the conditions, which a satisfactory set of moral beliefs must fulfil, for it is not even necessary that an ideal observer should have any moral beliefs. It is his emotional reactions to actions, or the reactions which he would have, if he existed, and not his beliefs, which determine whether our moral beliefs are correct or incorrect; indeed, it is this very same thing which would determine whether the ideal observer's own beliefs, if he had any, were correct or incorrect, but it is not at all necessary that he should have any. So long as he reacts to actions by approving or disapproving of them, this is all that is necessary: it is not necessary that he himself should know what his own reactions are.

Though the characteristics which we must ascribe to an ideal observer are not the same as those which any satisfactory set of moral beliefs must fulfil, there is at least one characteristic which may be required of the ideal observer, which is necessary if our beliefs are to fulfil the conditions which we decided any satisfactory set of moral beliefs must fulfil. If he reacts favourably to an action, person or situation, then he must react favourably to any other precisely similar action (performed by a similar person in similar circumstances), or person or situation. If he does this, it must be possible to find a set of moral beliefs which are about open classes – for the ideal observer will react favourably or unfavourably to actions because of their features. He will react to them because they are cases of promise-keeping or debt paying, and the features of things are characteristics which determine open classes. Hence he will disapprove of such things as promise-breaking or lying, not promise-breaking by Jones or lying by Smith. The same thing will also mean that it is possible for us to find a set of moral beliefs which are universal. If the ideal observer is such that, if he reacts favourably to a given action, he will react in the same way to any similar action performed by a similar person under similar circumstances, this will give rise to the fact that *all* actions which possess the features which these actions have are right.

When we consider the other conditions which any satisfactory set of moral beliefs must fulfil, we see that some of these characteristics, though our moral beliefs ought to have them, are not ones which any conceivable ideal observer could deprive our belief of. It is our own fault, so to speak, not his, if our moral beliefs are inconsistent with one another. His reactions could not possibly be inconsistent, in the sense of justifying us in asserting inconsistent moral judgments, for what is inconsistent cannot happen, and so it cannot possibly be a property of the ideal observer that he makes true both of two inconsistent beliefs.

The same is true of completeness. If our moral beliefs are incomplete, that is our fault, not his, and it is our business, on an ideal observer theory, to make our beliefs more nearly complete by finding out more about what the reactions of an ideal observer would be. It might be argued that the reactions of an ideal observer might be incomplete in the sense that there were some actions of which he neither approved nor disapproved. The answer to this is that, since 'right' and 'wrong' are, in one sense, contradictory epithets, it seems reasonable to suggest that if an action is wrong means the ideal observer reacts unfavourably by disapproving of it, then if he fails to react unfavourably, this means that the action is right; since obviously the ideal observer must either disapprove of something or fail to disapprove of it, it follows that it must be possible to tell by his reactions whether any action is wrong or right in all possible cases.

Again, the precision of our moral beliefs, so to speak, is our responsibility, not that of the ideal observer, that is to say, it is up to us to describe what the reaction of an ideal observer to actions would be. One is tempted to say that we must lay down that the ideal observer must be discriminating, that is to say, that small differences in the nature of the actions he is approving or disapproving of make a difference to his reactions, but it would be a mistake to do this. Where scientific instruments are concerned, it is necessary that they should be discriminating, for the object of scientific instruments is to discover facts about a world which is what it is independently of the instruments. Where the ideal observer is concerned, however, his function is not to discover moral facts about a world which is independent of him, and which would be facts whether or not he registered a reaction to them. The ideal observer, in reacting favourably to some actions and unfavourably to others, is not being sensitive to an independently existing right and wrong. His reactions constitute or determine what is right or wrong, and are not a means of detecting it. Hence, if he is undiscriminating, in the sense that he reacts in the same way to very different actions, there is nothing wrong with this; indeed, one could not hold an ideal observer theory if one was going to criticize the reactions of the ideal observer, for it is these which constitute our ultimate court of appeal. If an ideal observer does react similarly to very different actions, then there is nothing for it, on an ideal observer theory, but to say that very dissimilar actions can all be right or all wrong. In any case, there is nothing impossible or even unusual about actions which are in some respects very dissimilar being in other respects very similar.

What characteristics, then, *are* we to attribute to the ideal observer, bearing in mind the fact that we must not prejudge any issue by laying down that he must react in one way rather than in another to any kind of action whose morality is to be determined by ascertaining what his reactions to that kind of action would be? I think it would be to prejudice the question of what an ideal observer would approve of if we lay down that the ideal observer must be impartial. A judge is said to be impartial if he applies the law to all people alike, regardless of their social status or wealth or personal relationship to himself. This does not mean, of course, that he treats all people alike, otherwise he would hang all men indifferently, regardless of whether or not they had committed murder. What it does mean is that he considers only the law, and ignores any characteristics of the people with whom he is concerned other than those which are by law relevant to his judgment. If the law says that only the poor shall be hanged for murder, then he is applying the law impartially if he condemns the poor but not the rich. With the moral as well as the positive law of a country, the case is not altered. A man is being partial, if he condemns a poor man or a beggarman or an enemy for an action, but does not condemn a rich man or a duke or a friend or a relative for a similar action, provided the moral law does not lay down that wealth or social standing or the relationship to the person making the judgment is relevant to the question of how an action ought to be morally assessed. In many cases indeed, the wealth or social standing or relationships of the person, the morality of whose actions is in question, *is* relevant to the question of whether or not the actions are right or wrong; if only to take a mundane example, it is right for a rich man to spend an amount of money which it would be wrong for a poor man to spend. Hence impartiality consists in applying the moral law alike to all cases except when the moral law lays down that these cases are different in some way in which it justifies us in making different moral judgments about them. Now in this sense of 'impartial', the ideal observer cannot be impartial. He does not apply the moral law – for, as we have seen there is no need for him to make any moral judgments at all – but determines by the nature of his reactions what the moral law shall be. Hence it is whether or not an ideal observer reacts in the same way or in different ways to actions when they are performed by the rich and when they are performed by the poor that determines whether the wealth or poverty of the man who performs these actions constitutes a difference between them which is relevant to how they ought to be morally assessed. If he reacts differently to them, then the wealth of the agent, on an ideal observer theory, is a relevant difference, and, since the reactions of the ideal observer are the ultimate court of appeal, it is not possible to say than an ideal observer, in disapproving of an action when performed by a poor man but not disapproving of it when it is performed by a rich man, is being partial. It might be argued that there is one sense in which the ideal observer must be impartial; he must approve of our judging to be right all those actions which are made right by his approving of them, and of our judging to be wrong all those actions which are made wrong by his disapproving of them, regardless of such things as the wealth of the man who performed them or the relationship of the man who performed them to the person making the moral judgment. Even this is not so, however. To believe an action to be right is one thing, to say so out loud, possibly in the presence of the agent, is another. Though, if an action is right, any other relevantly similar action is right, this does not mean that if it is right to say out loud that an action is right, it is right to say out loud that any other relevantly similar action is right. For example, of two actions which are similar in all relevant respects one might be performed by a relative of the person making the judgment while the other might be performed by a person who is not a relative of the person making the judgment, and from the fact that it is right to say out loud that an action not performed by a relative is wrong it does not follow that it is right to say out loud that an action which is performed by a relative is wrong. In other words, two actions may be similar in all the respects which are relevant to whether or not they are right or wrong, without being also similar in all the respects which are relevant to the question whether one ought to say out loud that they are right or wrong, or more generally, without being similar in ways which would make it right to treat them in a similar way. Hence the question whether it is right to be impartial, in the sense of *treating* in a similar way actions which are morally similar, even though they have been performed by people who are in other respects very different, is a moral question of substance, and as such, it can, on an ideal observer theory, be settled only by discovering what the reaction of an ideal observer to such behaviour would be. Hence we cannot *define* an ideal observer as one who approves of treating actions which are morally similar in a similar way without assuming that we know an answer to a moral question, that is, the moral question 'Ought actions which are morally similar be treated in a similar way?', which we are not, on an ideal observer theory, supposed to be able to answer until we know whether an ideal observer would approve of this or not.

There is no reason why the ideal observer should be consistent, in the sense that his moral beliefs should be consistent, for, as we have seen, there is no reason why the ideal observer should have any moral beliefs. Nor is it necessary that the ideal observer should be consistent in the sense that he reacts to similar actions in a similar way; this would make it impossible, on the ground that all cases of violence are similar to one another in that they are cases of violence, for him to approve of some cases of violence but not others. What is necessary is that every reaction of the ideal observer should be a case of a rule, so that, if he reacts unfavourably to a given action, this was because he reacts unfavourably to all actions of a certain kind, and this action was an action of that kind. Similarly, if he reacts favourably to an action, this must be because he reacts favourably to all actions of a certain kind, and because this action is an action of that kind. That he must do this would follow from the fact that, if he reacts in a certain way to a given action, he must react in the same way to all similar actions performed by similar people under similar circumstances. Of course, it may be the case that there simply are no actions which *are* precisely similar to this given action, but I do not think this affects the conclusion that his reaction to this action is a case of a rule, provided you allow that it is a rule to the effect that he would act in a similar way to any other action which was precisely similar to this one, if there were any such actions. In any case, the conclusion that his reacting in a given way to this action is a case of a rule only to the effect that he would react in a similar way to precisely similar actions, if there were any, need follow only if we assume that *all* the features of *every* action are relevant to how he reacts to it, which seems *a priori* unlikely to be true. If you state that many, if not most, of the features of an action are irrelevant to the manner in which he reacts to it, then it is very likely the case that there is a class of actions, of which this action is an instance, which is such that he reacts to all members of the class in the same way that he reacts to this action, and that this class of actions usually has many instances.

Should the ideal observer be unbiassed; that is to say, should we lay down as one of the defining characteristics which an ideal observer must possess to count as being an ideal observer at all, that he is unbiassed? If by saying that he is unbiassed we mean that his *judgments* about what actions are right and wrong should be unbiassed, it is not necessary that the ideal observer should be unbiassed for, as we have already seen, it is not necessary that the ideal observer should make any moral judgments. Should we say that his reactions must be unbiassed, meaning that whether he feels approval or disapproval of any action is not affected by certain things, for example, by his likes or dislikes, if he has any? I can think of an argument which would purport to show that we should say that the ideal observer must be unbiassed in this sense. If he is biassed by his likes or dislikes, then, because he likes some people but dislikes others, this may cause him to approve of an action when performed by one person, whom he likes, but to disapprove of another precisely similar action performed by a precisely similar person, whom he dislikes. The reply to this argument however, might be that, if he likes one of these two people but dislikes the other, they cannot be similar people – there must, after all, be some reason why he likes one of them but dislikes the other – and hence, even if the two actions are precisely similar, and performed in precisely similar circumstances, they are not performed by precisely similar people. Hence there is no reason why he should not react to one of the actions favourably and to the other of the actions unfavourably. Perhaps, if he liked some people but not others, not because of their characteristics, which other people could share, and which, if they were shared by others, would cause him to like the other people too, but on account of the relationship of these people to him, which might be different for people whose characteristics were similar, we could then say that his moral reaction must not be determined by his likes and dislikes – but how can an ideal observer, who is a purely hypothetical entity, in the sense that in talking about his reactions we are talking about the reactions which a being of a certain kind would have, if there were one, stand in any relationship to actual people? Perhaps, however, we might argue that, if whether an ideal observer felt approval or disapproval of something was allowed to be determined by his likes and dislikes, these might change, and, as a result, he might approve of an action at one time but, because his likes had changed, disapprove at another time of a precisely similar action performed under precisely similar circumstances by a precisely similar person. I shall say more about this a little later on.

If we say that the reactions of the ideal observer are to be unbiassed, in that they are not to be affected by his likes or dislikes, we presumably ought also to say that his reactions are not affected by his desires or by his interests. This, again, will be for the same reason that we would not allow his reactions to be affected by his likes and dislikes. If he has desires, then presumably, his desires may affect his reactions in such a manner that he disapproves of one action because it interferes with the satisfaction of his desires, and approves of another similar action because it facilitates the satisfaction of his desires. It might be argued that this would infringe the universalization principle. It would be better to say, however, since the ideal observer is a purely hypothetical being, that if he exists, then his reactions cannot be affected by his desires, if he has any, not that his reactions are not affected by his desires. Unfortunately, however, it is not clear that, if his reactions were affected by his desires and interests, the result *would* be that he approves of one action but disapproves of a precisely similar action, for, if one action interferes with the satisfaction of his desires, but another action facilitates the satisfaction of his desires, they are *not* precisely similar, and there is no logical reason why he should not disapprove of the one while approving of the other. There is, in fact, no reason why an ideal observer, or anyone else, for that matter, should not approve *only* of actions which promote his own interest, or the interest of some institution of which he is a member – his country, for example – provided he would approve of *all* actions which promote the interest of a being or institution of such-and-such a sort, and he is the *only* being of this sort (which the ideal observer would be) or the institution to which he belongs is the only institution of this sort. If he or his institution were not unique, the best he could do without infringing the rule that if he approves of one action, he must likewise approve of all similar actions performed by similar people under similar circumstances, would be to approve of his own actions, when it promotes *his* own interest or that of some institution to which *he* belongs, provided he also approved of other people's actions when they promote *their* own interest or the interest of some institution to which *they* belong. Such a reaction, however, could not be dictated by his interests, for, though his interests might make him approve of an action which promoted his own interests or the interests of some institution to which he belonged, his own interests could not make him approve of other people's actions when they promoted their own interests or the interests of some institution to which they belonged. A uniform reaction, however, could be produced by his desires, for he might, conceivably have a desire that everyone should promote their own interests or the interests of institutions to which they belonged.

Perhaps, as was suggested earlier, one could rule out desires from affecting the ideal observer's reactions by the consideration that his desires might change, in which case he would approve of an action at one time, but disapprove of a similar action performed by a similar person under similar circumstances, performed at a later time, because his desires had changed in the meantime.

One could not for this reason rule out his reactions from being determined by his interests, however, because if his interests had changed, and he approved of an action which formerly he disapproved of for this reason, the action which now he approves of is *not* precisely similar to the action which he once disapproved, for the latter action interfered with his interests, but the former action either did not interfere with his interests, or positively promoted them. Perhaps, then, one could say that this would even allow the reactions of the ideal observer to be affected by his desires, for, if his desires change, then there is a difference between the action which formerly he disapproved of, but which he now approves of; formerly he did not want it to happen, or it prevented the realization of something else which he wanted, but now he does want it to happen or it actually promotes the realization of something else which he wants. Hence there is no reason why the ideal observer should not approve of whatever he wants, or whatever gets him what he wants, or, to avoid the difficulty that sometimes his wants might conflict, approve of whatever he wants to happen most, or whatever gets him what he wants most. Hence there is no reason why the desires of the ideal observer, as well as his interests, may not be allowed to affect his reactions of approval or disapproval. I am afraid the same argument would show that his likes might affect his attitudes without any infringement of the universalization principle.

If we try to exclude his likes and dislikes having any effect upon his reactions, this must be because we *disapprove* of a being who allows his feelings of approval to be determined by his desires or his interests, because we think that it must be *wrong* to approve of actions which are conducive to one's own interest, or to the interests of the community to which one belongs, or which bring about what one wants. It must be because we have decided that it is wrong for anybody to approve of actions which are conducive to the interests of the agent, whoever he may be, or further the interests of the agent's community, whatever that may be, or bring about the satisfaction of the agent's desires, whoever the agent may be. In this case, however, we are claiming to know, in advance of knowing whether an ideal observer would approve of these things or not, that certain ways of behaving *are* wrong, and what these ways of behaving are; that is, we are claiming to know, before having 'asked the ideal observer', that it is wrong to approve of what is to one's interest, or to the interest of the community to which one belongs, and so on. Hence we are ruling out these things on moral or material grounds, not on logical or formal ones. We are defining 'ideal observer' in such a way that it becomes an analytic proposition that the ideal observer approves of such-and-such things, and so defining 'ideal observer' in such a way as to refuse to call a being an 'ideal observer' if he will not give the answers to our questions which, without previously referring to him, are the ones we have decided we want to get.

Hence the only things that on logical grounds we are entitled to demand of our ideal observer, and which are such that we are justified in defining 'ideal observer' in such a manner that any being whose reactions do not have these characteristics is not properly to be called an ideal observer, are that his reactions to actions, people and situations shall not be based upon ignorance or mistake, and that they shall be uniform or consistent, in that if he reacts in one manner to one action, person or situation, he must react in a similar manner to some similar action, person or situation.

This brings us to the question: 'How do we know what the reactions of the ideal observer to actions, person and situations will be?' There is obviously no reason at all for supposing that there actually is a being who answers to the description of an ideal observer, and, if there were, it would be a mistake for an ideal observer theory to make the truth of moral judgments depend upon the actual existence of an ideal observer – this would entail the embarrassing consequence that all moral judgments were false, or, at any rate, that none of them were true. Hence, as we have seen, on an ideal observer theory, moral judgments must all be hypothetical; they state not how an ideal observer does react to actions, people and situations, but how an ideal observer would react to actions, people and situations, if there were an ideal observer. This leaves us with the awkward problem of explaining how one finds out how an ideal observer *would* react to actions, people and situations.

The position of the ideal observer, on an ideal observer theory, must play the same part in our body of moral knowledge as ideal gases, or bodies not acted upon by external forces play, in our knowledge of mechanics or of kinetics. Since there are no ideal gases, and no bodies not acted upon by external forces, one cannot find out how ideal gases, and bodies not acted upon by external forces, behave by examining them and seeing what is the way in which they behave in actual fact. One is supposed to know how ideal gases, or bodies not acted upon by external forces, behave because, in so far as gases approximate to being ideal or in so far as bodies approximate to being not acted upon by external forces, they tend to behave in the way in which it is then supposed that ideal gases, or bodies not acted upon by external forces, would behave, if there were any. An ideal gas or a body not acted upon by external forces is a limit to a series of actual gases or of actual bodies, such that the more closely the actual gas or actual body resembles the limiting case, the more closely does it behave in the way in which the ideal gas, or body not acted upon by external forces, is supposed to behave. In the same sort of way, perhaps, we know how an ideal observer would react to things because, in so far as we resemble an ideal observer, that is, have those characteristics which we attribute to an ideal observer by definition, our reactions tend to approximate to reactions of a certain kind. More specifically, if we react in a certain kind of way to an action which we believe possesses certain characteristics, this, so far as it goes, justifies us in thinking that an ideal observer would react in the same way to an action which actually had the characteristics which we believe this action possesses. We are justified in assuming that our reactions would be those of the ideal observer to the extent that they are based upon knowledge or true opinion about matters of fact, and that they would not be those of the ideal observer if they are based upon ignorance or false opinion about matters of fact. We are also justified in assuming that our reactions would not be those of the ideal observer if we react in one way to one action, but in a different way to a precisely similar action performed under similar circumstances.

This, however, takes us practically nowhere at all. It would be idle to pretend that there is a law connecting our knowledge of matters of fact with our moral reactions to things in such a manner that the way in which we react to things, whether we react by approving or disapproving of them, is determined wholly by our knowledge or belief about them, and by nothing else at all. It is a known fact that people who have the same knowledge or beliefs about matters of fact concerning the objects of their moral attitudes react in very different ways; their moral reactions, besides being determined by their beliefs about matters of fact, are also dependent upon the upbringing and environment to which they have been subjected, their temperament, inclinations, policies, and interests, and the mood in which they happen to be at the moment.

Indeed, it would be impossible to exclude, as a factor determining the reaction of a given observer to the things of which he feels approval or disapproval, the state of his nervous system, glandular activity, and brain, for it is known that this exercises a simply enormous influence not only upon our beliefs but upon our temperament, our desires, our interests, and our moods. It would not be going too far, in the light of the available medical and physiological knowledge, to say that the kind of person we are is determined, to a simply enormous extent, by the kind of brain and nervous system we have, and the way in which our glands are functioning; some, indeed, would say that the kind of person we are is determined entirely by such factors, and this view is certainly not without a fair degree of plausibility.

These facts, to my mind, raise insuperable difficulties for an ideal observer theory. If an observer's reaction to the actions we are morally interested in is not determined wholly by his knowledge or beliefs about them, but by his knowledge or beliefs about them in conjunction with other factors such as those which we have been considering, then, in order to be able to know what reaction a being who knows all the relevant facts about an action will have, we will have to specify what sort of upbringing he has had, what sort of society he has been brought up in, and his position in this society; the sort of person he himself is; his temperament, desires and interests; his moods; and the sort of brain and nervous system which he has, together with the state of his glandular activity. But what sort of upbringing are we to say the ideal observer, if there were one, must have had, and what shall we say must be his social background, and what sort of society shall we say he must have lived in, and what sort of person shall we say he must be, and what sort of brain and nervous system and glands shall we say he must have? Upon what we say depends the way in which he will react to the various kinds of action the morality of which we want to determine; but what principle can we use to say that a reaction may be determined by his upbringing, say, but not by his endocrine balance, or that it may be determined by whether or not he went to a public school, but not by whether or not he is good-tempered? There seems to me no way whatsoever of saying that one sort of thing may be allowed to influence the ideal observer's reaction but not another sort of thing.

The only way of excluding some things from having this influence is by saying that nothing shall be able to influence the ideal observer's reactions in such a way as to prevent him from coming to correct conclusions. This, however, is illegitimate, for one thing, because the ideal observer, as we have seen, does not himself need to come to any conclusions at all; we, on an ideal observer theory, come to conclusions about what the reactions of an ideal observer would be, if there were one, but the ideal observer himself need not come to any such conclusions. Even if he did, to say that his *conclusions* about what his reactions would be must not be affected by the state of his digestion or whether or not he went to a public school, though it is obviously true, is quite a different matter from saying that his reactions *themselves* must not be affected by the state of his digestion or by whether or not he went to a public school. To say that the ideal observer's reactions must not be influenced by anything which would cause him to come to an incorrect moral opinion is illegitimate for another thing, because as has already been said, we are not supposed to know what is right and what is wrong before we know how the ideal observer would react to them, and hence we cannot exclude anything from affecting his reactions on the grounds that they would influence his reactions for the worse, by making him disapprove of what was right or approve what is wrong.

If, as we must, we refuse to say that the ideal observer's reactions may not be influenced by anything which would lead him to a wrong conclusion, then I personally cannot see what possible criterion we could use for saying that some things may be allowed to influence his reactions, but not other things. It would, indeed, be quite absurd to demand of our ideal observer that he should have a brain and a nervous system of a certain sort, or that he should have had an upbringing of a certain kind. Yet if we do not specify some such factors as these, the reactions of the ideal observer will be left wholly undetermined, for it is simply not the case that the only thing which is necessary to produce a reaction of approval or disapproval to a class of actions in a rational and feeling being is knowledge of the nature of the actions whose morality is at issue. If we do not specify what the nature of the ideal observer in these respects shall be, it will be totally impossible to know how he will react to things; but, on the other hand, if we do attempt to specify what his nature shall be, there is no principle, which we may use to exclude some things from affecting his reaction but to allow other things to affect it, which does not presuppose that we already have answers to our moral questions, which answers, on an ideal observer theory, we are not supposed to have until we first know what his reactions will be. In any case, it seems very unlikely that there are some factors such as a person's education or his temperament or his brain's being in a certain state, which always affect one's moral judgment for ill, and other things of the same kind which always affect one's moral judgments for good. It entirely depends on the circumstances whether a man's education or his temperament affect his moral judgment for good or ill; a conservative education may predispose him to accept the moral judgments which most of his community already accept, and this will be a good thing if these are sound, but a bad thing if they are unsound. A good digestion may make him more lenient in his moral judgments, but, though this may be a good thing if the actions which he is called upon to judge are seldom evil, it may be a bad thing if the morals of his fellows are too lax, and are treated by other people in a too lenient way.

It may even be argued that the ideal observer cannot fulfil what was one of the conditions which, we agreed, on logical rather than on moral grounds, he ought to fulfil, that is, that if he reacted in one way to an action, he should react in a similar way to any similar action performed in similar circumstances by a similar person. If it were possible, which we have just seen that it is not, to specify the nature of the ideal observer in such a manner that his moral reactions to actions were wholly determined by his nature and could be predicted infallibly from a knowledge of it, it would follow that he always reacted in the same way to similar actions performed by similar people under similar circumstances. That he reacted to similar actions in a similar way, however, would be a fact at all only if there were psychological laws which allow his reaction wholly to be determined by certain factors of the kind we have specified. But it is just a *contingent* fact, if it is a fact at all, that there are psychological laws of the kind in question, which lay down that, given the nature of the ideal observer in other respects, his reactions are determined entirely by his knowledge of matters of fact, in such a way that, when he is in possession of the same information, the same reaction always follows. It is conceivable that psychological laws might not operate, in which case sometimes he would react to an action by approving of it, but, since, in the absence of psychological laws, his reactions are unpredictable, at other times he would react to an action about which he had precisely the same information by disapproving of it. If the ideal observer's reactions were like this, then, on an ideal observer theory, I think we would just have to say that one action could be right and another precisely similar action wrong; for all this would mean, on an ideal observer theory, would be that the ideal observer could approve of one action and disapprove of a precisely similar action, and we have just seen that he could do this. However, I think that, even if an ideal observer, defined in some such way as we have suggested, could approve of one action and disapprove of a similar action, we would still refuse to say that an action could be right, and another precisely similar action could be wrong. In other words, it is a logical feature of the way we use the words 'right' and 'wrong' that we are not prepared to admit that an action can be right and another precisely similar action wrong. It is a feature of the expression 'approved of by an ideal observer' that an action cannot be approved of by an ideal observer and another similar action not approved of by an ideal observer. Hence the logical features of 'right' and 'approved of by the ideal observer' and the logical features of 'wrong' and 'disapproved of by the ideal observer' are different, and it is in consequence impossible to say that the meanings of the words in each of the two pairs of expressions are identical.

There is yet another reason for rejecting an ideal observer theory. An ideal observer, in moral philosophy, plays a part which is somewhat similar to that played by the standard observer in the theory of perception.[1] One quite plausible way of defining 'is red' – as opposed to 'looks red' – is to say that something is red, even if it does not look red to me from here now, if it would look red to a standard observer. A standard observer is then defined as an observer with a standard eye and nervous system and brain, who is observing the object, whose colour is

---

[1] Since David Hume, though he sometimes seems to suppose that moral judgments are about people's sentiments, suggests ways in which we may make corrections to these, it would not be too far-fetched to regard him as holding some approximation to an ideal observer theory.

in question, from a certain standard distance – not from too close nor from too far away – under certain standard conditions – when white light is falling upon the object, and there is nothing but unpolluted air between the object and the standard observer's eye. The question is not whether this definition is correct – I am quite ready to admit that it is not – but that there is a certain reason for not minding about what colour an object turns out to be, given this definition of 'is coloured so-and-so', which is not a reason for not minding whether an action is right or wrong, given the definition of 'right' as meaning 'approved of by the ideal observer'. If it turns out that something one thought was one colour is, according to the definition just given, another colour, since it looks to the standard observer a different colour from the one we had always thought it was, one accepts the fact, perhaps with surprise, but without argument or regret. With right and wrong, however, it is quite a different matter. If we could discover what the reactions of an ideal observer to any given kind of action were, and it turned out that his reaction was wholly different from the one we expected it to be, and that this difference between his reaction and ours was not due to our ignorance of matters of fact or a mistake about matters of fact, I do not think we would just accept, without argument, that an action we had always thought wrong was right, or that an action we had always thought right was wrong. We would need personally to be convinced that any action, which it turned out he would approve of, but which we thought was wrong, was really right, and *vice versa*. We would want to know *why* the ideal observer approved of it, and to be satisfied that his reasons for approving of it were good ones. On a moral matter, such as the ones we have been discussing, we are not prepared to say that since a standard or ideal person would have the reaction of approval, that settles the matter; we would want to be shown that he was right to feel approval of the action in question. Hence we do not regard the reactions of a standard or ideal observer as settling our moral questions for us beyond the possibility of appeal; we do appeal, and, as it happens, appeal away from the other party, who in this case is the ideal observer, to our own moral judgment, and test the validity of the moral judgments which, on an ideal observer theory, would turn out to be true, by whether or not they would accord with our own. If an ideal observer theory were true, this would not be possible, and a knowledge of the nature of the reactions of the ideal observer would settle the matter. Since they do not settle the matter, the ideal observer theory must be rejected.

The ideal observer theory, nevertheless, is a much more plausible theory than any of the subjectivist theories discussed earlier. At least it does not allow an action to be right simply because it is approved of by some person or group of persons, even when the beliefs which cause them to feel this approval are mistaken. Hence it does draw attention to the fact that any moral judgment founded upon ignorance of, or mistake about, matters of fact must be regarded as inadequately based, even if it turns out by accident to be a true one in fact. The ideal observer theory, indeed, is not a subjectivist theory at all. Even though it identifies being right and being wrong with the manner in which some being or other reacts to the thing which is right or wrong, it does not make being right or wrong dependent on the existence of this person and the existence of his feelings. Moral judgments, on an ideal observer theory, are hypothetical judgments about the way in which an ideal observer would feel about an action, if there were an ideal observer, and hence they may be true, even if there is not an ideal observer to have these feelings. The truth of a moral judgment, too, is, on an ideal observer theory, quite independent of who it is who makes the judgment. The sentence 'An ideal observer would approve of breaking promises which have been extracted from one by means of force', if it expresses a true proposition, will express a true proposition whoever it is who uses this sentence and, if it expresses a false proposition, will express a false proposition whoever uses it. Hence if one person says that a thing is right, and a different person says that the same thing is wrong, they will be contradicting one another, whoever the people are who are making these at least apparently contradictory moral judgments.

If we assume the existence of unchanging psychological laws, which are such that if the ideal observer is of such-and-such a nature he will always approve of any set of actions if he has the same information about all of them, it will also follow that the truth of our moral judgments, on an ideal observer theory, will not depend upon the date at which the judgments are made. More accurately, if the sentence 'An ideal observer would approve of this' expresses a true judgment at one time, then it will express a true judgment at any other time, and if it expresses a false judgment at any one time, it will express a false judgment at any other time. Thus it will not be possible, on an ideal observer theory, for us to say such things as, 'The sinking of the French fleet in Oran harbour was quite justified, though, when at one time I said that it was unjustified, what I said was quite correct.' (It will be remembered that it was a difficulty with theories which identified right and wrong with the approval and disapproval of actual people that they all did allow that this *was* a perfectly permissible way in which to express ourselves.)

That this is impossible, however, depends upon the reactions of the ideal observer continuing to be governed by psychological laws, and by the assumption that these psychological laws cannot change. That psychological laws about the way in which observers react to actions do not change is, if it is a fact at all, a contingent fact, whereas the fact that, if we judge an action to be wrong, we must logically concede that our judgment was mistaken when we later judge that it was right, is a necessary truth. It is logically impossible for it to be true that we were right when we said that an action was wrong, if we are right when we now say that it was right. And, as we have seen, it is impossible for one action to be right and other precisely similar but numerically different actions performed by similar people under similar circumstances wrong, whereas, on an ideal observer theory, this is not impossible, but only impossible so long as the reactions of the ideal observer continue to be governed by unchanging psychological laws. That they are so governed, if it is a fact at all, is merely a contingent fact. Hence the expression 'approved of by the ideal observer' does not function quite like the word 'right', nor does the expression 'disapproved of by the ideal observer' function quite like the word 'wrong'. An ideal observer theory, therefore, must be rejected, in spite of the not inconsiderable merits we have seen it to possess.

If an ideal observer theory is true, moral judgments will be *synthetic*, for, as we have seen, it is important not to define the ideal observer in such a way that it becomes an analytic rather than a synthetic proposition that he approves of one thing rather than another. Moral judgments will be *contingent*, if the theory is true, rather than necessary. Their truth will be established *empirically*; we will argue that since human beings' reactions to actions are such-and-such in so far as they approximate to being ideal observers, the ideal observer's reaction will be such-and-such. Our premises that human beings reactions approximate to being such-and-such, is established by observation, and our conclusion, that the ideal observer's reaction would be such-and-such, is reached by a sort of inductive argument. It is reached by an argument to the effect that because the reactions of Tom, Dick and Harry approximate to being of a certain sort as Tom, Dick and Harry approximate to being like ideal observers, this tendency would be continued, or rather completed, in the case of an ideal observer, if there were one. Since an inductive argument is used to establish moral conclusions on an ideal observer theory, it will be committed to holding that moral judgments are *not basic propositions*. Moral concepts have to be *empirical concepts*, in the sense in which our concept of a unicorn or a centaur are empirical concepts; though we cannot ostensively define the words 'unicorn' or 'centaur' for there are no such things, we can define these words in terms of other words which can be ostensively defined. The concept of an ideal observer is defined in terms of the concepts of knowledge and approval, which are empirical concepts, together with certain syncategorematic or logical concepts, such as 'all' and 'if' and 'not'; it is the concept of a being, who would, *if* he existed, approve of such a thing, *since* he knows every matter of fact, and there are *not* matters of fact he does *not* know.

CHAPTER VIII

MORAL SENSE THEORIES; THE UNIVERSALIZATION PRINCIPLE

According to moral sense theories,[1] we know what actions are right and what actions are wrong because we are in possession of a moral sense. Just as it is the sense of sight which tells us that grass is green and that oranges are round, and the sense of touch that tells us that glass is smooth and sandpaper rough, so it is the moral sense which tells us that promise-breaking is wrong and truth-telling right.

This would appear at first sight to mean that we do not infer what is right and what is wrong, but that moral judgments are a species of basic proposition, and known to be true, when they are known to be true, without inference. It *seems* that we do not infer that grass is green, we see that it is, and we do not infer that sandpaper is rough, we feel that it is. Similarly, if a moral sense theory is true, it would appear that we do not infer that promise-breaking is wrong and truth-telling right, we perceive, by means of our moral sense, that this is so.

The theory that we know what actions are right and what actions are wrong because we have a moral sense is sometimes confused with intuitionism. This is, presumably, because both according to the moral sense theory and according to intuitionism moral judgments are known to be true without *inference*. However, according to intuitionism, moral judgments are known *a priori*; our reason gives us insight into the necessity of the connection between being a case of promise-breaking and being wrong, or into the necessity of the connection between being a case of truth-telling and being right, and our insight into this necessity is not based upon observation, and so not based upon sense-experience

[1] Moral sense theories are alleged to have been held by Shaftesbury, Hutcheson and Hume, but these philosophers do not appear always clearly to have distinguished between a moral sense theory and a moral sentiment theory, and all they clearly agreed on was that our knowledge of morality in *not* arrived at by reason. See Lord Shaftesbury, *An Enquiry Concerning Virtue, or Merit;* Francis Hutcheson, *Illustrations upon the Moral Sense;* and David Hume, *A Treatise of Human Nature*, Vol. III. See also D. Daiches Raphael, *The Moral Sense* (Oxford University Press, 1947).

of any kind. On a moral sense theory, however, it is just an empirical fact that promise-breaking is wrong and truth-telling is right, just as it is an empirical fact that grass is green and sandpaper rough. Our moral sense enables us to know empirically by observation that promise-breaking in fact has the property of being wrong, and that truth-telling in fact has the property of being right, but these actions might well not have had these properties, in which case our moral sense, if it were reliable, would inform us that they did not have them. Hence, on a moral sense theory, we do not have any rational insight into the necessity of a connection between being a case of promise-breaking and being wrong. We are aware, by means of our moral sense, of the property of wrongness which promise-breaking in fact has, and, because we are aware of its having this property, we are able to see, by direct confrontation with experience, that propositions such as that promise-breaking is wrong are true.

It has often been objected to moral sense theories that no one has ever succeeded in locating any sense organ which stands in the relation to our awareness of right and wrong that the eye stands in to our sense of sight, or the ear to our sense of hearing, or the surface of our bodies to the sense of touch. I am not absolutely convinced that there must be a sense-organ where there is a sense, or that it is impossible to have a sense without a sense organ. Though, in man, seeing is impossible without eyes, that it is so impossible is just an empirical fact, which we have discovered from experience of a concomitant variation between the state of our eyes and the state of what we see (or the state of our seeing what we see) but, so far as I can tell, though the view is unfashionable, there could be beings, even if there are not, who perceived even though they did not have bodies, and so did not have eyes either. Even ordinary human beings can have hallucinations of seeing, without their eyes being affected in any way.

However, even if we leave aside the question of whether there is or is not a moral sense organ, there do seem to be ways in which our awareness of right and wrong differs markedly from our perception by means of the other senses. In order to be aware of what an object looks like or of how it feels, our body has to be in a certain spatial relation with the object in question. For us to be aware of anything by touch, part of the surface of our body has to be in physical contact with the thing we are aware of, and for us to be aware of anything by sight, we have to be situated so that the object is neither too close to us nor too distant from us, and so that there is no opaque object between us and the thing we are seeing. Hence exploration of an object by touch or by sight involves altering the position of our bodies in familiar ways, such as getting closer to it, or rubbing our hands over it.

There does not seem to be anything analogous to this where our moral sense is concerned. If we are in doubt about whether some action is right or wrong, there is no physical movement which we can perform which will enable us to resolve our doubt. Getting close to it – or, rather, to the situation where it occurs – does not help, nor does coming into direct physical contact with it. In fact, if we are in doubt about whether an action is right or wrong, this is likely to be after it has happened, and so there can be no question of our examining it more closely, for it is a past event, and past events cannot be examined. Perhaps had we observed it more closely at the time at which it happened we might have been able to notice more about it, and, if we had noticed more about it, we might have had more information on which to base a judgment concerning its rectitude; but acquiring, by more acute observation, more information about the action to be morally assessed is not the same thing as perceiving, by more acute observation, whether it is really right or not. It seems, indeed, to be absurd to say that, had we been attending more closely, we might have noticed whether an action was right or not, though it is not absurd to say that, had we been attending more closely, we might have noticed whether Smith, who hit Jones with a poker, had been previously provoked by Jones, or whether Robinson, who was hit in the rear while executing a right turn in his car, had signalled his intention of doing so. Indeed, it really seems to make no difference at all, when we are assessing whether actions are right or wrong, how remote in space or time the action we are assessing is. What matters is the amount of information we have about it, and, given the same amount of information, it is just as easy or just as difficult to assess the rightness of an action performed in the vicinity as it is to assess the rightness of an action performed many thousands of miles away; given the same information, it is just as easy to assess the rightness of an action performed a moment or two ago as to assess the rightness of an action performed many years before the birth of Christ.

It might even be argued, with considerable plausibility, that when we are assessing the rightness or wrongness of an action, the most relevant fact about the action we assess is what the agent intended to happen; for example, that an unsuccessful attempt to kill somebody is just as wrong as a successful attempt, since the agents' intentions in the two cases were the same, and it was just a matter of luck that the second intention was fulfilled but the first was not. But, it may be continued, we are never aware of other people's intentions at all, but infer what people intend from what we see happening to their bodies, or from what we hear them say. In the first case what we perceive is their bodies, not their intentions, and in the second case what we perceive are noises emanating from their lips or marks on paper which they make with their hands, not the intentions themselves of which these physical movements or these symbols give us evidence. If, however, we are never directly aware of, or never perceive, other people's intentions, but moral judgments about rightness and wrongness are judgments about their intentions, then it seems to follow that we can never be aware of the rightness or wrongness of these intentions because we perceive this rightness or wrongness, for we could scarcely perceive this rightness or wrongness if we were not aware of the intentions themselves.

Even if, as many modern philosophers do, one says that there are no such things as hidden mental events (such as intentions have often been supposed to be) of which overt bodily movements are the outward sign, but that statements about people's intentions are hypothetical statements about what they would have done, if they had been able to foresee the consequences of their action, a similar difficulty remains. If there is no actual event, which consists of someone's intending something to come about, but merely the hypothetical fact that the agent would have done something if certain circumstances were realised which in fact were not realised, then there simply is nothing actual to perceive, and if there is nothing actual to perceive, it is difficult to see how we can perceive whether intentions possess the property of being right or the property of being wrong.

In addition to the difficulties I have already mentioned, there are a number of objections to the theory that we perceive by a moral sense what actions are right and what actions are wrong, which objections seem to me to be absolutely conclusive. Considering them draws attention to a number of important differences between rightness and wrongness on the one hand, and sensible predicates such as green or rough on the other.

In the first place, it seems fairly clear that right and wrong are resultant properties, if we may be allowed to call them properties at all, while greenness and roughness are not. When we say that an action is right or that it is wrong, we say this in virtue of other information which we possess about the action. We say that the agent killed his stepmother deliberately and without provocation, and so that what he did was wrong, or that someone helped a complete stranger who was in need, despite the fact that he incurred considerable inconvenience by doing so, and so that what he did was right. We do not, however, say that this cricket ball is round, hard, and made of leather and so it is red, or that this orange is a citrus fruit with an acid taste, and so it is, roughly, round. We see straight off that the cricket ball is red or that the orange is round; we do not say that the orange must be round in virtue of other properties which it possesses or that the cricket ball must be red in virtue of other properties which it possesses.

Hence, where the cricket ball or the orange is concerned, if it turns out that we are very much mistaken about them in other respects, we still do not need to withdraw our judgments that the one was red and the other round. Even if we were mistaken in thinking that the thing we judged to be red was a cricket ball, or that the thing we judged to be round was an orange, we still do not need to withdraw our judgment that the first thing we saw, whatever else it was, was certainly red at least, and that the second thing we saw, whatever it was, was certainly round at least. Since we did not pronounce the cricket ball to be red and the orange to be round in virtue of any other of the properties of these things, there is no need to modify our pronouncements when we find we are mistaken, even quite radically mistaken, about the nature of the objects, about which we make these perceptual judgments, in other respects. However, where right and wrong are concerned, we do need to withdraw, or regard as unfounded, any judgment we make when it turns out that we are radically mistaken about the facts upon which we based our judgment. If it turns out that Smith did not do what he did intentionally, or that Jones's motives were not what we supposed, then we feel we ought to revise our unfavourable judgments upon Smith's and Jones's actions.

It is, furthermore, possible to say that the *only* thing we know about this thing, which we can see but imperfectly, is that it is round, and that the only thing we know about this other thing, which we also see but imperfectly, is that it is red. Where judgments about the rightness or wrongness of actions are concerned, however, this is not possible. I cannot say I know nothing whatsoever about what Smith did at three o'clock yesterday except that, whatever it was, it was wrong; if I know nothing whatsoever about Smith's action, then I have no business to be making moral judgments about it, for I lack the information upon which any such judgments ought to be based. Perceptual judgments, however, are not based upon any information, and hence it is possible to make them quite correctly even in the absence of any other information at all about the nature of the things about which they are made.

Perhaps the most important difference between right and wrong and sensible predicates such as red, rough or round, however, is that right and wrong are universalizable, whereas red, rough and round are not. By saying that a predicate is universalizable, I mean that if one thing has it, then any other similar thing must also have it. There are two possible interpretations of this statement, one of which is trivial, and is true of all predicates without exception, the other of which is not trivial, and which applies only to some predicates, among which predicates are right and wrong. The trivial interpretation is this: if a thing has a predicate, then any precisely similar thing must also have this predicate. This proposition is trivial and analytic, because, if the second thing did not have the predicate which the first thing has, the second thing would not be precisely similar to the first thing. The interpretation which is not trivial is that, if a thing has a predicate, then any other thing which is precisely similar to it in all respects *except* that it also has this predicate, must *also* be similar to it in that it, too, has this predicate.[1]

The first interpretation, since it is true of everything, must be true of sensible predicates such as red, rough or round. If something is red, then anything else which is similar to this thing in all respects, including redness, must also be red; and the same is true of rough and round. The second interpretation is not true of all predicates, and is not true of sensible predicates, though it is true of

---

[1] This distinction appears to be neglected by Professor R. M. Hare, who holds the universalization principle in its trivial form. See *Freedom and Reason* (Oxford University Press, 1963), pp. 10 f.

right and wrong. If a lump of plasticine is red, then any other lump of plasticine which is similar to this lump of plasticine in all respects save redness does not also have to be similar to it in being red too. That the one lump of plasticine is red and the other lump some other colour may be the only difference between them. Though the *only* difference between two lumps of plasticine may be that one is red and the other some other colour, it cannot be that the *only* difference between one action and another is that the one action is right while the other is not. The same is true of wrong and, I think, all other ethical predicates.

The reason for this difference between predicates like right and wrong and predicates like red, rough and round is almost certainly connected with the fact that right and wrong are what have been called (by Sir David Ross)[1] resultant predicates, whereas red, rough and round are not. We say that an action is right because of other things we know about this action, whereas we do not say that something is red because of other things we know about it; we see that it is red straight off, and can know that it is red, even though this is the only thing about it which we know. Because right and wrong are resultant predicates, if being right results from a set of factual properties of the right action, then being right must also result from the same set of factual properties, even when they are possessed by a numerically different action; hence, if one action is right, any other action possessing the same factual properties must also be right. To put the matter in another way, we attribute rightness to an action in virtue of the other things which we believe about it; hence to be consistent we must make the same attribution of rightness whenever we have the same set of beliefs about another action not identical with the first.

Moral predicates are not the only predicates which are universalizable. If an argument is valid, then any other argument which is precisely similar to the first argument in all respects save validity, must also resemble the first argument in being valid. If anything is beautiful, then any other thing which precisely resembles the first thing in all respects save beauty, must also resemble the first thing in being beautiful.

It seems to follow from the fact that the universalization principle[2] applies to right and wrong that there are some true universal

---

[1] In *The Foundations of Ethics* (O.U.P., 1938), p. 168.

[2] The universalization principle must not be confused with Kant's first formulation of the categorical imperative: 'Act only according to that maxim by

propositions about right and wrong. From the fact that, if an action is right, any other action resembling this action in all respects save rightness must also resemble this action in being right, it logically follows that there is some set of properties such that whatever action possesses these properties, it must be right. That any action which possesses all the predicates, save rightness, which this right action possesses, must be right, is a universal proposition to the effect that all actions of a certain kind are right. It is true that it is not a very useful universal proposition. Since it is very likely the case that there is no other action which resembles this action in *all* respects, it is very likely the case that this action is the only instance of the universal rule that every action possessing all the properties which this right action possesses is right. Nevertheless, it does follow that there are true universal propositions about what actions are right, even if it does not follow that there are any useful true universal propositions about what is right, or any universal propositions which can give us guidance in other cases. To find a useful universal proposition to the effect that all actions of a certain kind are right, one must eliminate the properties of this right action which are irrelevant to its being right. For example, the colour of the hair of the man who performed the action will probably, though not necessarily, be irrelevant to the question whether what he did was right or wrong. If one does not eliminate irrelevant characteristics from one's generalization, this does not affect the *truth* of the generalization. If it is true that all promise-breaking is wrong, then it is true that all promise-breaking by red-headed men is wrong, and true even if being performed by a red-headed man has no tendency whatsoever to make an action wrong. But though including irrelevant characteristics in our moral generalization does not affect its truth, it does affect its usefulness, and the more irrelevant characteristics we can eliminate from our characterization of the class of actions which are being said to be wrong, and the more inspecific this class in consequence becomes, the more actions it will apply to, and so the more useful it will be.

Though a true moral generalization cannot *have exceptions* – for if some exceptional cases of promise-breaking are right, it cannot

---

which you can at the same time will that it should become a universal law.' It may be that this entails the universalization principle, but it is not entailed by it.

See Immanuel Kant, *Foundations of the Metaphysics of Morals*, trans. by Lewis White Beck (Bobbs-Merril, 1959).

be the case that all promise-breaking is wrong – there is no reason why it should not be *exceptive*, that is to say, there is no reason why the class of actions which is being said to be right or wrong should not be defined as 'all things which are so-and-so except such-and-suches'; for example, there is no reason why our generalization should not say some such thing as that all promise-breaking, except the breaking of promises extracted by means of force, is wrong. The converse of the process of eliminating irrelevant characteristics from the definition of the class of actions which are said to be right or wrong, which process makes our generalisation less specific and more useful, is the process of adding characteristics when a generalization to the effect that all of a certain class of actions are right is found to be so wide as to cover cases of actions which are not right. When this happens, the class of actions said to be right must be made more, not less specific, and more specific in such a way as to eliminate from the class of actions which are said to be right those actions which are in fact not right.

Once we have (*a*) eliminated from our characterization of classes of action which are said to be right all properties of the action which are irrelevant to its rightness, and once we have (*b*) made our characterization of classes of action which are said to be right (or wrong) more specific when this is necessary to eliminate from the class of actions which are being said to be right some actions which are not right, or to eliminate from the class of actions which are being said to be wrong some actions which are not wrong, the question arises: 'Will we be left with just one class of actions which are wrong, which class of actions includes all the wrong actions that there are, or will there be several different classes of actions, all of which are wrong?' I personally have a little leaning to the view that there will in the last resort turn out to be only one class of actions which are right, and only one class of actions which are wrong; that is to say, I am inclined to think that there is some characteristic or combination of characteristics which are common and peculiar to right actions, that is, some characteristic or combination of characteristics which all right actions possess and only right actions possess. If we liken the relationship, between being right and the characteristics which *make* an action right, to the relationship between a cause and its effect, I have some tendency to say both that whenever the effect is the same, the cause must be the same, and also that whenever a set of actions are similar in that they are all right, this must be for some reason which is the same in all cases. If this were so, of course, it would follow that there was some one characteristic or combination of characteristics which made actions which possessed it right and which was the only characteristic or combination of characteristics which made actions which possessed it right, but I do not myself know how much weight to attach to this argument.

If I am right about this – and I put it forward only very tentatively – it may be possible that philosophers who have thought that an action may be right for many different reasons have thought this because they confused characteristics which are immediately relevant to an action's rightness with characteristics which are only mediately relevant to an action's rightness. Let us suppose, purely for the sake of argument, that utilitarianism is true. If utilitarianism is true, there will be only one property of actions which is immediately relevant to the question whether they are right or wrong. They will be right if the agent could not have brought about more good by doing some other action; otherwise they will be wrong. But though being productive of good will, if utilitarianism is true, be the only property of actions which is immediately relevant to the question whether they are right or wrong, there will be many properties of actions which are mediately relevant to this. Whether an action is a case of promise-keeping or debt paying or truth-telling can be mediately relevant to whether an action is right or wrong, for promise-keeping, debt-paying and truth-telling usually do tend to bring about the maximum amount of good. Hence those philosophers who think that there is no characteristic or set of characteristics common to all right actions, but that some right actions are right for one reason and others for another reason, may well think this because they have failed to distinguish between characteristics which are immediately and those which are only mediately relevant to whether an action is right or wrong.

It should scarcely need pointing out that nothing whatsoever follows from the universalization principle about what actions or what kinds of action are right and wrong. The principle that right and wrong are universalizable is itself not a moral principle, but a second order principle, which implies that all moral judgments which are not themselves universal must be capable of being derived from moral judgments which are universal. No particular first order moral judgment can be deduced from it Indeed, the universalization principle applies indifferently to correct and incorrect attributions of rightness and wrongness. It does not matter whether I say truly that Smith was wrong to break his promise, or say falsely that Smith was right to break his promise. I am in either event infringing the universalization principle if, in the first case, I refuse to say that some other precisely similar action performed by a similar person under similar circumstances was wrong, or in the second case that some precisely similar action performed by a similar person under similar circumstances was right. In other words, the universalization principle is a principle more concerned with consistency than it is with truth. It holds that I am being in some sense or other inconsistent if I say that one action is right, but that a precisely similar action performed by a precisely similar person under precisely similar circumstances is wrong; but it is perfectly possible for me to be *consistent* without the moral judgments I make being in fact true.

Philosophers have objected to the universalization principle on many grounds, most of which rest upon confusion or misunderstanding. It is often said that no two actions ever could be or are precisely similar. The question whether two actions ever logically could be precisely similar is a difficult question, involving a consideration of the doctrine known as the identity of indiscernibles, which states that if of two things each has every attribute possessed by the other, these things are not two things, but are numerically identical with one another. Put in another way, it states, that if two things are not numerically identical, there must be at least one way in which they differ from one another. A discussion of this question, which would have to be very long and very complicated, I shall omit. It is nevertheless fairly obvious that no two actions ever do have all their attributes in common, that no two actions ever are *precisely* similar. The attributes of an action are very large, and possibly infinite, in number. It is, for example, an attribute of an action of promise-keeping that the man who performed it was bald, or that he had hair, or that he had become bald recently, or that he had been bald for a long time, or that he had 20,109 hairs on his head. If we take all these attributes into consideration, it seems quite certain that no two actions ever would have all their attributes in common.

The universalization principle, however, is multiply hypothetical; it does not state that any two actions ever are precisely similar, but that if they are, then, if one of them is right, the other must be right also. Even if no two actions are ever precisely similar, then there is still this difference between predicates like right and wrong and predicates like red and round. It is not true that, if two things are precisely similar in all respects save colour, then, if one of them is red, the other must also be red, or that, if two things are precisely similar in all respects save shape, then, if one of them is round, then the other must be round also. Hence, even if no two actions ever are precisely similar, it is still the case that there is this important difference between right and wrong and certain other predicates, sensible predicates for example. It is true that, as has already been said, the universalization principle is not *necessarily* of any practical use. It will not be of any practical use unless the characteristics of an action which make us say that it is right or wrong are sufficiently few in number to give rise to a principle, of the form that all actions which have these characteristics are wrong, which applies to a fairly large number of cases over and above this one. That this is so will not follow from the universalization principle itself, but only from the universalization principle together with the statement, which commends itself to common sense, that almost all the characteristics of an action are entirely irrelevant to the question whether it is right or wrong.

Philosophers have also objected to the universalization principle[1] on the grounds that whereas there are certain kinds of right act the rightness of which is universalizable, there are also certain other kinds of right act the rightness of which is not universalizable.[2] If I do right to keep my promise, then any other similar person keeping a similar promise under similar circumstances must also do right, but if I sleep with my wife or serve my country, I am acting rightly, it does not follow that anyone else – a Turk, for example – who sleeps with my wife or serves my country is acting rightly.

This objection, however, rests upon a mistake. The Englishman who fights for Germany is not performing an action which is

[1] Some of the following objections, or something approximating to them, may be found in 'What Morality is Not', by Alasdair MacIntyre, *Philosophy* Vol. XXXII, October 1957.

[2] See E. A. Gellner, 'Ethics and Logic', *Aristotelian Society Proceedings* Vol. LV, 1954–5.

G

similar to the action of the German who fights for Germany, so there is no exception to the universalization principle involved in saying that the former is doing what is wrong, but that the latter is doing what is right. The German is fighting for his country, but the Englishman is fighting for someone else's country. The universalization principle entails not that if Herr Schmidt is right to fight for Germany, anyone else who fights for Germany is acting rightly, but some such thing as that, if Herr Schmidt is right to fight for Germany, which is his country, then Mr Smith is right to fight for England, which is *his* country. And the actions of both are similar in that each is fighting for the country to which *he* belongs.[1]

It is sometimes objected to the universalization principle that it puts too high a premium on action done from principle, as opposed to impulsive action. Smith, who has certain moral principles such as that it is always right to pay one's debts, keep one's promises and tell the truth, and sticks to these principles, is not necessarily a better person than Jones, who has no systematic set of principles at all, but often performs acts of kindness and even heroism on impulse. This criticism of the universalization principle rests upon a mistake. Since, as I have already said, it says nothing at all about what kinds of action are in fact right and what kinds of action are in fact wrong, it does not say that actions done on principle are right, and impulsive actions are wrong, or even that actions done on principle are better than impulsive actions. What it does say is simply that if this action, done on principle, is right, then any other similar action done by a similar man on a similar principle in similar circumstances must also be right, and that if this impulsive action is right, then any similar impulsive action performed by a similar man under similar circumstances must also be right. It does not say whether men who act on principle are better or worse than impulsive men, simply that if a man who acts on principle is a good man, then any other similar men who act on similar principles must also be good men, and that if a man who habitually performs acts of kindness upon impulse is a good man, then any other similar man who performs similar acts of kindness in similar circumstances must also be a good man. It is not, in fact, a principle which recommends people to perform *acts* on principle, so much as a principle which recom-

[1] See R. M. Hare, 'Universalisability', *Aristotelian Society Proceedings* Vol. LV, 1954–5.

mends a certain kind of consistency in one's *judgments* about actions.

It is sometimes supposed that the universalization principle implies that whenever someone makes a moral judgment, he must *have in mind* some principle, to the effect that all actions of a certain kind, of which the action he is judging to be right is an instance, are right. Since this is obviously not always the case, the universalization principle is rejected. The universalization principle, however, does not imply that one must know what the principle is from which one's moral judgment that this action is right or that this action is wrong would follow. All it implies is that there must be some universal principle, from which one's particular judgments about individual actions would follow, not that one must necessarily or easily be able to elicit it. Hence even judgments such as 'Smith did wrong to break his promise' do not, according to the universalization principle, imply that all acts of promise-breaking are wrong. The universalization principle does imply that there is some set of characteristics, which this act of promise-breaking has, which is such that any action which was an instance of this set would be wrong. It does not, however, imply that we have necessarily *named* this set of characteristics when we describe the action which we say is wrong as, say, one of promise-breaking.

Does, however, my saying that Smith was wrong to stay at home *because* he had promised to go out with Jones, imply that whenever someone breaks a promise, he is acting wrongly. Though it has been held that it does, I think this is a mistake. If I say that I was late because my watch was slow, this does not imply that I am always late when my watch is slow. It does not imply, that is to say, that my watch's being slow is a sufficient condition of my being late. What it does imply is that, if all the other circumstances attending my lateness had been the same, but my watch had not been slow, I would not have been late. That is, it implies that my watch's being slow is a sufficient condition of my lateness, *all other things remaining the same*. Similarly the statement that Smith was wrong to stay at home because he had promised to go out with Jones does not imply that whenever anyone has made a promise, or a promise to a friend, or a promise to a friend to go out with him, he is acting wrongly if he breaks it. It simply implies that, if all other facts attending Smith's staying at home remained the same, he would not have been acting wrongly had he not promised to go out with Jones. Hence it is not being implied that the fact that Smith is breaking his promise to Jones is a sufficient condition of Smith's action being wrong, simply that it is a sufficient condition of Smith's action being wrong if all the other facts about it remain the same.

It is sometimes objected to the universalization principle that there are many actions where it is not at all the case that, if it is right for one person to do something, anyone else who does some action, in the same situation, which is different from this action, is acting wrongly. To take an undeservedly celebrated example from Sartre, during the Second World War a man is faced with a choice between staying at home with his widowed mother and joining the French resistance movement. He decides to join the resistance movement, and in doing so he is acting rightly, but, it is alleged, it does not follow that anyone else who, in the same situation stays at home with his widowed mother is acting wrongly. In general, it is argued that the universalization principle would demand too much uniformity of mankind, and would make it seem as if there were only one right and proper way of behaving in any situation, whereas there are in fact all sorts of different ways of meeting a situation, and from the fact that one man rightly adopts one of them, it does not follow that other people, who choose some action which is different, are acting wrongly.

This objection rests upon a gross logical confusion. The universalization principle states that, if an action is right, then any other action similar to that action in all other respects must also be right. It does not state that, if an action is right, then any action which is dissimilar from it must be *wrong*. To suppose that the latter proposition followed from the former would be a case of the fallacy of denying the antecedent. The statement that if an action is right then any other action similar to it must be right implies that any action which is not right must be *dissimilar* from the first action in some respect, but it does not imply that any action which is dissimilar from the first action in some respect must be wrong. It is indeed quite obvious that actions may be very dissimilar and yet all be right. The universalization principle does not even imply that if a man performs a right action in a certain situation, then anyone else doing something different in a precisely similar situation must be acting wrongly. Hence from the fact that the man, in the above example, who forsook his mother and joined the resistance movement was acting rightly, it does not follow from the universalization principle that he would not also have been acting rightly had he not joined the resistance, but stayed with his mother instead. In fact, there are many situations in which there are two or more alternative ways of acting, each one of which would have been right.

This, of course, implies that something I do could be right, without its following that if I omit this right action I am necessarily acting wrongly. If this conclusion sounds a little paradoxical, this may be because the word 'right' is commonly used ambiguously. Sometimes it is used with the implication that omitting to do what is right would be wrong, but at other times it is not. Sometimes 'right' means something like 'all right' or 'permissible' or 'not wrong', and omitting the permissible is not necessarily wrong. At other times it means something more like 'obligatory' or '*the* right thing to do' or 'that which it would be wrong to omit', Omitting the obligatory *is* necessarily wrong. One must infer from the context in which of these two senses the word 'right' is being used.

It is also sometimes suggested that acts of supererogation are ones over which the universalization principle breaks down. For example, when Captain Oates walked out into the snow to certain death in order that his colleagues might have a better chance of survival he was not acting upon any rule which demanded the action he performed. He was performing *more* than was demanded by any moral rule, and hence it is argued, because his action is not demanded by a universal rule, the rightness of his action is not universalizable. Again, I suspect that the philosophers who make this objection to the universalization principle are confusing the assertion that, if Captain Oates's action was right, any person who performed a similar action to it in similar circumstances to those which obtained in Captain Oates's case, must also be performing a right action, which assertion is implied by the universalization principle, with the assertion that if Captain Oates's action was right, anyone else who, in similar circumstances, does not perform a similar action must be acting *wrongly*, which latter assertion is *not* implied by the universalization principle. And it certainly does not follow from the universalization principle that if Captain Oates was right to walk out, he would have been acting wrongly if he had not walked out.

I am personally not sure how acts of supererogation are correctly to be described. It may be that Captain Oates, though he was acting rightly, was not doing his duty, but going beyond it. It may well be, too, that, though an act of supererogation is especially praiseworthy, it is not the case that one would be acting wrongly if one omitted it. But however acts of supererogation, as Captain Oates's is supposed to be, are defined, and whatever moral epithets are correctly applicable to them, it remains true that if a moral epithet is applicable to one act of supererogation, the same moral epithet must be applicable to any otherwise similar act of supererogation performed by a similar person under similar circumstances.

The question arises: How do we know that the universalization principle is true? How do we know that, if an action is right (or good, or praiseworthy, or one which ought to be done) then any other otherwise similar action performed by a similar person under similar circumstances must also be right (or good, praiseworthy, or one which ought to be done)? We have already seen that the universalization principle is not true for the reason that we would not say that any action which was wrong was *not* similar to an action which was right, on the grounds that one was right and the other was wrong; that is to say, the universalization principle is not analytically true in virtue of the meaning of 'precisely similar'. We were careful to say that 'precisely similar' meant 'precisely similar in respects other than being right'. Presumably, then, the universalization principle is true because of what is meant by 'right' (or whatever other word we claim the universalization principle applies to). Why this should be so is a question to which we must return in a later chapter.[1]

If the moral sense theory is true, moral judgments will be *contingent*, and so the theory is inadequate to the extent that it makes no attempt to explain their apparent necessity. Moral judgments will also be synthetic, for there is no need of anything analogous to perception in order to establish analytic propositions. They will also be established empirically, as perceptual judgments are established empirically.

I said at the beginning of this chapter that it seemed as if

---

[1] Chapter XIV. A discussion on universalization will be found in *Empiricism and Ethics*, by D. H. Monro (C.U.P., 1967).

moral judgments, if a moral sense theory were true, would have to be basic, for it seemed as if judgments to the effect that grass was green, when we could see the grass, were basic, but many philosophers – most philosophers until recently – would dispute this, and, I think, rightly. What we know without inference is that grass *looks* green to me personally from where I am now. If we assert that it *is* green, we are implying that it will look green to people other then myself, and to me from other places and at other times, and that it will do these things is something we infer from knowledge, obtained by experience in the past, that this, which looks green under these conditions, will continue to look green under other conditions.

It might be possible for a moral sense theorist to hold that moral judgments were not basic if he argued that there were certain judgments which were related to the judgment that some action was morally wrong, in the same sort of way that judgments about what colour a thing looks is related to judgments about what colour it is. Perhaps there is some judgment, say the judgment that some action *feels* right, which is related to the judgment that it is right in the way in which that something looks green is related to the judgment that it is green, and perhaps judgments to the effect that actions feel right are basic and judgments that they are right are inferred from them.

Though such a view is possible, I do not think it very plausible. It is not *too* gross an oversimplification to say that there are two senses of words like 'looks' and 'feels'.[1] In one sense, when I say that something looks green or feels hard, I am reporting something about its look or its feel, and, in this sense of 'looks' and 'feels' I am, when I say that something looks green or feels hard, asserting a basic proposition. But very often when I say that something looks green or feels hard, I am saying that it looks as if it were green, or feels as if it were hard, or I am judging on the basis of the way it looks or feels – because it looks as a green thing would look, or feels as a hard thing would feel – that it is green or is hard. In the first of these two senses of 'looks' or 'feels', it is perfectly possible to define without circularity 'is green' in terms of 'looks green', or to define 'is hard' in terms of 'feels hard', but in the second of the two senses of these words, this is not poss ble.

---

[1] It is, however, an oversimplification. See H. H. Price, 'Appearing and Appearances,' *The American Philisophical Quarterly*, Vol. I, January 1964; and J. L. Austin, *Sense and Sensibilia* (O.U.P., 1962), Chapter IV.

You can define without circularity 'green' in terms of 'looking green', for there is not in fact one word with one sense, that is, the word 'green' as it occurs in the sentences 'That is green' and 'That looks green'. There is in fact one word, 'green', and another phrase (and this would be clearer if it were hyphenated) 'looking-green', which has a different sense from 'green'. This is brought out more clearly in the sentence 'That is green looking'. In the second sense of 'looking green' or 'feeling hard', being green or being hard could not possibly be defined without circularity in terms of looking green or looking hard, for the word 'green' in 'looking green', and the word 'hard' in 'looking hard' have just the same meaning as they do in 'That looks green' and 'That looks hard'. It would be as impossible to define the former in terms of the latter as it would be to define being a steam engine in terms of looking like a steam engine. We could perfectly well understand the expression 'looks green' in a world where the looks of everything were so irregular and unstable that we had no use for the expression 'is green'; but we obviously could not understand what was meant by saying that something looked like a steam-engine if we did not understand what was meant by 'steam-engine'.

When we consider 'That feels right', it seems fairly clear that we are not attributing to some action the peculiar property of feeling-right. We are saying that it feels as if it were right, or that it feels as a right action would feel, and tentatively judging, because of this, that it is right. Hence to define being right in terms of feeling right would, unlike defining being green in terms of looking green, be circular.

CHAPTER IX

GOD'S COMMANDS AND MAN'S DUTIES

It seems not unnatural to pass from considering ideal observer theories to discussing the view that moral judgments are statements about what God has commanded, prohibited or approves of. God, of course, is a very different kettle of fish from an ideal observer. Though it was not necessary to conceive of the ideal observer as being absolutely omniscient, but only as knowing all the relevant facts about the actions he approved or disapproved of, God is usually thought of as being omniscient. Though the ideal observer was an abstraction – by saying he was an abstraction, I mean that it was necessary to conceive of him as having only some of the characteristics which an actual person would need to have in order to exist – God is not, like the ideal observer, simply omniscient, but is also capable of action. Indeed, he is by definition capable of succeeding in any enterprise he undertakes, which is to say that he is omnipotent, and the enterprises he does attempt are supposed always to be highly commendable, which is to say that he is conceived of as being perfectly good. It is generally also supposed that he created the universe, and that he has certain characteristics, over and above being omnisicent, omnipotent and perfectly good, if these are necessary to make him a fit and proper object for men to worship.

In the preceding paragraph I have spoken as if God were in time, whereas the majority of Christians believe that temporal predicates do not apply to him, but this last feature of the divinity, that he is not in time, is even more difficult than the others for us to conceive of adequately, and it is almost impossible not to speak of him as if he were in time, that is, to speak of him as if the commonly accepted theological view that he is timeless is false. He can, for example, be worshipped at one time by Smith, and not be worshipped at a later time by Smith.

If it is asked how we know that God is omnipotent, omniscient and perfectly good, I think the correct reply is that he is these things by definition. This means that it is customary to use the word 'God' in such a way that we would refuse to apply the word

'God' to a being who was very knowledgeable, but not quite omniscient, or very powerful, but not quite omnipotent, or very good, but not quite perfectly good. Hence the propositions that God is omniscient, that God is omnipotent, and that God is perfectly good are analytic, and the propositions that God is not omniscient, that he is not omnipotent, and that he is not perfectly good are self-contradictory. It is true, I think, that if it turned out that the universe was governed by an extremely powerful, very knowledgeable and very wise and good being who fell short of being quite omnipotent, or quite omniscient, or quite perfectly good, we would, very likely, decide to stretch a point, and call this being 'God', but, in doing so, we would be slightly shifting the meaning this word has at present. In its most commonly accepted usage, the word 'God' is used to mean a being who, among other things, must be omniscient, omnipotent and perfectly good, and hence that God is all these things can be elicited simply by analysing our concept of God.

It would be a mistake to conclude from all this that there must *be* a God who is omniscient, omnipotent, perfectly good and so on. From the fact that human beings have decided to use the word 'God' in a certain way, it could not possibly follow that there *was* a being who actually possessed the attributes which, by human convention, are connoted by this word. Hence the propositions that God is omniscient, omnipotent and perfectly good must be construed as being hypothetical, as meaning, that is, that *if* there is anything which can properly be described as God, *then* this being is omniscient, omnipotent and perfectly good.

There is a notorious attempt to say that, just as God can be omniscient, omnipotent and perfectly good by definition, so he can, by definition, also exist. This attempt is known as the onto-logical argument for the existence of God.[1] It runs as follows: God is by definition perfect. A being who did not exist would be less perfect than a being who did exist and possessed all the other attributes which God by definition has; hence God, in order not to be imperfect, when in fact he is by definition perfect, must exist. God is supposed to possess by definition every perfection; existence is a perfection; hence to say that God does not exist is to say that a being who by definition possesses every perfection lacks a perfection, namely existence.

It is fairly easy to see what is wrong with the ontological argu-

[1] See Anselm, *Proslogion;* and Descartes, *Meditations*, Book V.

ment. Existence is not an attribute, and hence cannot be a meritorious attribute, that is, a perfection. There are a number of reasons for thinking that existence is not an attribute. Where attributes are concerned, both the statement that a kind of thing possesses this attribute, and that it does not possess this attribute, presuppose that there are some of these things; both the statement that goats are cloven-hoofed and the statement that goats are not cloven-hoofed presuppose that there are some goats. The statement that goats exist, however, does not presuppose, so much as explicitly say, that there are some goats, and the statement that goats do not exist could not possibly presuppose that there were some goats, or all such statements would presuppose their own falsehood. Where an attribute is concerned, it is possible to say that some things possess this attribute while others do not; for example, one can say that some dogs beg but others do not. Where existence is concerned, this is not possible; it is not possible to say that some dogs exist, but others do not. Most importantly, it is possible to decide to withhold a given class name from any things which do not possess a certain attribute; for example, people can decide not to call a creature an insect if it has more or less than six legs and, if they do decide to do this, it then becomes true by definition that insects have six legs. But one could not do the same with existence, for this would mean deciding, for example, to withold the word 'insect' from anything I came across which had the other properties which things must have if this word is properly to be applied to them, but did not exist; but, of course, I do not and cannot come across anything which does not exist. For this reason, neither insects not anything else can by definition exist, as they can by definition have six legs, and the ontological argument, which amounts to saying that God can by definition exist, must be invalid.

It has been maintained[1] that though this is sufficient to show that God cannot necessarily and by definition possess existence, it does not show that God cannot necessarily and by definition, possess necessary existence. The proposition which the ontological argument shows is true, and necessarily true, by definition, is not the proposition 'God exists', but the proposition 'God necessarily exists'. 'God exists' cannot be necessarily true, but 'God necessarily exists' can be, and is.

[1] By Norman Malcolm, in 'Anselm's Ontological Arguments', *The Philosophical Review*, Vol. LXIX, 1960.

However, if the proposition 'God exists' cannot be necessarily true – and our criticisms of the ontological argument have shown that it cannot be – then the proposition 'God necessarily exists' cannot be true – for to say that 'God exists' is necessary and that 'God necessarily exists' are just to say the same thing in different ways. But if the proposition 'God necessarily exists' is not even true, it certainly cannot be a necessary truth, and so God cannot necessarily possess necessary existence, any more than he can necessarily possess existence. Indeed, the proposition that God cannot necessarily possess existence entails the proposition that God cannot necessarily possess necessary existence.

When we consider the relation between God's commands and man's duties, it seems to be a fairly good rough approximation to the truth to say that there are three possible views about the nature of this relation. In the *first* place, it is possible to say that God, since he is omniscient, always knows what is right and wrong, and, since he is perfectly good, always commands us to do what is right and prohibits us from doing what is wrong; he is pleased with us when we obey his commands, and do what is right, and displeased with us when we disobey his commands, and do what is wrong.[1] On this view, God's will is determined by his knowledge of right and wrong. *Secondly*, it is possible to say that what makes right actions right and what makes wrong actions wrong is that God has commanded the right actions and prohibited the wrong ones, and that being commanded by God is the *only* thing which makes an action right and being prohibited by God is the *only* thing which makes an action wrong. On this view, it is impossible for God, in commanding some actions and prohibiting others, to be guided by the fact that the actions he commands are right and the actions he prohibits are wrong, because, before he has commanded them, no actions are right, and before he has prohibited them, no actions are wrong. The *third* possible view is that there are not two pairs of different facts, being commanded by God and being right, and being prohibited by God and being wrong: to say that an action is right just *means* that it is commanded by God, and to say that an action is wrong just *means* that it is prohibited by God. Hence it is impossible to raise the question, which the first view answered in one way and the second view in another, whether it is the fact that an action is right that causes

_____
[1] This appears to have been the view of Aquinas and Bishop Butler.

God to command it or whether, conversely, it is the fact that an action is commanded by God that makes it right. On the third view there are not two different facts, being commanded by God and being right, such that we can ask whether the first is dependent upon the second or whether the second is dependent upon the first. There is just one single fact, which may be put indifferently by saying either that God has commanded something or that it is right.[1]

Which of these three theories one holds does not necessarily make any difference to what one thinks is right and wrong. It is perfectly possible, for example, for theologians who hold each of these three theories to agree that it is right for us to love one another, but the first kind of theologian will think that, though loving actions are both right and commanded by God, they are commanded by God because they are right. The second kind of theologian will think that though loving actions are both commanded by God and right, they are right because God has commanded them. The third theologian will think that, though it is true to say of loving actions that they are commanded by God and true to say of them that they are right, to say these things is not to make two different statements about loving actions, but to make one and the same statement in two different ways.

However, though which of these three theories one holds *need* not make any difference to what actions one actually thinks are right and wrong, there is one possible circumstance in which it *will* make a very great deal of difference. If there is no God, then, if you accept the second theory, that only what God commands is right, you are logically bound to say that there are no right and wrong actions, for, according to your theory, only one thing can make an action right, namely, that God commands it, and, if there is no God, nothing can be commanded by him. If you hold the third theory, and think that to say that an action is right just *means* that God has commanded it and that to say that an action is wrong just *means* that God has prohibited it, you will also, if you think that there is no God, be logically committed to holding that nothing is right and nothing is wrong, for, of course, if there is no God there will be no actions which God commands and no actions which he prohibits. If, however, you hold the first theory,

[1] See Henry Sidgwick, *Outlines of the History of Ethics*, 6th edition, enlarged (Macmillan, 1962), pp. 110 f.

it is possible for you to think both that there is no God and also to think that some actions are right and others wrong. Since, on this view, actions are right for some reason other than that God commands them – though God does command or prohibit them in fact – it is possible for actions which are right to go on being right, even if there is no God.

The three theories, though they need not make any difference to one's views about what actions are right and wrong, are nevertheless very different kinds of theory. One might describe the first as a sort of *psychological* theory about God's policy of action. It states that it is God's policy, in directing the behaviour of his creatures, always to command right actions and to prohibit wrong ones. The second theory is not a psychological theory about what makes God command some actions and prohibit others. It says nothing about what causes God to command a certain class of action, but simply says that, if God does command any class of action, it is right for us to perform actions of this class. Hence it is a theory not about God's policy of action, but a *moral* theory about what makes right actions right. The third theory says nothing about what makes actions right or wrong, nor anything about what makes God command some actions and prohibit others. It is simply a *linguistic* theory about the meanings of the words 'right' and 'wrong'. It says that the word 'right' simply means 'commanded by God', and that the word 'wrong' simply means 'prohibited by God'. Hence these three theories, though they do not necessarily – while they may – make any difference to one's views about what actions are right and what actions are wrong, are theories of very different kinds.

It would also seem, at first sight at any rate, that the three theories are incompatible with one another, and that no one ought to hold more than one of them. The first must be incompatible with the second, for how can anyone both hold that what makes God command any action is that it is right, and also at the same time hold that what makes it right is the fact that God has commanded it? The first must also be incompatible with the third, because how can anyone both hold that what makes God command any action is the fact that it is right, and also hold that the fact that it is right is the very same fact as the fact that God has commanded it, put into different words? The second must be incompatible with the third, because how can anyone both hold that it is the fact that God has commanded an action that makes it right, and at the same time hold that the fact that God has commanded it is the very same fact as the fact that it is right, expressed in a different way? To put the same argument again, it seems firstly, impossible that what God commands should depend on what he thinks is right, if what is right depends on what God commands, and secondly, that if the fact that God commands something is *identical* with that thing's being right, then they cannot be two different facts, about which the question which is dependent upon the other can be raised.

Though the second view and the third view appear to be the ones which are being attacked by those people who argue in favour of morals without theology, there is no necessary connection between either of these and the Christain or any other religion. There is no reason why a theologian should not hold the first of the three views, and many theologians, including Aquinas and Bishop Butler, have done so. If the second view or the third is the correct one, it will certainly be the case that, if there is no God, we do not have duties, either because, as would be the case if the second view were correct, the only thing which can make an action right is that it is commanded by God, or because, as would be the case if the third view were correct, the fact that an action is right just is the fact that it is commanded by God. If the first view is the correct one, however, and God, if he exists, always commands what is right and prohibits what is wrong, then presumably, since the reason why God commands some things and prohibits others is that they are right or wrong already, these things would still be right or wrong even if they were not commanded or prohibited by God; hence there is no reason why they should not continue to be right and wrong, even if God were not to exist and so were not to command or prohibit anything. Hence there is no reason why a theologian should hold that nothing would be right or wrong, if there were no God. Odd though it may seem, there is even no logical connection between which of these three views one holds and whether one believes that there actually is a God or not, though perhaps the first of the three is the most *natural* view for an atheist or an agnostic, since it is the only one of the three which can be adopted by someone who both wants to hold that some things are right and wrong and at the same time wants to hold that there is no God – and most atheists and agnostics do appear to wish to hold that some things are right and others wrong. One can hold the second view or the third and at the same time believe that there is is not a God, provided, of course, one is prepared to embrace the logical conclusion that, in that event, nothing is right and nothing is wrong. It is presumably partly extreme reluctance to accept that nothing is right and wrong which has driven most who think that there is no God, or that it cannot be decided whether there is a God or not, to embrace the first of the three views we have distinguished.

Though which of these three views one holds need not, (though it may) make a difference to what actions one thinks are right and what actions one thinks are wrong, there are a number of important differences between them. Though, whichever view one accepts, one *may* think that whatever God commands is right, and that whatever is right is what God commands, there will even so be a difference in the correct order of establishing whether or not something is right, and whether or not something is commanded by God. If the third view is correct, of course, there will be no such thing as an order in which one establishes what is right and what God commands, for there will not be two facts, that something is right and that something is commanded by God, but just one fact which we express indifferently by the sentence that God commands something or that that thing is right. However, the third view, since it consists in giving a definition of 'right' and 'wrong', does automatically carry with it implications about the correct manner of discovering whether anything is right or wrong. One finds out, if this definition of 'right' is correct, what is right and wrong in the same way in which one finds out what God commands and prohibits, whatever this way may be.

Whether one holds the first view or the second, though it may not make any difference to the actions one thinks are right and wrong, does make a difference to whether one thinks that one finds out *first* what God commands, or whether one thinks that one finds out *first* what is right or wrong. If the second view is correct, one must find out first what God commands, and then argue that, since everything God commands is right, this kind of thing, which God is supposed to command, is right. It is not, on the second view, possible to find out what is right or wrong first, without previously having determined whether or not God commands it; hence, on the second view, ignorance of God's commands or of his existence must imply an equal degree of ignorance concerning what actions are right and what wrong.

On the first view it is perfectly possible to argue from an antecedent knowledge of right and wrong as a premise to a conclusion about what God commands or prohibits. We may, on this view, argue that, since it is wrong for us to harm one another, and since God forbids us to perform any action which is wrong, God must forbid us to harm one another, or more accurately, that if he exists at all, he must forbid us to harm one another. That, if God exists (and there is a right and wrong which neither consists in the fact that he commands some things and forbids others, nor is *determined* by the fact that he commands some things and forbids others) he always commands what is right and forbids what is wrong would seem to follow from the fact that God is, by definition, perfectly good. If he sometimes commanded what was wrong or forbade what is right, this would be inconsistent with the way in which we would expect a perfectly good being to behave.

There are difficulties with each of these three views. The first view has difficulty in explaining how, if it is true, God can be omnipotent. If we accept the first view, we must suppose that God's will, and in particular what actions God commands men to perform and what actions he commands them to refrain from performing, is determined by a moral law which is not identical with his commands, as it is on the third view, nor determined by his commands, as it would be on the second view. This seems to imply that the fact that certain things are wrong and other things are right is something over which God has no control. If he could control it, then it would be extremely odd to suppose that his will was subsequently determined by what he had himself brought about. It would be a very extraordinary situation if, though God's will was determined by the moral law, he himself decided what the moral law which determined his actions should be. God's will might just as well not be determined by any law at all, as be determined by a law which he himself decided upon.

The most natural view of our knowledge of right and wrong to combine with the view that God's will, and in particular his will concerning the behaviour of mankind, is determined by his knowledge of a moral law which he himself cannot control, is intuitionism. According to intuitionism, as we have seen, we just see *a priori*, without argument, that certain propositions about the principles of morality are true, and we are able to do this because these principles are necessarily true, for we have *a priori* insight into what is necessarily the case. Hence, if intuitionism is true, morality, like mathematics and logic, becomes a branch of necessary truth. Just as God is quite commonly supposed to be unable to do anything about such mathematical truths that two and two are four, and nothing about such logical truths as that a thing cannot both be and not be, so he is, if intuitionism is true, unable to do anything about such alleged moral truths as that promises ought to be kept and debts paid. But this constitutes at least an apparent limitation upon his omnipotence, for if God cannot alter, at will, the fact that debts ought to be paid, it would appear that there is something he cannot do, and that, in consequence, he is not omnipotent.

It would be very difficult to combine the view that God's will is determined by his knowledge of an antecedently existing moral law with any view other than intuitionism. If moral judgments are just empirical propositions, say empirical propositions about what people approve of or about what conventions actual societies have established or what conventions have grown up, then God could alter the moral law, for he could certainly, if he is omnipotent, alter the fact that people approve of what they do, or the fact that they have the conventions that they do. Hence, if we try to combine the view that God's will is directed by his knowledge of an antecedently existing moral law with any form of empiricism, we are left with the difficulty that God's will is being determined by something which he has the power to alter, for no one has ever supposed that God, if he exists, has not the power to alter at will any empirical facts at all.

The second and third views apparently have no difficulty in accounting for God's omnipotence. On the second view, God, by deciding what actions he will command and what actions he will prohibit, actually decides what the moral law shall be, for whatever he commands becomes right for us, and whatever he prohibits becomes wrong. On the third view, he decides what shall be right for us and what wrong, for the fact that something is right just is the fact that he commands it, and the fact that it is wrong just is the fact that he prohibits it, and, presumably, he commands and prohibits what he pleases.

The difficulty the second and third view have is to explain how God can be good at all, let alone how he can be perfectly good. For one thing, the conclusion, which each of these two views entails, that whatever God were to command would be right for us, even if he commanded homicide, cannibalism or incest, is one which many people find shocking.[1] For another thing, it seems reasonable to ask how, if the second or third views are true, can it even make sense to raise the question whether God is good or not, for, to say that a rational being is good is to say that his will accords with the moral law. God, however, could be neither good nor not good in this sense, for the moral law, on both the second view and the third, is something which he himself lays down or determines; hence his will could not be determined by the moral law, for there simply is no moral law, independent of what he himself decides, to determine it. Though there is nothing immoral in his commanding anything he pleases – for he himself determines what shall and shall not be immoral – many find the idea that God is in that way above morality repulsive.

Quite apart from the fact that there is nothing, however outrageous human beings may find it, which God may not, so far as moral considerations go, do, there is also a logical difficulty involved in saying that God is perfectly good on these two views. For God cannot be perfectly good, in the sense that whatever he does is right, if what he does is not determined by his knowledge of what is right, as it would be on the first of the three views. Indeed, it may be argued that it is even circular to define God as a being who is, among other things, perfectly good, if we also want to say that a being is good if he does what is right, and that he does what is right if he does what God commands. We are, in other words, first defining, or partly defining, God in terms of *goodness*, and then subsequently defining goodness in terms of what is commanded by *God*.

Though, as I have said, the three views, that God commands us to perform actions which are right, that actions are right because God has commanded us to perform them, and the view that the fact that an action is right just is the fact that God has commanded it, are incompatible as they stand, it is possible to combine variants of the three with one another, provided these views are modified in a suitable way. Though I cannot see how it is possible to produce a variant of the third view, that the fact

[1] See Immanuel Kant, *op. cit.*, p. 62.

that something is right just is the fact that God has commanded it, it is possible, even if the third theory is true, to preserve God's goodness by identifying this, not with a disposition on his part to obey the moral law, but by saying that his goodness consists in benevolence. Since he is good, that is, benevolent, he commands his creatures to perform actions which are conducive to their happiness; hence such actions – since the fact that he commands them is identical with the fact that they are right – are actions which it is right for God's creatures to perform. There is no circularity in saying that God is benevolent; though, since he creates the moral law, any attempt to say that God is good, in the sense that he obeys the moral law, must be circular.

God's morality can also be preserved, if the second view – that it is being commanded by God that makes right actions right – is true, in the same way. Though, if the second view is true, God cannot be good in the sense that he obeys the moral law, for he himself decides what the moral law shall be, he can be good in the sense that he is benevolent, desires the happiness of his creatures, and so makes moral laws which are such that, if men obey them, their happiness will be brought about thereby.

It is possible to combine a variant of the second view with the first if one says that one thing, but not the *only* thing, which makes right actions right is that God has commanded them. Some actions, say Sabbath observance, are right simply because God has commanded them, but other actions, say actions of promise-keeping, are not right simply because God has commanded them, but for some other reason. On this view, being commanded by God is just one of a number of things which make it right for us to do something, but not the only thing which makes right actions right. It is then possible to argue that, since things like promise-keeping and honesty are right, and can be known to be right without its first being known whether or not God commands them, and since God is perfectly good, and will command us to perform actions which are right, he will command us to perform actions like keeping our promises and telling the truth. Since, on this view, being commanded by God is one thing which makes an action right, actions which are right for some reason other than that they are commanded by God now become right for *two* reasons; since they are right for whatever reason, God will command them, and since they are commanded by God, they will also become right because it is also right for us to obey his commands. Since God may also command some actions which are not antecedently right, there are some actions which are right only because God has commanded them; it will be impossible to infer that God has commanded *these* actions from a prior knowledge of the fact that they are right because, where these actions are concerned, they are not right until God has commanded them.

It might even be possible, on this view, to have a conflict of duties, a conflict between our duty to obey God's commands and our duty to perform an action which is right for some reason other than that God has commanded it. One might say that, when God commanded Abraham to sacrifice Isaac, Abraham was faced with a conflict of duties, a duty to preserve human life and to take care of his offspring, and a duty to obey God's commands. It might seem suitably pious to say that, in the event of such a conflict, one's duty to obey God's commands would take precedence over any other duty.

If there were no God, all the actions which were right for some reason other than that they were commanded by God, might still be right, though in this case they would be right for one reason only, instead of two. They would be right for whatever reason made them right in the first place – say that not to have performed them would have caused other people unnecessary suffering – but they would no longer be right because God, who commands us to perform every action that is right, has commanded us to perform them, for God does not exist. Hence, on this view, or combination of views, there will still be some right actions, if God does not exist, though not so many as there would be if God does exist. One will also have motives, if God exists, for doing what is right, which one will not have, if God does not exist. If God exists, one may wish to do what is right not simply because it is right, but to please the God who has commanded it, and possibly also because one believes that ill will befall one in this world or the next as a result of a persistent adherence to wrong-doing.

The question arises: 'How, on each one of the three views distinguished above, would we know what actions are right and what actions are wrong?' It would seem at first sight, that if you accept the first of these three views, it is left open for one to hold any theory whatsoever about how we know what actions are right and what actions are wrong. All the person holding this first view need say is that we know what is right and what is wrong in whatever is the appropriate way of answering such questions, and then infer that, since God is perfectly good, he commands us to do what is right, whatever that is, and to refrain from doing what is wrong, whatever that is. The possible ways in which one might hold that one does find out what is right and what is wrong are those which are considered in other parts of this book. There is a difficulty, however, which has already been discussed, that if one takes the the view that moral judgments are a species of contingent proposition, and are known to be true by observation and experience, one will have to hold that God, since he decides all contingent matters of fact, decides what is right and wrong, which is difficult to reconcile with the view that God's will is determined by the moral law.

If you hold the second view, according to which it is being commanded or prohibited by God that makes actions right or wrong, it might seem that you must hold that we know what is right or wrong in the same way in which we know what God commands and prohibits, whatever this way may be, but to think this would be a mistake. The mistake arises from failing to distinguish between the manner in which we know the hypothetical proposition, that if any action is commanded by God it is right for us to perform that action, and the manner in which we know that an action really is commanded by God as a matter of fact. The fact that something is commanded by God is a fact about God, and so must be discovered in whatever way, if any, we do discover facts about God. But the hypothetical fact, that if an action is commanded by God it is a right action, is not, on this theory, itself a fact about God, and so a different account will have to be given of the way in which we come to know that it is true from the account we give of the way we come to know facts about God. Now that if an action is commanded by God it is a right action, cannot be an analytic proposition on the second view, for, if it were, this could only be because being right was part of what was meant by being commanded by God, which would entail holding the third view, or something very like it, that moral judgments are just identical with certain facts about God's commands. Hence this judgment must be synthetic, and either synthetic and *a priori* or synthetic and empirical. Since God can always alter any synthetic contingent and empirical fact, then, if the proposition that whatever he commands is right is synthetic, contingent and empirical, God not only decides what to command his creatures to do, he also decides that whatever he commands his creatures to do is right, which is ridiculous. On the other hand, if the proposition that whatever God commands is right is synthetic, *a priori* and necessary, God, though he can decide what to command us to do, cannot, if he has not the power to make false a proposition which is necessarily true, do anything to alter the fact that if he commands us to do some action, then that action is right.

It is the third view, which holds that 'right' means 'commanded by God', and that 'wrong' means 'prohibited by God', which does lead to the conclusion that we find out what is right and wrong in the same way in which we find out what God in actual fact does command. What could this way be? One might argue that, since God is by definition benevolent, he will command us to perform those actions which are such that human happiness will be brought about if they are performed, but, though this will give us the hypothetical proposition that if there is a God, he will command us to perform actions which are conducive to human happiness, one cannot, as we have seen, from any definition of the word 'God', conclude that there actually is a God who commands us to perform actions which are conducive to human happiness. Hence one is thrown away from *a priori* argument, which rests upon definitions, to an empirical argument, if such is possible, by which we attempt to glean what information we can about the nature of God and his commands, from an investigation of the actual nature of the world.

There are two questions which must be distinguished from one another. There is the question: 'Is it possible to argue, from a knowledge of what happens in the universe, to the nature of God's purposes for man, and hence to what he commands us to do, given the assumption that everything that happens in the universe, with possibly the exceptions of the freely chosen actions of God's creatures, are things for which he is responsible?' There is also the question: 'Is it possible to argue, without this assumption, from a knowledge of the nature of the universe to the existence of a God who purposes certain things for his creatures, and in order to achieve these purposes, commands them to behave in certain ways?' The second question will be more difficult to answer in the affirmative than the first question, for in order to answer the first question we are allowed to assume a premise, the premise that there is a God, for which, in order to answer the second question, we must produce reasons. It may well be that we could conclude, in answer to the first question, that *if* there is a God, then he must have certain purposes for men, and command them to behave in certain ways, though we cannot, in answer to the second question, come to the conclusion that there is a God.

If there is a God, and he is omnipotent and omniscient, as by definition he is, then everything that happens in the universe, with the possible exception, already mentioned, of the free actions of human beings, must be something which he has intended or has allowed to happen, and has intended or allowed to happen for some reason. Hence, if something that happens is beneficial to mankind, God must have intended it to be so, and if something that happens is harmful to mankind, God must have intended this to be so also. Now, of course, a great deal of what happens in the world is of benefit to mankind; men are usually born with the tendency to develop abilities, in particular their intelligence, which are useful to them; they have been made sociable to quite a high degree, which enables them to augment their power and their productivity by co-operating with one another; in nature there is a not wholly inadequate supply of the raw materials which they need; and man is quite well adapted to the environment in which he lives. All this, on the assumption that there is a God who is responsible for every contingent matter of fact about the world being as it is, points to the fact that God is well-disposed to mankind. On the other hand, much of what happens in the world does not point to a God who is well-disposed to man. Man would be happier and more successful if he were even more intelligent than God has made him, if he were less prone to quarrel with his fellow men, less prone to physical and mental illness and deformity, had a more adequate supply of the commodities he needs, and was better adapted to his environment. Hence, on the assumption that there is a God, an investigation of the natural world would point to the fact that he is reasonably benevolently disposed to mankind, but by no means wholly so, and, moreover, to the fact that he is much more well-disposed to some men than he is to others. To some men, indeed, he would appear to behave in a manner worse than any human malevolence could possibly imagine or contrive.

Many attempts have been made to reconcile the apparent evil and imperfection in the world with God's benevolence, but they have not been very successful.[1] It has been suggested that some evil in the world enhances the goodness of the whole, much as a discord in music may enhance the beauty of the music or an ugly colour in a painting may enhance the beauty of the painting; it may be argued, however, that the dreadful suffering endured by many is too high a price to pay for this aesthetic beauty. It has also been suggested that the appearance of evil in the world may be due to the fact that man, being finite, sees only a small part of the whole, and that, were he to see the whole, he would realize that the evil in the part he does see is a necessary means to some over-riding good. But though this *may* be so, that it is so is simply a possibility – and a remote one, at that – which we have no means of testing unless we do view the whole that we cannot see. It has been suggested, too, that the causal laws which govern the universe make evil a necessary concomitant, and sometimes a necessary means, to a greater good. For example, the function of pain is to warn the person who feels it of something that will do him damage, and, though pain could be dispensed with, it would be at the price of endangering the organism which it is the function of pain to preserve. It is argued that even useless pain is still part of that price which mankind, or rather, sentient creatures in general, have to pay for their preservation, for it would be impossible to have the physiological mechanism which causes us to feel pain unless we also felt pain sometimes when it was too late or impossible for us to take the necessary avoiding action. The difficulty with this defence is that one cannot argue that the causal laws which govern the universe make it inevitable that we should experience pain if we are to be warned of danger, when God is himself supposed to have created the universe and made these causal laws what they are, and so must have the power to alter them at will. It has been suggested that man himself brings evil into the world by his own free will, and that the only way God could have prevented this was by creating men without free will; but a man without free will would be a less admirable being than a man with free will; hence evil is the necessary price we have to pay for freedom. The reply to this is obvious. Not all the evil in the world *is* the result of the operation of man's free will. Earthquake, famine and pestilence are not. It might even be argued that God could, if he had wished to do so, have created man both free and good. What we freely choose to do is to an enormous

[1] See John Hick, *Evil and the God of Love* (Macmillan, 1966).

extent dependent upon the physical state of our brain and nervous system. A woman taking therapeutic drugs for mental illness may freely choose to do many things which the same woman not taking drugs will not freely choose to do. Hence if an ordinary doctor, by giving someone drugs or some other form of treatment, can change the pattern of a person's free and voluntary activity for the better, it is difficult to see how God could find it difficult to have made people better than they are, and at the same time free. Hence, even if we concede that there is a God who for some reason or other brings about or permits everything that happens in the universe, it is difficult to see how one can arrive, by the unaided use of reason, at the conclusion that he is perfectly benevolent. (If you say, as I have suggested you should, that God is by definition perfectly benevolent, you must then say that it is difficult to see how you can arrive at the conclusion that the being who governs the universe is God.) For all these reasons one cannot, even granted that there is a God, or at least that the universe is ruled by an omnipotent and omniscient being, come to the conclusion that necessarily he commands us to perform those actions which it would be to our good to perform, for a God who will allow suffering might very well command actions which are *not* conducive to the happiness of his creatures.

If one does *not* allow oneself to assume that there *is* a God, it is still more difficult to produce any reason for thinking that God commands men to perform those actions which further their own happiness. In this case, we are not allowed to assume that there is a God, and simply show that he is benevolent; we must show that there is a God, and that he is benevolent. All the difficulties with the first argument, for the benevolence of God on the assumption that he exists, are also difficulties with the second argument, which purports to show that there is a God who is benevolent; and there are more as well.[1] The hypothesis that the world is governed by an unobserved but benevolent God is very unlike the hypothesis that there is an unobserved magnet in my pocket, which is causing a compass needle to behave in an unusual way, or that there is an unobserved planet, the existence of which is modifying the behaviour of other planets, even leaving aside the difficulty that it is in principle possible to observe the magnet and the planet, though they are at the moment unobserved, while it may be argued that God is in principle something which

[1] See David Hume, *Dialogues Concerning Natural Religion.*

it is impossible to observe. Where the hypotheses that there is an unobserved magnet in my pocket or an unobserved planet in the solar system are concerned, one argues to their existence from an apparent irregularity in the normal course of nature, an irregularity in the behaviour of the compass needle or in the behaviour of other planets, which irregularity can be shown to be only apparent if the magnet or the extra planet are postulated. The argument in fact goes as follows: something which happens appears to go against what we expect from what we know of the laws which govern nature; if however, there were an unobserved magnet or an unobserved planet situated in a certain position in space, we could explain what is happening without abandoning any of the laws which we already accept; hence there is very likely an unobserved magnet or an unobserved planet. In the case of the argument to the existence of a benevolent God, however, there *is* no interruption to the normal laws of nature. The fact that man is intelligent and is adapted to his environment can be perfectly well explained without the hypothesis that there is a God. If we discount, for the sake of simplicity, miracles ,which are in any case sporadic, unpredictable and imperfectly attested, the argument to the existence of God takes as its premise not apparent irregularities in the course of nature, but the fact that nature is uniform. There is no need, however, to postulate anything at all to explain the fact that nature is uniform. Indeed, it would be impossible to have any explanation of this. For normally the question 'Why' means 'Why in this case but not in that?' and it is impossible to ask the question 'Why is nature uniform in this case but not in that?' – which question *might* be answered by saying there is a God responsible for the uniformity in this case, though there is not in that – for, where the universe is concerned, the universe is the sum total of everything that there is, and hence there are no other cases. Hence, if we are not allowed to assume that there is a God, it is still more difficult to argue to the existence of a benevolent God who makes laws which it is in man's interest to obey.

Perhaps, however, we are wrong to try to make our argument to the nature of God's laws rest upon his benevolence. Perhaps we should argue, instead, that what God intends is the normal or the 'natural', and that deviations from the normal or 'natural' are contrary to his intentions, and so wrong. Hence suicide is wrong because God must have intended man to live out his normal life-span, unless this is shortened by illness which man has no power to control, and contraception is wrong because this is contrary to the normal or natural manner of having sexual intercourse, and sexual perversion is wrong for the same reason.

There are a number of difficulties with this manner of arguing. For one thing, it is very difficult to find any standard of normality other than what is usual or what happens most, and what happens most is obviously quite often wrong. For another thing, if God is omnipotent and omniscient, then he must have intended everything that happens, and be as much responsible for deviations from the norm as he is for the norm itself; hence we cannot argue that the norm is what he intends, but the deviations are not what he intends. And it is very difficult to argue that it is wrong to interfere with the normal course of nature by committing suicide or using contraceptives while stopping short of arguing that it must also be wrong to interfere with the normal course of nature by curing disease or using artificial fertilizers. In any case, the argument would at most allow us to argue to God's intentions given the assumption that there is a God, not at all to the *existence* of a God.

If we cannot argue to the nature of God's commands for man from a consideration of the nature of the world, perhaps we are able to know about him from what we are told about him in the Bible or in some other holy book. Certainly in the Bible we are told things about God, and what he intends, and what he expects of his creatures. The most serious difficulty is that part of the appeal of the Bible is a moral appeal. Christ, for example, is presented not simply as a man who worked miracles and who claimed to be, or to be in a special relationship to, God. He behaved in certain ways which most people regard with at least qualified approval and enunciated certain moral precepts which commend themselves to many people at least in some degree. But for the appeal of Christ to be a moral appeal, it must be presupposed that we have some standards of right and wrong already, by which Christ's behaviour can be morally assessed. For his precepts to commend themselves to us, we must have some insight into what is right and wrong which is independent of his testimony. I personally have no doubt that, if Christ behaved in ways which we would consider quite reprehensible, and enunciated precepts which most people would regard as being outrageous, the claims which he made on his own behalf and on behalf of the religion which he founded would command no serious attention.

It is true that, given that Christ's behaviour appeals to the standards of morality we already have, and given that many of his moral precepts commend themselves to the degree of moral enlightenment we possess at the moment, we may well be prepared to accept some *other* of his precepts simply on his authority, that is, on the authority of someone who has already shown himself to possess moral insight and to be in practice good. But such precepts would supplement the knowledge of right and wrong we already possess, rather than be the sole means of our having any knowledge of right and wrong. Hence the view that we acquire all our knowledge of right and wrong – that is, on the view that 'right' simply means 'commanded by God', all our knowledge of God's commands – upon the authority of some divine being, revealed in some divine book, must be rejected.

In any case, as has already been argued, all knowledge based upon testimony presupposes knowledge not based upon testimony. We may know that there are black swans in Australia or that Pythagoras's theorem is true because we have been told, and the person who told us may himself have been told by yet another person, but the chain of testimony must end at some point by someone's having observed the black swans in Australia, or worked out Pythagoras's theorem, for himself. Hence, though we may believe things about God's commands or man's duties on the authority of some holy person or book, there still remains the question how this holy person or the men who wrote the holy book themselves came to know what they claim to know.

Many people believe that our consciences provide a way of knowing what it is that God commands us to perform, and what kind of thing he wishes us to do. I believe that, for many people, conscience presents itself as of divine authority. These people, when they have a guilty conscience, feel as if God is actively displeased with their conduct, and, when they have a clear conscience, feel as if he is not displeased or is positively approving of them. Hence they imagine, if this is not too question-begging a word, their conduct to be under the perpetual review of a being who demands that they do what he enjoins, and that they refrain from doing what he prohibits. I doubt, however, whether conscience does provide us with any means of knowing what God's wishes for us are. For one thing, I do not think it is a universal phenomenon that conscience presents itself as the voice of God. Many who do not even believe in God have a conscience which demands that they behave in some ways and refrain from behaving in others.

For another thing, it is unclear whether conscience is supposed to provide us with a means of inferring what God's commands are, or whether it provides us with some form of direct acquaintance with the wishes of the divinity. If it were to provide us with a means of inferring the commands of the divinity, the argument would, again, have either to be one which rested *upon the assumption* that there is a God who causes us to feel guilty or self-approving in the way we do, and to have the conscientious scruples we do have, or it must itself provide us with a reason for thinking that there *is* a God who causes our consciences to operate as it does. The latter argument would only be plausible if the operations of conscience could not be explained in any other way, but these operations can already be partially explained as being a reaction to the pressures of our environment and the demands made upon us by our community, and it seems quite possible that psychologists will be able to produce a full explanation of the working of conscience in the course of time. And the argument that, *if* there is a God, he must intend us to refrain from performing those actions which are such that they would cause us to have an uneasy conscience if we did perform them is highly precarious. Conscience is moulded by social influences which often seem to have little to do with divine action, and is highly fallible, both because the person who possesses the conscience is mistaken about or ignorant of relevant matters of fact, and also because it appears to enjoin at one time things which we subsequently reject as being wrong. God, if he is omnipotent and omniscient, must be responsible for the deliverances of our conscience when these err just as much as when they do not err.

Perhaps, however, it is not so much a case of arguing to the existence of God, using facts about our consciences as premises, as that, through our consciences, we are brought into some form of direct contact with the divine will, and hence know what he commands not by inference but by something more like direct acquaintance with his commands. It is certainly true that, in many people, though not in all, conscience does present itself as if it were a form of immediate awareness, as if we did not need to infer, from the deliverances of conscience, what God's commands are, but knew them in some more intimate, less discursive way. If this were so, it is important to realize how very different would be our awareness of God's commands from our knowledge of the commands of our human superiors. Where these latter are concerned, we hear words, the meaning of which we understand, and which we believe to emanate from the bodies of the people who are commanding us, which bodies we suppose to be animated by minds, whatever being animated by a mind consists of. Hence we are not directly aware of some entity called a command; what we are directly aware of is a noise, or possibly ink marks on paper, and we infer from the occurrence of the noise or the ink marks that there is some being with a mind like ours who is doing what we are doing when we ourselves command others. In the case of our alleged *acquaintance* with God's commands, however, there can be no question of written marks being made on paper by some divine being, or of sound waves emanating from his vocal chords. We must, if we are aware of his commands at all, and especially if this awareness is supposed not to involve our making any inference, be directly aware of the commands without the intermediary of ink marks on paper producing light waves which modify the retina of our eyes or of noises produced by sound waves affecting our ears.

Personally I find it very difficult to conceive of what such an awareness, the awareness of a command of some being, which does not consist in the first instance of an awareness of symbols the meaning of which we understand, could possibly be. It is true that I am familiar with the experience of imagining myself disapproved of by some superhuman being, as I am with the experience of imagining myself disapproved of by other human beings, but *imagining* oneself disapproved of, even if it is accompanied by a tendency to believe that one actually is disapproved of, is a very different matter from being aware, in some unusual way, of the disapproval which these other beings are supposed to feel.

It is often the case that people who believe that there is some intimate connection between God's commands and man's duties hold their moral opinions with much greater firmness, a firmness which in some cases amounts to an intolerant dogmatism, than people who believe that moral beliefs are not beliefs about God's commands, whether or not these latter people also believe that there is a God who commands them to perform actions which they think are right. I cannot personally see any reason why the belief that actions are right because they are commanded by God, or the belief that 'right' simply means 'commanded by God' should by itself produce dogmatism or intolerance, but there is a reason why the belief that one arrives at least at some of one's moral tenets upon God's *authority* should produce such dogmatism. The reason, I think, is this. An omniscient being can scarcely be supposed to be mistaken about what is right and wrong; hence, if we are told that something is right upon the authority of an omniscient being, it is natural to suppose that we ourselves cannot be mistaken about this thing's being right. Though this is natural, however, it is mistaken. Though God's 'beliefs' may be superhuman and infallible, our beliefs, even when they are beliefs which we think that God has revealed to us, are all human and fallible. Hence, though God may know that adultery is wrong, and may have told us that adultery is wrong, it does not follow that we ourselves know that adultery is wrong, and it does not follow, therefore, that we are justified in maintaining that adultery is wrong with supreme confidence. For our belief that adultery is wrong, if we believe this because we believe God has revealed it to us, can be no better warranted than our belief that God *has* revealed it to us, and this belief is simply a human fallible belief of ours. We may feel that God has not only revealed to us that adultery is wrong, but has also revealed to us the fact that he has revealed to us that adultery is wrong, and hence that our belief that God has revealed to us that adultery is wrong has a divine backing which justifies us in holding it with a confidence which we would not have in it if we thought it was merely a human belief of our own; but this, again, is a mistake. To argue that we know that God has revealed some fact to us because God has revealed to us the fact that he has revealed this fact would be rather like the notorious argument that God exists because this is revealed in the Bible, which must be infallible, because it is the word of God. Any doubt about whether God has revealed something must imply a like doubt about whether he has revealed to us that he has revealed this. If God does not exist, for example, not only can he not have revealed to us that adultery is wrong; he also cannot have revealed to us that he has revealed that adultery is wrong. In any case, it is a peculiar kind of revelation which requires another and prior revelation of the fact that it is revelation.

If it is either the case that the only things which are wrong are things which God has prohibited, or the case that to say that something is wrong is just to say that God has prohibited this thing, it looks as if it is possible to produce a moral argument for the existence of God. If either of these two views is correct, we would not, as we have already seen, have any duties if there were no God. Hence it looks as if it were possible to argue that, since we do have duties, there must be a God. (It would not be possible to argue in this way if the first of the three theories distinguished above about the connection between God's commands and man's duties were the correct one, for on this theory it *would* be possible for man to have duties if there were no God.)

Such an argument, however, would not prove the existence of God. It is true that it is a valid argument (in the form of a *modus tollendo tollens*), that is to say, that if its premises are true, its conclusion must also be true. More, however, is necessary for an alleged proof to count as a genuine proof than that its premises should entail its conclusion, or that it should be valid. Its premises must also be *true* – and it is questionable whether one premise of this argument, that the second or third of our three views about the connection between God's commands and man's duties is acceptable, *is* true. Over and above this, it must be possible to show that its premises are true without first showing that its conclusion is true. Though, if the second or third theories about the connection between God's commands and man's duties is the correct one, the premises of this argument are true, it is also the case that, if either of these two theories were true, it would not be possible to show that we had any duties unless it were *first* possible to show that there was a God who commanded certain things and prohibited others. For if only the things God has commanded are right, or if to say that an action is right is simply to say that God has commanded it, then, if we are in doubt about the existence of God, we ought to be just as much in doubt about whether or not we have any duties. Hence it is not possible, on either of these last two views, to argue that God must exist because we do have duties, for any such argument would be circular.

H

The question finally arises: 'How does our view of the connection between God's commands and man's duties affect our view of the manner in which our concepts of right or wrong, etc., are acquired?' If we accept either the first or second of the three theories distinguished earlier in this chapter, that is, the view that God commands actions which are right and the view that actions are right because God commands them, then we are not restricted in any way in our choice of theories about how ethical concepts are acquired. On either of these two theories, the concept of something's being commanded by God and the concept of something's being right are two quite distinct, though connected, concepts; neither is reduced to the other, and so our views about the manner in which we acquire a concept of God need not affect our view of the manner in which we learn what the word 'right' means, that is, our view of how we acquire a concept of moral rectitude. On the third theory, however, being right is alleged to be identical with being commanded by God, from which it follows that our concept of moral rectitude is essentially tied up with our concept of a being who commands and prohibits certain actions, and so the two concepts must be acquired in the same way.

How do we acquire our concept of a God who commands some actions and prohibits others? My own personal view, which is somewhat old-fashioned, is that we acquire this concept by means of a process which used to be known as *compounding*.[1] For example, we acquire concepts of a lizard, of wings, of breathing, and of fire from having seen lizards, from having seen wings, from having seen creatures breathing and from having seen fire. Hence we can form the concept of a winged fire-breathing lizard, i.e. a dragon, although we have never actually come across one.

Where our concept of God is concerned, the situation is in some ways easier, in other ways more difficult. It is *easier* because our concept of God is partly the concept of a being who can act, and in particular create, who possesses knowledge and probably also sentience, and who possesses moral virtue, and, though we do not come across winged fire-breathing lizards in reality, we do come across creatures, viz. men, who do instantiate all these attributes simultaneously. It is *more difficult* because God is

[1] See John Locke, *Essay Concerning Human Understanding*, Book II, Chapter 11; George Berkeley, *The Principles of Human Knowledge*, Introduction; David Hume, *Treatise of Human Nature*, Book I, Part I, Section 1.

not simply supposed to possess the power to act, knowledge, etc., but to possess these things in an unlimited degree; there is supposed to be nothing he does not know, and nothing, except that the performance of which is logically contradictory, which he cannot do. However, if we have the concepts of God's acting, and knowing, and being benevolent, presumably we can have the concept of God's being able to do anything, knowing everything, and not being in any way lacking in benevolence, for these involve, besides the concept of doing, knowing and being benevolent, simply our ability to understand the words 'all' and 'not'; he can do *all* things; there is *nothing* he can *not* do. The more serious difficulties for the view that we have a concept of the deity arise from the fact that we do not observe him, and from the fact that his knowledge and action is supposed to be timeless; but if we can conceive of disembodied spirits, who cannot be observed, then presumably we can conceive of an omnipotent, omniscient and omnibenevolent disembodied spirit, who does not choose to reveal himself to many, and perhaps not to any; and perhaps the timelessness of God is not so essential to him as some theologians suppose.

In the foregoing argument in this chapter I have spoken as if God were, though not actually part of the furniture of the world, at least like a piece of furniture, though, perhaps, a piece of transcedent furniture, transcendent because lying outside space and outside time. God, though transcendent, is treated as an actual entity, and the possessor of attributes (human or quasi-human attributes) and a list of everything there was that left out God would to that extent be incomplete. This perhaps simple-minded view of the divinity is now considered old-fashioned by many philosophers of religion, if not by ordinary people or even by philosophers of religion when they turn from speculation to actual devotion. If we reject it, the sentence 'God exists', which by almost everyone until quite recently had been supposed to be used to assert that, among or transcending the furniture of the universe there was an actual entity, answering to a certain description, must be considered to be used for doing something different, for example, for expressing one's intention to lead a certain kind of life.[1]

[1] See R. B. Braithwaite, *An Empiricist's View of the Nature of Religious Belief* (C.U.P., 1955).

If God is not an actually existing entity, then he cannot be an actually existing entity of the sort which issues commands, and hence the question of the relation between God's commands and man's duties cannot arise. The most we can do is to *believe* we have duties, and think that faith in God, in a sense which does not involve believing that the proposition that he exists is true, manifests itself in their performance. Perhaps all that having faith in God consists of is doing one's duty, or in doing one's duty and at the same time telling oneself certain stories, stories to the effect that one is being watched over by a loving God, who is pained by one's transgressions and delighted by one's good actions; stories, however, which one is not expected to *believe*, though one may *pretend* that they are true if one finds this encouraging.

For myself, however, I find it difficult to believe that, when one says that God exists, one is not asserting the existence of a being who actually has the attributes of being omnipotent, omniscient and benevolent. Faith itself may not consist in *believing* that such a being exists, so much as assiduously and perserveringly acting as if there were such a being, and certainly this is the most, if it is not too much, that could be required of one as a duty; nevertheless, when one asserts that God exists, one is actually asserting the proposition that there is in the universe or 'beyond' it an actual being who possesses certain characteristics. It is very difficult to make sense of the religious attitude if all possibility of such an assertion's being a genuine proposition, and so of being true, is removed.

CHAPTER X

MORALITY AND MORAL CODES

Judgments about what actions are right or wrong are not judgments about what actual spectators feel about these actions, or even judgments about how an ideal spectator would feel about them, if there were one. Perhaps, however, if moral judgments are not judgments about people's feelings, they are judgments about people's moral codes. There are various possible views about the relation between right and wrong and the conventions actually in operation in given communities. One perfectly natural view is that the rectitude or otherwise of an action consists in its conforming or failing to conform to some set of rules which some group of men have actually adopted, or, which has, over the course of time, grown up. On such a theory it is fairly obvious that moral judgments would be empirical, for it would be a matter to be established by observation and experience what the moral codes of any community actually were. Moral judgments would be synthetic, for it is not plausible to suggest that communities are defined by their moral codes, and moral judgments would be contingent, for it would be just a matter of fact that communities had the moral codes they did; it would be perfectly conceivable that they should be otherwise. Moral judgments will not, on such theories, be basic. They will be inferred from what we hear people say and what we see them do. For example, if we hear people expressing disapproval of a certain class of action, divorce, for example, and taking hostile action towards those who perpetrate it, we may infer that actions of this kind are contrary to the moral rules of the community to which these people belong.

It would not be very plausible to suggest that the moral code to which an action must conform in order to be right is the moral code of the community *of the person making the moral judgment*. On such a view 'right' would mean 'in conformity with the moral code of the community of the person making the judgment' and 'wrong' would mean 'not in conformity with the moral code of the person making the judgment'. Since the person judging that polygamy, say, is wrong might belong to a different community from the person making the judgment that polygamy is right, the judgment made by the first person would not necessarily be incompatible with the judgment made by the second person; if they belonged to different communities, both judgments could be true. Hence, on this theory it would be possible to say to someone from a different community from oneself, 'What you say when you say polygamy is right is true, but polygamy is not right.' It would be perfectly possible for a person to make at one time the judgment that some action, say an instance of human sacrifice, was right, and at a later date make the judgment that the same act of human sacrifice was wrong, without having to withdraw his previous judgment, for his community's moral codes might have changed in the interval between his making the two judgments.

Furthermore, since a community's opinions about the nature and effects of any action must have something to do with whether or not this community has or has not a rule prohibiting or enjoining it, it is perfectly possible that some actions are prohibited or enjoined by a given community, which actions would not be prohibited or enjoined by that community if they were not ignorant of or mistaken about the nature and consequences of the action in question. However, on the view we are considering, whether or not they are so ignorant or are so mistaken would have no bearing whatsoever upon the truth or falsity of judgments about the rightness or wrongness of the actions this community enjoined or prohibited. So long as an action was actually prohibited, it would be wrong, and so long as an action actually was enjoined, it would be obligatory, whether or not it was prohibited or enjoined simply as a result of ignorance or mistake. Lastly, it is most implausible to suggest that what determines whether an action performed in China three thousand years ago is right or wrong is whether or not it conforms to the moral rules in operation in Britain in the twentieth century. That, however, is what on the view we are considering, does determine whether the moral judgments made by a contemporary Briton, about actions which took place in ancient China, are right or wrong.

A more plausible suggestion is that an action is right if it conforms to the moral rules in operation not in the community of the person *making the judgment*, but in the community of which the person who *performed* the action was a member. On this view, to say that an action is right is to say that it conforms to the moral rules which obtain in the community to which the agent belongs at the time at which the action is performed. On such a view, one person's judgment that some action is right would always be incompatible with some other person's judgment that the same action is wrong, whoever these two people might be, for an action could not both accord with and fail to accord with the moral rules in operation, in the agent's community, at the time at which the action was done. Nor is this view open to the objection that a man can at one time judge an action to be right, and at a later time judge the same action to be wrong, without having to say that he was formerly mistaken. If a person at one time judges that an action conformed to the rules in operation in the community of the agent at the time at which the action was performed, and at a later time judges that this very same action was not in conformity with those very same rules, one of these two judgments must be mistaken. The difficulty remains that whether or not the rules, which determine whether an action is right or wrong, are based upon ignorance or mistake about the nature and consequences of the action in question, is entirely irrelevant to the truth of the moral judgment about it. If it does conform, it is right, and if it does not conform, it is wrong, however ignorant or mistaken may be the beliefs which produced the rules to which it conforms or fails to conform.

This theory also has the demerit that it makes it very difficult to criticize the rules of one's own or any other community. In the special case when the agent and the person making the moral judgment belong to the same community, it seems perfectly possible for one to say that some action does conform to the rules of the community to which the agent belongs (which is also the community to which the person making the moral judgment belongs) and to say, without contradicting oneself, that the action is nevertheless wrong. There would, however, if this theory were true, be a flagrant contradiction in saying that an action was wrong, although it did conform to the rules of the agent's community, or that it was right, although it did not conform to these rules.

It is sometimes suggested that there are two questions which must carefully be kept distinct: whether an action is right or wrong, which question is settled by whether or not it conforms or fails to conform to the rules of the agent's community, and the further question whether these rules are good rules or bad rules. It seems implausible to say, however, that it is right to conform to a community's rule, however harmful having such a rule is. If one of a community's rules is very harmful indeed, then perhaps steps ought to be taken to change it; perhaps, then, it is right and proper to take steps to change it, but it is hardly plausible to suggest that to say that it is right to take steps to change it simply means that taking steps to change it accords with one of the community's rules; it might well, one feels, be right to take steps to change a community's harmful rules, whether this community had a rule to the effect that its members were to take steps to change its harmful rules for the better or not. And one perfectly good way of trying to change a community's rules is by breaking them oneself, and trying to persuade other people to break them also; but if, in order to change a harmful rule, it is right to break it, it cannot be that 'right' simply means 'in accordance with the rules of the community to which the person performing the right action belongs'.

It might be suggested that two conditions must be fulfilled for an action to be right. In the first place, it must conform with a rule actually in practice among the community to which the person performing the action belongs, and, in the second place, this rule must be a useful rule. Such a view, however, would be no more plausible than the one it is intended to replace. Clearly there is no contradiction in saying – and it would even be quite reasonable to say this – that some actions are right, even though they are not covered by a useful rule, because the consequences of omitting them would be very bad indeed. There is, too, no contradiction in saying – and it is even reasonable to say – that some actions are right, because they are covered by a rule which is not a useful rule, because, though the consequences of having the rule are bad, the consequences of one individual's departing from it, given that a community actually does have it, would be worse. Hence there is no truth in the view that 'right' means 'in accordance with a useful rule' and that 'wrong' means 'not in accordance with a useful rule'.

If we consider more carefully what it is to be a moral rule, or to have a moral code, it is difficult to see how the theory that 'right' means 'in accordance with the moral code of the agent's community' or 'in accordance with a moral rule which the agent's community accepts' is so very different from a version of subjectivism which we have already found to be inadequate. The reason for this is that it is quite plausible to suggest that statements about a community's moral codes or a community's moral rules are statements about the attitudes which members of that community have to the performance or omission of certain classes of action. For example, to say that an action is contrary to a given community's moral code may just mean that it is one of a class of actions which all or most members of that community consider to be wrong. This theory, as we have already seen, would be circular, for it defines 'wrong' in terms of being considered wrong. Also, there seems to be no contradiction in saying that all or most members of a given community think mistakenly that a certain class of actions is wrong, whereas, if this definition were correct, there would be a contradiction in saying this, for if most members of a community thought an action wrong, it would, on the theory, be wrong, and so could not be mistakenly thought by them to be wrong.

Perhaps, however, it is incorrect to define a community's moral codes in terms of the beliefs of members of that community about what is right and wrong. It would, however, be most implausible to suggest that statements about a community's rules or about a community's moral codes were not statements at all about the attitude of members of this community to the performance or omission of certain classes of actions. For example, to say that a given community has a rule prohibiting cousins from marrying one another is very likely to say something like this: when cousins do marry one another, most members of the community view this action with abhorrence; they take steps to prevent such marriages, treat them as being null and of no effect when they do take place, and inflict pain, inconvenience or deprivation of liberty or rights on those participating in them. Hence though statements about a community's moral rules are not statements simply about the beliefs of members of this community, they are statements about members of this community, partly about their feelings, but also about the manner in which they will behave towards breaches of these rules, should any occur. Hence such theories are bound to have the same type of difficulty as the subjectivist theories we have recently been considering.

One special variety of the theory that to say that an action is wrong means that it infringes the moral rules of the community of which the person who performed the action in question is a member is the view that to say that an action is wrong means that it is contrary to the positive law of the country to which the agent belongs (or should it be the country in which he is living at the time at which he performs the action in question?). Such a view, too, has no plausibility whatsoever. There is no contradiction in saying that an action is wrong, although there is no law prohibiting it; indeed, it would be impracticable and undesirable to prohibit every wrong action by law, partly because of the difficulty and expense of enforcing the laws, partly because of the amount of interference with people's liberty which this would involve. Similarly, there is no contradiction in saying that it is sometimes right to break the law, and indeed, not only is this not contradictory, there seems every reason to suppose that sometimes it *is* right to break the law.

It was once supposed that there was some special difficulty for the theory that morality was eternal and immutable, and independent both of man's will and of man's opinions, in that whether or not some action was contrary to law, which law was deliberately and freely created by human beings, could make a difference to what is right and wrong.[1] If morality was eternal and immutable, it was supposed, it could not be altered by human action, but if law made a difference to what it was right to do, it could be altered by the human action of creating the law or of altering it, and so was not eternal and immutable. There is, however, no difficulty in supposing that, though morality is eternal and immutable, what is or is not contrary to law makes a difference to what is right and wrong, provided, or course, that one does not *define* 'right' as 'in accordance with the law' and 'wrong' as 'not in accordance with the law'. The reason why there is no such difficulty is this. There is no reason why one item in the eternal and immutable moral law should not be a rule to the effect that breaking the positive law of the country to which one belongs is wrong or, at any rate, tends to be wrong. If there is such an item, then, of course, whether an action is or is not prohibited by law will have some bearing upon whether or not it is right or wrong, and hence one can alter the morality of an action by altering the positive law which prohibited it, or by creating positive law which enjoins it. Whether or not one

---

[1] This difficulty was discussed by Ralph Cudworth, in *A Treatise Concerning Eternal and Immutable Morality*, Book I, Chapter II.

decides to prohibit or to enjoin by law a certain class of actions, however, only makes a difference to their morality because of the truth of the rule, which is one item in the eternal and immutable moral law, that *if* any class of actions is contrary to law, performing actions of that class is, or tends to be, wrong.

Not only does one not alter the morality of the *class* of actions, actions contrary to the law, by altering the law, one does not even alter the morality of any given individual action by altering the law. If one repeals the law prohibiting sexual intercourse between consenting males, for example – let us suppose, for the sake of argument, that the fact that something is prohibited by law is *sufficient* to make it wrong – one does not cause actions which were wrong when they were performed *before* the law was repealed, to become right. What one does is to make other instances of the same class of actions, performed *after* the law was repealed, right. There is nothing whatsoever surprising about this, since circumstances, in that a kind of action which was once contrary to law is so no longer, have altered, and there is no reason why instances of a class of actions performed in one kind of circumstance should not be wrong, while other instances of the same kind of action performed in different circumstances are right.

Perhaps this is a convenient place to make a few remarks about the general nature of the connection between the morality of actions and whether or not they are prohibited or enjoined by law. Actions may be divided into three classes, those which are prohibited by law, those which are enjoined by law, and those which are neither prohibited by law nor enjoined by law. The class of actions which are neither prohibited by law nor enjoined by law need not here be considered.

Of the actions which are prohibited by law, there are firstly actions, like murder, which would be *wrong*, even if they were not prohibited by law. If we agree that the fact that an action is prohibited by law has some tendency to make it wrong to perform that action, such actions, when they become prohibited by law, become wrong on two counts, whereas before they were wrong only on one. Secondly, there are those actions which, if they were not prohibited by law, would have been *right* in the sense that they would have been permissible but not obligatory; these actions are such that, though they would have been right, it would not have been wrong to omit them. An example of such a class of actions would be taking brandy from France to England without declaring it. In the absence of a law prohibiting one from doing this, taking brandy from France to England would be right or permissible, but not actually obligatory. When a law is passed prohibiting actions such as these, it is likely that they will then become wrong, since the fact that an action is contrary to law has some tendency to make it wrong. Since this action was not obligatory before, there seems no reason why it should not be right to obey the law, as there might have been if that law had prohibited an action which, antecedently to being prohibited, was positively *obligatory*. (I think, however, that a situation might arise in which so many actions which, apart from being prohibited by law, were neither wrong nor obligatory, became prohibited by law that citizens might be under some obligation to disobey a proliferation of laws which grossly restricted their liberties. Whether they had such an obligation or not would depend on the circumstances.)

Lastly, there is a class of actions which would, if they were not prohibited by law, have been positively *obligatory*. If such a class of actions becomes prohibited, then it will depend upon the circumstances whether it is right to do the thing which would certainly have been obligatory, had it not been prohibited, or on the other hand to obey the law, and omit the thing which would have been obligatory had it not been prohibited. For example, a pacifist might consider it wrong to give a substantial part of his income to paying for arms, but if not to do this becomes prohibited, he has to consider whether his obligation to obey the law of his country outweighs his obligation not to pay for armaments, or whether his obligation not to pay for armaments outweighs his obligation to obey the laws of his country.

Parallel considerations apply without alteration to the case when actions are *enjoined* by law. Indeed, being prohibited by law and being enjoined by law may be considered as two different sides of the same coin. If an action is prohibited by law, then its omission may be considered as being enjoined, and if an action is enjoined by law, then its omission may be considered as being prohibited.

There are, of course, many sorts of rules, and moral rules are only one of these. Games have rules. So do corporations, limited liability companies and parliament; indeed, all manmade institutions would find it impossible to exist and carry out their functions without rules which co-ordinated the activities of the different individuals comprising them. Sometimes these rules have grown up in the course of time, at other times they have been deliberately and consciously formulated. They are all, however, alike in that they have been deliberately or accidentally produced by man in order to serve man's purposes, and can be altered by him if need be. Moral rules, however, are not like this. It is true that people's attitudes to actions can change, so that what is regarded by any community as immoral at one time, and is punished by it in one way or another, is not necessarily regarded as immoral by it at another time. But what is regarded as immoral by any community is one thing, and what really is immoral is another. Though it is possible to change the moral attitudes of members of one's community, and to persuade them to impose penalties for actions at present unpenalized or to relax penalties already in force, it is not possible to change something from being right to being wrong, or *vice versa*. Indeed, the notion of changing something from being right to being wrong, or from being wrong to being right, does not make sense, and the moral law can no more be changed than can the truths of mathematics. (The truths of physics cannot be changed either, but the idea of changing them is not incomprehensible; God, if he existed, could change the laws of physics, but not change the laws of mathematics.) Supposing that for some reason you did not like it that killing people was wrong – perhaps there was someone you particularly wanted to kill, but you were not prepared to do anything immoral, and so wished to alter the fact that it was immoral – what could you conceivably do, or what steps could you conceivably take to remedy this? You could, I suppose, try to convince yourself that killing people was not immoral, but, even if you succeeded, this would not make killing people not immoral; what you would have changed would simply be the fact that you yourself thought it *was* immoral. Similarly, you could try to convince other people that killing people was not immoral but, again, even if you succeeded, this would not make killing people not immoral, since, as we have seen, altering people's opinions about what is immoral is not the same thing as altering what is immoral. If you wish to change the law of the land in which you live, there are usually known procedures which may be adopted, but if you wish to change the moral law, there are no procedures, known or unknown, which may be adopted.

There is, indeed, something rather *like* changing something from being right to being wrong, which *may* be done. If it is wrong to disobey the law, then one can make something wrong – say, withdrawing one's children from school before the age of fifteen – by passing a law making it illegal to do this thing, which was not illegal before. But this, as we have seen, is not to make something wrong which was right before. If it is the case that breaking the law is wrong, there is nothing one can do to alter this fact; what one has done, by making illegal something which was not illegal before, is not to change this or any other moral fact; one has, in the above example, simply to change the circumstances, so that an action which, performed at one time, is not illegal and so not immoral, is, performed at a later time, illegal and consequently immoral.

Hence one extremely important difference between moral rules and other sorts of rule is that whereas other sorts of rule are man-made, and capable of being altered by human decision, moral rules are not man-made – perhaps because they are not *made* at all – and are not capable of being altered by human decision. Hence there is little to be said for Kant's view that the will is subject only to a law of which it can regard itself as the author.

I do not wish, in the foregoing pages, to give the impression that society's rules are irrelevant to what it is right or wrong for an individual member of that society to do. Most of these rules have grown up over a long period of time, and in the course of that time have become adapted, to a greater or lesser extent, to society's needs, and, in the interests of social cohesion and cooperation, it is necessary that most of them should be obeyed more often than not. Hence there is some presumption that if an action conflicts with an established social rule, it is wrong. However, even if this were not merely a presumption, but a universal rule, it would still not be the case that 'right' and 'wrong' could be defined in terms of conformity or otherwise to the rules which actual societies accept.

CHAPTER XI

EVOLUTION AND ETHICS

Though evolutionary ethical theories[1] are far from popular at the present moment, once upon a time they enjoyed a considerable vogue. After the Theory of Evolution was first propounded by Darwin in the middle of the nineteenth century, it seemed not unnatural to regard evolution as a kind of progress. If evolution is regarded as a kind of progress, it seems also natural to suppose that the direction of evolution, if this can be discovered, is some sort of guide to what is good morality. If evolution, as the rather misleading statement that the fittest survive would suggest, is a process of continual improvement, then all we need to do in order to find out what is better and what is worse is to find out in what direction the evolutionary process is going. If we assume that we ought to make ourselves and others better, then it would appear to follow that we ought deliberately to try to conform to the pattern of change that an examination of the evolutionary process would discover.

There are, however, a number of very strong objections to regarding the direction of evolution as any guide to progress. Even if, as a matter of fact, there is some tendency for the better to be favoured by the evolutionary process at the expense of the worse, this is only a tendency, which is sometimes overridden by stronger and contrary tendencies. Though it is true that the fittest tend to have the advantage in the struggle to survive over the less fit, the word 'fittest' in this context simply means 'fittest to survive', and there seems to be no particular reason why the qualities which we regard as admirable should necessarily make their possessors more fit to survive than other qualities. Health, for example, though it is normally regarded as an admirable, or rather a desirable, characteristic, usually is an advantage to its possessor in the struggle for survival, but it need not be; in time

[1] Evolutionary theories have been put forward by T. H. Huxley in his Romanes lectures, by Julian Huxley in *Essays of a Humanist* (Chatto and Windus, 1964 and Penguin, 1966), and by C. H. Waddington in *The Ethical Animal* (Allen & Unwin, 1960). The treatment in this chapter, however, is entirely my own.

of war, when healthy men are compelled to kill one another but unhealthy men are not, unhealthy men are much more likely to survive than healthy men, and hence unhealthy men will be fitter to survive than healthy men. Intelligence is usually regarded as being an admirable or desirable characteristic, but if intelligent men and women are able and willing to use contraceptives to limit the size of their families or to avoid having children at all, then stupidity will be a characteristic which in some ways is favoured by the evolutionary process at the expense of intelligence, and stupid men will be fitter to survive than intelligent men. And any characteristic, however frivolous, in men which is attractive to women, and any characteristic, however frivolous, in women which is attractive to men, will tend to be favoured at the expense of other characteristics, however admirable most people may think them, which are not attractive to the opposite sex. If gentlemen prefer blondes, then being fair of hair will be a characteristic which will be favoured by natural selection, and if women prefer men who are strong, or hairy, or good dancers, then these characteristics too will tend to be favoured. It is true that the evolutionary process started with amoebae and has ended in men, and men, who, unlike amoebae, write books on evolutionary ethics, are sufficiently prejudiced to think of themselves as being better than amoebae; but men are not the latest species to survive – species of virus are evolving all the time – and there is no reason to suppose that the characteristics which men have and other organisms lack will always enable men to compete successfully with other organisms, or to suppose that men will necessarily be replaced by supermen. A new species of influenza virus might wipe out the whole of mankind in a week or so, but this would not mean that viruses are fitter than men in any other way than that their characteristics have given them an advantage over men in the struggle for survival.

There are also a number of erroneous conclusions which are quite frequently deduced from the facts about evolutionary development. It is sometimes thought that knowledge about evolution ought to make us revise ethical views commonly held by educated Europeans. For example, most educated Europeans think that kindness, a disposition to sacrifice oneself and to put others before oneself, gentleness and non-violence are characteristics which it is proper to regard as admirable. Against this it is argued, however, that such traits will only handicap their possessor in a struggle for survival in which the fierce, the ruthless and the merciless must inevitably be at an advantage in competing with the good-natured and the meek. Even granting that if strength and ruthlessness were characteristics of advantage to their possessors this would not show that it is admirable to have these characteristics, it is not, or not always, a fact that these characteristics *are* of advantage to their possessors, or to the community to which the possessors of these characteristics belong. One characteristic which is of enormous advantage to some species, especially mankind, is their ability to co-operate with one another. If no man had ever been able to co-operate with any other man, it is very doubtful whether mankind would have been able to survive in competition with other animals, despite his superior intelligence. Hence there are many characteristics which tend to survive at the expense of other characteristics, even though they are of no immediate advantage to the beings who possess them, because they enable *other* individuals of the same species to survive. The disposition in some birds to risk their own lives for their offspring, though it is of no advantage to the mother bird itself, does give the chicks a better chance of survival, and so, in favouring the survival of the species, does tend to perpetuate itself where more egotistic behaviour in birds does not. The disposition in some bees to protect the hive by stinging intruders, even though doing so leads to their own death, is perpetuated, though it is no advantage to the individual bees themselves, because it is of advantage to the bee community, and so to the advantage of the species of bees. Altruistic behaviour in men – for example, the disposition to care for one's offspring and to succour and protect other members of the same community – tends to increase man's chances of survival for the same reason. If men were indiscriminately fierce, cunning and ruthless they would, like Cadmus's soldiers, have perished miserably at one another's hands many years ago.

When evolutionary ethical theories take the form of an attempt to *define* the words 'right' and 'wrong' 'good' and 'bad', they are not to my mind, at all plausible. For example, 'right' might be held to mean 'conducive to the survival of the race' or 'conducive to the survival of the community of which the agent is a member' or 'in accordance with the direction in which evolution is moving'. On such views, of course, moral judgments would be synthetic,

contingent and empirical, for statements about what is conducive
to the survival of the agent's community or the race or about
what accords with the direction of evolution are synthetic,
contingent and empirical. Such theories, however, are easy to
refute. Many people are quite sure, for example, that polygamy
is wrong, and wrong whether or not it is conducive to the survival
of the community which practices it. It makes no difference to
the force of this objection whether or not they are right or wrong
about this. The point is that, if 'wrong' *meant* 'inconducive to
the survival of the community', these people would be contradicting themselves if they thought both that a practice was wrong
and that it was not inconducive to the survival of the community
which had the practice. Since they do not appear to be contradicting themselves, this cannot be what they mean by the word
'wrong'. Similarly, one can – and most people do – believe that
something is wrong without knowing or even having any
opinion about the direction which evolution is taking, which
would not be logically possible if 'wrong' simply meant 'not
in accordance [with the direction of evolution'. When ordinary
people say that one man is better than another, they cannot be
making any statement which involves a knowledge of evolutionary
biology, for they feel themselves competent to make judgments
about good and bad, even though they are totally ignorant of biology.

It seems to me, however, that it is possible to produce an
evolutionary ethical theory of some kind which is more plausible
than any which has hitherto been elaborated by anyone I know of.
Certainly it would seem to me to be unlikely that evolution
should have no bearing whatsoever upon moral philosophy,
when it is considered that a community's moral codes have
evolved over a long period of time, and that the characteristics
of these codes must have at least something to do with the ability
to survive of the communities which have adopted these codes.

First of all, let me briefly state what I believe are the elementary
facts about the manner in which some characteristics are favoured
by the process of evolution, while other characteristics are not.
(I do not think it will greatly matter for my present purpose if
these facts are not wholly accurate.) In the first place, no living
organism lives indefinitely; it dies and is replaced by organisms
which it itself, usually in conjunction with other similar organisms, has reproduced. The living organism which it has reproduced

will tend on the whole to resemble its parents, but the resemblance will not be complete, and the offspring will differ both from their parents and from one another in various ways. Furthermore, parents will produce more offspring than can possibly themselves reach maturity and produce offspring. To some extent, which of the offspring will survive will be a matter of accident, but to some extent it will be because some of the characteristics in respect of which they differ from other offspring of the same or similar parents are of advantage to them in competing for food or mates or in escaping from predators. Hence offspring with certain characteristics will be more likely to reach an age when they can reproduce themselves, or more likely to rear their young successfully, than offspring without these characteristics, and, since they will tend to pass on these characteristics to their children, there will be a continuous pressure in the direction of spreading and improving upon advantageous characteristics, and weeding out or whittling away disadvantageous characteristics. Hence if having a long neck is of some advantage to a species, offspring with the longer necks will be more likely to reproduce themselves, and the still longer necked offspring of these offspring will tend to be favoured at the expense of the shorter necked, and so the process will continue until having a longer neck ceases to be of any advantage to the animals who possess it.

Now moral codes, it seems to me, are not wholly dissimilar from necks, for the following reasons. Communities compete with one another for survival, just as individuals do, and, just as with the characteristics of individual organisms, the moral codes of one generation resemble, but do not completely resemble, the moral codes of the previous generation. Furthermore, a community's moral code may be of advantage to it in competing with other communities, or it may handicap it. If the industry of a community is of advantage to it in competing with other communities for a limited supply of food and raw materials, then a moral code which encourages industry will tend to be favoured at the expense of a moral code which does not encourage industry. The industry, and the code which inculcates moral approval of industry, will tend to increase the prosperity of the industrious community; it will grow in number and wealth and annihilate or annex less industrious communities, and so its moral code will oust the moral codes of the less prosperous and successful. Similarly, if military prowess is of advantage to a community, a moral code which tends to inculcate the military virtues will give the community which possesses this moral code an advantage over communities which do not have such a moral code; this will make the community with this moral code more prosperous and successful than its rivals, and hence the moral code inculating the military virtues will tend to prevail over the moral codes of the less successful communities. It need hardly be said that a moral code which tends to favour a community in one set of conditions will not necessarily favour a similar community if conditions are different; hence there is no reason to expect uniformity in moral codes, any more than there is any reason to expect all species to have similar characteristics. It seems quite possible however, that the present enormous disadvantages of international warfare will tend to produce a single world community with an overall moral code, though this will probably vary in some degree or other over different parts of the globe.

It follows from what has gone before that moral codes are likely to be to a large extent utilitarian in nature, for moral codes will tend to survive to the extent that they are useful to the community which possesses them. It must not be expected, however, that moral codes should be wholly utilitarian, for the usefulness of its moral code is only one factor which enables a community to survive, and a community with a very useful moral code may nevertheless not prevail over a community with a less useful one, if the members of the second community are healthier, stronger, more intelligent or more richly endowed in natural resources than the members of the first community. That moral codes are not wholly useful to the communities which possess them is only what one would expect from the analogy with the other characteristics which enable living things to survive, for these living things are not perfectly adapted to their environment; a long neck has disadvantages as well as advantages; some characteristics are useless because the circumstances which produced them have changed, and the process by which living organisms come to be adapted to their environment is still continuing, and is never complete. Besides fingers, which are useful, man has toes, which are not very useful, and appendices, which are not useful at all. Hence the fact that moral codes have evolved because useful moral codes tend to prevail at the expense of less useful ones should not lead us to expect that all the items in a community's moral code should be of use to it, or that the useful items cannot be improved upon.

The fact that a community's moral codes have evolved because they are part of the manner in which a community adapts itself to its environment, and must roughly or predominantly be of advantage to the community whose moral codes they are, has a number of important implications for moral philosophy. In the first place, I think it follows that either man's moral beliefs are wholly irrational, or some form of utilitarianism is roughly true. My reason for thinking this is that, since in order to survive we should have to have moral codes which were roughly utilitarian in character, we should have to have approximately utilitarian moral beliefs, whether these moral beliefs were true or not. Hence, if utilitarianism is not even roughly true, and we cannot have rational utilitarian moral beliefs, we must have irrational utilitarian moral beliefs.

It is, in fact, very tempting to suppose that the theory about the connection between evolution and our moral codes which I have just put forward does imply that our moral beliefs are all irrational. In the form in which I put it forward, it is suggested that certain moral beliefs were arrived at in a haphazard or random manner, just as certain offspring of two parents have certain characteristics and other offspring of the same parents do not. On this form of the theory, just as one does not have a long neck from an appreciation of its advantages in obtaining food, so one does not have a belief in the rectitude of bravery from a rational appreciation of its advantages; the belief grew up irrationally, and tended to survive because it was useful. Such a theory would accord very well, for example, with some version of subjectivism, according to which moral beliefs are beliefs about what either oneself or one's community approves of. The evolutionary theory I have outlined would then explain how it comes about that one tends in general to feel approval of what is of advantage to one's community and disapproval of what is not. Such a theory, too, would fit in very well with some versions of non-propositional theory, to be discussed later,[1] according to which the function of ethical words is to express emotions or to formulate commands. Such theories could then be supplemented by an evolutionary explanation of how it comes

[1] Chapter XII.

about that we are disposed to have the feelings or issue the commands which it is roughly advantageous to the community we should have or issue.

There is no necessity, however, to take this rather pessimistic attitude. Among the main things which are of advantage to human communities in the struggle for survival is a knowledge of mathematics or of physical science. Hence communities whose science or mathematics is poor will tend to be weeded out at the expense of communities whose science or mathematics is good. This does not show that the beliefs, about science and mathematics, of the community which survived are irrational; rather, it must be the case that the mathematical and scientific beliefs of the surviving communities must have been more rational than the mathematical and scientific beliefs of the communities who did not survive.

The reason why the fact that certain *scientific* and *mathematical* beliefs have become prevalent because of their survival value does not show them to be irrational in this. Scientific and mathematical beliefs, from one point of view, are beliefs about the correct means to obtaining given ends. The mathematical belief that two and two are four, put in one way, amounts to the fact that if you want four things, and you obtain two things and two other things, you will have four things. Similarly, the scientific belief that water expands when it freezes amounts to the belief that, if you don't want anything to be destroyed by the solidification of water, you must take steps to prevent its freezing. Correct beliefs about the means to ends must obviously be of enormous value in any struggle for survival, and this is the reason why good science must inevitably drive out bad.

Moral beliefs, however, are not usually thought to be beliefs about the correct means to ends. There is normally said to be a difference between what is called the hypothetical imperative, which is not supposed to be a moral imperative, 'Do so-and-so if you want such-and-such', and the categorical imperative, which is supposed to be moral, 'Do such-and-such (whether you want to or not)'. Hence it is more difficult to explain how moral beliefs can be both evolutionally determined and be at the same time rational, than it is to explain how scientific beliefs can be both evolutionally caused and be rational.

However, evolution is not always a blind force, which selects certain characteristics, produced randomly, because of their survival value and rejects others, also produced randomly, because of their lack of it. This is the way in which the leopard got his spots and the Ethiope his skin, but it is not the way in which art, scientific or philosophical ideas, or the products of engineering or design, have evolved. Such things as these have been deliberately produced by man, and deliberately rejected by him when he has thought of something better or what seemed to him to be better. Hence in the evolution of these things, unlike that of the giraffe's neck or the chameleon's ability to change its colour with the colour of its background, man is not the slave of blind forces, but is himself consciously selecting things which he approves of, and rejecting what he does not approve of. It seems not too far-fetched a flight of fancy to suppose that in the future this process of deliberate selection will extend from the things man has himself created to man himself, and that by such means as selective breeding and the extended use of drugs and surgery man will himself freely decide to a much larger extent than formerly what sort or creature he will be.

When we consider the evolution of man's moral codes, I think it must be remembered that though in part they are like the white skin of the polar bear or the nocturnal habits of the owl, in that they have grown up unplanned, and have been accidentally selected by circumstances unenvisaged and unforeseen, they are also in part like the design of the motor-car or the rules of parliamentary procedure, in that man has changed his moral code to some extent in the light of experience of its disadvantages and of insight into the ways in which it can be improved. Mankind, though partially blind to the effects for good or ill of his moral practices, and though partially bound by inherited beliefs or irrational taboos, is not wholly so. To some extent he is capable of realizing the effects for good or ill of his moral practices and attitudes, and modifying these in the light of this realization. The process is partial, *ad hoc* and piecemeal; an immediate and comprehensive view of moral codes in the light of pure reason is out of the question. But to some extent review does take place, and moral codes are deliberately adopted or changed in the light of their advantages or disadvantages. Hence the theory of the evolution of moral codes elaborated earlier in this chapter, together with its possible implication that all our moral beliefs were irrationally selected by blind evolutionary forces over which man had no control, must at least partially be revised.

It remains the case that those moral codes with the highest survival value will prevail, other things being equal, over moral codes with a lower survival value, but man has the codes with the higher survival value partly because, in adopting his moral codes, he is deliberately selecting them, as he does his scientific and mathematical beliefs, because of their usefulness. To this extent, the more rational man's opinions of the usefulness of his moral codes are, the more likely these moral codes are to survive, and to this extent their actual success in the struggle for survival is not a proof of their irrationality, but a test of their rationality, just as the success in the struggle for survival of some kind of offensive and defensive weapons over other kinds is a test of the rationality of the principles on which they have been constructed, and the justness of the appreciation of their effectiveness in warfare.

Furthermore, the importance of survival must not be over-estimated, and survival in a sense becomes less and less important as man becomes more and more civilized. Within the overall requirement that man must *survive*, all sorts of different alternative ways of living are possible. The choice between these different ways of living cannot be determined by considering what will best enable those adopting them to survive, for they all equally well enable these communities to survive. And since, within this broad framework, *whatever* the way of life a community chooses, this way of life will survive, and the way of life it rejects will fail to survive, it cannot be said that the way of life which in fact survives must be the best. It is not that the way of life that survives is the best, but that it is the way of life which is chosen that survives, whether it is the best way of life or not. For this reason, evolutionary ethical theories are bound to be unsatisfactory.

There is perhaps, however, another way in which evolution has a bearing upon ethics, which way we have not yet considered. It seems unlikely that, in the consideration of what is the better or worse way of life for man to choose, man's nature is wholly irrelevant. In other words, the sort of way of life which is best for man must be adapted to his needs. To take a very simple example, all marriage rules, if any, that mankind adopt must somehow be related to the fact that it takes two sexes for mankind to reproduce himself, that reproduction is not possible before a certain age, that human children are born helpless, and do not reach maturity until a relatively large proportion of their life-span has elapsed. Now these things have come about because man has evolved to be the sort of being he is as a result of natural selection. Hence to the extent that man's morality must be adapted to his needs, it is determined indirectly by evolutionary forces. Even what is good and bad in art and literature is to some extent also so determined. Literature must be about things which man can understand and which appeal to him, and what appeals to him must be stories about beings roughly similar to himself, with similar emotions, aspirations and outlook. That man has these emotions, aspirations and outlook is determined by natural selection. In art, so long as it is not abstract, the things man enjoys seeing depicted are, roughly, nature and other men. That nature appears to man as it does is determined by the fact that he sees it with eyes which have come to be what they are by a process of natural selection, and that man looks as he does is also manifestly evolutionally determined. Even in music it can be argued that the forms man enjoys must not be too simple, or he will get bored, or too complex, or he will not be able to comprehend them, and that he is the sort of being to whom musical forms of a given degree of complexity appeal must be determined by the depth of his understanding, which has itself been made what it is by a process of natural selection. He must, too, have evolved ears, which some animals do not have. An animal who had evolved totally different sense-organs from man would appreciate totally different kinds of aesthetic objects, and on different planets in different solar systems of different galaxies it seems to me that there is no denying that very different sense-organs are possible.

CHAPTER XII

NON-PROPOSITIONAL THEORIES

So far, every possible account of the nature of moral judgments, and the manner in which we come to know them to be true, has turned out to be a blind alley. Moral judgments are not *a priori*, necessary, analytic, and such that they can been seen to be true because to deny them would be contradictory, an infringement of the ordinary laws which it is necessary to observe in order to think logically. On the other hand, though it follows from this that they are synthetic, it is implausible to claim that they are synthetic propositions which we are able just to see *a priori*, intuitively and without argument to be necessarily true. Attempts to show that they are synthetic, contingent and empirical judgments, known to be true by observation and experience, and about the natural world, also break down. First of all, efforts to identify moral judgments with some well-known independently identifiable kind of judgments about the natural world, such as judgments about what men approve of or judgments about human conventions all failed. And then the view that judgments about right and wrong, though not the same as any independently indentifiable class of judgments about the natural world, are, nevertheless, judgments about the natural world, the truth of which is discovered by means of a moral sense, had also to be rejected. So far, then, we seem to have reached an impasse.

It is very commonly held nowadays that the reason for the impasse is that the whole programme of investigation we have pursued hitherto rests upon a mistake.[1] We have been asking questions, such as whether moral judgments are analytic or synthetic, whether they are empirical or *a priori*, whether they are necessary or contingent, whether they are seen to be true by intuition, whether they are basic propositions, or whether they are known to be true by inference. In asking such questions we presuppose that the function of ethical sentences is to make judgments, or to assert propositions, or to make statements (which judgments, propositions or statements are capable of being true or false); and we

---

[1] See, for example, A. J. Ayer, *Language, Truth and Logic* (Gollancz, 1946).

then ask such questions as whether they are analytic or synthetic statements, or whether they are statements which are known to be true *a priori* or by means of observation and experience. But, it is frequently argued, to suppose that the function of moral sentences is to formulate judgments, propositions or statements at all is a mistake. Once it is seen to be a mistake, it will also be seen that all the questions we have been asking up to now are bogus questions, resting upon a false assumption, the assumption that the function of ethical sentences is to express propositions. It is not surprising then, if most modern philosophers are right, that the questions we have been asking are so difficult to answer. If moral sentences do not express propositions at all, either an affirmative or a negative answer to questions such as whether they express analytic or synthetic propositions, or whether or not they express propositions which are known to be true by observation and experience must be mistaken.

Although it makes sense to say of propositions that they are true or false, many of the things which we use English sentences to say cannot meaningfully be said to be true or to be false. It does not make sense to say of the command 'Shut the door' that it is true or that it is false, or of the request 'Please shut the door' that it is true or that it is false, or of the expression of a wish 'Would that the door were shut' that it is true or that it is false; nor does it make sense to say of a large number of other things, which we can use English sentences to say, that they are true or false. These things, other than propositions, which can be put into words by means of English sentences, will be considered in more detail in the next chapter, when I shall consider whether it is plausible to identify moral judgments with any of them. In the present chapter I shall consider difficulties which apply alike to all varieties of the view that it is not the function of ethical sentences to express propositions.

I shall use the word 'tenet', as the best neutral word I can think of, to describe what we use ethical sentences to say, intended not to beg the question whether what we are doing when we use ethical sentences is to assert a proposition or issue a command or express a wish or what have you. The trouble with non-propositional theories of ethics is that there are a number of notions, which seem, at first sight at any rate, to be applicable to our moral tenets, which one would normally consider were linked inescapability with truth and fasehood. For example, it would seem that when we are in doubt about what we ought to do, as we sometimes are, what we are trying to do is to find a *true* answer, or the right answer, to the question 'What is it that I ought to do?' When we are trying to discover what it is that we ought to do, we seem to be trying to make ourselves sensitive to something external to ourselves, which it is not within our power to alter, that is, to discover some true proposition to the effect that what we ought to do is so-and-so, the truth of which true proposition we have not the power to do anything about. Again, when we are trying to answer the question 'What ought I to do in this situation in which I find myself?', it looks as if we are trying to find *reasons* for thinking that one answer to this question is correct, and other answers to this question are incorrect; but reasons, it would seem, are normally reasons for thinking that something is true. If we try to convince *someone else* that what he ought to do is so-and-so, we again produce reasons for what we say, and the fact that we can produce reasons for what we say might tend to indicate that what we say is the sort of thing which can meaningfully be said to be true or false; for reasons, again, are frequently reasons for thinking that some proposition is true. If I think that what Smith ought to do is so-and-so, but he thinks that he ought not to do so-and-so, what he says and what I say are *incompatible* with one another, but to say that two things are incompatible with one another is normally to say that they cannot both be *true*. Again, my moral tenets may not only be incompatible with Smith's moral tenets, my own moral tenets may, if I am careless, be inconsistent with one another, and inconsistency, too, is usually defined in terms of truth; to say that two things are inconsistent with one another is usually said to mean that they cannot both be true. Similarly, some of my moral tenets may entail other moral tenets, which I also hold, or entail moral tenets which I do not hold, but would hold if I were completely rational, and entailment, too, is usually defined in terms of truth; to say that one thing entails another is to say that if the first thing is *true*, the second thing must be *true* also, or to say that if the first thing is true, the seond thing cannot be false. More, serious, from a practical point of view, than any of these, is the fact that if moral tenets cannot be true or false, it would seem as if we can never be either right or wrong about a moral issue, because for me to be right on a moral issue is for my moral tenet to be true, and for me to be wrong on a moral issue is for my moral tenet to be false. But if I can never be right or wrong on a moral issue, there would seem to be no point in my bothering at all about what moral tenets I hold. None can be right, and so none can be wrong; none can approximate closely to the truth, and none can be far from the truth. Hence all moral tenets would seem to be equally satisfactory or equally unsatisfactory, if it even makes sense to talk of them as being satisfactory or unsatisfactory at all, and true morality, if the phrase makes sense, would appear to be something not worth bothering about.

These objections can to some extent be answered.[1] For example, advice can neither be true nor false. If I say, 'Buy as much gold as possible' or, 'I advise you to buy as much gold as possible,' it does not make sense to say of this piece of advice that it is either true or that it is not true. Nevertheless advice can be good advice or bad advice, and some pieces of advice can be better than other pieces of advice. Hence it would be foolish to say that there was no need to bother about what advice you gave anyone on the grounds that all advice was equally impossible of truth and falsehood and no advice could be near to the truth or far from it. Again, though commands are incapable of being true or false, it is nevertheless possible for Smith's commands to be inconsistent with Jones's commands. If Smith says 'Shut the door' and Jones says 'Leave the door open' they are issuing incompatible commands, and it is logically impossible for me to obey both of them, just as it is logically impossible for two incompatible propositions to be both true. Similarly, I can issue inconsistent commands, just as I can hold inconsistent beliefs, and some commands can in some way or other involve others, just as some propositions entail others. If I say, at one and the same time, both 'Shut the door' and 'Leave the door open', my commands are inconsistent with one another; and if I say, 'Everyone on this train must get out at the next station', this would seem to involve that, if Smith is in this train, I am commanding him to get out at the next station. At any rate, he would be disobeying my command if he were in the train, and heard my com-

---

[1] See, for example, W. H. F. Barnes, 'Ethics without Propositions', *Aristotelian Society Supplementary Proceedings*, Vol. XII, 1948. See also, R. B. Brandt, *Ethical Theory* (Prentice-Hall, 1959), Chapter IX.

mand, and did not get out at the next station. The notion of giving reasons, too, is not so closely tied to the notion of truth and falsity as at first sight might appear. It is possible to give reasons for things which cannot be true or false; for example, it is possible to give reasons for doing one thing rather than another, but doing one thing rather than another is not a proposition, and it would not make sense to say that doing one thing rather than another was true, or that doing one thing rather than another was false. Finally, if it is possible for things other than propositions – pieces of advice, for example – to be better than one another, and if it is possible to give good or bad reasons for things other than propositions, our last objection to non-propositional theories would seem to be answered. It would then be foolish to cease to bother about what ethical tenets we held, on the grounds that ethical tenets were not capable of being true or false, if some were better than others, or if better reasons could be given for some than could be given for others. To do this would be rather like to cease to bother about what sort of advice we gave, on the grounds that it did not make sense to say of pieces of advice that they were true or that they were false.

However, though things, of which it does not make sense to predicate truth or falsity, can be better than others, have better reasons given for them than others, be inconsistent with one another and involve one another, it must be considered whether they are inconsistent, and so on, with one another in the *right ways*, that is, in the way in which moral tenets are inconsistent, and so on, with one another, and not in some other way. Another point must also be considered. Though some things which are not propositions can be inconsistent with one another, and though some things which are not propositions can have reasons given for them, it may be that there is no one thing, other than a proposition, of which can be said *all* the things considered above which certainly can be said of our moral tenets.

The things we can *say* of our ethical tenets are as follows. We can say that what Smith thinks on a moral matter, say, that hanging people is wrong, is incompatible with what Jones thinks, that hanging people is not necessarily wrong. We can say that Smith himself is being inconsistent in thinking both that hanging people is wrong and that it is right to hang Robinson, whom he particularly detests. We can say that Smith's belief that hanging is wrong entails that it would be wrong to hang Robinson. We can say that Smith has, or that he has not, given good reasons for thinking that hanging people is wrong. We can also say that we *think* that hanging people is wrong; that Smith thinks hanging people is wrong, though he is *mistaken;* that perhaps hanging people is *not* wrong. We can ask ourselves or someone else the question 'Is hanging people wrong?'; we can *wonder* whether hanging people is wrong and be in doubt about whether it is wrong or not; we can *disbelieve* that hanging people is wrong, or *believe* that hanging people is not wrong. We can say that we *know* that hanging people is wrong, or that we do not know whether hanging people is wrong or not. Almost the only thing we can say of some, but not all, propositions, which we cannot say of moral judgments, is that they are facts. We can say of the assertion 'The cat is on the mat' that it is a fact, i.e. that it is a fact that the cat is on the mat, but we cannot say 'Killing people is wrong' is a fact, or that it is a fact that killing people is wrong.

Now the *way* in which moral tenets are inconsistent with one another is this; if Smith is right in thinking that hanging people is always wrong, Jones must be wrong in thinking hanging people is sometimes right; if Smith is right in thinking that hanging people is wrong, he cannot also be right in thinking that it is right to hang Robinson. Moral tenets entail one another in the sense that if Smith thinks that no one ought to be hanged, he ought also to think, if the question arises, that Robinson ought not to be hanged. The reasons we give for our moral tenets are reasons for thinking them, not just explanations of how it comes about that we think them, but reasons for thinking that they are *so*, for example, that hanging, whatever anyone may say to the contrary, really *is* wrong. Now though commands, for example, can be inconsistent with one another, they cannot be inconsistent with one another *in the required way*; they cannot be inconsistent with one another in the sense that they cannot both be *so*, for it does not make sense to say of a command that it is so, nor can they be inconsistent with one another in the sense that one ought not to think that both of them are so, for it does not make sense to say of commands that one can *think* they are so, or believe them. One cannot think or believe *shut the door*, for example. And I do not think that there is any such thing as a reason for a command, as opposed to a reason for giving a command. A reason for giving a command is a reason for saying out loud some such thing as

'Halt' or 'Quick March', and such a reason will be that the person giving the command wants for some further reason the person or persons he is commanding to behave in the ways commanded, or that there is a certain established ritual about commands, laying down that certain commands are the proper commands to follow upon others. But a reason for giving a command is not at all the same thing as a reason for holding the command. Where beliefs are concerned, there are both reasons for beliefs, and reasons for saying out loud that we believe certain things, and the reasons one has for beliefs and the reasons one has for formulating them out loud are quite different from one another. My reason for thinking that the Conservatives will win the next election, or that God does not exist, are one thing; my reasons for saying so in company are quite another thing. I may think I have excellent reasons for thinking that God does not exist or that the Conservatives will win the next election, and at the same time also think I have equally excellent reasons for not saying so in certain kinds of company. Indeed I may even have excellent reasons for saying out loud certain things for which I have no reason, that is to say for which I have no reason for believing. With commands, requests and a large number of things other than propositions which I can use language to express, I can have reasons for formulating them out loud, but cannot have reasons for them, that is, reasons for believing them or thinking that they are so. I can have reasons for making a promise, for example, but no reasons for thinking or believing a promise, for it does not make sense to say of a promise that it can be thought or believed. In other words, I can have a reason for saying out loud, 'I promise to pay you five pounds before next Tuesday,' though it does not make sense to say, 'I have reasons for thinking I promise to pay you five pounds before next Tuesday.'

Perhaps one of the non-propositional utterances which corresponds most closely to moral tenets is advice. Some advice can be inconsistent with other advice, things can be entailed by what I advise – for example, the advice to sell all one's shares entails that one is advised to sell one's oil shares – and there can be good or bad reasons for a piece of advice. (There can also, as has already been pointed out, be good advice and bad advice.) But again, some advice cannot be inconsistent with other advice in the way in which some moral tenets can be inconsistent with other moral tenets. For moral tenets are inconsistent in the sense that they cannot consistently be held, while it does not make sense to say of advice either that it is held or that it is not held. Moral tenets entail one another in the sense that if you hold one, you must also hold the other, but again, it does not make sense to say of advice that it is held or believed. You can give reasons for a moral tenet in the sense that you can give reasons for holding it, or reasons for thinking that it is so. For example, you can give reasons for holding that no one ought to be hanged, or for thinking that, despite what anyone may say to the contrary, it really is the case that some people ought to be hanged. But again, you cannot give reasons for advice in this sense, for, as I have said, you cannot hold advice, nor can you think that what you advise is so. Furthermore, though advice can be good advice or bad advice, I do not think it ever makes sense to say of a moral tenet that it is good or bad, as opposed to being right or wrong. It is true that you can say 'You would be well advised to work harder,' or, 'It would be advisable for you to work harder', (as opposed to 'Work harder' or 'I advise you to work harder') that this is something that someone holds or thinks, and also that it is something which is so; Smith can hold or think that so-and-so is advisable, and can also think that it is the case that so-and-so *is* advisable. Similarly, reasons for thinking that something is advisable are reasons for thinking or holding something. But, this, so far from showing that moral tenets may be very similar to some form of non-propositional utterance, namely advice, would show, if anything, that someone saying some such thing as, 'It would be advisable for you to work harder,' or 'You would be well-advised to work harder,' is not in fact making a non-propositional utterance at all, but is simply asserting a proposition.

At the beginning of this chapter I defined 'proposition' a little narrowly, by implying that a sentence expresses a proposition if it is possible meaningfully to put the words 'it is true that' in front of it. Personally I think that it is possible to put the words 'it is true that' in front of ethical sentences, which would on this definition show that they are propositions. For example, it is possible to say, 'It is true that men ought to be punished, but they ought to be rehabilitated afterwards,' or, 'It is true

I

that his conduct has frequently been reprehensible, but nevertheless there is something very likeable about him.' However, I can see that this is something that many philosophers might wish to dispute.

If we define 'proposition' a little more widely, however, I do not see that there is any room for doubting that the function of ethical sentences is to express propositions or something very like them. A proposition, I think it might be said, is something which may be asserted or denied; something which may be believed or doubted or wondered about or disbelieved; something about which you may ask the question whether it is so or not; something about which you may disagree with other people; something you may argue about; something you may produce reasons for. It is true that, as we have seen, propositions are not the only things you may disagree with other people about, or about which you may argue, or which you may produce reasons for. You may, as I have said, argue about what to do, as opposed to whether something or other is so or not; you may disagree over whether to do one thing or another, as well as about what is or is not the case; you may produce reasons for doing something as well as produce reasons for thinking something. But where ethical tenets were concerned, it did seem as if you were disagreeing, not about what to do, but about whether or not something or other was so or was not so; it did seem as if you were arguing not about whether to do one thing rather than another, but about whether someone was *right in thinking* one thing rather than another; it did seem as if you were producing reasons not for doing something, but for believing that something was so.

Where the other marks of a proposition are concerned, marks which can be possessed by things which are propositions and not by anything else, it seems to me to be beyond question that our ethical tenets really do possess them. You certainly can assert that eating people is wrong, deny that eating people is wrong, believe that eating people is wrong, believe that eating people is not wrong, doubt that eating people is wrong, wonder whether or not eating people is wrong, ask the question 'Is eating people wrong?', say that Smith, who thinks that eating people is wrong, is mistaken, and agree with Jones in thinking that eating people *is* wrong. Anyone who holds that our moral tenets possess all these marks, and still thinks that they are not propositions or at least very like propositions, seems to me simply not to understand what a proposition is.[1]

It has been suggested that the fact that we say, 'I think capital punishment is wrong,'[2] does not show that 'Captial punishment is wrong' is a statement or assertion, because we sometimes say such things as, 'I think or believe I'll take that one.' when we are not asserting the statement *that* I will take that one, but expressing a tentative decision *to* take that one.

I think this is a correct account of 'think' as it is used in the sentence 'I think I'll take that one', but I do not think that the word 'think' *is* being used in this way in the sentence 'I think capital punishment is wrong.' When Robinson says of Smith that he thinks he will take that one, he is not doing what Smith is doing when he says, 'I think I'll take that one.' Smith is *expressing* a tentative decision to take that one, but Robinson is *reporting* Smith's state of mind as being one of having tentatively decided to take that one. The relation between Smith's saying, 'I think I'll take that one,' and Robinson's saying, 'Smith thinks he'll take that one,' is like the relation between Smith's saying, 'I promise to take thee, N. for my lawful wedded wife,' and Robinson's saying, 'Smith is promising to take her, N. for his lawful wedded wife.' Smith is making a promise, but Robinson is simply reporting that a promise has been made. Smith is making a promise, not making an assertion, and Robinson is making an assertion, not making a promise. However, when Robinson says, 'Smith thinks capital punishment is wrong,' he is not reporting even a tenative decision of Smith's. This is shown by the fact that he can say, 'Smith thinks capital punishment is wrong, and he is right (to think this).' Robinson cannot say, 'Smith thinks he'll take that one, and he is right (i.e. right to think this)', for this would suggest that Smith is believing a proposition about what he will do in the future, a proposition which Robinson thinks he would be right to believe. But the whole assumption of this argument is that, when Smith says, 'I think I'll take that one,' he is not saying that he believes any proposition at all, and so not a proposition about his future behaviour. Furthermore, one cannot say, 'I deny (assert etc.) I'll take that one,' unless 'I'll take that one' *is* being used to make a statement.

[1] See Robert J. Fogelin, *Evidence and Meaning* (Routledge, 1967), pp. 134-5.
[2] See H. H. Price, *Belief* (Allen & Unwin, 1969), p. 338.

However, in case this short way with non-propositional theories be considered unsatisfactory, perhaps it may be as well to consider in more detail some of the more prominent forms of non-propositional utterance, and the ways in which they differ from what we are doing when we use characteristically ethical sentences. This I shall now proceed to do.

CHAPTER XIII

MORAL JUDGMENT AND SOME
PRACTICAL USES OF LANGUAGE

One way in which we use language to modify the behaviour of other people is obvious, and has always been recognized. We may affect the behaviour of other people by supplying them with information which they lack, possession of which information may cause them to act in a different way from that in which they would have acted without it. On the other hand, we may try to influence the behaviour of other people without supplying them with extra information, and use for this purpose language which conveys no information. It would not be unreasonable to suppose that these two ways of affecting the behaviour of other people are found mixed in various proportions. In the lines:

'Ladybird, ladybird, fly away home;
Your house is on fire, and your children will burn'

both ways of modifying the ladybird's behaviour are used. The ladybird is given the information, which is presumably news to her, that her house is on fire. But the words 'fly away home' themselves convey no information, and may be regarded as an attempt to influence action in a more direct way. It is this more direct way of using language to influence action, the most obvious example of which is provided by the use of commands, with which I am primarily concerned in this chapter. It has been less closely investigated, and raises more recondite problems, than the other way. Incidentally, we will consider the question whether moral judgments fall into any of the classes of practical uses of language which we shall distinguish in the following pages.

COMMANDS[1]

I shall say little about commands for they have been much dis-

[1] See R. M. Hare, *The Language of Morals* (O.U.P., 1952), and *Freedom and Reason* (O.U.P., 1963). It is Professor Hare's view that moral judgment are not commands, but a species of imperative. See also G. H. von Wright, *Norm and Action* (Routledge, 1963).

cussed recently. However, the following points are worth mentioning.

Commands are not devoid of what may loosely be called 'cognitive content'. If I say, 'Shut the door,' the words 'shut' and 'the door' have just the same meaning that they have in the sentence 'The door is shut'. The two sentences 'Shut the door' and 'The door is shut' cause the hearer to envisage the same state of affairs, namely, the door's being shut. In the latter sentence it is asserted that the door is shut, and hearing this assertion will in most cases cause the hearer to believe that the door is shut, whereas the former sentence gives no information about what is or is not the case. (It is true that though someone saying, 'Shut the door,' does not assert that the door is not shut, hearing him would certainly lead the hearer to infer that he believes this, for otherwise his giving the command would be pointless, except to deceive.) The 'cognitive content' of commands is essential if they are to be useful as a means of modifying the behaviour of the hearer. If there could be such a thing as a command without cognitive content, it would command without indicating what was commanded. The function of the 'cognitive content' of commands is to designate some state of affairs or action which the hearer is commanded to bring about or to perform.

Since someone issuing a command is not making an assertion, it does not make sense to say of a command that it is true or false. This is not simply because commands are not asserted. The antecedent and consequent of a hypothetical statement are capable of being true or false, though they are not asserted.

A command implies some superior authority or superior power on the part of the commander. The fact that a command is made implies that the commander is in a superior position in some way or other to the person or persons commanded, or, at any rate, that the commander supposes, rightly or wrongly, that he is in such a position, or wishes to make his hearers believe that he is.

Anyone giving a command will normally be taken to believe that the person to whom the command is addressed can hear him, and that it is within his power to obey it.

It must not be assumed that everything verbally similar to 'Shut the door' is a command, nor that everything verbally dissimilar from it is not. 'Pass the salt', especially among people who know one another sufficiently intimately to dispense with formality, may be a request, and 'I expect you to behave yourselves' may be, if not actually a command, at least much more like a command than its verbal form would indicate.

Commands are the most brutal ways of using language to modify the behaviour of other people. No account is taken by the person commanding of the inclinations of the person commanded, and, though the commander may deliberately command someone to do something which he knows this person wants to do, this is no exception, because he is told to do what he wants to do, whether he wants to do it or not. There is no more than an apparent contradiction in this, since the wants of the person commanded, like those of any other person, may conflict, and he may both want to do and not want to do one and the same thing.

Commands can involve one another, as 'All children who have not done their homework stay in after school' involves the command 'Tom stay in after school' if Tom is a child who has not done his homework. Some commands are inconsistent with others, either formally, as are the commands 'Shut the door' and 'Don't shut the door' when these are addressed to the same person at the same time, or because of the impossibility of the person commanded obeying both of them simultaneously.

MORAL JUDGMENTS AND COMMANDS

I can say 'You ought to do X' without implying that I am in a position of authority over the person to whom I am speaking, and though it is known to myself and to him that I have no power to enforce X. It would be silly to say 'Do X', where the context shows that this expresses a command, under these circumstances.

I can issue either commands or moral judgments from any motives. In making the moral judgment, however, I am appealing to what may be called my hearer's sense of duty. When I issue the command, I am not appealing to anything in the hearer other than his fear of the consequences of disobeying me. The fact that I have commanded X, and that my hearer believes I will enforce what I have commanded, constitute for him a reason for doing what I have commanded. He could not have had this reason for doing X, however, before I had issued the command, whereas my hearer could have done X, because he thought he ought, even if I had not said that he ought. My issuing a command provides my hearer with a reason for performing an action, which reason did not exist before I issued the command. My making a moral judgment draws attention to a reason which would have existed, if it exists at all, whether I made the moral judgment or not.

If I command X, and the person whom I command does X, he may properly be said to obey me. If I say 'You ought to do X', and my hearer does X, he may not properly be said to obey me. If I command X, my hearer may say 'Yes', thereby indicating that he intends to do what I command him to do, or he may say 'No', indicating that he does not. It would not be sensible to respond to the moral judgment 'You ought to do X' by 'Yes' or 'No' in this sense, though it would be sensible to respond by saying 'Yes, I ought', or 'No, I oughtn't'. If my hearer says 'Yes, I ought', he is agreeing with me that he ought; if he says 'No, I oughtn't', he is disagreeing with me that he ought. One cannot, however, agree with a command, or disagree with it. The functions of 'Yes' in response to a command, and of 'Yes (I ought)' in response to a moral judgment, are different; the one expresses an intention to obey, the other expresses agreement. You may substitute 'Yes, I agree' for 'Yes, I ought'; you cannot substitute 'Yes, I agree' for the 'Yes' which is said in response to a command. The fact that 'Yes, I agree' may properly be said in response to a moral judgment, however, does not show that the moral judgment is a statement. It might be a proposal or a suggestion.

If I say 'Yes' in response to a command, and then do not do what I am commanded, then either when I said 'Yes' I was being deliberately misleading, or I changed my mind. If I say 'Yes (I agree)' in response to a moral judgment, and I do not do what I agreed I ought, then neither of these follow. I may agree that I ought to do X, without intending to do it, and omit X without having changed my opinion that I ought to do it.

If I command X, but do not command another action precisely similar to X, then I have not been inconsistent. If I say 'You ought to do X' to one man, and say 'It is right to omit X' to another, and these two men are in all respects precisely similar, I have, in some sense, been inconsistent. Hence making the moral judgment 'You ought to do X' commits me to the moral judgment 'All men like you ought to do actions precisely similar to X': issuing the command 'Do X' does not commit me to issuing the command, 'All men like you perform actions like X'. The particular command does not imply a universal command, whereas the particular moral judgment does imply a universal moral judgment.

'All men ought to perform actions like X' is not identical with

'All men, perform actions like X'. The former is a sensible thing for most people to say. The latter is not, for (*a*) we are commanding what everyone knows we cannot enforce and (*b*) we would be addressing people who are not, and cannot possibly be, listening. 'All men' is in the vocative in the latter expression; in the former it is the subject of the sentence.

This does not mean that a universal command is an impossibility. God or the devil, if we suppose him to be powerful enough to enforce his commands, and ubiquitous enough to be heard by everybody, could issue such a command. Neither would, however, be judging that the class of actions he was commanding is right or obligatory. The devil could command a class of actions which are generally agreed to be wrong, and perhaps this is what he does. He might even command all men to perform actions which he himself thinks are wrong. Commanding a class of actions generally agreed to be wrong cannot consist in judging that a class of actions generally considered to be wrong is right. If this were so, the devil would be a moral reformer.

REQUESTS

Like commands, requests have a 'cognitive content', and would not be useful if they had not. Like commands, too, requests are not capable of being true or false, and no assertion is being made, or information conveyed, by the person who makes the request, though the making of a request is an occurrence, and the person requested may draw inferences from this occurrence, as he may from any other occurrence, and someone hearing me say, 'Please tell me,' is entitled to infer that I believe that I have not been told. Again, there is no hard and fast line of demarcation between the language used to make a request and the language used for other purposes. As I have said, 'Pass the salt' is probably a request – perhaps albeit a rudely expressed one – though it is verbally similar to a command. 'Please leave the room instantly' will probably be a command, though the word 'Please' is, in English, usually used to indicate that a request is being made. Whether a form of words expresses a command or a request depends not only upon the words themselves, but upon the tone of voice in which they are uttered and upon the context in which they are spoken. 'Would you like to go to the pictures with me?' looks like a question, but is in fact in many respects more like a request, for a person answering 'Yes' would not be supplying information which the person who made the request lacked, but accepting an invitation. Again, 'I would be very pleased if you could manage to come to dinner on Thursday' is not a statement about the speaker's state of mind, but a request. Someone answering 'Would you?' would be rudely evading accepting or refusing, and the proper reply would be 'Yes, I should like to' or 'I am afraid I cannot manage it', which, if the request were a statement about the speaker's state of mind, would simply be silly.

The difference between a request and a command is that in a request account is taken of the inclinations of the person to whom the request is addressed, while no account is taken of the inclinations of the person to whom the command is addressed. 'Please', which usually, though not necessarily, prefaces a request, means 'If you please'. There is no question of a request being enforced, though commands are usually made by people who have the power, or at any rate wish the person commanded to suppose that they have the power, to enforce their commands. As I have already said, there is something in a command rather like a verbal shove. In a request, the shove is still there, but it is less forcible and is also conditional upon the inclinations of the person requested being favourable to complying with it; the person to whom the request is addressed is urged to pass the salt, but only *if* he pleases.

It must not be supposed that the difference between a command and a request is that the former is unconditional while the latter is not, for there may be conditional commands, e.g. 'Put on your overcoat, if it is cold'. Perhaps the difference is that all requests are conditional, whereas commands are frequently unconditional, and, furthermore, that requests are conditional upon the inclinations of the person to whom the request is addressed being favourable to the requested action.

PLEADING

Pleading is like requesting in having a cognitive content, which the usefulness of the plea presupposes, and in that a plea conveys no information, though again, inferences may be drawn from the fact that it is made. Pleas, like commands and requests, are incapable of being true or false.

A plea is more like a command than a request in that the verbal shove is stronger. If we plead with someone to do something, we are urging him more strongly (perhaps even desperately) than if we simply request him to do something. On the other hand, pleas are more like requests than commands in that the person pleading does not assume authority or power over the person with whom he is pleading, as the person commanding does assume authority or power over the person he is commanding. Unlike requests, pleas are not conditional upon the inclinations of the person to whom the plea is made. There is a 'take it or leave it' character about a request which is absent from a plea. A person making a request is asking someone to do something, if it pleases him; but a person making a plea is trying to get the person with whom he is pleading to do something, whether he wants to or not; only he is not, as he is when he is commanding, suggesting that he has the power to impose sanctions if the plea is ignored. It is scarcely unfair to say that he is trading on his weakness rather then on his strength; he is throwing himself on the mercy of the person with whom he is pleading in a way in which he is not when he is simply making a request. The effectiveness of a plea depends on the charity, good nature, the capacity for pity, etc., of the person to whom the plea is made. Though a request is of the nature 'Please me, if it pleases you', a plea is of the nature 'Please me, whether it pleases you or not'. Hence, whereas a person making a request is not putting himself in an inferior position to the person requested, a person making a plea is. The inferiority, of course, is not moral inferiority, for the plea may be one which ought to be made, and to which the person to whom it is made ought to listen; it may even be for the good of the person to whom it is made that he should listen.

PRAYERS

Prayers are again like the aforementioned forms of language in having a cognitive content, in only being useful in so far as they have a cognitive content, and in that no assertion is made and no information, true or false, conveyed, though inferences can be made from their occurrence about the beliefs of the person doing the praying. It is usual, within the context of a highly evolved religion like Christianity, to think of prayers as being made to an omnipotent and omniscient God. This is not an essential characteristic of prayers, and they may not only be made to Gods who are not omnipotent and omniscient, but to human beings, for example, the Queen. They could not be made to inanimate objects, unless the person making the prayer supposed that they were in some sense animate.

A prayer is an attempt to get the person or the being prayed to, to produce some desired state of affairs, indicated in the prayer. As in commanding and requesting, a verbal shove is involved, but it may be of any degree of strength. A prayer, like a request, may be conditional upon the 'inclinations' of the being to whom the prayer is addressed.

I am inclined to think that prayers are simply species of requests or pleas, differing from other sorts of requests and pleas not in their 'intrinsic nature', but in the nature of the being to whom they are addressed.

Being, or trying to be, actually or allegedly, in some sort of communication with a being superior to ourselves, is frequently called praying, but it is a different sort of praying from that I have just mentioned, though doubtless the two are often or even mostly found together. It is not my purpose to say anything about praying in this contemplative sense, since it does not consist in an attempt to modify the behaviour of the being prayed to.

Praying must not be confused with worshipping, though no doubt they often accompany one another, and may be almost inextricably intermingled. I shall say nothing about worshipping in so far as it involves emotional and non-verbal behaviour, but make a few remarks only about the verbal expression of worship. Worship is usually verbally expressed in the form of statements, which may be loosely and too mundanely described as 'complimentary' or 'adulatory', and which are capable of being true or false.

Statements are often found in prayers, as subordinate clauses, e.g. 'Our father, *which art in heaven* . . .' It would be odd to speak of a prayer, containing such a subordinate clause, as being true or false, nor can the subordinate clause itself be said to be true or false. But perhaps, any such subordinate clause can be detached from the prayer, and, when suitably modified, can be said to be true or false; the prayer can be said to be 'appropriately based' (though not necessarily appropriate) if the statement or statements extracted from it are true statements.

Those taking part in the controversy concerning the truth of fundamentalism should carefully consider their position in the light of the fact that so much of what is expressed in the Bible cannot sensibly be said to be true or false.

The fact that so much of the verbal expression of worship is poetic has no bearing upon the question whether it is true or false, since truths and falsehoods may be poetically expressed, as can almost anything which is not too technical or too mundane. It must not be supposed that poetry is necessarily, though it often is, a species of fiction. The fact that metaphorical expressions are so frequently used in the verbal expression of worship may well have some bearing on the question, but this is a problem into which it would be outside my scope to enter.

Worshipping may be used as a means, whether successfully or not it is not my business to enquire, of affecting the behaviour of the being worshipped, since the worshipper may suppose that the being worshipped may look upon him more favourably if he worships than if he does not. This does not mean, however, that worshipping may properly be classified as a means of modifying the behaviour of the person worshipped. For the person worshipping is not, like the person praying, urging the being worshipped to perform some action. He is simply himself performing an action which he thinks the being worshipped will approve of, as he is for example when he goes to church or gives to charity.

MORAL JUDGMENTS AND REQUESTS

I do not think any philosopher in his senses would hold that ever, when we make a moral judgment, we are making a request.

MORAL JUDGMENTS, PLEADING AND PRAYING

To make a moral judgment is not to plead or to pray. One can quite consistently say 'I know it is your duty to hang me, but I pray you not to.' Furthermore, the correct reply to someone who pleads with you to do something or prays you to do something is to say, 'No, I refuse.' It would be senseless to reply to someone who says it is my duty to do something by saying, 'No, I refuse' – though one might say, 'I agree it is my duty, but nevertheless I refuse to do it.' One can only plead or pray to someone directly, that is, one can plead with Jones to do something or pray him to do something, but you cannot say to Jones, 'I plead with you that Smith will not hang me.' One can, however, quite properly say to Jones, 'Smith ought not to hang me,' or, 'It is Smith's duty to let me go unscathed.'

ADVISING

Advice is most naturally expressed in the imperative mood, e.g. 'Sell it, if it is too large for you', and truth or falsity cannot be meaningfully predicated of it. It goes without saying that advice has 'cognitive content', and that its usefulness depends on this.

A piece of advice, unless it is unsolicited, is an answer to the question 'What shall I do?' or to more specific questions, such as 'Shall I sell my house or not?' It is most naturally answered by an expression in the imperative mood, e.g. 'Do such and such' or 'Sell it as soon as you can'. A slightly evasive answer may consist in a statement or set of statements, which provide the person asking for advice with information which the adviser hopes will enable him to make up his own mind, e.g. 'The value of houses is likely to fall in the near future'. It is quite natural to answer a request for advice by saying, 'I would sell it, if I were you.' This is a hypothetical statement about the adviser, but the person asking for advice may extract from it what he requires by means of an inference: What my adviser would do, if he were me, is what he would consider it advisable for me to do: hence he considers it advisable for me to sell my house. The phrases 'is advisable' and 'well advised' also serve for the communication of advice. The estate agent may say 'You would be well advised to sell' or 'It is advisable to sell as soon as possible.' The first statement is roughly equivalent to: 'If anyone did advise you to sell, the advice would be good.' The difference between this and 'Sell' is like the difference between 'Jones is a liar' and 'If anyone were to say that Jones was a liar, he would be telling the truth'. Anyone hearing either of these remarks would be justified in inferring, in the first case, that the speaker thinks it is advisable to sell, and, in the second, that he thinks Jones is a liar. In neither case would the hearer be misreporting if he said, 'He said Jones was a liar,' or, 'He advised me to sell.' Any difference between 'You would be well advised to sell' and 'It is advisable to sell' is entirely unimportant, 'advisable' performing the same function as 'well advised' though, of course, you could not substitute 'well advised' for 'advisable' in *any* sentence in which either occurred and produce a result which made sense.

Advice is usually concerning the means to ends. The estate agent assumes that his client wants to get as much money for his house as possible, and advises him accordingly. Hence such advice is frequently prefixed by 'If you want to get as much money for your house as you can. . . .' or 'To get the best price . . .'

Advice which is concerning the means to ends may be good or bad (though it cannot be true or false, unless it takes the form 'You would be well advised to . . .') and the criteria for whether it is good advice or bad advice is very simple. 'To get the best price for your house, sell it now' is good advice if the statement 'The house will fetch a better price if sold now than at any other time', is a true statement. Whether or not this is a true statement will be decided by empirical evidence, which means that the goodness or badness of such advice is tested on empirical grounds. This account, however, needs a little elaboration, for it does not explain how the goodness or badness of such advice may admit of degrees. I think the reason for this is that ends are not simply realized or not realised; they may be partially realised, or nearly but not quite realised. A man's object, of getting as much money as possible for his house, is partially or incompletely or nearly but not quite realized if he gets a good price for his house, though not the highest possible price. In this case the advice which enables him to get it is good advice, though not the best advice. It should also be pointed out that advice may be bad advice, or, at any rate, not the best possible advice, if taking it interferes with other ends which the person asking for advice may have, among which ends may be moral ones, for his end may not simply be to get the best possible price for his house, but to do this without cheating, or to do this without a tiresome waste of time on haggling.

'Such-and-such advice is good advice' is a statement, unlike the advice itself, and so may be be true or false. Its truth conditions have already been given. As has already been hinted at, someone making, in the presence of the person seeking advice, the statement that certain advice, not yet taken, is good advice, is not simply making a statement about advice; he is also at the same time advising. Hence advice can sometimes be expressed in the form of a statement, though this is comparatively rare. It should be noted, however, that advising does not simply consist in making the statement, for if the statement is made when the person seeking advice is not present, or after the occasion for taking or not taking the advice has passed, no advice is being given.

Advice concerning the means to given ends may be expressed by the use of the word 'ought', e.g. 'If you want to get the best price for your house, you ought to sell now'. By using the word 'ought' the estate agent does not intend to imply that it is the customer's duty to sell now. But this use of the word 'ought' in 'You ought to sell now' is not as different from what we may provisionally term the 'moral' sense of the word 'ought' as is sometimes alleged. In both the speaker is giving a verbal shove, is urging the person to whom he is speaking to perform a certain action. It is a precondition of both uses of the word 'ought' that the action towards which a shove is exerted must be one which the person shoved can perform, otherwise shoving would be futile. And in both, the speaker, though he does not evince disapproval of the omission of the action, for it has not yet been omitted, does signal the fact that he will disapprove of its omission, if it is omitted. The type of disapproval will differ, however. The former type will be evinced by such expressions as 'He is a fool'; the latter by expressions such as 'He is a rogue'.

I do not think there is any difference between 'If you want to get the best price for your house, sell now' and 'If you want to get the best price for your house, you ought to sell now'. This is *prima facie* evidence for an imperative theory of this non-moral sense of 'ought'. I do not think, however, that the 'Sell now' in the above sentence can be described as an imperative except in so loose a sense that it obscures more truth than it reveals. Though grammatically an imperative, 'Sell now' is in fact used to give advice; and giving advice is very unlike issuing a command; when a person gives advice, he is not indicating that he will apply sanctions if it is not taken, as he is when he issues a command, nor is he suggesting that his position gives him power over the person he is advising. Furthermore, advice may be backed by reasons. The estate agent may back his advice by saying that it is now spring, and houses fetch more in the spring than at any other time of year. A command, however, cannot be backed by reasons, though it may be reinforced with threats.

Advice is universalizable. If to advise a given action is to give good advice, then to advise any similar action to a similar person in similar circumstances must also be good advice. This is not to say that a man who advises a given action is committed to advising the same action in similar circumstances. There may be alternative ways of achieving a given end which are equally good, or different ends at which it is equally sensible to aim.

MORAL JUDGMENTS AND ADVICE

Making moral judgments is never to advise *to*. There is no contradiction in saying, 'It is your duty to help him, but I advise you not to,' or, 'You are really under an obligation to visit him, but I wouldn't if I were you,' or, 'He is a good man, but don't try to be like him; the effort would be too much for you.'

PERFORMATIVE UTTERANCES[1]

The best examples of performative utterance are a number of sentences containing verbs in the first person present tense, for example 'I promise', 'I swear', 'I N take thee N', 'I declare this foundation stone well and truly laid'. In uttering such words *in an appropriate context*, the person uttering them has completed a performance, which performance may be described by sentences containing the same verb in a different person or tense or both, e.g. 'He is promising', 'He swore'.

Performative utterances cannot meaningfully be said to be true or false, and the person making them is not communicating information, though information can be gleaned from the fact that he makes them. They have cognitive content, however; the word 'promise' in 'I promise to marry you' has the same meaning that it has in 'To promise and not perform is reprehensible'. If it had not, there would be no indication that the person saying 'I promise' was promising, and not swearing or baptizing a baby.

Of course, whenever we utter a sentence, we are engaged in a performance, namely, the performance of uttering certain words, or conveying information, or asserting, or persuading somebody to do something. What, then, is the point of calling them performative utterances? The reason, I think, is that saying them has normally the function of changing the ritualistic or legal status of something. Someone who says 'I promise' incurs obligations which he did not have. If he says 'I give you this', his property becomes my property. If someone says, 'I baptize you . . .' to a baby while making the sign of the cross on its forehead, it is now baptized, whereas before it was not. Before certain performative utterances are delivered in the appropriate circumstances, someone was not a privy councillor, or a bachelor of arts, or a curate, or a

---

[1] See J. L. Austin, *How to Do Things with Words* (O.U.P., 1962).

pope, or a parson; after these magical formulas have been proclaimed, he is one.

MORAL JUDGMENTS AND PERFORMATIVE UTTERANCES

Moral judgments are not performative utterances. An essential feature of performative utterances is that someone using a verb in the first person present perfect tense, is actually doing that which is *described* when the same verb is used in other persons or in other tenses. Someone saying 'I promise' for example, is not saying that he is promising, but actually doing the promising. To say that someone is promising is to say that he is saying the words 'I promise' under appropriate circumstances.

It should be quite obvious, however, that someone saying of a third person that he ought to do something, or that it is a duty to do something, or that he would be acting wrongly if he did not do something, is not saying that this person has used the words 'I ought . . .' or 'It is my duty . . .' or 'It would be wrong for me not . . .' Furthermore 'I have a duty to go' said by Smith is equivalent to 'Smith has a duty to go' said by Jones of Smith. 'I promise to go', said by Smith, is not equivalent to 'Smith is promising to go' said by Jones of Smith. Moral judgments can be made indifferently by any person, but performative utterances can only be used in the first person perfect tense by the person actually going through the performance, which other people can only describe.[1]

PERSUADING

Though persuading is an activity usually accomplished by means of the use of words, there is no such class of expressions as 'persuasions'. In this respect persuading is unlike advising or commanding or requesting, for there are classes of expressions, commands, pieces of advice, requests, etc., corresponding to the analogous activities. Though one may issue a command, or make a request, or give advice, one cannot issue or make or give a persuasion.

Persuading is a fairly general name for trying to get someone to do something. When I am persuading I may be advising or pleading or imploring or requesting or praying, or some or all of these together. I may also be making statements, which are capable

[1] See Alasdair MacIntyre, 'What Morality is Not', *Philosophy*, Vol. XXXII, 1957, pp. 326 f.

of being true or false. If I am trying to persuade a customer to buy a car, I may do so by saying it is fast and reliable and new and inexpensive.

To persuade is not the same thing as to command, nor is it to threaten, or to implore or to plead. In persuading, though one may cheat it is true, one is generally appealing to someone as a rational person, or as an equal. In these others one is either treating him as a superior, or as an inferior and frankly disregarding his own interests and inclinations.

MORAL JUDGMENTS AND PERSUADING

We have seen that there is no class of verbal expression, called persuasions, corresponding to the activity of persuading. We can persuade someone to do something in a variety of different ways, by adducing *facts* about the course of action, which we are trying to persuade someone to adopt, which will tend to make it attractive in his eyes, or by *asking* him to adopt it, *pleading* with him to adopt it, *imploring* him to adopt it.

One thing we may say about a course of action which we may think will make it more attractive in the eyes of the person we are trying to persuade is that he ought to do it, that it would be wrong to omit it, or that it is his duty. This tells us nothing about what we are doing when we say these things, however, for we might equally well try to persuade someone to do something by making ordinary statements about it, for example by telling him that it was to his advantage to do it, that he would enjoy doing it, or that not to do it would hurt someone he cares about. Though saying that something is someone's duty *may* feature in the activity of persuading him to do that thing, just to say that it is his duty is not by itself to persuade him. We are not trying to persuade someone if we say, 'It is your duty, take it or leave it,' but only if we say it is his duty as one means, among others, of getting him to do it, and if we prepared to adopt other means of getting him to do it, if telling him that it is his duty fails.

EXPRESSING ATTITUDES [1]

Expressing an attitude is like persuading, in that there is no class of expressions, 'expressions of attitudes', which correspond to it.

[1] See W. H. F. Barnes, 'Ethics without Propositions', *Aristotelian Society Supplementary Proceedings*, Vol. XXII, 1948.

I may be expressing a favourable attitude to a class of actions by requesting, advising, imploring, commanding, etc., my hearer to perform an instance of it. I may be expressing an unfavourable attitude to a class of actions by requesting, advising, imploring, commanding, etc., my hearer *not* to perform an instance of it.

An unfavourable attitude may be expressed in statements as well as by issuing commands, etc. If I say that a man is a liar, I am expressing an unfavourable attitude to him, and at the same time making a statement, which may be true or false, about him. It may be, however, that favourable or unfavourable attitudes can only be expressed by emotively-laden words such as 'liar', 'honest', etc. If I find another word having the same descriptive meaning, but not emotively-laden, then I can describe him without expressing either an unfavourable or a favourable attitude to him. My attitude is shown by my choice of words (and also by the manner in which I say them), by my selecting a word which is calculated to evince and evoke favourable or unfavourable emotions, or no emotions at all.

Just as it was roughly true, but unhelpful, to say that the function of ethical discourse is to persuade (or deter) so it is roughly true, but unhelpful, to say that the function of ethical sentences is to express an attitude, for expressing an attitude does not designate a class of expressions, though it does designate a class of verbal performances. To say that ethical sentences express an attitude does not commit us to saying that to use one is or is not to command, to advise, or to assert or convey information.

Since to express an attitude may be to command, advise, state, etc., this affects other people's behaviour in the way in which commanding, advising, stating, etc., have already been described as doing.

When one says that a man is good, one is using language improperly if one does not have a favourable attitude to this man, though one is not, as we have seen, asserting that one has this attitude. Similarly, when one says that some action is wrong, one would be using language improperly if one did not have a hostile attitude to the performance of this action, though, again, one is not asserting that one has this hostile attitude. This tells us no more about the meaning of 'good' and 'wrong', however, than does the fact that one is using language improperly if one says that X is a dodecahedron, but does not believe that it is a dodecahedron, tells us about the meaning of 'dodecahedron'.

MORAL JUDGMENTS AND EXPRESSING AN ATTITUDE

Though we certainly do express a favourable attitude to someone or something if we say that he or it is good, this tells us very little about what we are doing when we say that something is good, for a favourable attitude can also be expressed by statements such as that someone is a hard worker, or a famous athlete, particularly if we do this in an approving or admiring way. We are expressing a favourable attitude to something when we say anything about it which is likely to cause our hearers to *infer* that we have a favourable attitude to it, though this, of course, does not mean that we are *stating* that we have a favourable attitude to it, or that what we say is false if we do not have such an attitude. The fact that an attitude to something may be expressed by making statements about that thing does not, on the other hand, mean that we are making statements when we make moral judgments, for an unfavourable attitude to something may, as we have seen, also be expressed by means of commanding or exhorting people not to do or bring about that thing. In fact, saying that moral judgments express attitudes, though true as a general rule, does not tell us very much of importance about their nature. Almost any kind of utterance can express an attitude if it is said in a manner or in a context which will tend to make the person hearing the utterance draw inferences about the attitude of the person making it.

RULE MAKING

Rules may be expressed in words, and obviously rules affect people's behaviour, in so far as they are effective, and if they are not effective, there is no point in making them. Promulgating a rule is a linguistic performance. Words or other symbols are necessary to indicate the class of actions which the rule enjoins or prohibits or permits. I do not think it makes much difference from a linguistic point of view what sort of rule we consider; whether we consider parliament making laws or the M.C.C. making rules; or whether we consider rules made by an individual, like a headmaster, or a collection of individuals, like a city corporation.

Rules are generally formulated before they are promulgated, or, where previous discussion is unnecessary, in the act of promulgation. When they are formulated in these circumstances, the sentences which formulate them do not state facts, and cannot be true or false, though they must, of course, have cognitive content. Let us suppose that a committee are sitting to draw up a set of rules for a new card game. It may be proposed that the person who draws the highest card shall deal first. The sentence 'I propose that the player who has the highest card shall deal first' does not then make a statement. It is, of course, a proposal. What is being proposed is that it shall be made a rule that the player with the highest card shall deal first.

After a rule is proposed, it may be promulgated. A rule may be promulgated by being spoken aloud or by being written down and published. In either case, the enunciating of the rule will not consist in asserting anything true or false.

Promulgating a rule is like issuing a command, since a rule, like a command, implies sanctions. But (*a*) the body promulgating the rule may be identical with the body which has to observe it, though a command is issued from one person to another; (*b*) a command may be particular, in that a particular person may be commanded to perform a particular action, whereas a rule must be fairly general, i.e. a class of actions must be enjoined, prohibited, or permitted for a class of persons. The class of persons or actions need not be open classes, though they will often be; 'citizens of Great Britain' or 'members of the Athenaeum' does not describe an open class, though rules may be made for such people and such people only. And (*c*) rules may be permissive, though a command can only enjoin or prohibit. (Though commands cannot be permissive, there is a 'permissive utterance', for which there exists no English name, which is expressed by the words 'You may'. 'You may go out', unlike 'You can go out', does not express a statement. It may be particular or fairly general. I shall say more about this point later.[1])

After a rule has been promulgated, the very same words which were used to propose that the rule should be promulgated, or to promulgate it, may serve to make the statement that the rule exists. After the rules of the aforementioned imaginary game have been set up, and the game has achieved some popularity, a player – or someone else, for that matter – may say, 'The player who draws the highest card deals first'. This is a statement, and is true if there is a rule of the game which lays down that the player who draws the highest card shall deal first, false if there is not.

[1] Pp. 293–6.

MORAL JUDGMENTS AND RULE-MAKING

There is a great difference between making moral judgments and promulgating rules. When an authorized body, say the M.C.C., promulgates a rule prohibiting throwing, throwing subsequently becomes illegal. After the M.C.C. has said with due form and ceremony, 'No bowler may throw', or whatever they do say on such occasions, any person saying, 'No bowler may throw', is making a true statement, though, had it been made before the M.C.C. had promulgated this rule, he would have been making a false statement. It is not the case, however, that moral judgments can be made only by persons having authority to legislate for others. Anyone can make them. And it would be quite ridiculous to say that there was any person, such that after he said, 'Promises ought to be kept', it became a true statement that promises ought to be kept, though before this to say this would have been false. Hence moral rules cannot be promulgated.

For this reason they cannot be made or modified or unmade. That this is so is shown by the fact that there is no conceivable procedure for doing any of these things, as there is a procedure for changing the law of England or the rules of chess. The idea of a committee of people meeting together to decide upon the moral law is absurd.

Some philosophers may have wrongly supposed that the moral law may be promulgated because, just as any change in our situation may alter our duties, an alteration to the law may alter our duties. Hence, if there is a law forbidding taking cannabis, it may be wrong to take cannabis, though not wrong to do this when the law is repealed. This is not because parliament has altered the moral law, however, but because if one item in the moral law is that it is wrong wantonly to disobey the law of the country in which one lives, one will be disobeying this moral law if one takes cannabis when this is forbidden by law, but not when this law has been removed from the statute book.

SENTENCES AND VERDICTS (GENERAL)

Where there are rules, someone has to decide when they are infringed, and, if the penalty attached to infringement, if any, is not rigidly specified in the rules, what the penalty for infringement shall be. It is not essential that this function should be assigned to a special individual or a number of special individuals. In a game, for example, the players themselves may decide when the rules have been infringed. This is more easily done in games than in life, for in games the stakes are usually smaller, and amateurs, at any rate, are more keen on enjoying the game – which will not be possible if the rules are not observed, and the proper penalties not exacted for non-observance – than on winning. But in life, from which one cannot withdraw so easily as one can from a game, the stakes are greater; there is consequently more likely to be disagreement concerning whether the rules have been broken, and what penalty should be imposed if they have. Consequently, it is expedient that the function of deciding whether the rules have been infringed or not be entrusted to some disinterested party – 'disinterested' at least in the sense that *his* interests will best be forwarded by applying the rules impartially.

This disinterested party (or these disinterested parties) will have three functions to perform: (*a*) they will have the function of deciding what in fact occurred; (*b*) they will have the function of deciding whether what in fact occurred infringed a rule; (*c*) they will have the function of determining the penalty for infringement, where this is not laid down in the rule, or where the rule allows latitude. These three functions may be and sometimes are, carried out by different persons or bodies.

Deciding what occurred *looks* like a plain decision on a matter of fact, and it looks as if the sentences which express the decision will be statements, capable of being true or false. A decision on a question of fact seems to be a decision on whether what occurred was of a certain sort; a decision on a question of law seems to be a decision on whether actions of that sort are not prohibited by a rule. I am not so sure, however, that the decision on whether what occurred is of a certain sort *is* always a decision on a matter of fact. In clear cases it will be. Deciding whether what occurred was of a certain sort is deciding whether the symbol used to describe things which are of this sort, is properly applicable to what occurred or not. There will be cases where it obviously is or is not properly applicable, but there will also be borderline cases, where it is a matter of doubt whether the symbol is properly applicable or not. In this case, the function of the person who has to decide on what occurred will be to decide whether to apply the symbol to what occurred or not. This will not be a decision upon what is in fact the case or not the case, but a decision on whether to do something or not. If he decides to apply the symbol he will, as a result of his decision, say, for example, of a woman who has had artificial insemination by a donor without her husband's consent, 'This is a case of adultery'. This looks like a statement, but in fact it is not. It expresses the decision to use the word 'adultery' in a certain way, e.g. a wider way instead of a narrower way. It is more like saying 'Let us call it adultery,' which expresses a resolution, than like saying 'It is called adultery', which expresses a statement. If the use of the word 'adultery' becomes determined, then, as a result of this, subsequent uses of 'What occurred was adultery' will express statements, though not the same statements that they expressed before the decision was taken.

The decision whether to apply a symbol to what occurred is a linguistic decision. It cannot, however, be made upon purely linguistic grounds, i.e. upon grounds of how or how not it is convenient to talk. For the person making the decision will know that there is a law prohibiting actions of a given sort; hence by deciding to call what occurred by the word for actions of the sort which are prohibited, he will be bringing what occurred into a class of actions prohibited by rule, but by deciding not to describe what occurred by this word he will be excluding it from this class. Hence his decision on how to use the word is going to have other than linguistic effects; a man may be hanged as a result of his deciding one way, set free as a result of his deciding another. Hence his decision cannot be taken on grounds of purely linguistic convenience, but wider considerations of expediency and justice must enter into it.

The view that the person who must decide whether or not to call what occurred by a certain word must do so by taking into account the intentions of those who 'drew up' the rules prohibiting occurrences described as being of this sort is not tenable. According to this view, the person who decides whether what in fact occurred is properly described by a given word or not, must decide to call what occurred by this word if those who drew up the rules would have used that word, and must decide not to call it by this word if those who drew up the rules would not have used it. This is quite impossible, for those who drew up the rules presumably had not envisaged the kind of case which is giving rise to the difficulty, and so could no more have had intentions about it than anybody else.

The view that the person, whose function it is to decide whether

what occurred is or is not a case of a certain sort, has simply to dis-
regard the intentions of those who drew up the rules, but simply
to use the words in question in the usual way is – since it will be
impossible to discover what these were – equally untenable. For
in the circumstances we are considering, there will be no usual way
of using these words.

The function of the person applying the law, in the general
sense of deciding on questions of law and on questions of fact,
will therefore be quasi-legislative. For since those who promulgated the law which he is applying were using words which were
not governed by completely precise rules, he, in making these
rules more precise, is altering the law, not in the sense of giving
it one meaning where previously it had another, but in the sense
of giving it a more specific meaning where previously it had.

VERDICTS[1]

A verdict is apparently a statement of fact, for the person expressing the verdict seems at least to be saying that the accused did
or did not commit the crime of which he is accused, and this is a
statement of fact. He is not, however, simply describing what the
accused did or did not do. He is also bringing what the accused
did or did not do under a class of actions prohibited by law, or
excluding it from this class.

In fact, of course, a jury are not experts in law, and will have
been asked to make up their minds on a question of fact. The
judge, in his summing up, will have explained to them whether
the accused will or will not have commited, a crime, i.e. infringed
a law, *if* he has performed an action of this or that sort. This does
not absolve them of all law-interpreting responsibility; they are
not penny-in-the-slot machines, which automatically respond
to various stimuli; they will have to remember the judge's remarks
on points of law, and interpet these; and interpreting the judge's
remarks on questions of law is not a different sort of activity,
though it is to be hoped that it is a rather less difficult activity,
than interpreting the law. They will also have to make linguistic
decisions, which decisions will determine whether the accused is
guilty or not, (*a*) in deciding on how what the accused did is to be
described, and (*b*) in deciding how the words the judge uses are
to be interpreted. Hence the foreman of a jury, in pronouncing the

[1] See G. J. Warnock, *Berkeley* (Penguin Books), pp. 183 f.

accused to be guilty or not guilty, is, in a clear case, making a combined statement of law and of fact. He is saying or implying both that the accused killed in such-and-such circumstances, and that killing in these circumstances is murder.

Though the foreman of the jury, in pronouncing the words 'guilty' or 'not guilty' is making a statement, this is not all he is doing. Someone other than the foreman of the jury may make the statement that the accused is guilty, but this other person is not pronouncing a verdict. Certain consequences, of one sort or another, will follow from the words pronounced by the foreman of the jury, which will not follow from the words pronounced by a spectator. If the foreman of the jury says 'Guilty', it will then be a true statement that the accused was *found* guilty, whereas if a spectator says that he was guilty this will not thereby become a true statement. It will be possible for a spectator to say that he was found guilty, though he was not guilty (or for a court of appeal to do the same).

MORAL JUDGMENTS AND VERDICTS

There is some resemblance between moral judgments and verdicts.[1] When the foreman of the jury says that the accused is guilty, he means that the accused has performed some action which is a breach of the law of the land. When we say that someone has done something wrong, we are saying that he has performed some action which is a breach of the moral law. This has no tendency to show that moral judgments are not statements, for we have seen that when the foreman of the jury says that the prisoner is guilty, he *is* making a statement. There is an important difference between what the foreman of the jury is doing when he says that the prisoner is guilty, and what an ordinary person is doing when he says that someone, perhaps himself, has done something wrong. No legal consequences follow as a result of the second pronouncement, though as a result of the first a judge has to make up his mind whether to sentence the prisoner, to put him on probation, or to let him off with a warning.

SENTENCING

Sentences are a species of performative utterance. The judge who

[1] See P. H. Nowell-Smith, *Ethics* (Blackwell, 1957; Penguin, 1954), pp. 164–5.

says 'I sentence you to three years hard labour' is not making a statement, which will be true or false, but sentencing the prisoner. It is impossible for a judge to say these words, in the appropriate context, and not to sentence the prisoner. Hence there is no question of the judge saying, in appropriate circumstances, the words 'I sentence . . .', and not sentencing, as there would be if he were making a statement, which could be false, in which case he would not have pronounced a sentence. Furthermore, though a judge in saying 'I sentence . . .' will be making a performatory utterance, anyone else in saying 'He was sentenced' will not be making a performative utterance, but a statement to the effect that sentence has been passed, that a performative utterance has been issued in the appropriate circumstances, in court, by a judge, and so on.

MORAL JUDGMENTS AND SENTENCING

Making a moral judgment does not resemble what a judge does when he pronounces sentence upon a prisoner. When a judge says, 'I sentence you to ten years hard labour,' his utterance is performatory, and we have already seen that moral judgments are not performatory utterances. Also, when a judge says some such thing as this in the appropriate circumstances, unpleasant consequences follow, in accordance with a set of rules, for the person he is addressing, who is, as a result, sent to prison, or fined, or both. No such unpleasant consequences follow when we make moral judgments, even adverse moral judgments, upon someone's character or behaviour, even when we are addressing him personally.

The moral judgments most like a sentence are, I imagine, those in which it is said that someone or other, perhaps the person to whom we are speaking, deserves to suffer in some way or other. But to say that someone deserves to suffer is not to sentence him to suffering, and we may tell someone that he deserves that ill befall him without any ill befalling him as a result of our disinterested remark.

PROPOSALS

Proposals may or may not be made by using the words 'I propose'. 'I propose that we go for a walk' does involve these words; 'Let us go for a walk' does not, yet the person using either is making a proposal.

There is a difference between proposing *to* and proposing *that*. When one says one proposes to do something, what one proposes is always to do or to refrain from doing something oneself, for example, to give up smoking. Saying 'I propose to give up smoking' is rather like declaring one's intention of giving up smoking, about which much has already been said by other philosophers. 'I propose to give up smoking' is also rather like a performative utterance, in that it does not serve to make a statement, though 'I proposed to give up smoking' and 'He proposes (proposed) to give up smoking' do serve to make statements.

'Proposing that', however, must always involve someone else as well as the speaker, and may involve only people other than the speaker. Hence we can say 'I propose that we get married' or 'I propose that you get married' but not 'I propose that I get married'.

There is a class of things called proposals, which one can put forward by using the words 'I propose that' or some other words. In this respect, proposing is like commanding, but unlike persuading, for there are commands, but not persuasions. When I say I propose to do something, I am not putting forward a proposal. Though a proposal is not capable of being true or false, it is capable of being good or bad. It is a good proposal if acting on it produces the ends which the proposal was made to bring about, otherwise it is not.

MORAL JUDGMENTS AND PROPOSALS

When someone makes a moral judgment, even in the first person, he is never proposing *to* do something. There is no contradiction in saying, 'I know I ought to work harder, but I don't propose to.' Someone proposing that is making a species of performative utterance, which someone making a moral judgment never is. Though someone saying 'We ought to do X' or 'It would be wrong not to do X' is not making a proposal, saying these things is one way of *backing up* a proposal.

One might be tempted to say that someone saying that some group of people of which he was a member *ought* to do something could be described as proposing that that thing be done, but I think this would be a mistake. Someone saying 'We ought to save more' is not actually proposing that we save more, though he is coming very near to it. It is something one might say in the discussion preceding the actual making of a proposal, though it is not the actual making of a proposal. And there is no inconsistency in saying, 'I think we ought to save more, but I propose we don't', or, 'I think we ought to save more, but let's not bother.'

If moral judgments ever were proposals, they could only be so in certain circumstances. A member of the British Cabinet who said, 'I think we ought to try to join the Common Market,' might just possibly be described as making a proposal, but an American who said, 'I think Britain ought to try to join the Common Market,' could not be.

SUGGESTIONS

Above I distinguished between proposing to and proposing that. There is no analogous distinction where suggesting is concerned; one can only suggest *that*.

When I suggest that, however, I can be suggesting that a certain statement is true, or I can be suggesting that a certain course of action be adopted. I can suggest that the works of a given philosopher have been misinterpreted, or I can suggest that a philosophical conference be held to consider them. When I make the former sort of suggestion, what I suggest is capable of being true or false. Suggesting in this case is a way of making a statement, but of making it fairly tentatively, though it can often be used rhetorically to put forward a statement pretty confidently. When I make the latter sort of suggestion, what I suggest cannot be true or false.

As when I command, I issue a command, and as when I advise, I give advice, so when I suggest, I make a suggestion. When I make a suggestion of the latter kind, what I suggest is some course of action which involves myself and other people (that *we go* to to the pictures) or other people alone (that *you* go out for dinner). I can also suggest that I do such-and-such a thing, but I would make such a suggestion because my doing this thing involved other people, e.g. I could suggest that I minded the baby so that my wife could go to the pictures. I can propose to work harder, but I cannot suggest to myself that I go the the pictures.

Though suggestions cannot be true or false, they can be good or bad. A suggestion is made to solve a problem. The problem may be a theoretical one, concerning what is or is not the case, in which case the former sort of suggestion distinguished above would be made, or a practical problem concerning what course of action or policy to adopt, in which case the latter sort of suggestion would be made.

The former sort of suggestion is a good suggestion if the statement suggested is true, or likely to be true on the available evidence. The latter sort of suggestion is a good suggestion if the course of action suggested will produce, or is likely to produce, the results desired by the people to whom the suggestion is made. Since a statement can be more or less likely to be true, and results can be more or less likely to be brought about, the goodness or badness of a suggestion will be a matter of degree.

A suggestion will probably, though it need not, be supported by the person who makes it. If he is suggesting that such-and-such is the case, he will support it by reasons for thinking that this is the case, and no more need be said about this. If he is suggesting that such-and-such a course of action be adopted, he will probably support it by reasons for thinking that adopting this course of action will produce the results the suggestion was made to produce. There are, however, other ways in which he may support this latter sort of suggestion. He may persuade those to whom he has made the suggestion to adopt it, which persuading may consist simply, again, in producing reasons, good or bad, for thinking that adopting the suggestion will produce the results desired, but may also consist in advising (which advice may be backed up by the same reasons as before), pleading, imploring, and generally using emotively laden words to make those to whom the suggestion is made look upon it in a favourable light.

MORAL JUDGMENTS AND SUGGESTIONS

Making a moral judgment can always be a case of suggesting *that*. Just as one can suggest that perhaps Harold at the battle of Hastings was not killed by an arrow in the eye, so one can suggest that Richard III was not as *bad* a man as Shakespeare supposed, or that the law about abortion *ought* to be obeyed.

Sometimes when we make a judgment in which the word 'ought' figures, we can be described as making a suggestion, but I am not quite sure what sort of suggestion it is. When I say 'I think we ought to save more', I can certainly be described as making a suggestion, but am I properly described as suggesting that we save more, or as suggesting that we *ought* to save more? Only if the former description is correct can I be described as suggesting a course of action, rather than as suggesting that something, in this case, that we ought to save more, is the case. I am inclined to think, however, that in either event I may be described as suggesting that we save more. This suggests that saying 'I suggest we save more' and saying 'I think we ought to save more' are two different ways of making the same suggestion. Perhaps this is because it would be very odd for me to suggest that we save more, if I do not think we ought to save more. This again is because I suggest that we save more as a means to having longer holidays, and because, when I say I think we ought to save more, I say we ought because I think that only so will we be able to have longer holidays. This seems to imply that my suggestion that we save more as a way of having longer holidays is a *good* suggestion if and only if we *ought* to save more in order to have longer holidays. It does not follow from the fact, that when I say, 'I suggest that we have longer holidays' I cannot be described as saying something true or false, that when I say 'I think we ought to have longer holidays' I cannot be described as saying what is true or false, though, of course, this may be the case in fact. I am inclined to think that we can say that it is true or false that we ought to save more, and we can certainly assert that we ought to save more, deny that we ought to save more, ask whether we ought to save more, wonder whether we ought to save more, agree that we ought to save more, assert that we ought not to save more.

The equivalence between a suggestion's being good, and its being the case that we ought to do what is suggested, only holds where *hypothetical* imperatives are concerned.

QUESTIONS

It goes without saying that to ask a question is not to make a statement. It is to ask for information or advice, or to be told what to do. A question need not be answered by a statement. If I ask the time, I hope for a statement informing me what the correct time is. If I ask the way, I hope for directions, which will normally be expressed in the imperative mood, e.g. 'Take the second turning on the left'.

A question is very like a request, which might be described as asking *for* and, if I ask a question, what I do may not inaccurately be described as requesting advice or information. For example, if I say, 'Could you tell me the way?' I am doing something which can both be described as asking a question and as requesting directions; only a very simple man would answer, 'Yes, I could tell you the way,' and say no more.

'Where', 'Why', 'How', 'What', 'When', etc., are all linguistical luxuries, and could be dispensed with. Perhaps a question can be regarded as a request that a blank be filled in in a verbal framework. For example: ' "The time is . . ." Please fill in the blank in the preceding sentence in such a way that the result expresses a true statement.' ' "To get to the Albert Hall, you . . ." Please fill in the blank in the preceding sentence in such a way that the result directs me correctly.' The words 'Where', 'When', etc., serve to indicate the sort of filling in desired, that is, whether the information is about spatial location, temporal location, motive, method, or what have you.

There are two different sorts of *asking*, which must be distinguished, namely asking *to* and asking *whether*. If I ask someone to come to dinner with me, I am asking that a given action be performed. If I ask someone whether it is raining, I am asking for information. Neither of these raise any interesting questions which have not already been discussed.

MORAL JUDGMENTS AND QUESTIONS

It would be absurd to suggest that to make a moral judgment was to ask a question. Questions, however, do throw some light on the nature of moral judgment. The fact that you can ask 'Ought I to keep my promises?', 'Is it my duty to keep my promises?', 'Would it be wrong of me not to keep my promises?' is a reason for thinking that moral judgments are not commands; someone saying this would appear to be asking for an opinion, e.g. an opinion about what he ought to do.

The proper response to someone who says, 'Ought I to keep my promises?', is not 'Yes, do' or 'Yes, you may' but 'Yes, you ought', that is to say, someone asking this question is not asking to be told what to do, or to be given permission to do something, but to be told what he *ought* to do. He is doing something very much more like asking for information or an opinion which will help him come to a decision, than it is like asking to be told what to do, which latter a man would do in order to avoid having to think or decide for himself.

The statement 'The door is shut' can be changed into a question

K

by changing the position of the word 'is', viz. 'Is the door shut?'
Similarly, from 'Promises ought to be kept' you can obtain a question by changing the position of the word 'ought', viz, 'Ought promises to be kept?' But from the commands 'Shut the door' and 'Keep your promises' no question can be obtained by any such manipulation.

There are three quite distinct questions, 'What shall I do?', 'What will I do?', 'What ought I to do?' The person asking the first wants to be told what to do. The person who asks, 'What will I do?', wants information or a prediction about his future behaviour. The person who asks, 'What ought I to do?', wants to know neither what to do, nor what he will do, but what he ought to do.

AGREEING

Just as it is possible to distinguish between proposing *to* and proposing *that*, asking *to* and asking *that*, it is possible to distinguish between agreeing *to* and agreeing *that*. I may agree to buy someone's house, or I may agree that it is an old house. In the latter case, I am agreeing upon the truth of a statement; in the former I am agreeing upon a course of action, which action must concern both of us. In the second case, I agree when someone has made a statement; in the first case I agree when someone has made a request or put forward a proposal.

Two people may be said to agree if they share one another's opinions, or because they get on amicably, whether they share one another's opinions or not. It is possible for people to have all their opinions in common but to get on very ill, because their temperaments and inclinations and policies of action are different.

Sometimes 'I agree' means 'What you say is true'. At other times, it does not mean this, but 'I share your preference'. When I say 'The world is round', and my friend says 'I agree', his agreement is of the former sort. When I say 'I hate television' and my friend says 'I agree', he does not mean that he agrees that I hate television; he means that he hates it too.

OFFERING

I may offer to do something, or I may offer something. I may offer someone a cup of coffee, or I may offer to give someone a lift. Offering a cup of coffee may be done non-verbally, by holding out the coffee-cup. Offering to give a cup of coffee must be done verbally (or, at any rate, symbolically).

There is no class of verbal utterance which stands in the relation to offering that commands do to commanding. One usually offers by asking a question like 'Would you like a cup of coffee?' when it is clear from the context that I do not just want this information from disinterested curiosity, but will give the person, of whom I ask the question, a cup of coffee if he replies in the affirmative.

ACCEPTING

I may accept an offer, or I may accept a thing offered. Accepting a thing offered may be done by taking that thing, or taking it over, if it is too big to be taken, or by saying 'Yes' if someone offers to give me that thing. Accepting an offer is always done by saying 'Yes' if someone makes an offer, or by some other suitable symbolic device, e.g. by nodding my head or by waving my pipe at an auction sale.

CONSENTING

I must always consent to; it is not good English to talk of consenting that. Generally I consent to a request. Sometimes it is a request that I do something. Sometimes it is a request from the person making the request for my permission to do something. This is in fact a species of request that I do something, i.e. give my permission. I may consent to do something which involves both me and some other party, perhaps the person making the request, but always what I consent to do is to do something myself, e.g. to go for a walk with the person making the request to which I consent. I cannot consent that someone else do something, though I can consent to allow someone else to do something.

Connected with consenting is the performative utterance 'I consent . . .' You do not have to use the words 'I consent' in order to consent, however, any more than you have to use the words 'I promise' in order to promise, and consenting is usually accomplished without using them.

SAYING 'YES'

The word 'Yes' has a number of functions. One of its functions, as we have seen, is to express assent to or compliance with a request.

Another function is to indicate willingness to obey a command (not the same thing as obeying the command; but if what I am commanded to do is to say the word 'Yes', saying the word 'Yes' is then obeying the command, but *not* indicating willingness to obey the command).

Another function of the word 'Yes' is to answer a question, though only certain sorts of question can be answered by saying 'Yes', for example you could answer the question 'Is it on the mantelpiece?' by saying 'Yes', but not the question 'Is it a boy or a girl?'

The word 'Yes' can be used to accept a proposal, and, possibly in conjunction with other words, to indicate one's intention to accept advice.

The word 'Yes' can be used to express one's agreement to a proposition, though it is sometimes used to reply in the affirmative to the question whether the proposition, just expressed by the speaker, is true or not, as in 'It is a fine day, isn't it?'

'Yes' can, as we have seen, be used to accept an offer.

The word 'Yes' also has certain 'third-party' uses. If A is asking B to do something, C may say 'Yes, please do', indicating that he supports B in making the request. He is, of course, requesting, not consenting to a request, but his use of the word 'Yes' presupposes that a request has already been made, and would be pointless and unintelligible had no request been made. The request need not have previously been made by some person other than the person using 'Yes' in this way, but by that person himself, i.e. 'Yes' may be used to repeat a request made by the person using the word 'Yes', and not by some other person. Similarly, C may use the word 'Yes' to command what A has already commanded B to do, to advise B to do what A has already advised him to do, to enable C to join with A in pleading with B, or imploring B, to do something, and so on. But I do not think 'Yes' is ever used by itself for these purposes. One would normally say, not 'Yes' alone, but, 'Yes, do', or, 'Yes, please do', or, 'Yes, that is what I would do too'.

The word 'No' can have the opposite of all the varying functions already ascribed to the word 'Yes'.

PERMITTING AND PROHIBITING

The sentence 'You may leave the room' is ambiguous. It may mean that it is possible that the person to whom I am speaking will leave the room, that I do not know that he will not leave the room. (Perhaps we ought always to say 'You *might* leave the room', when this is what we mean.) It may be a statement about a set of rules, to the effect that there is no rule prohibiting the person to whom I am speaking from leaving the room. In both these cases its function is to express a statement or proposition, which proposition will be true or false. But sometimes the words 'You may leave the room' do not state the fact that leaving the room is either possible or permitted. When I say these words, I am not saying that it is in fact already permissible for the person to whom I am speaking to leave the room, I am actually giving my permission for him to leave the room.

Giving my permission is rather like commanding, in that, if I say 'You may leave the room', this implies that I believe that either I have superior authority or power over the person to whom I am speaking. The words 'You may leave the room' are also like performatory utterances, in that just as when I say 'I promise' I am not stating that promising is occurring or has occurred, but actually doing the promising, so, when I say 'You may leave the room', I am not saying that permission is being or has been given, but actually permitting a certain action or kind of action to be performed.

Simply refusing permission may be described as forbidding. When to forbid is simply to refuse permission, it may be done simply by saying the word 'No' or by saying 'You may not'. When to forbid is to legislate against something or to command its non-performance, it may be done in words like 'No undergraduate shall (or may) entertain a woman in his room after eleven o'clock'. Both when permission is being refused and when a class of actions is being prohibited or forbidden, sentences like 'You (or undergraduates) may not . . .' do not express statements, and cannot be true or false. They are more like performative utterances. The same words, however, when used to say that something is in fact prohibited, or that permission has been refused, do make a statement, a statement which, of course, one needs no special power or authority to make.

MORAL JUDGMENT, AGREEING, OFFERING, ACCEPTING, CONSENTING, REFUSING AND SAYING 'YES'

Making a moral judgment is obviously neither to offer nor to accept. Agreeing, consenting and saying 'yes', however, all throw some light on moral judgments. If someone says to me, 'We ought to go out oftener,' or, 'You ought to work harder,' and I say, 'Yes, I agree to do that,' my using these words would show that I had misunderstood what he said. This shows that someone who says either of these things (and the same applies when they are said in response to 'It is your duty to work harder' and 'You are wrong to work no harder than you do') is not agreeing to a proposal, or to a suggestion that a course of action involving both him and the person with whom he is talking be adopted. When someone makes any moral judgment, the proper response is always 'I agree that that is so'; for example, I agree that promises ought to be kept, that it is my duty to be there, that eating people is wrong, and never 'I agree to'. This is a further reason for thinking that moral judgments are very much more like statements that they are like anything else.

Again, when someone makes a moral judgment, it is quite appropriate to say 'Yes'. This 'Yes' is the 'Yes' of agreement to a statement, and not the 'Yes' of consent or the 'Yes' which indicates willingness to do something. It means 'Yes, I agree that . . .', not 'Yes, I agree to . . .', or 'Yes, I consent to . . .', or 'Yes I will'. This is further reason for thinking that when we make moral judgments, we are making statements.

When we say 'You may go', we may be giving the person to whom we are speaking permission to go, and when we say to him 'You may not go', we may be prohibiting him from going. (The words 'Yes' and 'No' can serve instead of either of these two expressions, provided they are made in response to a question.) The same two expressions, too, can serve to *state the fact* that permission to go has been given or refused.

It could be held that to say 'You ought not to do X' is to prohibit X, and to say 'X is right' is to permit X. This theory would be in some respects like a command theory, for prohibiting X is like commanding non-X, and permitting may be held to be like not prohibiting.

The identification of 'X is right' with 'You may do X' is rendered plausible partly because of the logical analogies between must', 'must not' and 'may' on the one hand, and 'ought' 'ought not' and 'right', on the other. These can be exhibited as follows:

A₁ X is wrong	B₁ It is wrong to omit X
A₂ X ought not to be done	B₂ X ought to be done
A₃ X must not be done	B₃ X must be done
A₄ It is a duty not to do X	B₄ X is a duty
C₁ It is not wrong not to do X	D₁ X is right
C₂ It is not the case that X ought to be done	D₂ It is false that X ought not to be done
C₃ X may be omitted	D₃ X may be done
C₄ It is not a duty to do X	D₄ It is not a duty not to do X.

In this square of opposition the A propositions are contradictories of the D propositions and the B propositions are contradictories of the C propositions. The A propositions imply, but are not implied by, the C propositions, and the same relation holds between the B propositions and the D propositions. The A propositions and B propositions are contraries, and cannot both be true. The C propositions and the D propositions are subcontraries and cannot both be false.

However, it is comparatively rare, though cases do arise, to express the judgment 'It would be right for you to do X' in the words 'You may do X'; comparatively rare to express the judgment 'You ought to do X' in the words 'You must do X'; comparatively rare to express the judgment 'You ought not to do X' in the words 'You must not (may not) do X'. ('You must not do X' means 'You must do non-X'; 'You may not do X' means 'It is false that you may do X'; hence 'You must not do X' and 'You may not do X' are equivalent.) It is much more usual to use the impersonal forms 'X must be done', 'X must not be done', 'X may be done'.

When we do say 'You must not do X', 'You may do X', or 'You must do X' we are not prohibiting X, permitting X, or prohibiting the omission of X; what we are doing is stating that an action is impermissible, permissible, or that its omission is impermissible, i.e. that it is obligatory. This is much more like what counsel is doing when he gives an opinion concerning whether an action is prohibited, permitted, or enjoined by a set of rules, than like actually ourselves doing the permitting or prohibiting. It would be absurd to substitute for 'You may do X', when this is equivalent to 'It would be right for you to do X', the performative utterance 'I permit you to do X'. It would also be absurd to substitute for 'You may not do X', when this is equivalent to 'It would be wrong for you to do X', the performative utterance 'I do not permit you to do X' (or, 'I prohibit you from doing X'). Only a person having power or authority to permit or prohibit may properly make the performative utterances 'I permit . . .', etc., whereas anyone may properly make the moral judgments, whether having power or authority or not. The view is made to seem plausible, however, by the fact that the sentence 'You may do X' may sometimes be equivalent to the performative utterance 'I permit you to do X' or may at other times be equivalent to the judgment that X is permitted by a set of rules. When 'You may do X' expresses a moral judgment, it is more like the latter than the former, though, as we have seen, the rules which permit X are in this case not rules which anyone has made.

RECOMMENDING

There does not seem to me any peculiar, distinctive class of utterances corresponding to the activity of recommending, in a wide sense, something or somebody. It is true that we can recommend a car by saying that it is a good one, but so we can by saying that it is fast, economical and reliable, which are ordinary statements.

Normally, when we recommend something, we are simply making statements about it, Not any statement, however, can feature in a recommendation. The statements have to be of the kind which will make the person to whom the recommendation is made see what we are recommending in a favourable light. They do not, however, have to be statements which make the person making the recommendation regard the thing recommended in a favourable light. I may recommend a car by saying it is fast, because I know the person I am talking to wants a fast car, though I myself do not like cars to be fast. Though recommendations consist of statements, to recommend something is not simply to make statements about it, but to make statements about it with a view to satisfying the wants or needs, of the person we are addressing, for a thing or person of a certain sort.

In a narrow sense, one can only recommend something by

using the words 'I recommend'. Someone saying, 'I recommend you to take a French cook (or a Chinese wife),' is not making a statement to the effect that he is or was recommending something; he is actually doing the recommending. His utterance is therefore performative, and so not capable of being true or false. One can, however, recommend something without using the verbal formula 'I recommend'; some testimonials contain these words; others do not. Though, when I say 'I recommend', I am not making a statement which can be true or false, I make *statements* in support of my recommendation, and these are true or false.

Though recommendations may consist of statements, which are true or false, recommendations cannot properly be said to be true or false. They can, however, be described as sensible or sound or worth adopting or worth very serious consideration. This is perhaps because the important thing about a recommendation is not the academic consideration of whether the statements it contains are true or not, though people given to making false statements in their recommendations are known as unreliable, but whether or not to adopt the recommendation. The fact that all the statements in the recommendation are true does not at all mean that the recommendation ought to be adopted, or that it would be wise to adopt it. Whether or not it is wise to do the thing recommended will depend upon whether doing this thing will satisfy the need on account of which the recommendation was originally requested.

It is possible to recommend someone or something, or to recommend *that* some course of action be taken.

MORAL JUDGMENTS AND RECOMMENDING

To the extent that one can recommend something by making any statement about it which puts it in a favourable light, one can recommend something by saying that it is good. The fact that one can recommend something in this way by saying that it is good does not show anything about the nature of this moral judgement, other than that most people do regard what is good in a favourable light, and it certainly does not show that anyone making it is not making a statement.

Moral judgments are not equivalent to recommendations in the sense of performative utterances which start with the words 'I recommend . . .' It is perfectly possible to say 'That is the best one, but I recommend you to take this one, as it is cheaper.' We can recommend a car by saying that it is a good one only in the sense in which we can recommend it by saying that it is a fast one.

If it is possible only to recommend things or people, but not actions, then saying that some action is a duty, or that it ought to be done, or that it would be wrong to omit it, cannot be to recommend it. If it is possible, as it probably is, to recommend actions, moral judgments about actions will still not be such recommendations, for it is possible to say such things as, 'It is your duty to see him, but I recommend that you don't, as he is quite impossible,' or, 'Well, it would be wrong, but I recommend you to be a devil for once.' You cannot, however say, 'I think you *ought* to do so-and-so, but I don't recommend it.'

Hence someone saying, 'We think the course of action which ought to be taken is so-and-so', can be described, perhaps loosely, as recommending the course of action. This recommendation can be described as a good one if adopting it brings about the ends which the person or committee of persons making the recommendation was asked to find means to, or which solves the practical problem, which will be one of finding ways of accomplishing a certain end. It does not follow from this that saying that something ought to be done is not to make a statement about it. We can say 'I believe' or 'I think' or 'I know' or 'I wonder whether such-and-such ought to be done'. It is even possible to say that it is true that something ought to be done. To this extent saying that something ought to be done consists in making a statement. Nevertheless, whether or not something *ought* to be done will not depend so much on whether this thing has the characteristic which the speaker says it has, as on whether adopting the course of action in question brings about the desired results (and brings them about economically and without harmful side-effects).

When someone says 'X ought to be done', we can say 'His recommendation is sound and worth adopting', and this recommendation *will* be worth adopting if adopting it does serve the ends it was designed to serve. There is a close connection between the recommendation to do something, or the recommendation that something be done, and the judgment that the thing *ought* to be done. If the recommendation is a good one, then that thing really ought to be done. For example, someone's recommendation to me to take more exercise is a good one if and only if I ought to take more exercise. This equivalence applies only to *hypothetical*

imperatives. The recommendation that I must take exercise if I
want to be healthy is a good one if and only if it is the case that I
ought to take more exercise if I want to be healthy.

I still cannot help thinking, however, that only someone
using the performatory utterance 'I recommend . . .' can, strictly
speaking, be described as recommending, and that whenever we
use 'recommend' of anything other than this, we are using the
word somewhat loosely.

COMMENDING

Someone is normally commending some person, thing or action
if he makes statements about it ascribing characteristics to it
which are commonly considered to be desirable.

One can also commend something by using the performative
utterance 'I commend'. In such a case, one is not saying anything
about the person, thing or action one commends, though, doubtless,
one does commend it because one believes it has characteristics
which are commonly considered to be desirable. If one commends
so-and-so by means of the performative utterance 'I commend . . .',
mistakenly believing that he or it has certain desirable characteristics, then what one says cannot be false. One can, however, be
said to have commended it wrongly.

The sense of 'commend' in which one can commend oneself to
one's maker, or ask to be commended to one's mother, are of no
interest to moral philosophers. To commend oneself to one's
maker is to put oneself in one's maker's care. To ask to be commended to one's mother is to ask to be remembered to her.

Commending, unlike recommending, can be done 'disinter-
estedly', in the sense that someone commending some person,
thing or action, is not necessarily suggesting to the person he is
addressing that he take that person or thing, or perform that
action, for whatever reason.

We say that something commends itself to someone when he
has a favourable attitude to it. Something can commend itself to
someone as a means to something else, or for its own sake.

CONDEMNING

Condemning is often performed by means of a performative
utterance, like 'I condemn you to death'. Condemning does not

have to be accomplished by means of an utterance, however; putting a black mark against a name on a list may serve as well.

Sometimes to condemn something is to make a statement of a derogatory nature about that thing, like, 'He is the laziest and stupidest boy I have ever taught.'

When condemning is accomplished by means of a performative utterance or an equivalent, the person doing the condemning must have power or authority such that ill befalls, or is likely to befall, the person condemned as a result of his condemnation. If a forestry officer puts a mark on a tree, he may be condemning it, but if I were to put a similar mark on the same tree, I am not condemning it, for I lack the authority and power to see that the tree is cut down. No special power or authority, however, is needed to condemn something in the sense of making derogatory statements about it.

MORAL JUDGMENT, CONDEMNING AND COMMENDING

To judge that a man is bad, or that what he has done is wrong, is not to condemn in the sense in which condemning is performatory. No special authority is needed to condemn: anyone can do it, and everyone does. No harmful consequences follow or tend to follow, in accordance with a set of rules, for the person condemned as a result of my condemnation, as the man who is condemned to death by a judge is quite likely to be hanged. In any case, we have already seen that moral judgments are not performative utterances.

Someone who says that a man is bad, or who says that what he did was wrong, may be described as condemning the man or his action in the second sense of 'condemn' we distinguished above. Nothing of any consequence for the nature of moral judgments follows from this, however, for in this sense of 'condemn' someone making quite ordinary factual statements about him or his action, such as that he does not wash and that he did it out of jealousy may, perhaps loosely, be described as condemning.

Since anyone making a statement about someone, ascribing to him some characteristic which most people regard favourably can be described as commending him, the fact that we commend a man when we say that he is good shows nothing at all about what we are doing when we describe someone as good. There is this difference, however, between commending something by saying that it is good, and commending something by saying that it is fast, symmetrical or large. Being fast, symmetrical or large may or may not be desirable attributes, but being good must be a desirable attribute. It may be that 'good' is a word which signifies that the thing which is described as good possesses some desirable attributes in a more than average degree.

Obviously, when someone says that some action is a duty, or is obligatory, or is wrong, he is neither condemning nor commending anything.

EXPRESSIONS OF INTENTION [1]

There is a difference between what I am saying when I say 'I will drown' and when I say 'I shall drown', and also a difference between what I mean when I say 'You will drown' and when I say 'You shall drown'. The difference between 'You will drown' and 'You shall drown' is that when I say the former, I am predicting that the person to whom I am speaking will in fact drown; when I say the latter, I am expressing my determination that the person to whom I am speaking shall drown. Similarly, when I say 'I *shall* drown', I am making a statement which is a prediction of what will happen to me in the future, when I say I *will* drown I am expressing my intention to drown.[2]

It is sometimes alleged that expressions of intention, though they look like statements, are not statements in fact. 'I will drown', it is said, is neither a statement about my present intentions, nor a statement about my future destination. I personally, however, cannot see that sentences like 'I will drown' do anything different from stating the fact, which is a fact about oneself, that one is determined to drown. However, in certain contexts, 'I will be there' (or 'I shall be there', if we are ungrammatical) does do something over and above make a statement about one's intentions. It serves to make a promise, and someone who says, 'I will be there,' when it is known that his hearers are intended by him to be able to rely upon his future whereabouts, and the question whether he will be there or not is not purely academic, has made a promise just as much as if he had actually said, 'I promise to be

---

[1] See S. N. Hampshire and H. L. A. Hart, 'Decision, Intention and Certainty', *Mind*, Vol. LXVII, 1958.

[2] This rule, apparently, does not apply to Scots and Americans. See Sir Ernest Gowers *The Complete Plain Words* (Pelican Books, 1962), pp. 215–6.

there.' It may be, however, that one reason for regarding our obligation to keep this promise as less stringent than our obligation to keep some other promises is that we did not make this promise in a manner which was fully explicit.

Some philosophers have regarded all statements about the future, which are such that it is within our power to make them true or make them false, as promises.[1] It is not the case, however, that statements about the future which we make in idle or academic conversation, simply to satisfy the curiosity, about our future behaviour, of the people to whom we are talking, are promises. Furthermore, the important thing is not whether or not it *is* in our power to make the statement about the future true or false, but whether we and our hearers *believe* at the time the statement is made that this is within our power. We can make a promise too, not only by making a statement about the future, but also by making statements about our present intentions about what to do in the future; we may acquire some degree of obligation to do what we have said we intend to do if we have reason to believe that, through our saying this, those to whom we were speaking will come to expect us to carry out our intentions.

Though, in what has gone before, I have spoken as if, when I said 'I shall be there', I was making a statement about the future which was also a promise, I am not sure whether perhaps the correct account of the situation is not that, instead of making a statement about the future, I am making a promise.

MORAL JUDGMENTS AND EXPRESSIONS OF INTENTION

The only moral judgment which it is plausible to identify with an expression of intention is the judgment 'I ought to do X'. 'All men ought to do X', presumably, would have to be construed as an expression of intention to exhort other people to do actions like X, and this, presumably, would mean that 'You ought to do X' was not an expression of intention – intention to exhort – but the actual exhorting.

Even moral judgments about what one ought to do in the future cannot be regarded as expressions of intention. If I say 'I ought to work harder', and do not, I cannot properly be accused of

[1] See Richard Price, *Review of the Principal Questions on Morals*, (O.U.P., 1947), pp. 155 f.

not doing what I resolved, whereas if I say 'I intend to work harder', I can properly be accused of this. If I say 'I ought to insure my life', it is proper for someone else to say, 'Yes, you ought' or 'Yes, I agree you ought' or 'Ought you?' or 'I don't think so'. None of these responses would be proper if I had said 'I intend to insure my life'. A proper response to 'I intend to insure my life' is 'Do you?', which is not a proper response to 'I ought to insure my life'.

GENERAL CONCLUSIONS

The result of this chapter has been to confirm what was asserted in the chapter before, namely, that moral judgments, since they can be asserted, denied, believed, disbelieved, wondered about, and so on, are more like statements than like any of the species of practical discourse considered in this chapter. Nevertheless, if they did belong to any of these categories, or something resembling them, they would not be utterly lacking in any tie to reality which would make it a matter of indifference whether we accepted or rejected them. For advice, proposals, suggestions, recommendations can be good or bad, and whether they are good or not will not depend in any way on the opinions of the person who puts them forward about whether or not they are good or bad.

CHAPTER XIV

TO BE OR NOT TO BE

There is one possible answer to the question, 'What are we doing when we say that an action is right or that it is wrong?', which we have not yet considered. We have seen that, when we say that actions are right or wrong, we are not commanding or prohibiting them; we have neither the power nor the authority to do anything so absurd. Yet there is a class of sentences with which it may be more plausible to identify sentences expressing judgments about right and wrong. These are judgments to the effect that some action or other is or is not *to be* done. For example, we say that a certain climb is not to be attempted by beginners, that a certain kind of firework is not to be held in the hand, that a certain kind of chemical preparation is not to be used with any other chemical preparation, and so on. It is true that such sentences can with no plausibility whatsoever be identified with sentences which say that something or other is morally wrong. The person who says that a certain climb is not to be attempted does not mean that it would be morally wrong for beginners to attempt it (though he may think this as well). Nevertheless, considering such sentences may give us some clue to the nature of moral sentences. For this reason the subject is worth pursuing.

To say that a climb is not to be attempted by beginners is not the same thing as to command or order beginners not to attempt it. One experienced climber may remark to another that such-and-such a climb is not to be attempted by beginners, but the first climber cannot be ordering the second climber not to attempt it, for the second climber is not a beginner; nor can he be ordering anybody else, for there may be no beginners within earshot. Even if an expereinced climber does say to beginners, 'Do not attempt this climb,' he cannot be saying to them that the climb is not to be attempted by beginners; he *may* be ordering them not to attempt the climb *because* it is a climb not to be attempted by beginners, but he may also be issuing this command for a variety of other reasons. He might be telling them not to attempt the climb because they had not the right sort of equipment, or because it was Sunday, or because the weather was bad. Saying 'This climb is not to be attempted by beginners' is in this way more like giving information about the climb than it is like commanding any beginner not to attempt the climb.

It is possible for someone to be *mistaken* in thinking that a climb is not to be attempted by beginners. He may have read in his guide book that climb A is not to be attempted by beginners, but confuse climb B with climb A, and say, mistakenly, that climb B is not to be attempted by beginners. It would be possible to argue in reply that all he was mistaken about was the fact that it says in the guide book that climb B is not to be attempted by beginners, but I think such an argument would be mistaken. For someone, without reading any guide book, or consulting any other expert, might decide for himself, on the basis of his knowledge of the difficulty of the climb and his experience of the capacities of beginners, that such-and-such a climb was not to be attempted by beginners. If it turned out that he had grossly overestimated the difficulty of the climb, or grossly underestimated the capacities of the normal beginner, then he would have to say that he was mistaken in thinking that the climb was not to be attempted by beginners. Hence, when someone says that a certain climb is not to be attempted by beginners, there does seem to be some objective fact, which obtains independently of his opinion, about which he can be mistaken.

Similarly, it is possible for two people to agree or to disagree about whether a certain climb is or is not to be attempted by beginners. If Smith thinks that it may be attempted by beginners ('This climb may be attempted by beginners' is equivalent to 'It is not the case that this climb is not to be attempted by beginners') and Jones thinks that it is not to be attempted by beginners, then what Smith says is incompatible with what Jones says. Hence the meaning of the sentence 'This climb is not to be attempted by beginners' does not depend upon who the person is who utters it.

Nor does the meaning of the sentence 'This climb is not to be attempted by beginners' depend upon the time at which it is uttered. Provided the nature of the climb has not changed, nor the capacities of beginners improved or deteriorated, if anyone is right in thinking that a climb is not to be attempted by beginners when he says this at one time, he must be wrong in thinking that it may be attempted by beginners when he says this at a later time, and *vice versa*. Nor, of course, does the place at which the statement is made, or the nation or social class or cultural back-ground of the person who makes it, make any difference to whether the person who says, 'This climb is not to be attempted by beginners,' is right or wrong when he says this. All that the truth or falsity of what he says *does* depend on is the difficulty of the climb, and the capacity for climbing which beginners have.

Just as moral judgments are resultant, so are judgments such as 'This climb is not to be attempted by beginners'. Someone making the pronouncement that a certain climb is not to be attempted by beginners makes this pronouncement in virtue of certain facts he knows or thinks he knows about the nature of the climb and the capacity for climbing which beginners have. It is because this climb has certain features, such as overhanging rocks or poor foot and hand holds, and because beginners are not likely to have had experience of climbs having these features, that one pro-nounces that it is not to be attempted by beginners. If one possessed no information whatsoever about the climb and its difficulty, nor about the capacities of beginners for making climbs, one would not be able to come to any decision on the question whether the climb was one which beginners might attempt or not. Just as it could not be that the only thing we knew about an action was that it was wrong (though it could be that the only thing we knew about an object was that it was red), so it could not be that the only thing we knew about a climb was that it was not to be attemp-ted by beginners, unless, of course, we had simply taken this upon the authority of someone else, and not made up our own minds on the question.

Judgments of the kind 'Climbs of such-and-such a degree of difficulty are not to be attempted by beginners' also resemble moral judgments in that they are, on the face of it, *a priori*. If someone knows how difficult the climb is, and what the capacities of beginners are, there are no further observations he needs to make in order to decide whether the climb is or is not one which is not to be attempted by beginners. This is something which he must decide on the basis of the evidence which he already has, and there are no further observations which he could conceivably make in order to be in a position to make up his mind on this question. Hence the decision whether, given certain information about the difficulty of the climb and the capacities of beginners, the climb is or is not one which is not to be attempted by begin-ners, resembles the decision whether, given that all men are mortal and Socrates is a man, Socrates is mortal, in that it must be made on the basis of the facts provided; no further investigation of matters of fact is necessary or even possible.

For the same reason, the connection between the fact that the climb is of more than a certain degree of difficulty, and the fact that beginners have only a certain limited amount of climbing skill, and the climb's being one which is not to be attempted by beginners, is a *necessary* connection, not a *contingent* one. It does not just so happen that the climb is of the degree of difficulty it is, and the capacities of beginners are as limited as they are, and that the climb is also as a matter of fact one which is not to be attempted by beginners. If it is of this degree of difficulty, and if beginners are no better at climbing than they are, then the climb must be one which is not to be attempted by beginners. There is no possibility, given the difficulty of the climb and the capacities of beginners, of its not being a climb which is not to be attempted by beginners.

The judgment that the climb is one which is not to be attempted by beginners is also, like the judgment that something is right or that it is wrong, *universalizable*. If a given climb is one which is not to be attempted by beginners, then any other climb, which resembles this climb in all respects other than in being one not to be attempted by beginners must, since all other circumstances, in particular the difficulty of the climb and the capacities of beginners, are similar, also resemble this climb in being one which is not to be attempted by beginners. In other words, if, of two climbs, one is not to be attempted by beginners, and the other is not, then there must be some further difference between the two climbs, which accounts for the fact that one is not to be attempted by beginners and the other is one which may be attempted by beginners.

We saw that, of judgments about right and wrong, some were analytic whereas others were synthetic, but that the analytic ones were all practically useless as a guide to conduct, for the reason explained earlier in the book.[1] Doubtless some judgments about what is not to be done are analytic. If a climb is described as a Grade A climb, and a Grade A climb is one which is to be attempted only by experts, then it follows analytically and logically that it is one which is not to be attempted by beginners. However, the judgment that if a climb involves negotiating overhanging rocks,

[1] Chapter IV.

and beginners have not the skill to negotiate overhanging rocks, then this climb is not to be attempted by beginners, is not obviously analytic. Something does seem to be added, when we say that a climb is not to be attempted by beginners, to the fact that it contains overhanging rocks which beginners are unable to negotiate. In saying that it contains overhanging rocks, and that beginners cannot negotiate these, one has not actually said that it is not to be attempted by beginners.

On the other hand, though the judgment, that if a climb contains overhanging rocks which beginners cannot negotiate it is not to be attempted by beginners, is not analytic, and is also not a contingent judgment known to be true by empirical observation, it would be very odd indeed to suggest that some special intuition was needed in order to see that a climb which beginners could not negotiate was a climb not to be attempted by beginners. To suggest this would be rather like suggesting that in order to know that anyone who said that the answer to the question 'What is the sum of seven and twelve and nine?' was twenty-eight, was giving the right answer to this question, a special faculty of intuition was needed, or to suggest that a special faculty of intuition is needed in order to know that, if, of two roads, one went to Bath and the other went to Bristol, a man who wanted to get to Bristol and took the road to Bristol had taken the right road.

A question about moral judgments, which has been discussed earlier, is whether or not, when I say that some action is wrong, I am providing some further information about it, over and above the information on the basis of which I judge that it is wrong, or whether I am simply repeating some of this information in different words – the answer which the naturalist would give; alternatively, perhaps, I am not giving any information about the action at all, but doing some such thing as expressing the emotions which contemplating the action arouses in me, or commanding others not to perform it. If we ask the same question about judgments to the effect that something or other is not to be done, the answer is somewhat ambiguous. As we have already seen, it does not look as if someone saying that a certain climb is not to be attempted by beginners, because it is too difficult for beginners to negotiate successfully, is simply repeating the fact that beginners cannot successfully negotiate a climb of this degree of difficulty. On the other hand, it does not seem at all plausible to suggest that, as well as all the facts about the climb and the climbing abilities of beginners, there is, in addition, some further fact, namely, the fact that the climb is not to be attempted by beginners. When the degree of difficulty of the climb is known, and the capacities for climbing of beginners established, there seems to be no further fact to be discovered in order for one to pronounce upon whether the climb is one which is or is not to be attempted by beginners; hence that a climb is not to be attempted by beginners is not an additional fact about the climb. This would suggest that when I say that a climb is not to be attempted by beginners I am not so much stating a fact about the climb, as commanding or enjoining or advising beginners not to attempt it. But, as we have seen, it is possible to say, 'I think this climb is not to be attempted by beginners,' or to say, 'Yesterday I was mistakenly of the opinion that this was a climb not to be attempted by beginners,' or 'I wonder whether this is a climb which beginners may attempt or not.' Questions such as these cannot be raised about such things as commands, injunctions or pieces of advice. It is not possible to say 'I think *do not attempt this climb*,' still less, 'I mistakenly thought that *do not attempt this climb*.'

At least part of the reason for this is that judgments like 'This climb is not to be attempted by beginners' are anchored to reality in a way in which commands are not anchored to reality, but statements are. It is possible to issue a command which it is morally wrong to issue. For example, it is possible to order a guard to shoot a prisoner, and this would generally be held to be morally wrong. It is also possible to make a statement which it is morally wrong to make, for example it is possible to tell a lady that she is fat, which is unkind. But the fact that commands can be ones which it is morally wrong to issue and statements can be ones which it is morally wrong to make, does not alter the fact that a statement can be one which it is right or wrong to believe, whereas the question of believing, disbelieving, or being in doubt about a command is one which cannot possibly arise. Indeed, the statement 'You are fat' is one which it may be wrong to make, even though it is not at all a statement which it is wrong to believe, since it may be true. (It is perhaps even ruder to make it if it is true than if it is false.) Hence there is a dimension of appraisal, where statements are concerned, which simply does not exist where commands are concerned, and this is the dimension of appraisal which concerns how they are anchored to reality in being true or false, accurate or inaccurate. Since commands do not provide information, they cannot provide true information or false information, accurate information or inaccurate information. Hence commands are not tied to reality in a way in which statements are. One can command anything without fear of being wrong, except in the sense that one has given a command which it is morally wrong to give, or which is not the command laid down in the rule book to be given in just those circumstances, or which is the wrong command to give in the sense that it is ineffective in bringing about the end which issuing it was intended to bring about.

Judgments to the effect that something or other is not to be done, are fastened to reality in a way in which commands cannot be. This is shown by the fact that I can say that I was mistaken in thinking that a climb was not to be attempted by beginners. Nevertheless, judgments to the effect that something or other is not to be done are not tied to reality in quite the same way in which *ordinary* statements are tied to reality. This is shown by the fact that there is no extra piece of information about a climb, that it is not to be attempted by beginners – unless, of course, we mean, as we sometimes do, 'This climb is classified as one which is not to be attempted by beginners' – about which we can be ignorant or mistaken. That this is a climb which is not to be attempted by beginners is a decision about the climb which one makes upon the basis of possessing all the relevant information concerning it. How, then, are judgments to the effect that something or other is not to be done tied to reality?

Judgments to the effect that something or other is not to be done are action-guiding in a way in which *ordinary* statements are not. Statements guide actions in that they provide people with information which may tell them how ends which they are seeking may or may not be obtained. Commands are action-guiding in that, though they do not provide anyone with information, they give a shove in a certain direction. 'This climb is not to be attempted by beginners' does give a shove to beginners in the direction of not attempting the climb, but it claims to be an informed shove, not a brutal shove, so to speak. The appeal is not, as it is in the case of commands, simply to *force majeure*, but to reason. The suggestion is not that the person who ignores what is said, and does in fact attempt the climb, is to be scolded, imprisoned or shot, but that, if he ignores what is said, he will find himself in a predicament which the normal person would not choose to be in. It is not because it is dangerous that the climb is prohibited; one can command people not to do things which one believes it is not in their interest to do, but then the appeal is still to force, and there is no question of being able to say that the command was a mistaken command, in the sense that one mistakenly thought, 'Don't attempt that climb' (though, as we have seen, it could be a command which one was mistaken to give). However, if one says, 'That climb is not to be attempted,' because one supposes that it is dangerous, and one subsequently discovers that it is not dangerous, one does say, 'I thought that climb was not to be attempted, but I was mistaken.' Why is it that one can be mistaken, though in saying that a climb is not to be attempted, one is not saying anything about the climb which adds anything to anyone's stock of information about it, from which it follows that one cannot be saying something correct if the extra information provided corresponds to the facts about the climb, and saying something which is incorrect if the extra information provided does not correspond to the facts about the climb?

I think that the answer must be in part that, though when I say the climb is not to be attempted, I am not providing any extra information about the climb, but giving a push to beginners in the direction of not making the climb, the formula, 'This climb is not to be attempted by beginners,' unlike the formula, 'Beginners, do not attempt this climb,' arouses, in the context in which it is used, expectations in the minds of those hearing me use this form of words about the sort of reason I have for what I say. If I say, 'This climb is not to be attempted by beginners,' this causes my hearers to expect that I say this because the climb is dangerous for beginners. 'This climb is not to be attempted by beginners', unlike 'Do not attempt this climb', is not a push which relies for its effectiveness upon superior force or blind acceptance of authority, but a push to beginners in the direction in which they might reasonably be supposed to want to go, since it is reasonable to suppose that beginners will not want to attempt a climb which is dangerous beyond a certain point. Hence the person saying 'This climb is not to be attempted by beginners' will not still want to give the push if he discovers that he has overestimated the danger of the climb, or that he is wrong in thinking that beginners do not wish to kill themselves by attempting excessively dangerous climbs. Hence he is prepared to say,

'I think this climb is not to be attempted by beginners,' meaning that the push he is giving is one which he is prepared to withdraw if the supposed facts which caused him to give it turn out not to be facts; and if, after having acquired fuller knowledge of the facts, he does wish to withdraw the push he has given, he will be prepared to say, 'I was wrong in thinking this climb was not to be attempted by beginners.'

The rest of the answer is that there are reasons for thinking that a climb is not to be attempted by beginners, whereas there are no reasons for a command, as opposed to reasons for issuing a command. One can think that a climb is not to be attempted by beginners because one thinks it is very steep, and then one can say one was *mistaken* in thinking that it was not to be attempted by beginners if it turns out that it is not as steep as one had supposed, or if one decides that the fact that it is steep is not a good reason for thinking that it is not to be attempted by beginners.

But suppose that there is an eccentric man, with unusual wants, who *wishes* beginners to be killed on the climb. Will he be right when he says something like 'This climb is not to be omitted by beginners'? The answer is that he will not be right. If he had simply been ordering or commanding beginners not to omit the climb, there could be no question whether, when he said, 'Beginners, climb this mountain,' he was saying anything which was right or wrong, though, very likely, he would be saying something which it was wrong *to say*. But it is a convention governing the way in which it is permissible to use sentences such as 'This climb is not to be attempted by beginners' that it is only used to guide the behaviour of beginners in directions which it is likely that they will want to go. To take another example, if, on Brand X, it says, 'Brand X is not to be used in conjunction with any other product used for the same purpose,' it must be assumed that the reason why this is said is because using Brand X with any similar product is dangerous or deleterious or likely to impair the efficiency of Brand X, and that people using Brand X are not likely to want to do anything which is dangerous or deleterious or likely to impair the efficiency of product X. If it turns out that the makers have been wrong in supposing that using Brand X in conjunction with some other product is dangerous or will impair its efficiency, then one will have to say that, when the makers said, 'Brand X is not to be used in conjunction with any similar brand,' they were mistaken.

In other words, the difference between commands or orders and sentences like 'This climb is not to be attempted by beginners' or 'This product is not to be used in conjunction with any other similar product' is that, whereas a command may, without linguistic impropriety (though not without moral impropriety, and not without the possibility of the command being the wrong command to issue in the circumstances) be used for any reason whatsoever, expressions such as 'This climb is not to be attempted by beginners' must be assumed to be made for guiding the people to whom it applies in some direction which it is assumed that they are likely to want to go. If the assumption that it will guide them in this direction is mistaken, then, it is possible to say that the person who used the form of words in question was saying something mistaken, though it is not possible to say of commands that they are mistaken.

There is also another class of judgments, consideration of which may well throw some light on the nature of moral judgments. These are judgments to the effect that some class of actions must be done, or may be done, or must not be done.

There are various judgments which make use of the word 'must'. (1) We can say that it must be the case that two and two are four. (2) We can say Smith must be the murderer, because only he had both an opportunity and a motive. (3) We can say that a gas must expand if it is heated. (4) We can say that in order to open a tin, one must have a tin-opener. (5) We can say that a white tie must be worn with tails, or that a bishop must move diagonally. (6) We can say to someone over whom we have authority, 'You must go to bed immediately.' (7) If we are inventing rules for a new game or a new constitution, we can say, 'The player with the highest card must bid first,' or, 'The President must secure the consent of congress before taking any decision which commits armed forces.' (8) We can say, 'Justice must be done, but inhumanity must be avoided.' In all the above cases, similar judgments may be made by using the words 'may' or 'must not'.

Although all these might be said to be propositions involving necessity, only the first of them is a necessary proposition. The examples mentioned under (6) and (7) are not propositions at all. Anyone saying, 'You must go to bed immediately,' is not making a statement but giving an order; anyone saying, in the process of inventing a game, 'The player with the highest card must deal first,' is not making a statement, but promulgating a rule.

The question arises whether the word 'must' is being used in different senses in the examples given above. I am inclined to think that it is not. There are different sorts of necessity, but a different sort of necessity is not the same thing as a different sense of 'necessity'; large animals and small animals, though different sorts of animal, are not animals in a different sense of the word 'animal'. The root idea of necessity seems to be the same in all these cases, namely, the idea of only one alternative being possible. The first states that there is no alternative admitted by logic to a proposition's being true. The second states that there is no alternative to Smith's being the murderer. The third states that there is no alternative to something's happening (the gas expanding) if something else has happened (the gas being heated). The fourth states that there is no alternative way of opening a tin to using a tin-opener. The fifth states that the rules of etiquette allow no alternative to wearing a white tie if you are wearing tails. The sixth and seventh are attempts to preclude any other alternative than a child's going to bed or the player with the highest card dealing first. The eighth, perhaps, states that there is no morally permissible alternative to justice's being done and inhumanity avoided.

As with judgments saying that something is to be done, or is not to be done, there is a close resemblance to the logical properties of at least some of these judgments and the logical properties of judgments about right and wrong. Not to do X is wrong, X ought to be done, X is a duty, X is obligatory, omitting X is impermissible, are all very like X must be done. X is (all) right, it is not the case that non-X is obligatory, non-X is not a duty, and X is permissible are all like X may be done. X is wrong, X ought not to be done, non-X is a duty, non-X is obligatory, X is impermissible, are all very like X must not be done. And the logical relations between judgments in these three groups are the same. Any judgment in the first group is the contrary (to say that two statements are contrary is to say that they cannot both be true, though they can both be false) of its parallel in the third group. Any judgment in the second group is the contradictory (to say that two judgments are contradictory is to say that they cannot both be true *and* cannot both be false) of its parallel in the third group. Any judgment in the first group entails its parallel in the second group. (This, incidentally, does not imply that any judgment in any group is equivalent to any other judgment from the *same* group.)

Furthermore, if we omit examples (6) and (7) it is possible to say of statements expressed in sentences using 'must' and 'may' that we were mistaken in thinking them, or that someone else is mistaken in believing them. Anyone saying '. . . must . . .' or '. . . may . . .' is saying something incompatible with what someone else is saying who says 'It is not the case that . . . must . . .' or 'It is not the case that . . may . . .', and if we ourselves say '. . . must . . .' we are committed to holding that formerly we were mistaken when we said 'It is not the case that . . . must . . .' or 'It is not the case that . . . may . . .'. And since the place at which these statements are made is irrelevant to whether the person making them is saying what is true or what is false, such judgments are, like moral judgments, not dependent for their truth upon the place at which they are made, the person who makes them, his social background or the community from which he comes, or the time at which they are made.

Obviously moral judgments about what is obligatory are not much like judgments of the kind, 'If you want X, you must do Y,' or, 'You must do Y, in order to bring about X.' These latter judgments are like the so-called hypothetical imperative, 'If you want Y, you ought to do X,' and only tell you what to do in order to achieve some desired result. Moral judgments, however, are commonly supposed to be *categorical*, and to tell you what you must do, whether you want to or not. Moral judgments, then, must be like judgments of the sort 'You must do X', when it is not understood that you must do X, in order to bring about some some desired end.

However, there is no reason why one should not say 'You must do X' because one thinks that certain consequences will result from or be avoided by doing X, and no reason why these consequences one is thinking of should not be the good or ill of society. Saying 'X must be done', because one thinks the good of society will result from X's being done, is not at all to say, 'You must do X, if you *want* the good of society.' One must distinguish, too, between saying, 'You must do X, in order that harm to society be avoided,' and saying, 'You must do X,' in order that harm to society be avoided. It is the latter, not the former, whose similarity to and possible identity with moral judgments I am considering.

Even if we say 'X must be done' because we believe that harm to society will result from X's not being done, this does not mean that we can establish that X must not be done simply by establishing that harm to society will in fact result if X is not done. All we have established is that X must not be done, *if* harm to society is to be avoided, from which it follows that X must not be done, if in fact harm to society *is* to be avoided. This takes us back to the first kind of judgment which we considered as a model for moral judgments, that is, judgments of the kind 'X is to be done'.

A third class of judgments, consideration of which may throw some light upon the nature of judgments about right and wrong, are judgments about what is enjoined, permitted or prohibited by certain rules. If we make the assumption, which seems not unreasonable, that whatever is not expressly prohibited by a rule is permitted, the judgment that X is enjoined by rule (which is analogous to X is obligatory), the judgment that X is permitted by rule (which is analogous to X is right in the sense of all right, or permissible) and X is forbidden (which is analogous to X is wrong) will stand in the same relationships to one another that X is obligatory, X is all right, and X is wrong respectively stand in to one another. We have seen that sometimes 'X must be done. means 'X is enjoined by a rule'; that 'X may be done' sometimes means 'X is permitted by a rule' and 'X must not be done' sometimes means 'X is prohibited by a rule'.

Such judgments have many of the logical features which we have seen that moral judgments have. We are capable of being mistaken about them. Judgments about them are genuinely incompatible with the apparently contradictory judgments made by other people, at other places, and from different countries or social backgrounds. On the other hand, as we have seen, rules can be changed, although the moral law cannot be, and judgments about what is enjoined, permitted or prohibited by rule are clearly synthetic, contingent empirical matters of fact, established by observation and experience. And any *actual* set of rules may sometimes enjoin actions which are wrong, and any *sensible* set of rules will certainly sometimes fail to enjoin actions which are right.

Perhaps, however, to say that an action is obligatory, is to say that it would be enjoined by a set of rules which are to be adopted; to say that it is all right is to say that it would be permitted by these rules; and to say that it is wrong is to say that it would be prohibited by these rules. Perhaps we think that the rules which are to be adopted are *ideal* rules. And maybe we think they are ideal rules if they are ideal for the purpose of furthering society's interests and welfare.

At this point some clarification of the nature of an ideal rule is necessary. It may be that, in an ideal society, there would be no violence. This does not mean that we ought not to be violent; we do not live in an ideal society. Nevertheless, an ideal set of rules would be one which would tell you both how you ought to behave in an ideal society, where there is no violence, and in this society, where there is violence. One thing, indeed, which an ideal set of rules will take into account, is the fact that there are actual laws, which may sometimes be very far from ideal, and sometimes even enjoin actions which would certainly be wrong if they were not enjoined by law. In a situation like this an ideal rule might demand that you conformed to the law, even though the law enjoined an action which would have been wrong had it not been enjoined by law, and which an ideal rule would have prohibited had it not been contrary to the law.

One must distinguish, therefore, between the view that an action is wrong, if it is prohibited by an ideal rule, and the view that an action is wrong if it is the sort of action which, in an ideal society, would not be performed. Obviously, it would not necessarily be wrong to perform an action in *this* society which would be wrong in an ideal society, where circumstances would be very different, but this does not mean that right action does not consist in acting in accordance with an ideal rule. It is the latter view, of course, that I am suggesting, though the two views are very commonly confused.

By suggesting that when we say an action is obligatory we mean that it accords with a set of rules which are to be obeyed and that we often say they are to be obeyed because they would secure society's happiness, I do not mean by 'rules' a set of rules which, like the positive law or like social conventions, needs to be *enforced*. If this were so, then we would have to think that every wrong action carried sanctions, either legal or conventional. All I am suggesting that we are saying when we say that an action is wrong is that it belongs to a class of actions such that we think that ideally they would not be performed. (We may say this because we think their performance substracts from the welfare of society.) We are not saying that the performance of actions of this kind has to be prevented. The only sanctions that such rules carry with them is, what is inevitable, that performance of them incurs moral disapproval from those who accept these rules, and it is not even necessary that this moral disapproval has to be *expressed*.

Just as when we said that certain actions must be done, it turned out that we might be saying this because we thought that they must be done if the happiness of society was to be brought about, and because we thought that the happiness of society *was* to be brought about, so when we say that an action is obligatory if it is enjoined by a rule, we are saying this because it is enjoined by a rule which we think must be observed if the happiness of society is to be brought about, and because we think that the happiness of society *is* to be brought about.

So much, for the time being, for a rough approximation to the meaning of the words 'right' and 'wrong'. This takes us to the question: 'How do we *know* that certain actions are to be done, or that they must be done, or that they are enjoined by a rule which is to observed?'

I think that in many contexts of moral discussion, it is *assumed* that what is being discussed are ways of bringing about the happiness of society, of making life as satisfactory as possible. Hence, when in these contexts we say that something must be done, or is to be done, or is enjoined by a rule which is to be observed, we just assume that we are discussing what is to be done if the happiness of society is to brought about. Hence, given this assumption, our moral problems are settled by showing that the performance of a type of action does or does not lead to the happiness of mankind.

But this assumption, that the happiness of society *is* to be brought about, is itself in need of justification. Fairly obviously, that the happiness of society is to brought about is not analytic; there is no contradiction involved in saying that the misery of society is to be brought about. It does not seem that we can establish by observation and experience that the happiness of society is to be brought about. Nor does it seem at all plausible to suggest that one can intuit that the happiness of society is to be brought about. When someone says that the happiness of society is to be brought about he is, however, not issuing an arbitrary command or imperative, as he would be if he said, '*Bring* the happiness of society about.' When a man says, 'The happiness of society is to be brought about,' he is putting something forward for other people to consider and accept or reject. But strict proof is inappropriate in a case like this. What in fact happens is that a man who says, 'The happiness of society is to be brought about,' is hoping that what he says will commend itself to the people to whom he puts it forward. To say that that the happiness of society is to be brought about commends itself to people is to say that they are in favour of the happiness of society's being brought about. The only reason why they can be in favour of this must be that they want it to be brought about. Since people live in society it is only natural that they should want the happiness of society to be brought about.

However, many rules which are such that they must be observed if the happiness of society is to be brought about will in fact enjoin upon individual people in certain circumstances actions which will *not* bring about *their* happiness, or which will necessitate actions of positive self-sacrifice on their part. How can they then be in favour of such a rule, or how can such a rule's being observed commend itself to them? The answer is that, when they are in favour of such a rule's being observed, and of actions which bring about the happiness of society's being performed, they are considering the matter from an impersonal point of view. That is, they are considering whether they are in favour of such a rule, whether they want such a rule to be adopted, without considering the question of the position they would have in society with regard to the rule, or how they would be personally affected by the adoption of the rule. It is as if they were asked if they would want to live in a society which had such a rule, without being told how they themselves would be situated with respect to the rule. They would know that the rule would bring benefits to many people and enjoin sacrifices upon some people, but they would have to pronounce in favour of or against the rule without knowing whether they would reap the benefits, or have to make the sacrifices, or both. Their position in this respect would be rather like that of the man watching a play, who (logically) cannot be affected by the actions of the characters.

When, of course, they are actually living in a society which operates the rule, they will find it enjoins actions of sacrifice upon them personally sometimes. In such a case, there may be what Kant calls a contradiction in their will. They will remain in favour of the rule when they consider it from the impersonal point of view described above, but naturally they will not want to perform the action which this rule, of which they are in favour from an impersonal point of view, enjoins upon them.

It seems a natural view to take that moral rules have a purpose, the purpose of securing society's welfare, and preventing actions from being done which are detrimental to this welfare. If moral rules have purposes, then it seems that one might very well say that, when one said that some kind of action was not to be done, actions of this kind really were not to be done if the rule that they be not done is a good rule, and that the rule that they be not done *is* a good rule if it serves the purposes which moral rules have, that is, the purpose of subserving society's welfare.

The difficulty with this, however, is that moral rules, as we have seen, are not man-made. Since they are not man-made, they cannot be made for a purpose (because they are not made at all), and so cannot be good rules or bad rules according as to whether they do or do not subserve the purpose for which they are made.

I think this difficulty can be answered in the following way. When you say that some class of actions are not to be done, you are doing two things. You are saying that they are not to be done and, over and above this, *by* saying that they are not to be done, you are doing something to get the practice of not doing them adopted. Whether or not a practice is adopted *is* something which men, collectively if not individually, decide. Hence a rule can be one which is or is not to be obeyed, according as to whether the purpose of adopting it, viz. promoting the welfare of society, is or is not served. The fact that *if* a rule is adopted, its adoption would be beneficial, and so the rule is to be obeyed, is not something men can do something about. Hence, since they adopted the rule for a purpose, we can be right or wrong in saying that these rules are to be adopted, according as to whether the purpose of having them is fulfilled. However, the rule, that rules are to be adopted if the purpose of having them is secured, is not the sort of rule which can be right or wrong according as to whether *its* purpose is secured.

Those rules which are or are not adopted in order to secure

society's welfare, and the rule that rules are to be adopted if they serve society's welfare are, incidentally, rules in different senses of the word 'rule'. The first is a rule in roughly the sense of 'practice'. The second is a rule in roughly the sense of 'principle'; that is, in the sense that what is implied by a true proposition is true is a rule. It is, then, a rule about a rule, or more precisely a *principle* about *practice*.[1]

It is certainly not the case that 'wrong' means 'not to be done' or 'prohibited by a rule' or 'must not be done', where these are hypothetical, and mean 'not to be done, if you want so-and-so' or 'prohibited by a rule which must be observed by those who want so-and-so' or 'must not be done, if you want so-and-so'. But though sometimes, as we have seen, these are *not* hypothetical, and do not have either a stated or an unstated if-clause of the kind 'If you want so-and-so', even when they are categorical, they are not equivalent to 'wrong'. It would be idle to pretend that 'not to be done' or 'must not be done' or 'prohibited by a rule which is to observed' ever give a wholly adequate account of the meaning of the word 'wrong'. Indeed, it would be unlikely that this word has any exact equivalent in the English language, which is fairly economical in that there are seldom two expressions which have exactly the same meaning. This is what gives plausibility to the contention that 'wrongness' is unique and unanalysable. There do in fact seem to be two elements in the meaning of 'wrong' which are left out of the expressions which I have suggested are its rough equivalents.

In the first place, the word 'wrong' has an emotional aura which the expressions 'must be done' and 'are to be done' lack. Though, when someone says that something is wrong, he is not, as we have seen, making a statement about his attitude to the performance of the action, it is possible, from the fact that he uses this word and not some other, to draw inferences about the nature of his attitude to the action he says is wrong. When someone says that something is wrong, he is not only saying that this thing is not to be done, he is expressing a special kind of unfavourable attitude to its being done. He is showing that he would have some tendency to feel guilt if he were to do it himself, and self-approval if, though tempted, he did not do it himself. He is showing that

[1] See John Rawls, 'Two Concepts of Rules', in *The Philosophical Review*, Vol. LXIV, 1955.

he would tend to be antagonistic to anyone who performed the action which was wrong, however this person might be related to himself personally, and that he would, at the least, not feel displeased, and might feel positive satisfaction, if harm resulted to or was inflicted on the person performing the wrong action, not because he dislikes the wrong-doer, or because he has been personally harmed by the wrong done, but because the wrong-doer has done something such that he will feel satisfaction at harm resulting to him in consequence, whoever the wrong-doer is, and however the wrong-doer is related to him personally.

The second feature of our use of the words 'wrong', which is absent from the phrase 'not to be done', is that when we say that something is wrong we tend to regard ourselves as saying this on account of intrinsic features of the action, which make us feel that, the action being the kind of thing it is, we cannot but say that it is not to be done. We say that the actions which we regard as wrong are not to be done on account of the abhorrence the thought of their being done arouses in us, but it never appears to us that it just so happens that the performance of those actions arouses abhorrence in us. It seems to us unthinkable that they should do anything else but arouse this abhorrence in anyone, and it comes as a surprise to us if we discover that there is anyone who does not regard such actions with abhorrence. It is, furthermore, almost as if we thought of the abhorrent nature of the actions we regard as wrong not so much as a dispositional property of the action to arouse feelings of abhorrence in us, but as an intrinsic quality of the action itself, much as (though in fact the redness of a red thing is only its disposition to look red to normal observers) ordinary people tend to think of the redness of a cricket ball as being as much an intrinsic property of it as that it is round. Similarly, the disgustingness of excrement will seem to those who find it disgusting to be an intrinsic quality of the excrement, and it may come as a surprise to these people that there are some animals, and even some humans, who do not find excrement disgusting. An Indian of a high caste will think that there is some intrinsic quality of an untouchable, on account of the possession of which he may not be touched, and will not realize that the only essential difference between an untouchable and any other Indian is the sentiments inspired by him in Indians who are brought up in a certain kind of environment. And the divinity which, it is alleged, doth hedge a king will seem to those who feel this way about kings as much a part of him as the colour of his eyes and the length of his beard.

The difference, then, between 'not to be done', 'must not be done' and 'prohibited by a rule which is to be observed', on the one hand, and 'wrong' on the other, is that the latter includes all the meaning of the former, but that the former has some, but not all, of the meaning of the latter. Someone cannot consistently assert that something is wrong without also asserting that it is not to be done, but he might assert that it is not to be done without wishing to assert that it is wrong. One reason why he is not prepared to assert that it is wrong might be that he feels some dissatisfaction with using expressions like 'Such and such is wrong' as a means of causing people to act in a manner in which he regards as desirable. This may be because he does not have, and knows that the people to whom he is speaking do not have, the feelings of abhorrence which one usually has to the performance of actions which he wishes to say are not to be done. Indeed, if he wishes to say that actions, which are not commonly regarded as wrong are not to be done, because he thinks he can foresee disadvantages from their performance which others cannot, it is unlikely that he or they *will* have feelings of abhorrence towards the performance of these actions, for the simple reason that neither he not they have been brought up to have them. It may be, too, that he thinks that conversation about what is right and wrong engenders more heat than light; that people, in expressing their opinions about what is right and wrong, are guided largely by inculcated prejudices which have no rationale, or the rationale of which they do not see, so that, in discussion about what is right or wrong, there is bound to be no satisfactory procedure for settling the questions which are at issue. Indeed, if what they are looking for is some intrinsic quality of the actions which they regard as being right or wrong – and they may suppose that those actions have such a quality because they project the feelings, which the actions arouse in them, on to the actions themselves – their search is doomed to failure, for there is not, and cannot be, any such intrinsic quality. For some people, indeed, the idea that being wrong is an intrinsic quality of the actions which they regard with abhorrence is so strong that they are in reality attributing this very property to the action which they say is wrong, rather than saying it is wrong on account of believing it to have such a property. When such people assert that an action is wrong, what they say is simply false, for all actions can do is to arouse feelings of abhorrence in the people who contemplate them. The conservatism which manifests itself in the use of the words 'right' and 'wrong' is dangerous, for those actions which have to be done in one situation in order to secure human happiness and even survival are constantly changing, and changing at an accelerating pace. On the other hand, of course, saying that actions are wrong is likely to have a persuasive force which simply saying that they are not to be done lacks.

It is necessary to consider how those various features of the way in which we use the word 'wrong' which have been elicited in previous chapters, apply also to 'not to be done' or 'must not be done', as they must do to the extent that the latter give an adequate account of the meaning of the former.

We can say that we *think* or *believe* that an action is not to be done, and we can say that perhaps we are *mistaken* in thinking that this kind of action is not to be done. It is obvious, I think, that someone saying that certain things are not to be done is saying something incompatible with what someone else is saying who says these things may be done, regardless of who these people are, and to what country, community or social or religious group they belong. And it is also obvious that someone who says a certain kind of action is to be done is saying something incompatible with what he said on some previous occasion when he said that it was not the case that actions of this kind were to be done. Hence some, at least, of the features of moral discourse noted earlier, are adequately accommodated by the view that 'wrong' means 'not to be done'.

Since moral judgments of the kind 'Promises are not to be broken' do not report facts, there is no reason why they should not be *a priori*. If they did report a fact, it is difficult to see how we could know that the fact they reported *was* a fact otherwise than by observation. They are *a priori* in that someone saying that promises are not to be broken is not reporting an extra fact about promising, which he has discovered or inferred, so much as, as we have seen, giving a push in a certain direction. He will have to decide whether such a push be given on the basis of all the facts at his disposal, and this is not a question of discovering more facts.

We established earlier that, though there were some analytic moral judgments, any moral judgment which was to be of any practical use had to be *synthetic*. On the view that 'wrong' means 'not to be done', moral judgments *are* synthetic, because in describing an action, we have not prohibited it, and in saying that something is not to be done, we are doing something rather like, though certainly not quite like, prohibiting it.

The *difference* between saying that something is not to be done and simply prohibiting it is this. Someone prohibiting something is simply making use of his superior power or authority to prohibit it arbitrarily. He may have excellent reasons for making the prohibition, that is, excellent reasons for *saying* some such thing as 'Undergraduates must not smoke during lectures' with the intention of prohibiting smoking during lectures; but this is not the same thing as there *being* reasons for 'Undergaduates must not smoke during lectures'. Only certain specially qualified persons can make prohibitions, whereas anyone at all can say something like 'Promises are not to be broken'. And someone saying 'Undergraduates must not smoke during lectures' after someone in authority has said, in order to prohibit smoking during lectures, 'Undergraduates must not smoke during lectures,' is not himself making a prohibition, but simply making the factual statement that smoking during lectures has been and still is prohibited by someone, whereas someone saying, 'Promises are not to be broken,' is always doing precisely what anyone else is doing who says, 'Promises are not to be broken'.

The *similarity* between saying 'Promises are not to be broken', and prohibiting promises from being broken, is that there is no extra fact about promises, that they are not to be broken, which the judgment 'Promises are not to be broken' reports. When I say 'Promises are not to be broken', I am doing something more like giving a reasonably based directive, which I hope will commend itself, than I am reporting a fact.

This leaves us with the question of what account we are to give of the *necessity* of moral judgments on the view we are considering. To those who say that actions are not to be done because they feel abhorrence at the thought of them, it will tend, as we have seen, to seem necessary that they should feel abhorrence of the actions which are abhorrent to them. But where suggestions about what is or is not to be done are made because they commend themselves to the person putting them forward and because he hopes they will commend themselves to others, the necessity of these proposals is different.

I am inclined to think that the statement that actions of a kind, the performance of which brings about a maximum of advantages over disadvantages, are to be done is of a different logical status from the statements that promises are to be kept, debts paid, and so on. I said that when one said that a rule was to be observed, one said this because that this rule was to be observed commended itself to one, and because one hoped it would commend itself to others. If a rule commends itself, this is quite likely because one supposes that the advantages of having it outweigh its disadvantages. Now though any given rule may commend itself because the advantages of having it outweigh its disadvantages, it is logically impossible for the rule that rules are to be adopted if their advantages outweigh their disadvantages should commend itself because its advantages outweigh its disadvantages. Though rules may be adopted because of their good consequences, the higher-order rule that rules be adopted because of the goodness of their consequences cannot be adopted because of the goodness of its consequences. Or perhaps it would be better to say that the rule that rules be adopted because their advantages outweigh their disadvantages must have advantages, and cannot have disadvantages, and so the question whether it has advantages or disadvantages cannot sensibly be discussed.

We argued earlier that we could say that moral judgments were true or false. For example, we can say, 'It is true that most promises ought to be kept; nevertheless, there are a few which ought to be broken.' It may seem odd that we can say that it is true that something or other is not to be done, if saying that something is not to be done does not report some feature of the thing, which is such that what we say will be true if the action really does have the feature we say it has, but false otherwise. However, we have seen that statements to the effect that actions of a certain kind are not to be done do have a dimension of appraisal which commands, say, or requests lack. They are anchored to reality in a way in which commands cannot be, in that, if we say that some class of actions is not to be done on account of the disadvantages of actions of this class being done, and the doing of these actions does not have the disadvantages we suppose, what we are suggesting as a rule is a bad rule. And one way of reacting to the fact that a suggested rule is a bad rule is to say that it is false that actions of these kinds are not to be done.

We have seen that we can say that we *believe* that something is wrong, and also that we can say that we *know* that something is wrong. On the view we are considering, this means that we can say that we believe that something is not to be done, or that we can say that we know that something is not to be done. What is the difference, on this view, between knowing that something is not to be done and believing that something is not to be done?

Presumably we will say that we know that something is not to be done, as opposed to believing this, if we are quite sure that it is not to be done. We may be quite sure that it is not to be done because the thought of doing it is very abhorrent to us, and because we are quite sure that this action really does have the characteristics on account of which it is abhorrent to us. If we say that an action is not to be done because of its harmful consequences, then we can say we know that it is not to be done if we think we know that it will have the consequences which we consider harmful, and are quite sure that these consequences are harmful.

Where *other people* are concerned, we will say that *they* know that something is not to be done if we ourselves are sure that it is not to be done, and believe that they are sure that it is not to be done. We will be right in thinking that they know these things are not to be done if we are right in thinking that they are not to be done, and if we are right in thinking that they are sure that they are not to be done. Most philosophers think that, for someone properly to be said to know something, it is not sufficient that he should be sure of it and be right in being sure; he must also have arrived at his opinion in the right way. For reasons which would take me far too far from my present topic, I am very doubtful whether this third condition is necessary.

The feature of 'wrong' which we discussed in an earlier chapter, that it was universalizable, in that if any action is wrong, then any other *otherwise* precisely similar action must also be wrong, is preserved by 'not to be done' for the following reason. If we say of any action that it is contrary to a rule which is to be observed, and the rule mentions *kinds* of actions only, then it will follow that any precisely similar action is an action of the same kind, and so follow that it, too, is not to be done. Since it is on account of the features of an action that we say that it is or is not to be done, if we say of one action that it is not to be done, but say of a precisely similar action that it is to be done, or that it is not the case that it is not to be done, then we are behaving in an inconsistent way. It is as if we had put a tick beside one sum, and then put a cross beside another precisely similar sum, or as if, following the directions to put eggs of different sizes in different boxes, we had put one egg in one box and then put a precisely similar egg in a different box.

I said in the chapter on Ideal Observer theories, that a set of moral rules had to be complete, universal and precise. On the view that 'wrong' means 'not to be done', the universality of moral judgments presents no problem. It would be odd indeed if anyone thought that one action was to be done, but another precisely similar action was not to be done. Since anyone who thinks something is not to be done must have reasons for thinking this, the reasons he has for thinking one action is not to be done must also be reasons for thinking a precisely similar action is also not to be done. Since he always says that an action is to be done or not to be done on account of its features, there must always be universal rules capable of being elicited even from his statements that particular individual actions are to be done or not to be done; to be consistent, he must say that any of the actions which have the features on account of which he says this action is not to be done are all not to be done. Of course, he may not always be able to say explicitly what it is about an action which makes him say that it is not to be done, and so he will not necessarily be able to produce some rule, which will satisfy him, to the effect that all actions of a certain kind are not to be done. But he may try, by a sort of experiment in imagination, to find out what these features are, by asking himself such questions as: Would I say of another action, which had all the features which this action has except, say, that the man who did it had been very badly wronged by the man upon whom he inflicted an injury, that it too was not to be done? By this process, he can discover which of the features of an action are the ones on account of which he says it is not to be done, and, when he has elicited these, he is in a position to say that all actions having these features are not to be done.

The view that 'wrong' means 'not to be done' accounts for the need for completeness and precision in the following way. It is not that there is some set of independently existing moral facts, of which a complete and precise account must be given. In saying that certain kinds of things are to be done, and others are not to be done, we are trying to put forward and get adopted a set of rules, which we think will be good rules. One feature of good rules is that they should be complete, in that they never leave it an unsettled question whether any given action is to be done, not to be done, or whether it is not the case that it is not to be done, (i.e. whether it is permissible). Another feature of good rules is that they should be precise, in that they should never leave it unclear whether any given action falls under the rule and is not to be done, or does not fall under the rule, and so is not to be done.

We saw earlier that moral rules were not man-made. This means that, unlike man-made rules, they cannot be promulgated, though I sometimes speak as if saying that something is not to be done is rather like promulgating a rule. This is because when one says that something is not to be done, one is doing something which one hopes will be a move in the direction of getting it to become a general practice that this thing is not done. The logical fact which reflects the truth that moral laws are not man-made, and that moral rules cannot be promulgated, is the fact that there is nothing analogous, in the language of 'not to be done', to the difference between saying that something is not to be done before and after this has been said by some accredited or authoritative person. If I, who am not an authoritative person, say 'No girl may walk in the Arboretum after dark' *before* the headmistress, who is an authoritative person, has said 'No girl may walk in the Arboretum after dark', I am making a false statement. If, on the other hand, I say this *after* the headmistress has said the same thing, I am making a true statement. Even in the case where the makers of a certain medicine write, 'Not to be taken internally,' someone else saying that this medicine is not to be taken internally is not simply reporting some fact which has been brought into being by the makers saying this, as someone saying 'The bowler must not throw' is reporting a fact which has been brought into being by the M.C.C. having pronounced, after following the proper procedures, some such words as 'The bowler must not throw'. To report this fact, he would say something like, 'It *says on the bottle that* this medicine is not to be taken internally.' If he says 'This medicine is not to be taken internally' he is in fact committing himself, showing that he himself is against this medicine's being taken internally, and doing just what the makers themselves are doing when they write these words on the bottle, though I and the headmistress are doing different things when we each say 'No girl may walk in the Arboretum'. Hence there is no body of people whose having said the words, 'Such-and-such is not to be done,' with due procedure subsequently makes it true for anyone else to say these words; hence moral rules cannot be promulgated, and so cannot be man-made.

It might be argued in reply that the phrase 'not to be done' is ambiguous, and that it can mean three different things. Sometimes, when we say that something is not to be done, we are simply commanding our hearers not to do it, as when I write, 'Not to be opened until Christmas day,' on a parcel. Sometimes I am simply reporting the fact that an action is contrary to a rule, as when I say that in chess the King is not to be moved more than one square at a time. And sometimes I am in fact doing what I have given the impression we are always doing when we use these words, that is, making an utterance which is like a command in that it gives a push in a given direction, but not quite like a command, in that reasons can be given why something is not to be done, whereas reasons cannot be given for what is expressed by an utterance like 'Shut the door'.

I doubt, however, whether the phrase 'not to be done' really does have these three different uses. When we write on a parcel, 'Not to be opened until Christmas day,' we are not simply saying, 'Do not open until Christmas day.' It can be that a parcel is not to be opened until Christmas day because it is a Christmas present, and hence there is a reason for what is written on it – as distinct from a reason for *writing* what is written on it – whereas if what is written on the parcel is the command 'Do not open until Christmas day', there cannot be a reason for what is written on it though there can be a reason for writing what is written on it. And I doubt whether 'The King is not to be moved more than one square at a time' does simply report the fact that moving the King more than one square at a time is prohibited by a rule of chess. A person saying this is not simply saying that this is prohibited by a rule; he is himself putting pressure on someone not to move the King more than one square, and his *reason* for thinking that the King is not to be moved more than one square is that this is prohibited by a rule of chess.

If we did sometimes use the expression 'not to be done' to report the fact that an action conflicted with a rule, and at other times to issue something like a command or recommendation, this would accord with one feature that the word 'wrong' is alleged to possess. Sometimes, it is held the word 'wrong' simply reports that an action is contrary to a rule accepted in my society; at other times, it is said, it is used in a more properly moral way to prohibit an action on account of my own personal attitude to it. I am not sure that this is true, but, if it is true, it is another reason for thinking that the phrase 'not to be done' gives a not wholly unsatisfactory account of the meaning of the word 'wrong'.

What account of the nature of moral *concepts* are we to give, if the view that 'wrong' means 'not to be done' is correct? If this view *is* correct, there will be no such things. Our having a concept consists in our being able to abstract some feature of a thing or action which feature it shares or may share with other things. It may partly manifest itself in our applying some word correctly to the things which have this feature. But there is no feature of the actions which we say are not to be done, over and above the ordinary 'factual features' of these actions. When we say that actions of a certain kind are not to be done, it is not because we have detected some feature of these actions, which we might otherwise have overlooked. It is because we have decided that, in view of the features which they do have, they are not to be done, and, in saying this, we are not so much reporting that they have another feature, as attempting to prevent these things from being done. Hence, though the words 'not to be done' have a use, which I have attempted to elucidate, and though the statements made by means of sentences containing these words stand in certain logical or quasi-logical connections to other statements, which relations I have tried to describe, their use, and the fact that they have a meaning, is not constituted by their being a 'name' for a feature which a number of particular things or actions may have in common.

How does the theory that 'wrong' means 'not to be done' stand in relation to Naturalism? In the chapter in which I discussed Naturalism, I argued both that there was no reason why ethical concepts should not be defined in terms of non-ethical concepts, and also that there was no reason why ethical concepts should not be held to be ordinary natural concepts. However, if 'wrong' means 'not to be done', it will neither be possible to hold that wrong can be defined in terms of non-ethical concepts nor possible to hold that they are ordinary natural concepts, or that they can be defined in terms of these. This is for the simple reason that, as we have seen, there is no *concept* of wrongness, and so the question of whether wrong is a concept which can be defined in terms of non-ethical concepts or is a natural concept cannot arise. Hence, in the usual sense of 'naturalistic' our theory will not be naturalistic.

However, in a wider sense of 'naturalistic', the theory of the meaning of 'wrong' which I am putting forward is naturalistic, as it implies that wrongness is *not* a non-natural concept. This follows from the fact that 'wrongness' is not a concept at all, for, if it is not a concept, it cannot be a non-natural concept. Hence this theory is an economical one, in that it does not need to postulate any non-natural concepts over and above those natural concepts we acquire by observation and experience of the natural world.

A question sometimes discussed is the question whether a being with reason, but no feelings, would be able to tell the difference between right and wrong.[1] What answer to this question is given by the theory which I have put forward? Obviously, a being with no feelings would never say that actions are not to be done simply because the thought of them aroused in him *feelings* of *abhorrence*. In this respect, if I am right, he would be positively better off than we ourselves, for this tendency in mankind to say that certain things are not to be done for this reason, without considering the disadvantages of doing them, is a positive handicap in trying to find rules which make possible a satisfactory way of life. It would also follow that such a being would have no incentive to say that certain kinds of things were not to be done because, if he had no feelings, he would simply not care whether these things were done or not, regardless of how much misery doing them caused.

On the other hand, such a being would be able to observe that a community had certain rules, and that these rules subserved the interests of this community to some extent, but that these interests

[1] See H. H. Price, *Belief* (Allen & Unwin, 1969), pp. 420 f.

might be better served by different rules. Hence he would be able
to say that some of its rules were good rules, others bad, and that
some rules which it did not have might be better than the ones it
actually had. Hence such a being would be able to see that, if any
member of this community were to enjoin a class of actions the
performance of which would be of advantage to it, he would be
making a sensible recommendation. He could not himself correctly use the phrases 'to be done' and 'not to be done', for
he would have no incentive to use them, and he would lack the
feelings which these phrases commonly imply, but he would be
able to see that the people who said of these things that they were
to be done were pushing people in what is the right direction for
them to go if their community's needs are to be met and their
wants satisfied.

At this point I should like to say a few words about the derivation of moral judgments from factual judgments, or, more specifically, about the derivation of the judgment that some kind of
action or other is not to be done from a set of factual judgments
which describe what sort of action it is. The factual judgments
will not entail the statement that this kind of action is not to be
done, and there will be no contradiction involved in accepting the
factual description of the action, and at the same time asserting
that it is to be done, or that it is not the case that it is not to be
done. Hence, on this view, a 'logical gap' between factual judgments and moral judgments is preserved. On the other hand, there
will be a rationale behind saying that the actions to which a given
set of factual descriptions applies are not to be done, rather than to
be done, for one is, in saying that certain actions are not to be
done, engaged in something rather like legislation. Though one
is not, because one has not the power or the authority, making
laws which other people have to obey whatever they may think of
them, one is putting forward what might loosely be described as
proposals about what is or is not to be done, which proposals have
to commend themselves to people, and can only sensibly commend
themselves because of the advantages or disadvantages of their
adoption. Hence if it is a good thing, or a good idea, that certain
things be not done because the disadvantages of doing them are
great and the advantages small, the proposal is a rational one.
Otherwise it is not.

What, then, is the answer which this theory offers to the moral sceptic of our second chapter, who wanted some proof that some things were right and others wrong? Assuming, what seems obvious, that there really are advantages in certain kinds of thing being done, and certain other kinds of thing not being done, the question arises: 'How can it be shown that the things, the doing of which have advantages, are to be done, and the things which would have disadvantages if they were done are not to be done?'

To ask for a *proof* of this, however, is misconceived, for, though you might prove that something or other had or lacked some property, *to be done* does not consist in having a property, and *not to be done* does not consist in lacking a property. To the extent that, in saying a certain action is to be done we are engaged in the quasi-legislative process described above, that is, the process of trying, by what we say, to get a practice adopted, then we justify the view that certain actions are to be done by showing that doing them has advantages, and consequently that the rules put forward are good rules. Since we say that certain things are to be done, hoping that that they are to be done will commend itself to rational people, we are justified in what we say if the idea of doing these things does commend itself to rational people, or would commend itself to people if they were rational. And rational people just are those people who among other things adopt rules on account of the advantages of having them, who think that things are to be done if doing them has advantages, and think that things are not to be done if doing them has disadvantages.

In the foregoing pages I have sometimes spoken as if someone saying that actions of a certain sort are to be done is making a statement. At other times I have spoken as if he is doing something much more like issuing a command or recommending a practice or attempting to make something become a practice. The truth is that saying 'Promises are to be kept' is in some ways like making a statement; in other ways it is more like commanding or rule-promulgating. It is like a statement in that we can say we think, believe, do not believe, know, wonder whether, do not know whether, may be mistaken in thinking, or that it is true that promises ought to be kept. Saying that promises are to be kept is more like issuing a command or promulgating a rule in that there is no fact about promises, that they are to be kept, which is there to be observed or discovered. There is just a class of actions, the performance of which one has to decide whether to be for or against or indifferent to. The reason why we can say that we think, or might be *mistaken* in thinking, or that it is *true* that promises are to be kept is that when we say this we are not just making an arbitrary command. We are making a proposal, about what is or is not to be done, which we think is sensible and advantageous, and which we think will commend itself to rational people, and so we will withdraw it as being wrong it it turns out not to be sensible or advantageous or one which will commend itself to rational people.

One interesting feature of the actions which we say are to be done or not to be done on account of their being advantageous or the reverse is that very often the consequences of the performance of any one action of that kind will depend upon whether or not other actions of the same kind are also performed. Just as, if one man stays off work in a factory, no harm may be done, but if all the men employed on a similar task stay off work, the organization of the factory will break down, so one promise may be broken with more good than harm resulting, but if all similar promises are broken the loss of that confidence, which is necessary for the successful functioning of society, may be completely destroyed. Hence, where cases like these are concerned, in saying that classes of actions are to be done or not to be done, we must consider not the advantageousness or otherwise of their being done singly, but the advantageousness or otherwise of all of them being done.[1]

The view that 'wrong' means 'not to be done' enables us to explain the fact, which earlier we found puzzling, that it is odd to speak of *remembering* that some class of actions are wrong. Of course, one might perfectly well remember, or forget, that members of a certain class of action were or had been prohibited. That they have been, or are, prohibited, is just an ordinary matter of fact about them, which can be remembered, or forgotten, just like any other matter of fact. But, as we have seen, saying that actions of a certain kind are not to be done is doing something more like, though not quite like, prohibiting them, and, of course, one cannot remember or forget something like 'Let no man kill'. In other words, sentences like 'I remembered (or forgot)

[1] See Michael D. Bayles, *Contemporary Utilitarianism* (Anchor Books, 1968); M. G. Singer *Gerneralisation in Ethics* (Eyre and Spottiswoode, 1963); and David Lyons, *Forms and Limits of Utilitarianism* (O.U.P., 1965).

336 OUR KNOWLEDGE OF RIGHT AND WRONG

"Let no man kill" ' do not make sense. Nor, of course, do sentences like 'I remembered (or forgot) "Keep your promises" ' make sense. Hence, to the extent that saying something is not to be done consists in giving a push in a certain direction, that something is not to be done cannot be remembered or forgotten.

However, though 'I remember "Let no man steal" ' does not make sense, 'I remember that that is not to be done' seems to make perfectly good sense. Perhaps one can remember that something is not to be done, while one cannot remember that something is wrong, because to say that something is wrong is not simply to say that it is not to be done, but to say it, so to speak, in the appropriate tone of voice and expressing sentiments of the appropriate kind. And even if one could remember that something is not to be done, feeling the sentiments which one must feel if one is to say that something is wrong is not something that can be remembered or forgotten. Alternatively, perhaps, the suggestion made earlier, that sometimes 'That is not to be done' simply reports the fact that it has been classified as something not to be done and at other times enjoins that that be not done, is correct, in which case it would be possible for one to remember what is not to be done in the first sense, but not in the second.

Similarly, one cannot believe a command on the authority of others, because a command is not the sort of thing which can be believed, or disbelieved, for that matter. Can one accept on the authority of some other person or some ecclesiastical institution that something is wrong? If I am right in suggesting that one cannot use the word 'wrong' properly of anything without feeling hostile sentiments towards its performance, then one cannot accept this on authority, for one cannot feel sentiments on the authority of others. Perhaps, however, one may have such respect for the person or persons whose authority one is accepting that one does feel sentiments of disapproval or abhorrence towards actions which he or they say are wrong. Again, *if* one can accept that something is not to be attempted on the authority of someone else, this is perhaps only if there is a sense of 'This is not to be done' in which it means 'This is classified as not to be done'.

If we say that actions are not to be done on account of the feelings of abhorrence which they arouse in us, there will never be any way of settling any moral dispute. The same kind of actions just do arouse feelings of abhorrence in some people, but not in others, and if neither party to the dispute is ignorant of or mistaken concerning any matter of fact about the action, then the only way of producing agreement will be by one of the disputants altering the feelings of the other by means of various rhetorical devices, or by subjecting him to an environment where it is normal to have the feelings of abhorrence which he lacks. Though such procedures may be successful or unsuccessful in securing the desired change, and may alter a person's feelings for good or for ill (for good if someone comes to feel abhorrence of actions the performance of which are disadvantageous, for ill if he comes to feel abhorrence of the performance of actions which are advantageous), there is no way in which, simply by considering how we feel, we can settle any moral issue, or arrive by any sensible procedure at any rule about what is not to be done.

It is an extremely fortunate fact, however, that there are excellent evolutionary reasons why the actions of which we feel abhorrence should by and large be those which are disadvantageous to our community. Otherwise our community would not be able to survive, and compete successfully with other communities for a limited means of subsistence. Nevertheless, in so far as we say that those actions are not to be done because we feel abhorrence of them, our adoption of advantageous rules is blind. We are in favour of useful rules and against harmful ones not because we foresee their usefulness or harmfulness, but because feeling abhorrence of advantageous actions and *vice versa* has been weeded out in the struggle for survival. It is something produced by nature, not by design.

To the extent that one reason, though not the only reason, why men feel abhorrence towards some actions is that they inflict injury upon those with whom they sympathize, there is a further reason why they should tend to feel abhorrence of those actions which are disadvantageous to their community, for actions which inflict injury upon other members of a community usually are disadvantageous to that community.

If we persist in saying that actions are wrong, instead of saying that they are not to be performed, when we think that the actions which are not to be performed are those from which ill to society results, our using the word 'wrong' has a positive disadvantage in that it suggests that we think that questions of right and wrong can be settled by our deciding that actions are wrong, if it so happens that the thought of their being performed arouses abhorrence in us. However, since there is no motive for the performance of those actions, which we think are to be performed, over and above the desire to procure advantages for, and to avoid disadvantages to, the society in which we live, and this is not the strongest of all the impulses which move creatures as frail as we, we might well regard it as politic to say that actions which are inconducive to the welfare of society are *wrong*. This is because, in saying this, we are doing something, though perhaps not much, to cause our hearers to take up, to these actions, the same sort of attitude which they now have to those actions which they regard as wrong. To the extent that we succeed in doing this, we will have produced or redirected some motive for omitting these actions, over and above that of desire for the welfare of society, namely, a desire to avoid doing those things which are morally abhorrent to us.

But given that it can be shown that doing something has certain *consequences*, how can it be shown that its having these consequences is an *advantage* or a *disadvantage*? Given that we know what are the *results* of its being the rule that a certain kind of action be performed, how do we decide that this is a *good* rule?

I think that a rule is a good rule in the sense in which a car is a good car; the car or the rule is good if it serves the purposes to satisfy which the car was made or the rule adopted. Since *moral* rules are not adopted, however, they cannot be good in this sense; but it can be the case that an action is not to be done if it is a member of a class of actions such that, if it is a rule that they are not performed, in the sense that their performance is generally disapproved of, this rule that they are not performed is a good rule.

A good rule will be a rule whose advantages outweighs its disadvantages. One can consider the advantages or disadvantages of a rule from a personal point of view, i.e. consider the advantages or disadvantages of the rule to oneself. Alternatively, one can consider the advantages and disadvantages of the rule from an impersonal point of view, i.e. examine its advantages or disadvantages to society, without raising the question of how one oneself would be situated with respect to the rule, or the actual place in society which one would have. Only if one approves or disapproves of the rule from this impersonal point of view is one's attitude to the rule a moral one.

This, however, still does not tell us what an advantage or a disadvantage is. I am inclined to think that something is an advantage or a disadvantage to oneself if it secures the ends which one in fact has, and an advantage or a disadvantage to society if it secures the ends which society in fact has. Hence an advantage is what helps to satisfy man's wants and needs, and a disadvantage is what frustrates these. Obviously, rule-abidingness, in the sense of a disposition to obey those rules which it is advantageous for society to adopt, is an advantageous character-trait – advantageous, that is, to society, even if it is not always advantageous to the individual, who may sometimes have to obey the rules at great personal cost to himself.

The results of having a rule are *good* results if they are things people want or need. Hence what is good or bad in this sense is dictated by the nature of man; if he wanted or needed completely different things, different things would be good or bad.[1] It is possible to want things which are bad only in that one want may prevent the satisfaction of others, or in that one person's want may prevent the satisfaction of other persons' wants. Since we are bound to have a favourable attitude to what satisfies our wants, when we say that something is good, because it is determined by our natures to be one of our ends, we are bound to have a favourable attitude towards this thing, which attitude we express when we use the word 'good'.

In some moods I am tempted to suggest that we even abandon using the words 'right' and 'wrong', and simply say that things are or are not to be done instead – though I am sufficiently realistic to know that this recommendation would stand no chance of being accepted. The reason for my making this suggestion will already be apparent: the language of 'right' and 'wrong' is so rooted in the myth of false objectivity, that being wrong is some intrinsic character of actions, and there to be discovered, that we simply find it in actions which we have been accustomed from childhood to regard as wrong. Hence its use makes moral disputes impossible to settle. If, instead, we talk about what is or is not to be done, in contexts where it is clear that we are talking about what is or is not to be done in order that mankind may lead the most satisfying kind of life, moral disputes would be much easier, though still not easy, to resolve.

[1] See Ralph Barton Perry, *General Theory of Value* (Harvard University Press, 1967).

I should like to make one final observation, or raise one final problem, before closing this chapter. The ethical (as opposed to meta-ethical) theory to which I have committed myself in the preceding pages is broadly utilitarian. However, when I consider what I really think, I seriously doubt whether I am as much in favour of Utilitarianism as I have given the impression of being. This is not for the usual reason, namely, that promises ought to be kept, debts paid and justice done, even when the consequences of this are harmful rather than beneficial. It is because I very much doubt whether I really *would* want to live in a world in which everybody was guided by rules dedicated to the good of society. I cannot help but feel that such a world might be very dull, and that a community of people who were guided solely by utilitarian principles would contain nothing but men with the combined mentality of social workers and higher civil servants. This, however, is not a difficulty I feel with Utilitarianism only. I doubt whether I even want to live in a world where everyone was good all the time on any theory about what the good man ought to do.

There are ways in which this difficulty with Utilitarianism might be overcome. One might put forward a relaxed version of utilitarianism, in which one said not that actions were to be done if they were of a kind which is beneficial, but said that actions must not be done if they were harmful *beyond a certain point*. Oddly enough, one might recommend this kind of Utilitarianism by pointing out the *advantage* of people not always being guided by the advantages and disadvantages accruing to society from what they did.

Another way of dealing with the problem would be to say that though actions which are inconducive to human happiness were not to be done, it is a very good thing that people do not do what is to be done all the time. There are virtues other than what might be called moral law-abidingness, and it is inevitable that these virtues should sometimes prompt men to disobey the moral law. And even a man who had no vices, and a world which contained no men who were vicious, might have drawbacks. A play with all heroes and no villains would be very tedious.

CHAPTER XV

SOME OTHER MORAL JUDGMENTS

Having explained the meaning of 'wrong' little need be said about the meaning of the word 'right', since very often 'right' simply means 'not wrong', and a definition of the former carries a definition of the latter along with it. Sometimes, however, as has already been pointed out, 'right' has a stonger sense than this, and means 'that which it would be wrong to omit'. Even so, however, 'right' is still defined in terms of 'wrong', and nothing more need be said about it. So far as right and wrong go, actions may be divided into three classes, actions which are wrong, actions which it is not wrong to do, but which would also be not wrong to omit, and actions which it would be wrong to omit. To put the same thing in another way, all actions are either wrong or right, in the sense of the latter word which means simply 'not wrong', but the class of actions which are right in this sense may be subdivided into those actions which it would be right to do, but which it would be also right to omit, and those actions which it would be right to do, but which it would *not* be right to omit.

There are, however, many moral judgments which can be expressed without using the words 'right' and 'wrong', though I think myself that the judgments expressed by the words 'right' and 'wrong' are by far the most difficult to give a satisfactory account of. To these other moral judgments we must now turn, though the treatment they are given must inevitably be cursory.

DUTY

It is often said that to say that some action is some person's *duty* is to say that he would be acting wrongly if he failed to perform that action. This is not so. For one thing, it is a perfectly good answer to the question 'Why would it be wrong for me not to do that?' to say, 'Because it is your duty to *do* it.' Hence to say that something is someone's duty cannot just be to say that it would be wrong for him not to do it. And there are many actions which, though wrong, cannot without absurdity be described as neglect of duty. For example, the attempt by the German government before and during the second world war to exterminate the Jews, atrocious though it was, could hardly be described as neglect of duty – those responsible for it could, with some plausibility, even claim to be doing their duty – and it is much worse than most cases of neglect of duty are.

To say that something is someone's duty is to say that it is a task which is his, and which arises from his station in life.[1] Hence a father has a duty to care for his children, a policeman to apprehend criminals, a judge to sum up impartially, a dustman to empty refuse, and so on. In this sense, not only are not all wrong acts cases of neglect of duty, it is not necessarily the case that it is wrong not to do one's duty. It was the sentry's *duty* to stay at his post, but, in these exceptional circumstances, he acted quite rightly in leaving it to rescue a baby from the path of an on-coming tank.

In this sense of 'duty', it is relatively easy to find out what one's duty is; one simply finds out what functions arise from one's station in life, and the question whether something is one's duty or not is simply a question of fact. But moral philosophers, and ordinary people to a lesser extent, have used the conception of a moral duty as equivalent to any action the omission of which they would wish to describe as wrong. I suppose that it is useful to do this, in that 'duty', used in this way, is free from the ambiguity of the word 'right'. Though 'right' in one sense means that which it is not wrong to do, in another sense it means that which it would be wrong to omit. Duty, on the other hand, always means that which it would be wrong to omit. Hence what has already been said about 'wrong' applies automatically to 'duty' when it is being used in this sense, though it is possible that saying an action is one's duty makes it seem more urgent that one perform the action in question than simply saying that it would be wrong to omit it. For this reason, 'duty' is not wholly suitable as a word for any action which it would be wrong to omit, for sometimes, when one does a wrong action, what one does is not *very* wrong.

Not only do we say that someone has a duty to *do* something, we also speak of having a duty *to* some person or institution, for example, to God, to one's country, or to one's father. To say that one has a duty to some person or institution can mean one of three things. One can be doing one's duty to someone if one

[1] See F. H. Bradley, *Ethical Studies* (O.U.P., second edition, 1927), Essay V, 'My Station and Its Duties'.

is doing something which is one's duty, and if this is a task which this person has allocated to one. One can have a duty *to* some person or institution, because one is under an obligation to him or it. (Often these two will go together, as when one is under an obligation to the person who allocates one's tasks.) Finally, one can have a duty to someone if it is one's duty, in the sense of one's allocated task, to care for the welfare of that person. This is the sense in which a father can have a duty to his children, though he is not under an obligation to them, and though they have allocated to him no tasks. It is possible that this sense of 'duty to' may overlap with the other two – although it does not in the example just given – for one of the tasks one has, which are allocated to one by some person or institution, to which one is under an obligation, precisely may be to care for the welfare of that person or institution. Hence one's country, to which one is often conceived of as being under an obligation, may have allocated to every citizen the task of caring for his country.

To the extent that the notion of duty involves anything over and above the factual one of the allocation of tasks, which notion presents no problems which are peculiar to moral epistemology, 'duty' can be defined in terms of 'morally wrong' – e.g. as a task which it would be morally wrong to omit – and hence it has by implication already been dealt with.

OBLIGATION

To say that one is *obliged* to perform an action, and to say that that action is *obligatory*, are usually held to be equivalent to one another, and both are also usually held to be equivalent to saying that an action is one which it would be wrong to omit. It is interesting, however, that, though both the sentences 'That action is obligatory' and 'I was obliged to do that' are ambiguous, they are ambiguous in very different ways. That is to say, the statement which could be alternatively expressed in the same words as the first statement is a quite different statement from the one which could alternatively be expressed in the same words as the second statement. Though 'I was obliged to shoot him' can mean that shooting him was obligatory – or, more accurately, that I shot him because shooting him was obligatory – it may mean that I had to shoot him as a necessary means to some desired end, say, his not foiling my attempt at bank robbery. Though I can say something is obligatory, without implying that it is morally obligatory – for to say that a white tie is obligatory with tails is not to say that it is morally obligatory with tails, but that it is demanded by a rule of etiquette – I never say that something is obligatory if I simply think that it is a necessary means to some desired end.

Common to all these senses of 'obligatory' and 'obliged' is the idea of necessity or coercion, i.e. there was no alternative to shooting him, if my attempted bank raid was to be successful; there was no alternative to shooting him, if I was to act rightly; there was no alternative, if etiquette was to be observed, but to wear tails.

It is also possible to say that we are under an obligation to *do* something, such as pay Jones five pounds, or to say that we are under an obligation *to* Smith. I think the latter notion, that of having an obligation *to* someone, can be defined in terms of the former, that of having an obligation to *do* something. One has an obligation *to* Smith if there is some tendency for one to be under an obligation to do something for Smith, because of some past action of Smith's, such as his having been very kind to one. Being under an obligation to do something is rather narrower in its range than the notions of being obligatory and being obliged. We tend to restrict being under an obligation to do something to those cases where the obligation arises from a contract or agreement or promise, or where it arises from past favours received. Hence we can speak of putting ourselves under an obligation, when we voluntarily enter into such a contract or accept such a favour, or putting someone else under an obligation when we give favours to him.

The essential notion in the various senses of 'obligation', 'obligatory', etc., which we have just discussed is the notion of an action to which there is no permissible alternative, the notion of a favour or a debt which one has no acceptable alternative but to return or pay, just as the essential notion of duty, in one sense, was that of an allocated task which one had no permissible alternative but to perform. Hence they can be defined in terms of 'wrong', and have, by implication, also already been dealt with.

'WICKED' AND 'IMMORAL'

A wicked action is the same as a wrong action, only worse.

An immoral action is often the same as a wrong action. Sometimes, however, the word 'immoral' is used solely for wrong acts where the misconduct, supposed or otherwise, is sexual, e.g. for adultery. Sometimes 'immorality' is used as a factual description, without or almost without any implication of moral condemnation, for departure from the generally accepted, or supposedly generally accepted, rules governing sexual practice.

A wicked man is the same as a bad man, only worse.

An immoral man is the same as a bad man, except that, again, it is sometimes being suggested that his badness consists solely in acting wrongly where sexual matters are concerned, and occasionally the word 'immoral' is used simply as a description of a man who does not adhere to the commonly accepted sexual rules, without or almost without any suggestion that he is necessarily bad.

'GOOD'

All the theories about the meanings of the words 'right' and 'wrong' reviewed in the first part of this book could be also held about the meaning of the word 'good'. It is obvious on a little reflection that they are no more plausible about 'good' than they are when they are held about 'right' and 'wrong', and the same objections which dispose of them when they are held about 'right' and 'wrong', also dispose of them when they are held about 'good'.

To say that something or other is good is generally to say that it is better in some way than most things of a certain kind, just as to say that something is a large mouse is to say that it is larger than most mice – though it may, of course, be smaller than most *rodents* or smaller than most *animals*.

To say that a man is a good man is to say that he is better than most men, and to say that he is better than most men is to say that he acts rightly a higher proportion of the time, and when subject to greater temptations and under more difficult circumstances, than most men do. Hence 'good', in this sense, can be defined in terms of 'right', and so in terms of 'wrong'. The question arises, however, whether we say that a man is a good man if he does what the person so describing him thinks is right, or if he does what he himself thinks is right. There is no hard and fast answer to this question. We do not refuse to say a man is good because the things he thinks are right differ somewhat from the things we think are right; on the other hand, if the divergence is very great, so that the things he thinks are right, or obligatory, are things which outrage us greatly, we do refuse to say that he is a good man. Whether we say that a man is good because he does the things he thinks are right, or because he does the things we think are right, 'good' can in either event be defined in terms of right.

Of course, goodness in this sense is not the only desirable attribute in a man. Strength, intelligence, tact, etc., are also desirable attributes. We do not, however, allow these to count towards whether the man who possesses them is a good man. We do, however, have the expression 'a fine man' for a man who possesses attributes such as these. It is possible to be a good man, without being a fine man, and to be a fine man, without being a good man. Goodness is not so important that it can never be better to be less good, but to have more of those attributes the possession of which makes us say a man is a fine man.

An alternative account of the meaning of 'good' would be this. A man is a good man if he possesses a certain number of characteristics from a list of characteristics, for example, being kind, honest, generous, courageous, reliable, sympathetic, industrious, imaginative, and so on. It is unnecessary for him to possess all these characteristics to be a good man, yet there is a certain minimum number of them which he must have. The word 'good', on this account of its meaning, is vague in three respects. It is vague, first of all, because there is no definitive number of these characteristics, which a man must have in order to be good. Some numbers of them can definitely be said to be enough, and other numbers of them can definitely be said to be too few, but, in between, there will be yet other numbers of them where it is not clearly laid down whether they are enough or too few. In the second respect, goodness is vague because the possession of each of these characteristics admits of degrees; one can be more or less kind, more or less honest, more or less courageous, and so on. Thirdly, goodness is vague because some of these characteristics are more important than others. A man may 'score more points' towards being good, so to speak, if he is more than average honest than if he more than average generous.

The whole question is made still more complicated by the fact that one must weigh the possession of a small number of important characteristics against a large number of unimportant characteristics, or the possession of a small number of characteristics in a high degree against the possession of a large number of these characteristics in a low degree, or the possession of important characteristics in a low degree against unimportant characteristics in a high degree.

It would be possible, if one were sufficiently myopic, to argue from what has just been said to the conclusion that good men need have nothing in common.[1] Let us suppose, for the sake of argument, that there are just three characteristics the possession of which counts towards a man's being good: characteristic A, charactereristic B, and characteristic C. Smith may be good because he is A and B, though not C. Jones may be good because he possesses A and C, though not B. Robinson may be good because he possesses B and C, though does not possess A. Hence, neither A nor B nor C will be possessed by Jones, Smith and Robinson. Jones, Smith and Robinson, however, do have something in common, which is that they each possess two from the list of the three characteristics, A, B and C.

Over and above this it is usual for a man who describes something as good to have a favourable attitude to that thing, though he is not, when he says that it is good, *asserting* that he has this attitude. If a man says something is good when he does not look favourably upon it, he will be misleading his hearers, so that they make mistaken inferences about the nature of his attitudes to the thing he describes as good, but he will not be saying what is false.

Suppose X has a favourable attitude to things which possess characteristics A, B and C, and an unfavourable attitude to things which lack these characteristics, and Y has a favourable attitude to things which possess the characteristics, P, Q and R, and an unfavourable attitude to things which lack these characteristics. In such a case X will describe aomething which is A, B and C, but not P, Q and R as being good, but Y will say that this thing is not good. In one way they will not be contradicting one another, because it is both true that it *is* A, B and C, and also true that it is *not* P, Q and R. However, there will be a conflict of attitude between X and Y, because X will look in a favourable light upon this thing, and regard it as something to be imitated or sought after, whereas Y will not. Hence, if X persuades Y to regard this thing as good, he will not have altered Y's opinions about it, which were

---

[1] See L. Wittgenstein, *Philosophical Investigations* (Blackwell, 1953), pp. 31 f.

not mistaken, but he will have succeeded in altering Y's attitude to it.[1]

The difference between the first account of the meaning of 'good' and the second is not as great as might be supposed, since we normally think that it is wrong not to be honest, wrong not to be generous, wrong not to be kind, and so on.

When we say of a tool, machine or instrument that it is good, we say so because it performs its function well, or better than most instruments, tools or machines of that kind. Men and women cannot be good in this sense, for, *qua* men, they are neither tools, intruments nor machines; we can however speak of good postmen, mechanics or footballers in this sense, because postmen, mechanics and footballers do have functions. To say that a machine or a mechanic is a good machine or a good mechanic if it or he performs its function well does not, *pace* Aristotle, help very much, however, for it leaves unanswered the question 'What do we mean by "well"?'

We say that a machine or a postman performs its or his function well because it accomplishes the end for which we make or buy machines or employ postmen, and brings about this end more quickly, reliably, efficiently and with fewer attendant disadvantages than most machines or postmen. Since someone who makes or builds machines or employs postmen will be making or building these machines or employing these postmen in order to secure the ends for which the machines are built or made or the postmen employed, it can be assumed that he will want these ends, and will look more favourably upon machines or postmen which or who do their job well than upon other machines or postmen. It is also obvious that since anyone who wants a machine or a postman will normally want this machine or that postman in order to secure for himself or for others the ends which it is the function of machines or postmen to bring about, the fact that some machine or some postman is a good machine or a good postman will, providing it or he has no incidental disadvantages such as being more expensive than most machines or most postmen, be a reason for choosing a good machine or a good postman, if he is going to choose a machine or a postman at all.

Where tools, instruments and so on are concerned, they are wanted and made for what can be produced or brought

[1] See C. L. Stevenson, 'Persuasive Definitions', *Mind*, XLVII, 1938.

about by using them. Tools or instruments are not made for their own sake, but for the sake of some end which they can be used to bring about. It would be totally mistaken to think that this end must be a good end. Tools or instruments can be made to serve any purpose, good or bad, and, if they serve this purpose better than most similar tools or instruments, then they are good tools or good instruments, regardless of the goodness or badness of the end they are used to bring about or the purpose they serve.[1]

However, not everything that can be described as good or bad is a tool or an instrument. Good or bad men, as we have seen, are not good or bad tools or instruments, and are not good or bad because they do anything well or badly. Pictures, sculpture, music, and literature are not good and not bad because there is anything they do well or badly, because these things do not do anything at all. The artist, composer or writer who produced them may have been doing something well or badly, but a good book is not a book which is written well, nor a good symphony one which is composed well. Rather, to say that a symphony is well-composed or a book well-written is just to say that the composer has produced a good symphony, or the writer has produced a good book. Of course, there are other things which, very likely, a composer or writer must be able to do well in order to produce a good symphony or a good book, though I cannot think what, in these cases, they are. But a good sculptor, presumably, has to be able to handle a chisel well (though someone who writes a good book does not need to be able to handle a pen well; that is something almost anybody can do) and a good painter, presumably, must be able to handle a paint-brush well.

Works of art – I use the expression without the implication, which it is sometimes supposed to have, that a picture, say, which is a work of art must, by definition, be a good picture – are not usually means to any further purpose, and so cannot be called good or bad because they serve this purpose well or badly. Nor can they be described as good or bad according as to whether the man or woman who produced them successfully achieved what he was trying to achieve; since his purpose is usually to produce a good sculpture, a good symphony, a good piece of music, or a good poem, such a definition would be circular.

[1] See Georg Henrik von Wright, *The Varieties of Goodness* (Routledge, 1963), Chapter II, 'Instrumental and Technical Goodness'.

However, though works of art are not good in the sense in which tools are good, because they serve some purpose well, nor good because they achieve the purpose that the artist who produced them set out to achieve, I find it difficult to believe that they are called good or bad by the people who so judge them irrespectively of whether or not they in some way or other give satisfaction. It is true that one can get more pleasure from a detective story than one can from a novel which one believes to be a better story, and one can believe, on the testimony of others, and perhaps even on one's own judgment, that a work of art is a good work of art, although one oneself gets no pleasure from it at all. Nevertheless, if no works of art ever gave anyone any satisfaction at all, I do not think that anyone would ever describe them as good. I suspect that perhaps one thinks that they would be good, even if no one got any satisfaction from them at all, for two reasons: because they certainly would have all the other features they have now, even if no one got any satisfaction from them, and because the view that 'good' means 'gives satisfaction to some group of people' has already been refuted, by implication, in the earlier discussion of similar views about the meaning of the word 'right'. But, though a work of art which gave no one any satisfaction of any sort could be described in all the ways in which we describe it now, when it does give us satisfaction, except by being described as good, it could not be described as good, because one of the functions of saying that a work of art is good is to give people information about what sort of work of art to look at, listen to, or read. And if this work of art gave and could give no human being any satisfaction, it would not be appropriate to describe it as good, for if anyone were to hear a work of art being described as good he could legitimately infer that the speaker thought that it would give at least somebody at some time – if not *he* himself at the present time, connoisseurs, or he himself when his tastes had become educated, or connoisseurs when their tastes had been educated – some satisfaction. This does not mean that anyone who says that a work of art is good is saying that it gives satisfaction, but that it can be inferred from his saying that it is good that he believes it will give someone some satisfaction.

However, works of art are not the only things we describe as good, although they are not tools or instruments, have no function, and serve no purposes of ours. It is customary for philosophers

to say such things as that beauty is good, that truth (or, more properly, knowledge) is good; that pleasure (or happiness) is good;
that virtue is good. I do not quite know how much importance to
attach to the point I am about to make, but this is not quite how a
man who was not a philosopher would talk. He would quite possibly say that anyone who enjoyed and had access to art, music
and literature, who had a mind well-stocked with information,
and enjoyed solving problems, even philosophical ones, who had
many friends and enjoyed their company, and who got pleasure
from the multifarious activities on which he was habitually
or incidentally engaged, was living his life well. And he might
say that it was good to enjoy art, music and literature, acquiring
and possessing information, the company of one's friends, and to
get pleasure from one's daily activities. I doubt, however, whether
he would say anything similar about virtue, if this is taken to mean
goodness in the sense in which a man is good, though this,
I dare say, is not so much because saying so conflicts with ordinary
usage, as because he does not think it is true. The commonest,
and most sensible, attitude to take to virtue is not so much that it
is an element in a good life, as that it is a necessary restriction imposed upon individuals' liberty to enjoy themselves, so that others
living with them in the same community can enjoy themselves
too. Obviously, however, though these things are certainly ingredients – though I would not like to say that they were the
only ingredients – in a good life, they are neither valued nor good,
save incidentally, for any end they serve to bring about, but for the
immediate satisfaction they give.

For this reason, philosophers sometimes describe these things
as 'good as ends', though this is not the way in which anyone
not contaminated by philosophy would talk. Philosophers also
frequently describe other things as good as a means if they have
things which are good as an end as their consequences; they also
sometimes identify being good as a means with being useful.
Being good as a means is certainly not identical with being useful;
tools and instruments are, as we have seen, good tools and instruments, provided they serve their purpose well, and the purpose
they serve is the purpose they were created to serve; they do not
however, have to produce goodness, beauty or truth. The way in
which we in fact differentiate between events and actions which are
productive of good consequences and those which are not is by

describing the former as fortunate and the latter as unfortunate. And sometimes we say of these actions or events that it is a good or bad thing that they were performed or happened.

Sometimes we describe something as a good action or a good deed. It has been argued that a good action or a good deed is not anything different from a right action; it has also been argued that a good action and a right action are different, since one can act rightly from bad or indifferent motives, in which case one's action is right but not good, and can also act wrongly from good motives, in which case one's action is wrong but not bad.[1] I am personally inclined to the former of these two views, and can see no objection to saying that a man did a good deed from bad motives. Hence nothing more need be said about 'good' in the sense in which it is applied to actions. We say that a motive is good because a permanent or relatively permanent tendency to act from that sort of motive is one of the features which make a man a good man, and the sense of 'good' in which it is applied to men has also already been discussed.

The question must arise: 'How do we *know* that things which I have said can be described as being good are in fact good?'

If by saying that a man is good we mean that he acts rightly more often than most men, then we find out *how* he acts by ordinary empirical means, and decide whether or not the things he is doing are things which are to be done or not in the manner described in the previous chapter. If by saying that a man is good we mean that he possesses certain characteristics, then we find out by ordinary empirical means that he possesses these characteristics. But, since we use the word 'good' to describe these characteristics, and using this word implies that we have a favourable attitude to their possession, the question arises whether those characteristics *are to be* imitated or sought after, and questions about our knowledge of what is to be done have, again, already been discussed in the previous chapter.

We know that instruments or tools are good instruments or tools by ordinary empirical observation of how effectively they achieve the purposes for which they were used or made. Though our using the word 'good' to describe them implies that we have a favourable attitude towards tools which are efficient, etc., it is inevitable that we should have this attitude, for it is inevitable

[1] Sir David Ross, *The Foundation of Ethics*, (O.U.P., 1938), Chapter VI.

that, if we make and use the tools for certain purposes, we should be pleased with them to the extent that they achieve the purposes for which they were used and made. Hence there can be no question of one person saying that a tool is good, and another person saying that the same tool is bad, when they are agreed upon all the empirical facts about the tools, and have the same purpose in view in using them.

We describe works of art as good if they satisfy certain very complex criteria, and we know that they do satisfy these criteria, again, by ordinary empirical means. And we use the word 'good' because we have a favourable attitude to things which satisfy these criteria, and it is just a matter of fact that we do have this favourable attitude to things which fulfil these criteria, because of the satisfaction which they give us. We imply, however, that this satisfaction is of a special kind, of a high order, and lasting, in the sense that it will survive closer inspection of the 'work of art' which gives it and comparison with other works of art of the same kind. If different things give satisfaction to different people, then the situation is without remedy. They will not be contradicting one another, in that the criteria which one says are fulfilled will be different criteria from those which the other says are *not* fulfilled, but the attitude which the one expresses will be different from that which the other expresses, and the recommendations about what to read or see or hear which the one implies will be different from those which the other implies.

To say that knowledge, beauty, pleasure, and so on, are good is to say that they are goods. Knowledge is a good because it satisfies a human desire, viz. curiosity, and because knowledge is, among other things, knowledge of the means by which other goods may be obtained. Beauty is a good because it satisfies, and pleasure is a good for the same reasons. We find out what is an object of human satisfaction by finding out whether something does satisfy us. The proof of the pudding is in the eating. When we say that something is a good, we not only *assert* that it satisfies, or is a means to that which satisfies, we also evince a favourable attitude to it because it satisfies. Moral virtue, or moral-law-abidingness, is a good partly because it is useful, because it is necessary that we have and obey rules, and partly because we are so constituted that it satisfies, probably for evolutionary reasons. *Good deeds* are good partly because they arouse a favourable attitude in

M

spectators, and so are agreeable, and partly because they are a means to goods, and so are useful. Good motives are good because they are the kind of motive which as a general rule disposes us to bring about that which satisfies, or is useful, especially moral-law-abidingness. All these things are discovered empirically. Though what we are asserting when we say that something is good will vary with the context, in all cases we express or evince a favourable attitude to something which we call good, and imply, though we do not assert, that it *is to be* imitated or sought after.

VIRTUES AND VICES

We say that thrift and industry are virtues, that extravagance and laziness are vices. We also talk about the virtues of a book, a work of art, a piece of music, a plan or project, a tool, or a medicine. The virtues of a tool are those featues of it which tend to make it a good tool; hence hardness is a virtue, and malleability a vice, in a screwdriver, since hardness helps, and malleability prevents, its performing its functions of screwing screws well. The virtues of a medicine are those characteristics which make it beneficial to human beings. The virtues of a book, a work of art, or a piece of music are those of its features which tend to make it a good book, a good work of art, or a good piece of music. The virtues of a plan are those features of a plan which tend to make it a successful plan, or more successful than alternative plans, in achieving the ends the plan was devised to achieve. A characteristic of a man is a virtue if it tends to enable him to succeed in his enterprises, or if it inclines him to undertake enterprises which enable him to lead a good life, or tends to make it easy for him to lead a good life, or if it enables him to help others to succeed in their enterprises, or inclines him to help others in their enterprises, or tends to make it easy for them to lead happy and successful lives. In a nutshell, Hume was right when he said that the virtues were characteristics which were either useful or agreeable to their possessor or others.[1]

Moral goodness, which has been dealt with already, is just one virtue among others. Some philosophers, for example, Sir David Ross,[2] assess its value so highly that they think that the smallest conceivable amount of moral goodness is greater in value than the

[1] See *An Enquiry Concerning the Principles of Morals.*
[2] Sir David Ross, *The Right and the Good* (Clarendon Press, 1930), pp. 150, 275.

largest conceivable amount of any virtue other than moral goodness. However, it is simply obvious that it would be a very one-
sided and useless person who was very good but possessed no
kindness, intelligence, humour, sympathy or imagination, and
there is no contradiction in saying – indeed, it is obviously true
– that some men would be better men if they were kinder, more
intelligent, more sympathetic and imaginative than they are, even
if this were purchased at the cost of their being less morally good.
Moral goodness may perhaps be a stand-in for some other virtues,[1]
in that a man who is not by nature courageous may still stay at
his post from a strong sense of duty, and a man who is not by
nature kind may still perform acts which benefit others from the
same motive. It cannot be a stand-in for all other virtues, however,
for no man can be intelligent, humorous or imaginative from a
strong sense of duty.

It is sometimes supposed that an ideal man would possess
all the virtues to the highest possible degree. An ideal man in this
sense is not possible, however, for some virtues are incompatible
with others. The hardiness, for example, which is a virtue in a
soldier may be incompatible to some extent with the gentleness
which is a virtue in a woman.

The question arises, again, how we *know* that such-and-such
things are virtues. This is simply the question how we know that
certain features of a plan are likely to make it successful, or how
we know that certain characteristics of a man are useful and agreeable to himself and others, or how we know that certain features
of a medicine enable it to cure the diseases it is intended to cure.
This is a matter of ordinary empirical fact. Again, when we
say that such-and-such is a virtue, we evince a favourable attitude to it, but not only is it inevitable that we have this attitude
to what is useful or agreeable, the question whether we are justified in having such an attitude cannot arise. We can raise the question whether we are justified in having this favourable attitude to
X, and this question will be settled by finding out whether X
really is useful or really is agreeable, but the question whether we
are justified in having a favourable attitude to useful or agreeable
things does not make sense. Similarly, we can ask whether we are
justified in being frightened of X, and the answer will be that we
are justified in being frightened if X is dangerous, but the question

[1] See P. H. Nowell-Smith, *Ethics* (Penguin, 1954), pp. 258–9.

whether we are justified in being frightened of dangerous things cannot arise. Or again, we can raise the question whether we are justified in accepting a given argument, and this question is settled by determining whether it is a valid argument, but the question whether we are justified in accepting valid arguments cannot arise.

'OUGHT'

The word 'ought' is used in a variety of different ways. We say that a certain horse ought to win a race, because, although perhaps it will not win, it would be reasonable to expect, in view of its past performance and the performance of the other horses in the race, that it will win. We say there ought to be an eclipse of the sun at four o'clock, because that is the time when, if calculations are correct, there will be an eclipse. We say that a train ought to arrive at twenty-five minutes past seven, because that is when it is due. We say that Smith ought to be at his desk by now, because this is the time at which he is supposed to start work, or because this is the time at which he usually does start work. In these cases it is not that anyone is doing anything wrong, or neglecting any duty, or failing in any moral obligation, when something that ought to happen does not happen. Trains, eclipses and horses cannot have obligations, and even a man is not under an obligation to do what he usually does. The idea common to these senses of 'ought' is that of a scheme of things in which some event, the eclipse, or a certain horse's winning the race, has a place, but the scheme of things is only ideal or projected or envisaged, so that what would happen, if this scheme of things were to be actually exemplified, is not necessarily what will happen in actual fact.

Of course, from the fact that the horse did not win the race, and the train did not arrive when it was due, one cannot deduce that they ought not to have, so it looks as if an 'ought' cannot be deduced from an 'is'. Nevertheless, from the fact that this horse has had a more successful record than any other horse in the race, from the fact that careful calculation shows that the eclipse is to be expected at four o'clock, from the fact that the train is due at twenty-five minutes past seven, and from the fact that Smith is always or almost always at his desk at nine o'clock, it does follow that that horse ought to win, that the eclipse ought to happen at that time, that the train ought to arrive then, and that Smith ought by now to be at his desk.

When we come to uses of 'ought' which approximate more closely to the so-called 'moral' senses of the word 'ought', the situation is slightly, but not entirely, different. There is still a scheme of things in which the action which ought to be done has a place, whether in fact it is done or not. If a mother makes a rota according to which Roger washes the breakfast dishes, Kate washes up after lunch, Timothy after tea and John after dinner, then it follows that Roger, who has not washed up the breakfast dishes, ought to have, and so on for the others. If a football team makes a plan of attack which involves the centre-forward being at a certain place at a certain time, then the centre-forward ought to be at that place at that time. It is not that there is necessarily any moral condemnation implied if Roger does not wash the dishes, or if the centre-forward is not at the place planned. Roger may have the most excellent reasons for not washing the dishes, and the centre-forward may have broken his leg. It is just that since, in the plan, that is what they were to do, that is what they ought to do. Hence the fact that one ought does not imply that one can. The centre-forward ought to have been there although, since he had broken his leg, he could not be. For since this *was* where it was planned that he should be, that is where he ought to have been, whether he was able to be there or not. It is, however, pointless to tell the centre-forward in a reproachful way that he ought to have done such-and-such, if the reason why he did not was that his leg was broken.

The case is not altogether different when we say that people ought to pay their debts and keep their promises. Debt paying and promise-keeping are part of a plan or scheme of things necessary in order for society to function correctly; hence it is part of this plan that debts be paid and promises be kept, so debts ought to be paid and promises ought to be kept. However, there now creeps in an element which was absent in the case of the eclipse and the train, and not present very strongly in the case of the dishes and the centre forward. Where promise-keeping and debt-paying and so on are concerned we are much *more likely* to say to Smith, who is contemplating not keeping a promise or not paying a debt, that he ought to keep that promise, or ought to pay that debt, in an encouraging or admonitory or exhortatory manner. But still, what is being said is that, if some ideal (in the sense of not necessarily realised) plan or scheme were realised, something would happen, which might not happen, because the plan or scheme might not be realised. In the cases when we say that debts ought to be paid and

M*

promises kept there is in addition the fact that we are usually evincing approval of the scheme which demands that these things be done. By saying that we are evincing approval I mean, again, that though we are not asserting that we approve of the scheme which demands that these actions be performed, anyone hearing us say that these actions ought to be performed is entitled to infer that we do approve of their performance. Again, 'ought' does not imply 'can'; there is no contradiction in saying that Smith ought to have kept his promise, but could not.[1] What is true is that there is no *point* in saying to Smith in an admonitory or accusing manner 'You ought to keep that promise' if Smith is unable to keep it, and that it would be unfair to Smith to say to some third person, 'Smith ought to have kept that promise,' in a manner such as to suggest that Smith was not to be relied upon to keep his promises, if Smith was unable to keep this promise.

It is often said that people ought always to act rightly, and never wrongly, and that they ought always to do their duty, presumably in the sense of 'duty' in which to say that something is someone's duty is to say that it would be morally wrong for him to omit it, but to say this more urgently. In the sense of 'duty' in which one's duty is one's appointed task, there clearly is no contradiction in to say that a man sometimes ought to neglect his duty. There were, no doubt, officials in concentration camps whose duty it was to administer gas to the Jews imprisoned in them. The relationship between 'ought' and 'wrong' (and so between 'ought' and 'duty' in that sense in which to say that something is someone's duty implies that he would be acting morally wrongly if he did not do it) seems to me to be this. Whenever someone does something which is morally wrong, he is failing to do what he ought, but the converse is not the case; whenever someone fails to do what he ought, or whenever something which ought to happen does not happen, it does not follow that some person is acting morally wrongly, or that something morally wrong is being done. Both when a train is late, and when a promise is not kept, something happens which ought not to happen, but only in the latter case is anything wrong being done. (In the case of the eclipse, of course, nothing at all is being done.) This is because, though both in the case when something wrong is being done, and in the case when something which ought not to happen is happening, a plan is not being adhered to,

[1] See ' "Ought" and "Can" ', by A. Montefiore, *The Philosophical Quarterly*, Vol. VIII, 1958.

or an expectation is not being fulfilled, or a rule is not being obeyed, only in the cases when there is some hope of causing, by putting pressure on an individual, that individual to keep to the plan, fulfil the expectation or adhere to the rule, do we say that not to keep to the plan, not to fulfil the expectation, or not to adhere to the rule is morally wrong, or that the plan is *not to be* departed from, the expectation *not to be* let down, the rule *not to be* disobeyed. There would be no point in saying that eclipses are not to be omitted, because heavenly bodies can neither control their own movements, nor can anyone else control them.

We also quite often say that, if someone wants such-and-such an end, then he ought to perform the action which is a means to that end. For example, we might say to someone who was habitually late, 'If you want to be at work on time, you ought to get up earlier,' and we might say to an unsuccessful burglar, 'If you want to avoid leaving finger-prints, you ought to wear gloves.' In these examples, the word 'ought' occurs in that part of the sentence which expresses the consequent of a hypothetical proposition, but it would be a mistake to call them, with Kant, Hypothetical Imperatives.[1] If we think that someone *does* want the end mentioned in that part of the sentence which formulates the antecedent of the hypothetical, we can say simply 'You ought to get up earlier' or 'You ought to wear gloves', and neither of these are hypothetical at all. Furthermore, it is a mistake to conceive of the difference between 'If you want to avoid leaving finger-prints, you ought to wear gloves' and 'It is your duty to care for your children' – by analogy with the difference between a hypothetical and a categorical proposition. For a hypothetical proposition, together with an assertion of the truth of its antecedent, entails the truth of its consequent, but 'If you want to avoid leaving finger-prints, you ought to wear gloves' does not, in conjunction with 'You do want to avoid leaving finger-prints' entail 'It is your *duty* to wear gloves'.

Again, when we say that a burglar ought to wear gloves (if he wants to avoid leaving finger-prints) we are saying that an action, if it were performed, would accord with some ideal scheme, but that it may or may not be performed. In this ideal scheme, people always adopt as means to their ends actions which in fact bring about these ends. Again, the statement that someone is wearing

[1] See Immanuel Kant, *Foundations of the Metaphysics of Morals*, trans. Lewis White Beck (Bobbs–Merril, 1959), pp. 31. f.

gloves does not entail that he ought to be. But the statements that wearing gloves would enable him to avoid leaving finger-prints, and that he wants to avoid leaving finger-prints, do entail that he ought to wear gloves, for to say that he ought to wear gloves is to say that wearing gloves accords with an ideal scheme, in this case, an ideal scheme in which men adopt, in order to secure their ends, means which in fact bring about those ends.

Hence someone saying that someone ought to do something, if he wants something else, is not using 'ought' in a different sense from the sense in which he is using it if he says that he ought to do something, whether he wants to do this thing or not. In both cases he is saying that something would happen if an ideal scheme were realized, an ideal scheme in which people adopted effective means to their ends, or an ideal scheme in which people always refrained from doing actions which were not to be done. At this point a difficulty arises. It is often the case that a man ought to make a lying promise, because this is the only way in which he can obtain money which he wants and badly needs, and also the case that he ought not to make lying promises, because lying promises are not to be made, or because making lying promises is wrong. But if it is the case both that someone ought, and that he ought not, to make lying promises, then must it not follow that the word 'ought' is being used in two different senses, so that it is true in one sense that he ought, and in a different sense that he ought not? This conclusion, however, does not follow. It can be true of a cat that it is larger than a mouse and also true of it that it is not larger than a dog. This does not mean that the expression 'larger than' is being used in two different senses, but that 'larger than' is a relative term, and the animal to which the cat stands in the relation 'larger than' is a different animal from the one to which it does not stand in the relation 'larger than'. The same is true of 'ought'. The scheme of things which would mean that an action was done, if this scheme were realized, is a different scheme of things from the one in which the same action would not be done, if *it* were realized. Hence it can be true of one and the same action that it ought to be done, in relation to one scheme of things, and that it ought not to be done, in relation to another scheme of things.

OUGHT TO BE DONE

We sometimes say that something ought to be done. For example, we sometimes say of some technique or process, 'That is the way it *ought* to be done,' leaving open the question whether anyone actually is doing it that way. I may say of a certain process or technique, 'That is the way it ought to be done,' although I do not think that any of the people engaged in making the things which would involve this technique or process ought to *do* it that way. They may have instructions from their employer to do it some other way, and it may be the case that they ought to carry out these instructions. Nor need it even be true that the employers ought to make their employees do things in the way they ought to be done, for perhaps the process is too expensive. It follows that 'ought to be done' does not imply 'can be done'.

The meaning of the word 'ought' in the phrase 'ought to be done' is the same as its meaning in the phrase 'Smith ought to do that'. It implies a comparison between an actual state of affairs and an ideal one. The ideal state of affairs, in the example used above, is the way in which it would be most successful to perform the operation in question.

RIGHTS

If it could be shown that, whenever we talk of people's rights, what we are saying is always equivalent to something which can be expressed by means of the word 'wrong', there will be no need to say anything about the manner in which we know that people have rights;[1] what has been already said about the manner in which we know that some actions are wrong can be applied automatically to rights. In what follows I shall be talking of moral rights, not of legal rights. It is clear that I can have a moral right to do something which is legally prohibited. Questions about people's legal rights are simply questions about empirical matters of fact, and need not be considered here.

The expression 'a right' can occur in a variety of different sentences. (1) We can say that men have a right to liberty, or to life, or to the pursuit of happiness. Here the word which follows the expression 'a right to' is what might roughly be called an 'abstract noun'. (2) The expression 'a right to' can occur in sentences like 'I have a right to the money' or 'I have a right to his co-operation'.

[1] See the 'Symposium on Rights', by John Plamenatz, W. D. Lamont and H. B. Acton, in the *Supplementary Proceedings of the Aristotelian Society*, Vol. XXIV. See also Stanley Benn and R. S. Peters, *Social Principles and the Democratic State* (Allen & Unwin, 1959).

(3) We can say, 'Men have a right to do as they please with what is theirs'. Here men are not being said to have a right to something, but to have a right to do something. (4) We can say, 'He has a right to be told.' In this case, what he is said to have a right to is not to do something himself, but that others should do something. (5) We can say, 'He has a right to know.' Here what he is said to have a right to is not to do something, or to have something done *to* him, *for* him or *on his behalf*, but to be in a certain state.

The third kind of sentence, where people are said to have a right to *do* something is probably the easiest to translate into a sentence involving the word 'wrong'. To say that someone has a right to do what he likes with what is his seems to me to mean either (i) he is not acting wrongly in doing what he likes with what is his, or (ii) anyone trying to stop him from doing what he likes with what is his would be acting wrongly, or (iii) anyone not trying to stop people from stopping him from doing what he likes with what is his would be acting wrongly, or (iv) either some combination of two of these, or all three of them. It seems to me unlikely that anyone would hold (iii) without holding (ii) – for I do not see why we should consider it wrong not to stop people preventing other people from doing what they like with their own unless we consider it is wrong to stop people from doing what they like with their own. Hence the possible combinations are as follows: (i), and (ii); (ii) and (iii); or (i), (ii) and (iii). I am inclined to think that it is not sufficiently clear what we mean when we say that someone has a right to do something, for us to be able to say which of these possibilities gives us the correct account of the meaning of 'Men have a right to do what they like with what is theirs'. However, some important consequences depend on which account of the meaning of this sentence one adopts. If you think it involves (i), then it will be an analytic truth that people, so long as they are doing what they have a right to do, are not acting wrongly. If you think, however, that it does not involve (i), it will be possible to exercise a right wrongly, that is, to do something which, though wrong, is something one has a right to do. If you think it involves (ii), it becomes an analytic proposition that rights are to be respected, and, if you think it inolves (iii), it becomes an analytic proposition that bystanders, or society, ought to see that rights are respected. On whatever combination of (i), (ii) and (iii) we adopt, it is a synthetic proposition that a man is not acting wrongly in *claiming* his rights, and this analysis leaves open the possibility that it is sometimes right to waive one's rights, to surrender them, or not to insist that they be enforced.

It is sometimes said that rights and duties are correlative. If this means that a person cannot have rights without also having duties, this does not follow from the meaning of the expression 'a right to'; this, of course, does not mean that it is not true, though I see no reason for thinking that it is true. If, however, saying that rights and duties are correlative means that one person's having a right entails that other people have duties, this will be true (in the sense of 'duty' in which some philosophers wish to say that it is always our duty to do something if not doing it involves doing something morally wrong), provided we think that the account of the expression 'a right to' involves propositions (ii) or (iii) above. On the other hand, if we think that the correct account of the meaning of expressions like 'Men have a right to do what they like with their own' involves (i) only, then rights and duties will not be correlative in this sense.[1]

If 'a right to do . . .', as it occurred in the *third* example of sentences involving this expression given above, can be defined in terms of 'wrong', and all other sentences involving the expression 'a right to' can be shown to be equivalent to sentences of this *third* kind, then it would follow that all uses of the expression 'a right to' could be defined in terms of 'wrong'. 'A right to', however, is not always a right to *do* something. It is fairly plausible to say that to have a right to liberty is to have a right to do something, to speak freely, for example, but in the other cases, the case when I say he has a right to the money, that he has a right to know, or that he has a right to be told, his having a right does not seem to imply a right to *do* anything at all. Perhaps, however, these other expressions can be defined directly in terms of 'wrong', even though they cannot be defined indirectly in terms of 'wrong' *via* being defined in terms of expressions of type (3) in the manner suggested above; even in the case of sentences like 'Men have a right to liberty', I do not think that it is very plausible to hold that they have quite the same meaning as sentences like 'Men have a right to speak freely'. It seems to me that, when we say that men have a right to speak freely, we are laying emphasis not on their not acting wrongly in speaking freely – speaking freely may,

[1] See Sir David Ross, *The Right and the Good* (Clarendon Press, 1930), Chapter II.

sometimes, be very wrong – so much as on the wrongness of other people's stopping them from speaking freely, or on the wrongness of people not stopping other people from stopping them from speaking freely.

I suspect that what we mean when we say 'He has a right to the money' is something like 'It is wrong for the person who actually possesses the money not to give it to him', or 'Some third person, having to decide whether to give the money to him or someone else, would be acting wrongly if he did not give it to him'. I think 'He has a right to be told' means something like 'It would be wrong not to tell him' or, perhaps, 'It would be wrong not to tell him, if he asks'. 'He has a right to know', I think, means either 'He has a right to try to find out' (which would mean that he would not be acting wrongly if he tried to find out, that other people would be acting wrongly if they tried to stop him from finding out, etc.), or simply that he has a right to be told. Hence the notion of rights can always be defined in terms of 'wrong',[1] which has already been discussed, and decisions about people's rights are decisions about what is or is not to be done.[2]

The expression 'It is my right' simply means 'I have a right to do it'. The expression 'That is mine by rights' simply means that I have a right to that, together with the suggestion that I do not actually possess it.

We also speak of wronging people, or of doing them a wrong. To wrong somebody is to do him a wrong. Doing someone a wrong is not to do him, wrongly, any sort of injury, but to do him an injustice. Injustice will be discussed later in this chapter.

DESERT

We sometimes say that someone deserved to be punished, whether he was punished or not. We sometimes say that someone deserved what happened to him, even though what did happen to him was not deliberately inflicted upon him by other human beings, nor

---

[1] Or 'tends to be wrong' (which means 'is wrong in normal circumstances').

[2] Rights will be inalienable, in that rights are defined in terms of 'wrong', and no one, as we have seen, can (logically) have the power to alter what is right and wrong. In another sense, however, rights are alienable, in that a change in circumstances may make a difference to what it is right for a man to do, or to how it is right for others to treat him, and in that some of these changes of circumstances may be deliberately brought about.

was even the consequence of the actions or traits of character which make us think the man who performed those actions, or possessed those traits of character, deserved the ill which befell him. Sometimes, of course, people deserve reward, as well as punishment, and deserve that good should befall them as well as ill.

To say that someone deserved to be punished for what he did is not to say that anyone ought to punish him, or that it would be wrong not to punish him. Again, to say that he deserved to be rewarded is not to say that anyone ought to reward him. Nor is there such a thing as a utilitarian theory of desert, for utilitarianism is a theory about the nature of the characteristic which is common and peculiar to all actions which are morally right, and so not at all a theory about what causes an action (or trait of character) to be of good or ill *desert*. The view that people ought to be punished if and only if they deserve to be punished, and that they ought to be rewarded if and only if they deserve to be rewarded, is a synthetic proposition, not an analytic one, and, fortunately for most of us, is not true.

Perhaps the sort of situation in which we say that a man deserves what he gets is a situation in which he might reasonably be expected to have foreseen that what has in fact happened to him would happen to him, and in which he could have avoided having this evil thing happen to him if he had taken more trouble, or when he would not have had this good happen to him, if he had not taken the trouble he did. Perhaps we speak of the deserved success of a burglar, if his success in crime is the result of his care, effort and skill, and not the result of what are, for him, fortunate accidents. It might be suggested that we say that his punishment for burglary was deserved for much the same reason that we say that his success in burglary was deserved; his punishment would have been deserved if pain, fine or imprisonment had been inflicted upon him as a result of something which he had done, and which he could have known would make him liable to pain, fine or imprisonment; whereas we say that pain, fine or imprisonment was not deserved if it happened to him not as the result of his doing something which he could reasonably be expected to know would lead to it, but as a result of causes of quite a different sort. But, surely, we do say that a man deserved his punishment even if his being caught and punished at all was the result of a fortuitous accident, which he could not reasonably have been expected to foresee, and we even say that a man deserved that ill befall him if the ill which befell him was not a result of the actions which make us say that he was of ill desert, but happened accidentally. For example, if a man who deserves ill in a more than usual degree dies of cancer, we say that he deserved to die like that, even if his dying of cancer was not a result of the deeds which make us say he deserved an unhappy fate, but happened for quite some other reason, and would have happened, whether he had behaved in the way which makes us say he deserved an unhappy fate, or had behaved in some totally different way.

Hence we cannot define desert in terms of the good or ill which the deserving or ill-deserving person could reasonably be expected to foresee would result from his actions, nor in terms of the good or ill which are the normal or usual consequences of manifestations of the character traits which we say are deserving of good or ill; for a person may deserve ill, even if he cannot reasonably be expected to foresee that ill would result from what he does, and a person may get the ill he deserves, even if the ill he got did not result from the character-traits which make us say that he deserves this ill. 'Desert', so far as I can see, must be defined in terms of a proportion between the goodness or badness of his actions or his traits of character and the happiness or unhappiness of his subsequent fate. We can grade some actions or some traits of character as better or worse than others, and some fates as happier or unhappier than others; we can then say that the better the action, or the better the trait of character, the happier is the fate which the man who performs the action or possesses the trait of character deserves. This, however, only enables us to say that the better the action or trait of character, the happier is the fate deserved; it enables us to put the goodness or badness of character traits or actions in the same order as the happiness or unhappiness of fates; but this is not enough. It is compatible with the worse actions or traits of character having much unhappier fates than they deserve, or the better actions or character traits having much happier fates than they deserve, or both; it is compatible with the worse actions or character-traits having much happier fates than they deserve or the better actions or character traits having much unhappier fates than they deserve; it is even compatible with all actions and character traits having very happy fates, or very unhappy fates, so long as the worse actions or traits of character have less happy fates, or more unhappy fates, than the better actions or traits of character.

Hence being in proportion to the badness of an action or a trait of character is a necessary, but not a sufficient, condition of a happy or unhappy fate being deserved.

In practice there are excellent utilitarian reasons for inflicting happy fates, where possible, upon good actions or traits of character, and unhappy fates upon bad actions or traits of character, for the good ones are the ones we wish to encourage, and the bad ones are the ones we wish to discourage.

But though there are these excellent utilitarian reasons, within the very considerable limits imposed by the expense of arranging it, the difficulty of organizing it, and the undesirability in interfering past a certain point in people's private lives, for seeing that happiness is the fate of the good and unhappiness the fate of the bad, this still does not tell us *to what extent* the good should be happy and the bad unhappy. There are, however, also excellent utilitarian reasons for thinking that the punishment which ought to be meted out to wrong-doers should be proportionate to the seriousness of the crime. Given that, on a utilitarian account, the seriousness of an offence varies with the amount of harm it does, there will also, in many cases, be a stronger incentive to do acts which are harmful in a greater degree than to do acts which are harmful to a lesser degree. Stealing a lot of money is a more serious offence than stealing only a little money; it also does more harm to steal a lot of money than to steal a little money, and also a stronger disincentive is needed to stop people from stealing a lot of money than to stop them from stealing only a little money. To inflict serious injury on someone is a more serious offence than to inflict only a minor injury upon him; it also does more harm to inflict serious injury upon someone than to inflict a minor injury upon him; hence it is more important to stop people from inflicting serious harm on others than it is to stop them inflicting only a little harm; and the incentives to inflict serious harm on someone you dislike may be greater than the incentive to inflict just a little harm on someone you dislike. This still only gives us the conclusion that (*a*) unhappiness should be made to result (within the limits mentioned above) for those who do wrong, and happiness for those who do right, together with (*b*) the proposition that the amount of unhappiness should vary with the seriousness of the offence. But if you take these two propositions together with the proposition that the amount of pain or unhappiness inflicted in the form of fine, imprisonment, physical pain or death should be the minimum necessary to prevent offences of that degree of seriousness (for inflicting punishment is expensive, harmful to those whose duty it is to inflict it, and on the whole unpopular) you do get a conclusion about how much unhappiness – measured in a rough and ready way by the amount of the fine, the severity of the term of imprisonment, or the number of strokes of the birch – should be inflicted.

This tells you how much suffering *ought* to be inflicted upon wrong-doers, but still does not tell you how much suffering wrong-doers *deserve* to have inflicted upon them for, as we have seen to say that someone *deserves* a fate unhappy to a certain degree is not to say that he *ought* to have that fate inflicted upon him. Sometimes one ought to be merciful, and inflict on someone a fate less unhappy than he deserves. Sometimes the necessity of preventing some crime which is difficult to detect may make it desirable to inflict a more severe punishment than is deserved upon those who are caught. Perhaps, however, to say of someone that he deserves a fate of a certain kind is not to assert the categorical proposition that he ought to have the fate inflicted upon him, but to assert the hypothetical proposition that it would be the case that he ought to have that fate inflicted upon him, if there were no reasons why this should be inexpedient. To say that someone deserves to suffer, on this view, would be to say that he ought to be made to suffer, provided that making a law prohibiting the kind of action of which he is guilty is not too expensive, difficult to enforce and provided that the consequences of interfering with people's liberties are not bad beyond a certain point. Even this will not do, however, for I can myself see no contradiction in someone saying that he does not think that anyone ought to be punished for any offence, provided punishing these offences is not essential for their prevention. It is necessary to punish these offences, in order to protect society against the offenders, but should it somehow become unnecessary, or futile – because the world is going to blow up in an hour or two's time, anyway – then it would not be the case that they ought to be punished, even though it still *would* be the case that they deserved to be punished.

The most plausible definition of desert that I can think of is this: a happy or unhappy fate is deserved if it is *as* unhappy as the action on account of which we say it is deserved is wrong. If this definition is correct, we will have succeeded in defining desert in terms of 'wrong', which has already been defined. The question arises, however, whether an action can be as wrong as a fate is unhappy, whether two such disparate things as degrees of wrongness and degrees of unhappiness can sensibly be said to be equal. Personally, I think they can be. We certainly make such comparisons in other spheres; we say such things as: 'She was as good as she was beautiful', 'She was as poor as she was honest', 'If he had been as industrious as he was clever . . .'. Though it is difficult to make sense of the idea of a degree of industry being equal to a degree of cleverness, or a degree of poverty being equal to a degree of honesty, the fact that we have these expressions does seem to suggest that sense can be made of it. Hence there is no reason why sense should not also be made of a degree of wrongness being equal to a degree of unhappiness.

JUSTICE

Some philosophers have tried to equate justice with the whole of morality, and injustice with the whole of immorality. Such an attempt does not, except for a biblical sense of the word which is now archaic, have the slighest plausibility.[1] Murder, rape and violence can scarcely be described as acting unjustly. And justice, or being just, is only one of the traits of character which make a man a good man. One can be just without being merciful, kind, industrious, generous, sympathetic, or imaginative, and perhaps without being very truthful or reliable or honest. Indeed, the number of opportunities the ordinary man has for being just or unjust is not enormously large. He can show his justice in dealing with his children, but not everybody has children. He can show his justice in dealing with his employees, but not everybody has employees. He can show his justice in the manner in which he conducts some sphere of public life for which he is responsible, but few people *are* responsible in such a manner. He can show his justice in the manner in which he interprets the law and pronounces sentence, but still fewer people have the opportunity to do this. It is not unjust, though it may be wrong, to tell lies, to break one's promises, to fail to pay one's debts, to injure people, or to neglect opportunities of doing good. In the narrow sense of 'duty', defined above, it is few people who have a *duty* to be just.

[1] See W. Frankena, 'The Concept of Social Justice', in *Social Justice*, ed. by R. B. Brandt (Prentice-Hall, 1962).

A judge will have a duty to be just since, if he is not just, he will not properly be performing his function or carrying out his allocated task, but a window cleaner will still be carrying out *his* appointed task whether he is just or not.

Not only do we speak of just actions and just men, we also speak of just laws, and just distributions. All justice has to do with the distribution of rewards and penalties, emoluments and burdens. Hence a man treats his children justly if he rewards them and punishes them justly, and if he distributes burdens and satisfactions justly. The same is true of a just judge or a just ruler. But what does it mean to distribute a burden, or an emolument, justly? If we could say that to distribute a burden or an emolument justly was to distribute it as it ought to be distributed, then we should have succeeded in defining 'justice', and defining justice in terms of a word which has already been defined, namely, the word 'ought'. But the view that to distribute a burden or emolument justly is to distribute it as it ought to be distributed is open to an extremely serious objection. Are there not some occasions when my obligation to distribute burdens and emoluments justly is overridden by other considerations, for example, by considerations such as that the just distribution of a burden or an emolument would have unfortunate consequences.[1] If it were known that giving a certain criminal his just punishment really would cause the heavens to fall then, surely, the sensible thing to do would be not to punish him; at any rate, there is no contradiction in saying that, though it would be just to punish him, he nevertheless ought not to be punished. And sometimes, perhaps, the rich must be taxed more than it is just to tax them, for the simple reason that no one else has the necessary money.

Perhaps to say that a man is just is to say that he habitually, that is, much more often than not, performs just actions. To say that an action is just is to say that the man who performed it chose not to infringe, rather than to infringe, someone's rights in circumstances where he had the choice of doing one rather than the other. (Simply to say that an action is just if it infringes no one's rights will not do, for my going to the pictures may infringe no one's rights, but is clearly not just.[2] Nor, of course, is it unjust.) A distribution is just if it involves the least possible infringement of people's rights, and a law is just if allocates to the people

---

[1] See W. Frankena, *loc. cit.*
[2] See John Stuart Mill, *Utilitarianism*, Chapter V.

governed by it their rights. If this definition is correct, we shall have succeeded in defining 'just' in terms of 'wrong', for rights have already been defined in terms of wrong.

There are, however, two difficulties with this definition of 'just'. In the first place, it is considered just to punish someone who has deserved punishment, but it would be odd to say that the person punished had a right to be punished. In the second place, a distribution of goods among similar people would be an even distribution. (If there were not enough goods to go round, the evenness of the distribution could be preserved by drawing lots for what goods there were, in which case everyone would have the same *chance* of getting something.) It seems to me that it is not merely a contingent matter that the just distribution in these circumstances is an even one; it is part of the meaning of 'just' that goods, or the chances of having goods, should be distributed equally among similar people. However, that people have a right to as large a share of goods as anyone else is a synthetic proposition, and that it is wrong not to give them even shares is also a synthetic proposition. Hence some ingredient in the meaning of 'just' is omitted if it is simply defined in terms of rights, and so in terms of what it is right to do (we shall see later that this element in the notion of justice *has* to be omitted since it is unhelpful and unclear).

Injustice always consists in treating similar people in a dissimilar way, or in a way which is more dissimilar than the dissimilarities between them warrant.[1] Someone who has been treated unjustly always feels himself wronged, because he has been treated worse than someone else whose case is not dissimilar from his own. This explains why someone who has been robbed, for example, does not consider himself to have been treated unjustly; he does not feel that he has been treated badly because he has been robbed, and the man next door has not. He complains because he has been robbed at all. The case might be different with an organization which, like Robin Hood's, set out to rob in a systematic way with some other end in view than simply acquiring money. If its object was to steal from the rich in order to give to the poor, then it might consider that the burden of being robbed ought to be distributed evenly among the rich, and a rich man who was robbed might consider himself unjustly treated if some other man, equally rich, was not robbed.

[1] This has been denied. See W. Frankena, *loc. cit.*

Not every case of treating similar people in a dissimilar way, however, is a case of injustice. If you ask a woman to marry you, other similar women whom you do not ask have no reason to complain that they have been unjustly treated. (This is sometimes regarded as being an exception to the universalization principle, but it is not. For if it is right to ask one woman to marry you, it would also be right to ask any similar woman to marry you, but not, perhaps, to ask both.) The reason for this is that justice is an administrative virtue; it has to do with the equitable distribution of goods or of the burdens which have to be incurred if society is to survive or achieve certain desirable ends, or with the legislation and enforcement of rules which are made necessary for the same reasons. Hence justice or injustice can be manifested only by those whose function it is to apportion those goods or burdens, or to make or enforce those rules, and injustice is always shown in a burden or a rule being made without good reason to fall more heavily upon one person or persons than another, or a rule being enforced in one case and not in another. Hence justice can only be manifested by a person who has authority over others, in his deciding how goods or burdens are to be distributed, or what rules are to be made and in enforcing those rules, in relation to the people over whom he exercises authority. Hence injustice cannot be manifested by a person who breaks such a rule or evades such a burden, which explains why it is not unjust to rob, nor by men in activities which are not in a wide sense administrative, which explains why it is not unjust to propose marriage to one woman but not to another whose qualifications for that happy state might seem more suitable.

Though we are unjust if, in an administrative capacity, we treat similar cases in a dissimilar way, this does not by itself tell us what dissimilarities make dissimilar treatment just, and what dissimilarities do not. A law which hangs blacks but not whites for similar crimes is not treating similar people in a dissimilar way, for their colours are different; nor is the judge, who impartially applies this law, treating similar cases dissimilarly.

Are we then to say that a man is just provided that, in his administrative capacity as a distributor of burdens and a maker and enforcer of rules, he treats similar cases in a similar way, or are we to say that this, though a necessary condition of being just, is not a sufficient condition of being just? In order to be just a man or a law or a distribution must not only treat similar cases in similar ways; he or it must also take account of the right sort of similarities and dissimilarities. If we regard treating similar cases similarly as being impartial, then it does seem that something more is needed than impartiality in order to be just.[1] A just man, or a just law, or a just distribution is not only impartial; it must also be equitable. A law, or a man, or a distribution, which treated blacks differently from whites would be the former but not the latter.

This latter ingredient in the notion of justice, however, is extremely difficult to give an account of. There are fairly obvious utilitarian reasons why it is better not to treat blacks differently from whites, or why the needy should be treated differently from those who are not needy, the industrious differently from the idle, the law-abiding from those who are not law-abiding, those who possess socially useful skills or abilities from those who do not, but the notion of justice is not fundamentally a utilitarian one. To say that it is unjust to have one law for the rich and another for the poor is not at all to say that this is harmful, even though it almost certainly would be harmful.

The notion of being equitable is not totally dissimilar from the notions of proportion or beauty or symmetry. A just distribution or a just law take account of certain features of the people among whom the distribution is made, or to whom the law applies, in something like the way in which a map takes account of the features of the country it maps. But there does not seem to be any precise means of specifying the way in which the equitable distribution or law takes account of these features. Certain ditributions or laws may plainly be equitable, and certain other distributions or laws plainly inequitable, but in between there is a wide spectrum of such distributions or laws where it is not possible to say whether or not they are equitable, since the notion of equity is insufficiently determinate.[2] It would be clearly inequitable to give pocket money to one child because you liked him and no pocket money at all to another child of the same age and needs. It would be fairly clearly equitable to allocate pocket money on some such principle as that the amount of the pocket money should be in proportion to the age of the child. There does not, however, really seem to be any way of saying whether certain other principles one might think of are equitable or not – it is not obviously inequitable to give

[1] See Ch. Perelman, *The Idea of Justice and the Problem of Argument*, trans. by John Petrie (Routledge, 1963).
[2] See John Stuart Mill, *Utilitarianism* (Fontana Library, 1962), pp. 310 f.

children of different ages the same amount of pocket money – or of choosing, on grounds of equity, between different principles, say, all the different ways one might think of of allowing for age in determining a child's pocket money. If I am right, equity is like the notions of symmetry and proportion, and so not a moral notion at all.

For these reasons it seems to me that, though we do have a non-utilitarian notion of equity, which has some similarity to the notions of proportion and symmetry, it is so vague and obscure as to be of very little practical use. Hence I am inclined to cut the Gordian knot and say that the nearest approximation I can get to the intelligible parts of the notion of justice is that a man in his administrative capacity as a distributor of burdens and benefits, or a law or a distribution, is just if he or it treat similar cases in a similar way, distribute these burdens and benefits as nearly as possible equally (in the sense of 'equally' which means allocating the same burden or benefit to everyone) and, in allowing for dissimilarities, allow for those dissimilarities which it seems *right* to allow for, for whatever reason. This definition, however inadequate, is at least economical, in that it defines 'just' in terms of 'right', and does not omit anything from the notion of justice which is worth preserving. The definition leaves it an open question whether a utilitarian or a non-utilitarian account is given of what dissimilarities are rightly to be taken account of.

One final difficulty remains. I argued earlier in this section that there was no contradiction in saying that sometimes one ought not to be just. But if a distribution or law is just only if it allows for those dissimilarities which it is right to allow for, does it not follow that there *is* a contradiction in saying that sometimes one ought to be unjust? However, a distribution or a rule, though it allows for those dissimilarities which it is right to allow for may, nevertheless, have to be set aside in unforeseen circumstances or in an emergency in an *ad hoc* and arbitrary way and, in such circumstances, it may well be that one ought to be unjust, for example, by setting aside the law, even a good law, which does treat similar cases in a similar way, and does take proper account of the differences which it is right to take account of. Justice, in other words, is a civilized virtue which may be something of a luxury in times of great stress, when it may be more important to do something quickly and effectively than to do it in a way which bears fairly upon the people concerned.

'NON-MORAL' SENSES OF ETHICAL WORDS

We not only speak of a morally wrong action; we speak of a wrong sum, a wrong way of doing something, a wrong turning, the wrong road, the wrong move, the wrong time, the wrong answer, and we sometimes say that clocks or watches are wrong. Someone has got the wrong answer to the question 'What is the sum of two and two?', if he gives an answer other than 'four'. Someone has given the wrong answer to the question 'What is the date of the Battle of Hastings?', if he says something other than '1066'. Someone has taken the wrong turning if he wants to go to Bath, but takes the road to Bristol (which is in the opposite direction from Bath). He has made the wrong move if he moves his Queen's pawn to Q6, if he could have mated in three moves if he had moved his Queen's pawn to Q8, and could not have mated in less than four moves if he had made any other move, and was trying to win as quickly as possible. A watch is telling the wrong time, and is wrong, if it tells some time other than the time it is (and has not stopped). The common thread in all these senses of 'wrong' is that one has done the wrong thing, selected the wrong object, made the wrong move, if one has not achieved what one was aiming to achieve, or taken the right means to what one was aiming to achieve. In most cases, this is obvious, but it is not so obvious in the case when I deliberately give the wrong answer, or when a clock is wrong, or when I am given the right tool for the job though, for some reason – perhaps because I *wanted* to do the job badly – I wanted the wrong one. In such cases we may hesitate; we want to say that Smith gave the wrong answer, because he said the Battle of Hastings was fought in 1166, and it was in fact fought in 1066; and we also want to say he gave the right answer, because he intended to give the answer 1166, knowing perfectly well that it was wrong. In these cases, one says that the tool for the job is the right tool if one thinks of the aims people usually have, or that it is the wrong tool if one thinks of the aims this particular person has in unusual circumstances, and one says that the true answer to the question is the right answer if one thinks of the aims people usually have, and that it is the wrong answer if one thinks of the aim this particular person has in unusual circumstances. One says a clock is wrong if it tells the wrong time, and one says that the time it tells is the wrong time if it does not tell the time it is, and one says that it is wrong if it does not tell the time it is because people who have clocks or watches usually want them, for obvious reasons, to tell the time it is.

The right tool may not be a good tool, and the right road may not be a good road, but it is difficult to see that the right way of doing something can be other than a good way of doing that thing, or that the right answer to a question can be other than a good answer. On the other hand, a good answer is not necessarily the right answer, and a good way of doing something is not necessarily the right way of doing it. However, it is not necessarily the case that the right way of doing something must be a good way, and that the right answer must be a good answer. Perhaps all the answers the examiner marks are right, but this one is not so well expressed or carefully presented as the others, and so it is worse than most answers, and so a bad answer. And the right way of eating spaghetti may not be a very good way, but the traditional way, and the way regarded as socially acceptable by spaghetti-eaters. Where people are concerned, a good man is not necessarily the right man to marry or to appoint; nor, even, is a man who is good at doing such-and-such a thing necessarily the right man to do that thing, for other people may do it better, and he himself may do other things better than he does that; even though he does not do anything better than he empties dustbins, and though nobody empties dustbins better than he does, he may still be the wrong man to empty dustbins for, since being a doctor is more important than emptying dustbins, he may be the right man to doctor rather than to empty dustbins, even though he is not as high up in the league of doctors as he is in the league of dustmen.

When we apply the word 'right' to tools or answers, are we using this word in a different sense from the sense in which we are using it when we say that actions are morally right? To suppose that we must be using it in a different sense, because we say that an action is morally right, but that an answer is simply right, would be like supposing we are using the word 'slow' in a different sense when we say that a train is dreadfully slow from the sense in which we are using it when we just say that it is slow. In this case, of course, going dreadfully slowly entails going slowly, for going dreadfully slowly is one way of going slowly. Even though a semi-quaver is not a sort of quaver and even though imitation mink is not a sort of mink – for being a semi-quaver entails *not* being a quaver, and being imitation mink entails *not* being mink –

SOME OTHER MORAL JUDGMENTS

the words 'quaver' and 'mink' are not being used in different senses when we say that a note is a semi-quaver or that a coat is imitation mink from the senses in which we use them when we say that a note is a quaver or a coat is mink.

Though it does not follow from the fact that we say an action is *morally* wrong, and a move at chess just wrong, that the word 'wrong' is being used in two different senses, a case can be made out for saying that the word is being used in different senses in fact. The analogy, in chess, with a morally wrong action is not so much an unsuccessful, ill-judged or strategically unsound move, as a move which conflicts with the laws of chess, though we do not, so far as I know, ever say of a move which conflicts with the laws of chess that it is a wrong move or the wrong move. (What we do say is that it cannot be done.) A chess move is illegal if it is forbidden by a generally accepted set of laws which are, in the case of chess, codified and written down. It is true that to say that an action is morally wrong is not to say that it conflicts with any actual set of rules; for a man can say, without contradicting himself, that an action does not conflict with the rules which his society (or any other society) accepts, but is nevertheless morally wrong. But it is tempting, however – and some philosophers have succumbed to the temptation – to say that an action is morally wrong, not if it conflicts with the rules a society actually does accept, but with the rules which it ought to accept, or rules of which it would be true to say that it would be a good thing if they were accepted, or which would have good consequences if they were accepted. Even this account of the meaning of 'morally wrong' will not do. For it may well be the case that a society *has* a rule making military service compulsory, and that it would be a very good thing, and productive of good consequences if it did not have such a rule, but this by itself does not mean that anyone accepting these two propositions is contradicting himself if he also says it would be wrong for men not to do their military service. For there seems no inconsistency in saying that we ought, sometimes, at any rate, to obey the rules we actually have, even though they are not very good ones, or positively bad ones. And it is perfectly possible that the action of breaking a rule which has bad consequences (and so is a bad rule) can itself have bad consequences (and so, perhaps, be wrong).

Nevertheless, we can, as we have seen, say that an action is right if it accords with a set of rules, which are to be accepted,

N

which rules will guide one how to behave in a society where there are actual rules which are far from ideal, and actual rules which are far from having good consequences. But even this does not mean that 'wrong' has a different sense when we say that something is morally wrong, i.e. is not to be done, because it conflicts with a set of rules which is to be acted on by everyone, and when we say that something is wrong in a non-moral sense, for example, because it is the wrong means to a given end. In both cases we mean that our action deviates from a norm, either a norm consisting of a rule which is to be followed, because not to follow it involves infringing some imagined taboo or producing socially harmful consequences, or a norm determined by actions which must be performed if certain desired ends are to be achieved, which deviates from that which we want (wrong screwdriver) or from the way in which something must go if it is to satisfy the need for which it was constructed (as when a clock or watch is wrong). There will, however, be emotional overtones in the so-called 'moral' and 'non-moral' senses of 'wrong'. For though in calling a clock and a case of promise-breaking 'wrong', we suggest that we have an unfavourable attitude to both these things, a preparedness to impose sanctions is evinced in the latter case which would be pointless in the former.

CHAPTER XVI

REASONS FOR ACTION

We have yet to consider our beliefs about right and wrong in their aspect of providing us with reasons for performing certain actions and avoiding others. It certainly seems obvious that we do some things because we think it is right to do them and refrain from doing other things because we think that to do them would be wrong; that we think that that something is right is a good reason for doing it and that that something is wrong is a good reason for not doing it. And some philosophers have contended that the right action is in one sense the rational action, and that it is the mark of a rational man that he does what is right and avoids doing what is wrong.

In the present chapter I shall mainly be concerned with four problems: the nature of the connection between the reasons for an action and the action which is performed for these reasons; the difference between good and bad reasons for doing something; whether acting rightly is really any more rational than acting wrongly, or the good man any more rational than the man who is not good; and whether the right answer to the question 'What is it right to do?' is the rational answer to this question.

In order to provide a satisfactory solution to these problems, it is first necessary to emphasize the difference between reasons for thinking or believing something, and reasons for doing something. The reasons for thinking something are always reasons for believing that some statement, proposition or judgment is true, or is the case, and the reasons we give for thinking these propositions or statements are true will also always themselves be propositions or statements. My reasons for believing the proposition or statement that the earth is round, for example, will always be other propositions or statements, such as that it is possible to travel round it, that distant objects sink below the horizon, that the sun and the moon and the stars look round, and that when there is an eclipse the earth always throws a round shadow on the sun or the moon. However, where reasons for doing something are concerned, that for which reasons are given, viz. doing something, is not a proposition but an action. Actions, unlike propositions, are not capable of being true or false, and are not capable of being believed or disbelieved; hence the reasons for an action cannot be reasons for believing that a statement or proposition is true or is the case, and, consequently, it would appear that different accounts must be given of the nature of reasons or good reasons for an action and the nature of reasons or good reasons for a belief. Obviously, one of the features of a rational man will be that he believes things if there are better reasons for believing them than for disbelieving them. Equally obviously, a different account must be given of a man who is rational in action from that which must be given of one who is rational in thought, for actions cannot be believed and so there can be no good reasons for believing them.

There are, however, different *kinds* of reasons for doing something. The question 'Why did you do that?' is ambiguous. It may mean 'What caused you to do that?', and an answer to it may take the form of stating some happening in one's past life, or giving some description of the state of one's brain or nervous system or endocrine activity, which is such that had not this event taken place, or had one's brain, nervous system or endocrine balance not been in the state it was, one would not have done what one did, but something else instead.

On the other hand, an answer to the question 'Why did you do that?' may take the form of saying what you hoped to achieve by doing that. For example, if what you did was to move your Queen's pawn to Q4, the answer to the question 'Why did you do that?' may take the form of saying, 'I moved my pawn to Q4 in order to release my bishop.' If what you did was to sell your oil shares, your answer to the question 'Why did you do that?' may be that you sold your oil shares in order to have enough money to buy a house. In this sense, the question 'Why did you do that?' is the same as the question 'With what end in view did you do that?' It is perfectly possible to do something with an end in view, and to wish to achieve this end as a means to some further end, but, of course, at some point or other, as Hume points out, it is necessary to stop with an end which, though you have it in view, you do not have it in view because it is a means to some other end you have in view. What this end is will vary from one person to another; one person may play squash in order to be healthy; another person may try to be healthy in order to play squash. And, of course, there are many things one does without any further end in view, simply because one enjoys doing them.

The question 'Why did you do that?' may also mean 'From what motive did you do that?', and the answer may be that you did it from pity, or jealousy or avarice or ambition. It might seem as if there was very little difference between specifying one's motive for doing something, and specifying the end one has in view when one does it. To say that one relieved someone's distress out of pity is, it might be argued, simply to say that one had no *further* end in view than to relieve his distress, and that one has a disposition or tendency to perform actions which relieve the distress of others. There are, however, two important differences between stating the end that someone has in view in doing something, and stating his motive. For one thing, having a disposition to seek certain ends is not all that having a motive consists in. Whenever one person or thing has a disposition which another person or thing lacks there must be some other, non-dispositional difference between the two persons or the two things, which explains why the one has the disposition, while the other has not. For example, to say that glass is fragile is to make a dispositional statement about it, that is, to say that if it drops it will easily break, but there must be some difference between the constitution of glass and the constitution of steel, which is not fragile, which explains why glass will break if dropped, but steel will not. Doubtless, in the case of motives, there is some physiological difference, known or unknown, which explains why one person has a disposition which the other person lacks, but there is also a psychological factor which most modern accounts of motives[1] forget about, namely, the fact that a person who has a certain disposition will have a felt tendency impelling him to perform certain actions, and making him feel distressed, frustrated or uncomfortable if he does not perform them. It is, in fact, because of this felt tendency, which seems to push us in a given direction, that motives are called motives at all.

The second reason why stating what someone's motive is and stating what end he has in view are different is this. To say that someone is acting from jealousy, for example, is to say more than that he has in view some such thing as the harm of someone else.

[1] G. Ryle, *The Concept of Mind* (Hutchinson, 1949), pp. 110 f.

It is also to say that he had in view harm to another because he believed him to be a rival, and that he would not have wished to harm him had he not believed this. Hence statements about people's motives frequently contain more information about these people than statements about their ends.

In general, whenever we seek a certain end, there must not only be some motive or desire, impelling us towards this end; there must also be a belief, a belief to the effect that performing the actions we do perform will result in the end which we desire to bring about or which has some feature towards which we feel an attraction. For example, the concert pianist, who practices for eight hours a day, must not only be motivated by something such as a desire to achieve fame by becoming a concert pianist; he must also *believe* that practising eight hours a day will enable him to become a concert pianist or, at least, improve his chances of becoming a concert pianist. Hence, one answer to the question 'Why did you do that?' may take the form of stating something which the person replying to this question believes. He may reply, 'I practise eight hours a day because I believe that in no other way can I become a concert pianist.' Motives and beliefs are closely interconnected. Given that a man wants a given end, it is possible to say that he believes that a certain action will produce that end if he performs it; given that a man believes that a certain action will produce a certain end, it is possible to say that he wants the end in question if he performs it. Hence, King Canute's action of commanding the tide to turn would, given a desire to stop the tide, be a manifestation of his belief that the tide would stop if he told it to; given a belief that the tide would not stop, his ordering it to stop would have to be a manifestation of some other motive, say, a desire to bring about the discomfortiture of his courtiers. Hence, whenever one says, 'I did so-and-so because I believed such-and-such,' a desire to do so-and-so or for the consequences of doing so-and-so is understood, and, whenever I say, 'I did so-and-so because I wanted such-and-such', a belief that doing so-and-so would result in such-and-such is understood.

Hence the answer to the question 'Why did you do that?' must be that I did it because of a desire for certain things which I believed would result from doing that, or because of a belief that certain things which I desired would result from doing that. As I have already said, the two are complementary; a desire cannot move us to action without a belief that what we do will satisfy it,

and a belief, as Hume pointed out,[1] cannot move us to action
unless it is a belief to the effect that some action has some feature
or some result which attracts us.

Having discussed what sorts of things are reasons for actions,
it is now necessary to consider the nature of the connection
between the reasons from which an action is done, and the action
done for these reasons.

The view, which was once taken for granted, that motives are
causes of actions, is nowadays unpopular. It has been held that a
motive is not a cause, but a disposition to perform actions of a
certain kind in certain circumstances, just as to say that something
is fragile is to say that it is disposed to break when dropped.[2]
This account of motives will not do, however. It leaves out the
fact that part of what is being said when one is described as having a
motive or possessing a desire is that one has an introspectible
feeling of being impelled towards actions which will satisfy that
desire, and an introspectible feeling of discomfort or frustration
when one does not perform actions which satisfy that desire. And to
have a motive cannot simply be to act in a certain way; it is to act
in a certain way, believing that acting in that way will satisfy a
want which one believes or knows one has. Hence to describe
motives as dispositions to act either leaves out something essential,
the fact that the actions which one is disposed to perform are
actions which one believes will satisfy a want, or is circular, for
to say that one believes an action will satisfy a want, is just to say
one believes one has a motive for doing it.

It might seem that both motives and beliefs must be causes of
actions, because it is sometimes true to say of an action that it
would not have been performed if the man who performed it
had not had a certain motive, or that it would not have been
performed if the man who performed it had not had a certain
belief. In reply to this it can be said that it is also the case that it can
be true to say that something would not have broken if it had not
been fragile; nevertheless, being fragile cannot be the cause of
something's breaking, for to say that something is fragile simply
is to say that if it is dropped it will break. Hence the causes of
one thing's breaking but other thing's not breaking may be that

---

[1] See David Hume, *Treatise of Human Nature*, Book II, Part III, Section III,
'Of the Influencing Motives of the Will'.

[2] See Gilbert Ryle, *op. cit.*, pp. 113 f.

the one thing is dropped but the other thing is not dropped, and the causes of one thing, which is dropped, breaking and another thing, which is also dropped, not breaking may be something to do with the nature of the materials out of which they are made; but the causes of one thing, which is dropped, breaking and another thing, which is also dropped, not breaking cannot be that the first thing is fragile but the second thing is not, for to say that the first thing is fragile is just to say that, if it is dropped, it will break, and to say that the other thing is not fragile is just to say that it will not break, even though dropped.

It is sometimes supposed that, to the extent that an action is done for a reason, it is not caused, and that, to the extent that it is caused, it is not done for a reason. If an action was wholly brought about by its causes, then it could not have been done for any reason, and so whatever reasons may have seemed to weigh with the man who performed it must be purely illusory. It may seem to him that his actions have reasons, that he would not have performed them if his beliefs had been different, but in fact, since his actions have causes, and reasons are not causes, he would have done just what he is doing now, whatever his beliefs about the nature of the action and its consequences were. A similar argument can be used in an attempt to show that, if beliefs have causes, they, too, must be irrational. For a belief is rational to the extent that the person who has it has reasons for what he believes, and if his belief has causes only – for example, if he believes what he does solely because he has a tumour of his brain, or because he was brought up to believe it, or because he wants to believe it – then it will not have reasons, and so, whether the belief in question is true or not, the person who has it will be believing it irrationally.

If, however, beliefs and motives are a special kind of cause, and not something other than causes, it is perfectly possible to say that actions can both be done from reasons and from causes, and it is also possible to say that my having a belief can both be caused and that I can have reasons for my belief, for if I have reasons for my belief, my belief is caused by the reasons I have. This is the view to which I am personally inclined. If I believe that the gun is not loaded, and so pull the trigger when I would not have pulled the trigger if I had not believed that it was not loaded, then my action is partly caused by my belief that the gun is not loaded; it is, of course, on this view also partly caused by a desire to pull the trigger for some reason – say a desire to test the mechanism – and I must, if it is to be the case that I would not have pulled the trigger had I believed the gun was loaded, also have had some other desire, a desire not to endanger human life, which would cause me not to pull the trigger if I believed the gun was loaded.

The view that beliefs and motives are a special kind of cause, however, is open to a very serious difficulty. It is usually held that the causal relation is one which holds between events which are distinct and logically separable, for example, between the lighting of a fuse, which is one event, and an explosion, which is another event; since either of these two events can be described without any reference to the other, there is no logical connection between the two events, and so there may be a causal connection. On the other hand, a man's being a bachelor cannot be the cause of his not having a wife, for these two things cannot be described separately, and so the connection between being a bachelor and not having a wife is logical, not causal. But, it is then argued, can it simply be a contingent fact that people who are hungry eat, or that a desire for food causes people to eat rather than sing, and that avarice leads men to seek after wealth and not to seek after power. Similarly, can it just be a contingent fact that a person's beliefs lead him to act in such a way as would enable him to satisfy his desires, if these beliefs were true? For example, if I want to catch a train, and have no other wants which would be interfered with by my catching the train, or which cause me to delay or procrastinate, can it just be a contingent fact that I go to the station roughly at the time I believe the train is due, and not ten hours later?

In the case of *motives*, I think the answer to the above difficulty is as follows. When you describe a motive or a desire, you describe it largely in terms of the ends which the person who possesses this motive or desire has a tendency to seek. Similarly, a balance-wheel or a main-spring is described in terms of the function these have. But, of course, that they have a certain function cannot be the only thing which is true about a balance-wheel or a main-spring. There must be something which has the function, and this thing must be capable of being described in terms other than those which describe what it does. For example, the balance-wheel and the main-spring must be made of certain material, have a certain shape, size, a position in relation to the watch, and properties like retaining their centre of weight through large changes of temperature or of being elastic. The same is true of motives. It cannot be that a motive is only a disposition to seek certain ends; there must be something which has this tendency, just as there is some piece of metal which performs the function of a mainspring. The situation, I think, is this. When we have a motive or a desire, there is an internal force pushing us in a given direction; these internal forces feel different from one another in ways which I am not very good at describing, but the important differences between them lie in the directions in which they push us, in the states of affairs which, if not realized, will cause us to feel discomfort and dissatisfaction, and the realization of which will cause us to feel pleasure and contentment. Hence these motives are defined in terms of the ends to which they incline us, but possess features other than that they incline us to these ends. Just as the fact, that what makes the hands of the watch turn round is the force applied to the cog-wheels by the main-spring, is not altered by the fact that it is an analytic proposition that it is the function of the main-spring to drive the cog-wheels, so the fact that I am caused to do the things I do partly by my motives is not altered by the fact that my motives are defined by the ends towards which they impel me. It is, indeed, an analytic proposition that avarice impels me to acquire and keep money, but this does not mean that my acquiring and keeping money is not caused by an impulsion towards acquiring and keeping money just as the fact that it is an analytic proposition that main-springs, when they are not broken or run down, drive the cog-wheels of watches does not mean that it is not a synthetic proposition that that piece of metal, with that shape, size, position in the watch and with those properties, is what causes the wheels of the watch to turn. Hence it is a synthetic proposition that I eat from an *impulsion* to eat, though it is an analytic proposition that an impulsion to *eat* is an impulsion which moves me to eat food; hence there is no reason why my impulsion to eat should not be the cause of my eating.

Where *beliefs* are concerned, the situation is somewhat similar. The difficulty, it will be remembered, with saying that my belief that the train left at four o' clock caused me to go to the station at a quarter to four to catch it, was that the proposition, that people who want to catch trains go, if they can, to the station in what they believe to be time to catch them, is an analytic proposition, not a synthetic one. My going to the station is not something which is caused by my belief, that is, it is not something which is caused by something which is distinct and separable from my going. My going to the station at the time is a manifestation of my belief, not an effect of it.

There is, however, to my mind a serious difficulty with the view that actions are manifestations of beliefs rather than effects of them. If it were the case that one's believing a proposition consisted in acting in a way which would be successful in satisfying one's desires, if it were true, then one would have to find out what one believed in the same way in which other people – to the extent, at any rate, that they have to make up their minds on this question independently of one's testimony about one's beliefs – have to find out what you believe, that is, by seeing what you do and say. It is surely absurd, however, to suggest that I know I believe the train leaves at four o' clock because I find myself going to the station at a time which would enable me to catch it, if it left at four. In the great majority of cases, I know what I believe in the same sort of way that I know that I have a pain or know that I can see a yellow after-image. I do not know what I believe because I infer it from what I do, any more than I know that I am in pain because I hear myself screaming, or know that I am hungry because I observe myself looking for food. Hence statements about what I believe cannot be statements describing my own behaviour, and statements about what other people believe cannot be statements describing their behaviour. The connection between believing a proposition or statement and acting in a manner which would be successful if it were true is not analytic, and so there is no reason why this connection should not be a causal one. But, could I decide, for example, that my train left at four o' clock, and that, in order to catch it, it will be necessary to get to the station at a quarter to four, and *not* decide to leave for the station in time to get there at a quarter to four? I could, and would, of course, if I didn't want to catch the train or if, though I did want to catch the train, there were other things that I wanted more. And I just might, I suppose, to try to act as if every belief I held, including my belief that the train leaves at four o'clock, were false, but then there would be something else I wanted to do more than achieve the results I would achieve by acting as if the beliefs I held were true, namely, to try to act as if my beliefs were false; hence, though to someone who did not know what was motivating me it would *seem* as if I was acting as if my beliefs were false, anyone knowing what my real motives for behaving in these strange ways were, would know that I was in fact acting as if they were true. I would be acting in a manner that would be successful in satisfying my desire to act as if my beliefs were false, if my belief, that these beliefs are true, is false.

The truth of the matter, however, seems to me to be this. The connection between belief and action is due to the definition of motives, not to the definition of beliefs. To act from a motive is always to act, not in a manner which will satisfy that motive, but in a manner which one believes will satisfy it. (This may be what Kant meant when he said that that whosoever wills the end wills the means – or, more accurately, what he believes to be the means – is an analytic proposition.) If you believe that A is a means (and the only means) to B, and you want B badly enough, you will do A; or, in other words, if you do not do A, either you do not believe A is a means to B, or you do not want B. But this does not show, as I think many philosophers have supposed, that *beliefs* have to be defined in terms of action; all it shows is that *motives* have to be defined in terms of action. It means that when I say I have a motive for seeking B, then, if I believe A will result in B, I will do A (provided, of course, I do not want anything else more than I want B, and am able to do A, and so on). In other words, though it is true that having a motive implies that if I have the belief, I will perform the action (which is equivalent to saying that if I have the motive and the belief, I will perform the action), this does not at all entail that, in order to understand what it is to have a belief, I need to understand what it is to act upon a belief. Hence having beliefs does not entail anything about actions, and there is not an analytic connection between belief and action, and so there may perfectly well be a causal connection between a belief and an action.

An analogous example may help to make this point clear. It is fairly obviously true that if a thing is fragile, this entails that if it is dropped, it will break (which is equivalent to saying that if it is fragile and it is dropped, then it will break) but this does not at all mean that in order to understand what it is to be dropped, you must understand what it is to break, or that being dropped entails breaking. The fact that if a thing is fragile and is dropped entails that it will break is due to the definition of 'fragile' in terms of breaking, not to any, obviously wrong, definition of being dropped in terms of breaking. Similarly, if I have a motive for seeking B, and believe A will result in B, that I will do A is due to motives having to be defined in terms of actions, not to beliefs having to be defined in terms of actions.

One reason why a person does something may be that he thinks he is under an obligation to do it, that he thinks that it is his duty, that he thinks that not to do it would be wrong. The most natural way to regard our doing something because we think it is our duty, or because we think that it would be wrong not to do it, is to think of it as being just like doing something because we believe that it is expected of us, or because it would be contrary to the law not to do it. If we do something because it is expected of us, or because we believe it would be contrary to the law not to do it, we first of all have a *belief*, that this action is expected of us, or that it would be contrary to the law not to do this action, and secondly a *desire*, a desire to do what is expected of us, or a desire to obey the law. As has already been said, a change in either our belief or our desire would produce a change in our action. At first sight, in the case of doing something because we believe that it would be wrong not to do it, it would seem that we also do that thing because we believe that not to do it would be wrong, and because we desire to do what is right. It also seems natural to say that we may desire to do what is right either for its own sake, that is, that the feature of the action which attracts us is simply that it is right, or that we do it because we believe that it is right, and because we believe that right actions have some feature, other than their rightness, and it is this other feature of the action which attracts us. For example, we may believe that right actions are rewarded in an after-life, and then we may perform the action because we believe that it is right, and because we believe performing right actions is rewarded, and because we want to be rewarded.

If, however, we accept some form of non-propositional theory about the nature of what we are doing when we use sentences containing ethical words, this natural account of moral reasons for doing something is barred to us.[1] We cannot do something because we believe that it is right, and because we want to do what is right, because there is no such thing as a *belief* that anything is right. The sentence 'That would be the right thing for

[1] See David Hume, *A Treatise of Human Nature*, Book III, Part I, Section 1.

me to do' does not express a proposition, and so does not express anything which possibly can be believed. Hence moral 'beliefs', if this view is the correct one, cannot affect actions in the way in which beliefs affect actions.

Now it does seem to me quite possible that other people's expressions of emotion, other people's commands, other people's wishes, requests, performatory utterances, and so on, may sometimes affect how I behave in a way different from the way my beliefs affect how I behave. If someone asks me to pass him the cheese, or tells me to pass him the cheese, or expresses a wish for the cheese, or his despair at not having cheese, it may be that sometimes I am prompted in a spontaneous way to act by such expressions, without the intermediary of any belief. Certainly this may actually happen when a well-trained soldier responds to a command. But more usually, hearing other people's commands, expressions of wishes, emotions, etc., affects my behaviour partly because they affect my feelings – and so my motives – and partly because they produce beliefs, for example, the belief that such-and-such a thing has been commanded, or requested, or the belief that Smith would be lost without it, which belief affects my behaviour because I want to do what has been commanded, or fear the consequences of not doing what is commanded, or want Smith to have what he wants. Where my own commands, requests, pleas, performatory utterances, expressions of emotion are concerned, these can hardly affect my own behaviour at all. My giving a command to others, or making a request, or expressing an emotion, can hardly provide *me* with any reason, incentive or stimulus for doing anything. My own moral beliefs, however, do seem to provide me with a reason for doing something. Hence they are genuine beliefs, or more like genuine beliefs than any of the things hitherto mentioned.

It is sometimes supposed that 'You ought to do that' is an answer to the question 'What shall I do?', and so affects my behaviour in a different sort of way from the way in which a piece of true or false information, so long as I believe it, affects my behaviour. It is not the case, however, that 'You ought to do that' is an answer to the question 'What shall I do?'; it is an answer to the question 'What ought I to do?' If I ask someone 'What ought I to do?' and he replies 'Do that', he is not answering my question but evading it, unless it is understood that he is not just telling me to do that, but means it to be understood from the context – that is, from the fact that the question I have asked him is 'What ought I to do?' – that what he means is not 'Do that' but 'That is what you ought to do'.

How do our beliefs that something is right or wrong affect our behaviour on the view that I have been putting forward, namely, on the view that when I say that something is wrong or when I say that it ought not to be done, I am saying that it is not *to be* done, and am doing something which is partly like making a statement, in that what I say can correctly be said to be something true or false, and which I can correctly be said to believe or disbelieve or be in doubt about, but which is also partly like attempting to promulgate a rule or issuing a directive? In the case of the relatively 'unsophisticated' people, who believe that 'not-to-be-done-ness' is an objective property of actions, essentially and inescapably inherent in them, then my belief that an action is wrong affects my behaviour in much the same way that anything else I believe affects my behaviour; in the case of believing that something is wrong, however, since I believe it is wrong because I project my feelings of disgust, abhorrence and antagonism on to the action itself, there *must* be some motives inspiring me not to perform any action I believe is wrong, namely, the feelings of disgust, abhorrence and antagonism already mentioned. What of those more sophisticated people, however, who do not believe that 'not-to-be-done-ness' is an essential property of actions, but who make a policy of saying that actions are not to be done when they believe that there are good reasons for this kind of action not being done by anybody? There is no discoverable property of 'not-to-be-done-ness', over and above the facts which make one say that these things are not to be done, and the attitude which makes these people hostile to it. In this case, what makes such people not do actions which they believe are wrong or not to be done is simply the hostility to the performance of the kind of action in question which makes them say it is not to be done, coupled with their beliefs about the nature and consequences of this kind of action. There is no extra fact about an action, viz. the fact that it is not to be done. However, in someone who thinks or says that something is not to be done, there is an extra motive for not doing this thing, over and above that provided by the desires this man has, and his beliefs about the nature of the action and its consequences. This motive is that, if he himself does an action which he thinks or says is not to be done, he will, as Kant, if I could understand him, may have pointed out, be guilty of a certain kind of inconsistency, the inconsistency of saying or thinking that an action is of a kind which is not to be done by anybody, and yet doing it himself.[1] (His motive is stronger, I think, if he has said out loud that this action is not to be done, for in that case it is strengthened by a different motive, namely, the desire not to be known by other people to be inconsistent, and not to be accused, publicly or privately, of inconsistency.) Of course, when I say that this is inconsistent, I do not mean that there is any logical impossibility in behaving in this way; obviously, people do in fact behave in this way, and so it cannot be logically impossible. Nor is anyone behaving in this way guilty of holding inconsistent beliefs. It is just that one of the ways in which the word 'inconsistent' is used is to describe this kind of behaviour, the behaviour involved in saying that a class of actions is not to be done by anybody, and nevertheless oneself performing actions which are members of this class. And it is just a psychological fact about some people, though not all, that they dislike behaving in this way, and so have a motive for not behaving in this way.

An action can be assessed as rational or irrational only to the extent that it is done for some reason, and this statement is true whether or not reasons may be regarded as a special kind of cause or not. We, of course, have come to the conclusion that reasons are a special kind of cause. If an action has only causes, (if reasons are not causes), or only causes other than reasons, (if reasons are causes), then the predicates 'rational' and 'irrational' cannot be applied to it. I now want to discuss the question: What is the difference between a good reason for doing something and a bad reason for doing something?

As we have seen, a reason is a good reason for *believing* something if it tends to support, or to support strongly or conclusively, what is believed. Since doing something is not a belief, we cannot have good or bad reasons for *doing* things in the way in which we can have good or bad reasons for *believing* things. Reasons for doing something, as opposed to believing something, can be either beliefs, or motives or desires. Very often a belief is a good reason for doing some action if the person who performed that action was aiming at some state of affairs, and if his action was performed as a result of the belief that his performing it would realize this state

---

[1] See Immanuel Kant, *Foundations of the Metaphysics of Morals*, trans. by Lewis White Beck (Bobbs Merrill, Library of Arts), p. 42.

of affairs, and if this belief is one for which he has good reasons. For example, if someone breaks a promise because he believes he will lose money if he keeps it, he has a good reason for breaking it in the sense that he has good reason for believing that he will lose money as a result of keeping it, and his aim is not to lose money.

There may also, though I am not sure, be a sense in which a motive can be a good reason for performing some action, if it is not a whim or purely ephemeral, or does not conflict strongly with the whole pattern of motivation which the agent has. Perhaps someone can be said to have a good reason, in this sense, for breaking a promise if he would be shot if he kept it, for the desire to avoid death, which is his motive, is not a whim, is not ephemeral, and seldom conflicts with a man's other motives.

In general, I have good reasons for *doing* something, as opposed to *believing* something, if I have strong and permanent motives for doing it, which are consistent with the whole pattern of my motivation, and if I have good reasons for believing that the action I am contemplating performing will satisfy these desires. The question now arises, is the belief that to omit an action would be *wrong* a good reason for doing it? And I think that the answer must be that it is a good reason for someone who wants to do what is right for its own sake, or who has desires, for example a desire to save his immortal soul, which would be satisfied by doing what is right, but that, for some people who have no such desires, it is not a good reason. In other words, by pointing out that what he is about to do is wrong you provide no reason at all for not doing this action to someone who does not care about right and wrong.

This would seem to suggest that right behaviour is not necessarily rational behaviour, and the good man not necessarily the rational man, which brings us to the third of the four questions outlined for consideration in this chapter. A little earlier we suggested that a man who was convinced that a certain kind of action was to be done, but did not do it himself, was being in a sense inconsistent. Though such behaviour is inconsistent, however, I cannot see any sense in which it is irrational, though it may seem odd that it may be not irrational to behave inconsistently. This is because I cannot see any sense in which wrong behaviour is irrational behaviour. The senses in which behaviour can be irrational are these. Behaviour can be irrational in the sense that the beliefs, upon which the person behaving in this way is acting, are irrational beliefs but, of course, a person may behave wrongly without having any irrational beliefs about what is wrong (if it is possible to describe one's moral beliefs as being rational or irrational at all, a problem which I shall come to later on). This follows from the fact, which some philosophers unconvincingly deny,[1] that people can do things which they believe to be wrong, and this is true whether their belief that something is wrong is an irrational belief or not.

Another sense in which a man's behaviour may be irrational is this. Somebody may be behaving irrationally although he has no irrational *beliefs*, if he pursues inconsistent *policies*, that is, if he pursues two polices which are so related that advancing the first policy hinders the second. In this sense, too, acting wrongly need not be irrational. A man may have a perfectly consistent policy of advancing his own interest, and do things which he believes are right when he thinks doing them advances his interest, and do things which he believes are wrong when he thinks doing *them* advances his own interest. Since saying something is one form of doing something, he will also say that he believes that actions are wrong when he believes that it is to his interest that other people avoid these actions, and thinks that his saying that these actions are wrong will cause other people to avoid them. This, presumably, will sometimes involve him in making inconsistent assertions that is, in saying to one person that some class of actions is wrong, in order to get this person to avoid doing them (because he thinks that it is contrary to his interest that this person should do them), and saying to another person that the same class of actions is not wrong in order to get this second person to *do* them (because he thinks that it is contrary to his interests that this person should *not* do them). There is nothing irrational about this (though his assertions certainly are inconsistent); he is quite consistently pursuing the policy of promoting his own interest, and taking the correct means to this end, and so there is nothing irrational about his behaviour, however reprehensible it may be. I conclude, therefore, that there is nothing necessarily irrational about performing actions one thinks are wrong, however blameworthy (and inconsistent in the sense explained above) such conduct may be.

[1] See R. M. Hare, *The Language of Morals* (O.U.P., 1952), p. 169.

Wrong conduct, however, though it is not necessarily *irrational*, may be, and perhaps always is, *unreasonable*. This is because among the meanings of the word 'reasonable' are those in which reasonable behaviour is fair behaviour, and in which it is unreasonable to make excessive demands.

The virtue of being reasonable manifests itself *par excellence* in situations where different people, who live together, have to decide when the needs, wants and interests of one may take precedence over the needs, wants and interests of others. Someone is described as being reasonable if he makes no more demands than it is reasonable he should make, or even less – in which case he may sometimes be described as being too reasonable – and as unreasonable if he makes more demands than are reasonable. But what is a reasonable demand?

It is tempting to suggest that a reasonable demand is one the satisfaction of which would be consented to by all parties. This will not do, however, because it is a characteristic of unreasonable people that they will not consent even to the reasonable demands of others, and to define a reasonable demand as one to which reasonable people would consent would be circular. Sometimes a reasonable demand in this context means an equitable demand, or one the satisfaction of which does not involve an inequitable distribution of goods, money, time or resources, whether material or non-material. Sometimes a demand is unreasonable because the person who makes it is asking incompatible things of one and the same person. Sometimes a demand is unreasonable because it involves asking too much of somebody, either absolutely, in that someone's resources are strained beyond endurance, or relatively to the benefit complying with the demands would yield to the person making it. In all cases, being unreasonable involves departure from rules the acceptance of which is designed to make living together possible with the smallest amount of sacrifice of the interests of the people involved.

It finally remains to answer the last of the four questions I posed at the beginning of this chapter, the question: 'Is the answer to questions like "What ought I to do?", "What actions are my duty?" and "What is the right thing for me to do?" the rational answer to these questions?'

In the sense of 'wrong' in which this word is used for a supposedly intrinsic property of the wrong action, or in which the fact that the action which is alleged to be one which is not to be done is grounded upon some supposedly intrinsic property of the action, then our moral beliefs are always irrational, for it is simply a delusion that there is any such property. All that can in fact be true of the actions themselves is that they have the power of arousing feelings of disapproval in certain people, and the view that what we mean when we say that an action is wrong is that it arouses feelings of disapproval in anybody at all has been conclusively refuted.

In the more sophisticated sense of 'wrong' in which we say that an action is wrong if we think actions of this sort are not to be done by anybody, regardless of their own personal inclinations, because we are opposed to the way of life in which the performance of such actions would be a part, or to the consequences of the performance of such actions, the situation is a little more complicated. Statements to the effect that a kind of action is not to be done cannot be logically derived from any description of the action which we say is not to be done, nor the circumstances in which it is performed, nor its consequences. Nor can we know by a process of inductive reasoning what is not to be done: it would be absurd to suggest that we knew that promises were not to be broken because we had observed that every action which was a case of promise-breaking in fact also possessed the property of not-to-be-done-ness, and so inferred that the next case of promise-breaking we came across would also possess this property; such an account would not answer the question how we know that the already observed instances of promise-breaking possessed the property of not-to-be-done-ness. It would not be at all plausible to suggest that we had some sort of special synthetic *a priori* insight into what actions were not to be done; and we certainly could not remember what actions were not to be done unless we had first found out what actions were not to be done in some other way than by remembering this, or had been told by someone else who had found out what actions were not to be done in some other way than by remembering. We have also shown that we could not have a special sense which told us what actions were not to be done. In what way, then, can our beliefs about what actions are to be done and what actions are not to be done be described as rational or irrational?

The only way in which I can see that our moral beliefs can be rational or irrational, when once we are rid of the delusion that there is some characteristic, wrongness, inherent in actions, the presence of which we may have rational grounds for believing in, is that the policies we propose, when we say we think that certain kinds of actions are not to be done by anybody, regardless of his inclinations, are rational or irrational policies for mankind to adopt. A policy is a rational policy for mankind to adopt if it serves the ends which mankind has. In this sense of 'irrational', it would be irrational of man to adopt a policy of keeping his promises, regardless of consequences, for the results of this would be inconducive to mankind's ends, and would not result in producing for him a satisfactory state of life. Furthermore, we can say that mankind has good reason for adopting a proposal that certain actions be not done, by anyone, regardless of their inclinations, in the sense that the motives which mankind has for adopting such proposals are not whims, are not ephemeral, and do not conflict with mankind's whole pattern of motivation.

There may seem to be some inconsistency between this contention, that it is rational for man to adopt a policy to the effect that certain kinds of action be not done if such a policy is conducive to man's interests, and my earlier contention that it is not irrational for individual men themselves to do actions which they think are not to be done. There is, however, no inconsistency. What is rational for mankind as a whole is not necessarily the same thing as what is rational for individual men. This is because what advances the interests of mankind, and what produces satisfaction for it, need not be what advances the interests of each individual man. Most men, fortunately, have strong motives which make them favour the welfare of the whole, both for its own sake, and because they see that they are likely to be happier in a community in which others are happy than in one in which they are not, but this coincidence of motivation is only partial, and many people, if not most, are too short sighted to notice that it exists at all. When the coincidence does break down, it is not irrational for men to act wrongly; this is why nature has not left to reason the function of enforcing morality, but has implanted in man powerful sentiments, sentiments which, as we have seen, tend to objectify themselves and to appear as an essential feature of the nature of things, and which impel men to do the things they regard as right, even when it is highly irrational that they should do them. And, of course, even those more sophisticated people who use the word 'wrong' for those actions which they believe are not to be done, without supposing that there is some intrinsic characteristic of not-to-be-done-ness, are making use of these sentiments to get their beliefs about what actions are not to be done enforced; for these sentiments are 'triggered off' to some extent by the word 'wrong', and anyone saying that some class of actions is wrong is, simply by doing so, doing something to persuade people to adopt, towards those actions which he says are not to be done, the attitude which they adopt to actions which they have been accustomed, from childhood upwards, to regard in this light.

Oddly enough, it seems to me to be perfectly possible that a situation should obtain in which, though it was rational for mankind to do certain things, it was not rational for any individual man to do these things. It is perfectly possible that it should be the case that, though it is to the interests of mankind that certain actions be done, it is not to the interests of any given man to do these actions. This is because it is perfectly possible that it should be to the interests of every individual man that other people, but not himself, should perform those actions which, if performed, will produce the greatest sum of satisfaction for mankind as a whole. In a situation like this, moral rules which are advantageous to mankind as a whole get put into practice, but not because each man imposes them upon himself, for this, to the extent that he is rational, and also has not moral motives to obey the rules as such, he will not do. They get put into practice because each man joins with other men in imposing moral rules on all men other than himself, and they join with others in imposing moral rules upon him.

The rational moral rules for men to adopt, then – rational in the sense of being the right means to man's ends – are those rules about what actions are or are not to be done which it is necessary that mankind should have for their own welfare and preservation. If mankind does not have rules which at the very least approximate roughly to this standard, he will certainly perish, and the farther away from this standard his moral rules are, the more miserable and unsatisfactory his life will be. In more technical language, the only rational set of moral rules for men is a broadly utilitarian one, and any departure from a roughly utilitarian standard must be due to mistakes about matters of fact, or prejudices in favour of thinking that certain moral rules which have been handed down by tradition are part of the nature of things. The least that can be said for a policy of saying that those actions are not to be done which are contrary to the general interest is that, so long as it is based upon adequate knowledge of matters of fact, it, by definition, cannot possibly do any harm!

INDEX